7⁰⁰

Ernest C

D1094962

James H. Taylor

"A BRIGHT SHINING CITY
SET ON A HILL"

Edited By Elizabeth Sue Wake

CUMBERLAND COLLEGE: WILLIAMSBURG, KENTUCKY

Published by Cumberland College, College Station Box 191, Williamsburg, Kentucky 40769.

DEDICATION

This book is dedicated to my wonderful wife Dinah and to our son Jim in recognition of their understanding, patience, and support.

Dinah has been a wonderful mother to our son and an understanding wife to me at a time when I've had to say all too frequently: ''I'm on my way to New York''; ''I'm headed for a meeting at Middletown or Cedarmore''; ''I'm in California''; ''I'm scheduled to speak at a convention''; ''I'll be late for dinner''; ''I won't be home then''; ''I'm sorry, I'm scheduled to speak in Lexington or Louisville or Harlan that Sunday.''

A college president must wear many hats: if you're away, you should be on campus; and if you are on campus, you should probably be out seeking support of one type or another. I can only be thankful and grateful for the patience and understanding and wholesome support of my wife and our son.

Jim is almost grown. Yet the Taylor household has invested its years in Christian educational opportunities for young people, primarily mountain youngsters, and we've never had a reason to regret it.

PREFACE

Since this book represents my first attempt ever to compile a history, and because this is a labor of love rather than the work of a trained historian, I hope I will not be judged too harshly. This history is much too light to be treated merely as a scholarly research project. Rather, this is a book written as a tribute to a special purpose liberal arts College which is located in and serving historically an economically depressed area which has become known as Appalachia. After all, I'm charging no royalties or accepting any type of compensation for the book. Frankly, my interest is in this College, since it has been serving the area long before the word "Appalachia" became fashionable.

Portions of this book come largely from the writings of three Cumberland College Professors: Miss Ida Janie Hall, Assistant Professor of History;[1] Miss Irene Peace, Assistant Professor of Health;[2] and Dr. Chester R. Young, Senior Professor.[3] Each of these people has given permission to be quoted liberally, and, of course, an exacting attempt has been made to document thoroughly through footnotes each person's contribution.

Since the College and the community are entwined and interrelated in the fabric called "community," I've made every effort to relate the College's history to local history. For this connection I have relied heavily on articles written for a number of years for *The Whitley Republican* by Congressman Eugene Siler[4] as well as those written by Judge Pleas Jones.[5]

Originally, while researching the institution's history, I made the trip to the College library to read, not to write. Finally, through an odd chain of circumstances and events, I became the "author-to-be" and simply sat down and began to write the Centennial history with the help of Dr. E. C. Masden, Miss Irene Peace, and Mrs. Sue Wake, in particular. Much credit, if not most credit, must be given to Mrs. Wake, without whom this book would never have been written. She must also be given credit for the editing and typing.

You will, I think, see as you read what I also saw as I wrote. And I've tried

---

[1] Ida Janie Hall, "The History of Cumberland College" (unpublished Master's thesis, University of Tennessee, 1962).

[2] Irene Peace, "The Contribution of Cumberland College" (unpublished monograph, Eastern Kentucky State College, 1963).

[3] Chester R. Young, *"To Win The Prize": The Story of the First Baptist Church at Williamsburg, Kentucky, 1883-1983* (Williamsburg: Centennial Committee, First Baptist Church, 1983).

[4] Eugene Siler, "Heads or Tales," *The Whitley Republican.*

[5] Pleas Jones, "Legend and Lore," *The Whitley Republican.*

to write readable writing without regard to splitting infinitives or dangling participles or ending sentences with prepositions. Yet, I've attempted to make my nouns notable and my predicates proper.

Frankly, I'm neither a historian nor a grammarian. On the other hand, I do confess to a deep and abiding interest in and appreciation for Cumberland's history, and I do want to see an accurate historical record preserved for posterity. Other historical works on the College have been excellent, but with the passing of time there has come a need to update the history. So Cumberland's story will be one of many scenes and many actors as they pass before us on the stage of time. The College's history cannot be told without telling the story of personalities as one travels back in the annals of time. Someone once said that all true history is biography. This book is really no exception. This history will be told in terms of people, not mere programs or projects.

Since 1889 Cumberland College, originally known as Williamsburg Institute, has provided unparalleled service against almost insurmountable odds. For goodness sake, one can spend hours reading of peoples' heroic contributions to this College. As you might imagine the official Minutes of the Board of Trustees were of inestimable value even though the early Minutes were written in longhand, long before this modern age of typewriters, lasers, and high speed printers. After reading the yearbooks, alumni publications, and other primary documents, an increasing appreciation for and understanding of the sweep of history was gained. One sees adversity and opportunity as well as the stewardship with which the College has been shepherded by its presidents, trustees, administration, faculty, students, alumni, and other friends since 1889.

Editions of the *Western Recorder, The Whitley Republican,* and *The Williamsburg Times* provided valuable historical information. Oddly enough, much of the information included in this history would not have been available in its entirety had modern technology not produced the microfiche and microfilm used so much in the preparation of this book. Interviews with older alumni and other citizens were helpful as they reflected on the past and provided meaningful memories and insights as the past paraded before us. Memories — how they linger!

The students who read the microfiche of the *Western Recorder, The Whitley Republican,* and *The Williamsburg Times* deserve recognition: Mrs. Terri Adams, Mr. Mark Adams, Miss Beth Hobson, Miss Teresa McHargue, Miss Kimberly Wake, and Mr. Allen Shepherd. Mr. Maynard Head should also be recognized. There are others to mention, too many to list here. You know who you are.

Mention should be made of Janus Jones who graciously provided a copy of the Mount Zion Association's original minutes which were helpful.

Special recognition must be given to Butch Housman for his preparation of the photographs appearing in this work, to Dr. E. C. Masden and also to Miss Irene Peace for their assistance and for their hours of work in researching specific topics assigned to them and compiling the data, to Miss Lisa Cox who assisted me endlessly, to my wife who encouraged me tirelessly, and to Mrs. Sue Wake who laboriously compiled data, read, edited, typed, reread, and assisted in the compilation, the writing, and the editing of this historical data and narrative. Enough cannot be said about Mrs. Wake's writing, editing, rewriting, and encouragement.

My purpose in writing the Centennial history, then, is to present the plain, unabashed story of Cumberland College as it unfolds page-by-page from all of those yesterdays which largely make today possible.

While some may claim this is revisionist history, and while others may say the book is not filled with enough dates and statistical data, my purpose in compiling the book was neither to be a historical revisionist nor necessarily to fill the book with dates and cold, impersonal numbers; but rather my purpose in writing is simply to tell the history as revealed to me through extensive research and through my first-hand association with this College for nearly a quarter of a century, first as a freshman, later as a teacher and administrator, and finally as its president. I readily admit to an emotional attachment to this College. Needless to say, this history contains a series of stories allegedly true. If I thought I could improve the story without being injurious to its historical authenticity, I have.

Early in the first week of my presidency at Cumberland in August of 1980, a stately senior citizen, a student, came to my office and in front of my administrative assistant, Mrs. Sue Wake, told me of her need to drop out of College. She said she desperately wanted to stay in College, but her husband had insisted she drop out because he didn't want her to become ''uppity'' or to get ''above her raising.'' Little did her husband know that this College turns out few ''hoity toity'' alumni. Rather Cumberland College is primarily for mountain youth and graduate students who are ready to serve, ready to place service above self, ready to redeem us from the curse of the commonplace.

Nonetheless, this woman insisted she tell me of a vision she had had of this College as ''A Bright Shining City Set on a Hill.'' She gestured with her hands and arms and hooked her finger at me. One could see the sincerity in her dark snappy eyes. She said she felt compelled and was under great conviction to tell me of her vision.

I was struck by her sincerity, by her integrity, by her intensity, and by what she had to say, because I, too, had also thought of this College as ''A Bright Shining City.'' She had, moreover, articulated my thoughts clearly and precisely and without ambiguity as she spoke of ''A Bright Shining City Set on a Hill,'' high and lifted up in all of its glory and majesty just as the Master himself had spoken of the Bright Shining City in the Scripture.[6]

---

[6] Matt. 5:14

Thus the title for this Centennial history had been spoken, and appropriately so by a genuine mountain woman in all of her sincerity, intensity, and without affectation.[7] Being a second generation Kentuckian myself, I was struck by her sincerity, her conviction, and her intensity.

Truly the founding fathers had envisioned "an institution devoted to illumination, and consecrated to enlightenment." They pictured young people "from humble homes filling its halls and coming forth from its shining portals, their faces radiant with the light of learning."[8]

Quite frankly, after listening to what this woman had to say and after reading the early College catalogues, yearbooks, Board Minutes, and alumni publications, I simply had to shed all pretense of detachment and roll up my sleeves and go to work writing the Cumberland College story, mostly in motel rooms from Mackinac Island, Michigan, to Miami Beach, Florida, and from the snowy chalets of Vermont to the sandy beaches of California, as I visited friends soliciting gifts and other forms of support and goodwill for the College.

In this College's panorama of history each president, each trustee, each professor, each staff member, each student, and each donor has made an unique, deep, and abiding contribution which is indelibly written in the pages of time. As in the early days of existence, the path to progress charted by the College has been accompanied by sacrifice and struggle. These people knew that life is essentially meaningless without interpersonal relationships. Thus, you are invited to step through the hourglass into days gone by as we reminisce about yesterdays which are largely responsible for today and for all of our tomorrows.

Good men and women should not be forgotten. Thus, an attempt has been made to recognize the good men and women who have worked unselfishly to make this College possible. As one person said, significant contributions for good must not go unnoticed or unrecorded, for surely men and women who fight against great odds for good serve as examples of all that which we might become. Not only did the stewards of yesterday serve as examples for us today, but we are serving as examples for those who will come tomorrow, purchasing the future with our actions today.

Today we stand on the shoulders of all of those who have gone before us. All of those yesterdays have gone to make today possible. And all of our todays will be largely responsible for the tomorrows, for surely we are only temporary stewards of this life as we pass the light of learning from one generation to the next.

---

[7] When Senator John Sherman Cooper, former Ambassador to India, visited Cumberland College on May 11, 1985, to receive an honorary degree, he also mentioned to me that the College had warmth, personality, and was "without affectation." In his unassuming and unpretentious way, this statesman said, "I've learned some things along life's way and one is the need for good, wholesome schools like Cumberland."

[8] E.E. Wood, "Dr. Gatliff's Vision," in *Doctor Ancil Gatliff* ([Williamsburg, KY, 1919]), pp. 13-14.

TABLE OF CONTENTS

CHAPTER 4, A NEW DAY DAWNING

CHAPTER 5, COMING OF AGE

CHAPTER 6, A MATURING INSTITUTION

ILLUSTRATIONS AND PHOTOGRAPHS

In the process of preparing many of the photographs for reproduction in this book, it was my pleasure to see, copy, and, in some cases, restore many interesting old photos and reproductions as well as paintings.

Since in the early days of photography, enlargements were difficult, if not impossible, to make, most photographers relied on large format equipment, generally exposing 8x10 inch or 5x7 inch negatives for portraiture. These cameras were capable of producing superb quality photographs. Two especially notable examples were the portrait of William Jennings Bryan and the picture of the Jellico dynamite explosion.

Unlike other artists, most photographers have been slow to sign or otherwise identify their work, so most of the photographers are anonymous. One notable exception was Jim Thompson of Knoxville, Tennessee. Mr. Thompson established a studio in 1902 and continued working until 1956 doing primarily commercial photography. Some of his pictures of architectural interiors appeared in early Williamsburg Institute Catalogues. These photographs were made with an 8x10 camera and lit by exploding magnesium flash powder in an open 18-inch tray yielding an attractive but smoky light.

As for style I felt many of the early portraits such as those in *The Eglantine* were very refreshing and "avant garde," especially compared to the "formula" portraits of later years.

— Butch Housman, Photographer

(Mr. Butch Housman was born 17 November 1946 in Dayton, Ohio. He received his professional training at Winona School of Professional Photography, Dayton Art Institute, and Art Center College of Design in Los Angeles. Mr. Housman holds a bachelor's degree from Cumberland College with an area of concentration in art. Since 1965 Mr. Housman has worked in advertising, illustrative photography, cinematography, and video tape. He now operates Housman Photography in Williamsburg.)

ABOUT THE EDITOR

Elizabeth Sue Wake was born in Harlan County, Kentucky. She attended Harlan County Public Schools and was graduated valedictorian from Loyall High School in 1963. After attending Southeast Kentucky Community College and the University of Kentucky, she transferred to Cumberland College where she was graduated with Honor in 1970 with a Bachelor of Science degree having majored in mathematics and minored in chemistry and history.

Upon graduation she worked in various positions at Cumberland College including library assistant, secretary to teacher education, director of instructional media, and part-time evening instructor. During this period she also continued her education and earned her Master's degree from Union College.

As I was preparing to assume the presidency of Cumberland College in 1980, I asked Mrs. Wake to serve as my administrative assistant. She accepted the position, and we have worked together since that time.

Mrs. Wake is married to Dr. Eric L. Wake who serves as the chairman of the history and political science department at the college. They have two daughters, Kimberly, who is currently attending Cumberland, and Jennifer, who attends the Williamsburg Independent School.

PROLOGUE

The Cumberland College campus is nestled in the mountains of eastern Kentucky and located on four hills in a city named Williamsburg.

Williamsburg, Kentucky, is located on Interstate 75 and is around eighty miles north of Knoxville, Tennessee, and approximately one hundred miles south of Lexington, Kentucky.

Within a radius of a relatively few miles from Williamsburg, one can see one of the most colorful small waterfalls seen anywhere. Cumberland Falls is commonly referred to as the place in the Western hemisphere where a moonbow can be seen. One hundred eighty miles to the west is the world-famous Mammoth Cave. To the east is Cumberland Gap through which Scotch-Irish settlers streamed. The list of beautiful attractions and other enticements could go on and on.

Williamsburg enjoys four distinct seasons of the year:

In the summer the beautiful mountains and valleys, the big blue sky, and the lush green grass abundant on the campus provide an inviting backdrop.

In the fall the rolling campus is carpeted with yellow, red, and auburn leaves as the trees are silhouetted against the sky.

In the winter those snowcapped mountains and valleys surrounding the campus remind one of a ski resort area in the Swiss Alps.

In the spring, naturally enough, flowers bloom and the redbuds and dogwoods give forth a fragrance of the newness of life.

Cumberland College, one of America's unique institutions, is located in the Cumberland Mountains, near the Cumberland River, Cumberland Falls, and Cumberland Gap.

The green, manicured campus is old, spacious, and pastoral with twenty buildings, most of which were built or acquired in the last thirty years and five of which are older. The buildings are blends of Antebellum, Edwardian, and historic Williamsburg architecture.

The campus beauty is unsurpassed with steeples sweeping up to the glory of God. At times clouds almost seem to surround the campus. In the midst of all the greenery of shrubs and trees and the big blue hue of the beautiful sloping mountains, the grounds of the Cumberland campus follow the natural elevation with valleys and peaks.

The natural beauty of the campus is inviting and is regarded as outstanding among college campuses.

This is no ordinary campus. Here youngsters have traditionally found a home away from home. This is a campus where professors give exceptional time and talent to the students. Good old-time values are taken seriously at Cumberland College as they are transmitted from one generation to the next.

Cumberland is one of those almost extinct institutions: a small college intimate and concerned in a setting of almost incomparable beauty. Meticulous would be the best word to describe the physical facilities, largely because of a dedicated maintenance staff supported by student labor. Many of the students are the first in their family ever to attend college, but they come from families which are rich in values.

The story of Cumberland College is a story about people.

Appendices I, II, III, and IV list the persons largely responsible for the work of Cumberland College since its founding. An exacting attempt has been made to list each person's name as it was recorded in the College's official catalogues: Appendix I lists the members of the College's Board of Trustees and the offices they have held; Appendix II lists the presidents (or principals as they were called earlier in the College's history) of the institution; Appendix III lists the academic deans and business officers; and Appendix IV lists the names of the College's employees from 1889 to the present as listed in the catalogues. Additionally, Appendix IV contains the names of the support staff as of May 1987.

No one could possibly tell the College's story without mentioning the contributions of hundreds of plain, everyday, ordinary people, each of whom had an extraordinary mission and each of whom made an uncommon, abiding, and enduring contribution by making life rich, rewarding, and worthwhile. These genteel people loom large on the stage of history. Many of these people are known and many others are unknown. Yet, all of these people left footprints in the sands of time as they fought an uphill battle to establish and sustain a College located in what has become known as Appalachia.

Thus the story about to be told is a story of tragedy and triumph, of obstacles and opportunities, of problems and possibilities, but most importantly, a story of "A Bright Shining City Set on a Hill."

"A BRIGHT SHINING CITY
SET ON A HILL"

AERIAL PHOTOGRAPH OF THE CUMBERLAND COLLEGE CAMPUS

"I will lift up mine eyes unto the hills, from whence cometh my help." Psalms 121:1.

(Photograph by Billy Davis, III)

CHAPTER 1
THE VISION

BEGINNING: A WEATHERBEATEN COUNTRY CHURCH

In September of the year 1887, there gathered at a little weatherbeaten country church in the mountains of Eastern Kentucky a few men representing eighteen churches. It was the annual meeting of the Mount Zion Association in a region having only one or two small schools that offered as much as a high school education.[1]

HIGHER EDUCATION FOR
KENTUCKY MOUNTAIN CHILDREN

Though these few men had only a meager common school education themselves, and some scarcely that, they, nevertheless, felt the responsibility of providing some means for the higher education of the children of the Kentucky mountains.[2]

The Association minutes show that the founders were poor — $366 was the total amount contributed by their eighteen churches during the year 1887-1888 to pastors' salaries. They, nonetheless, solemnly passed a resolution, through the encouragement of General Green Clay Smith and under the leadership of R. C. Medaris, looking toward the founding of a College.[3]

---

[1] Mount Zion Association, Record Book No. 1, pp. 23-24. Actually as early as September, 1886, the delegates to the Mount Zion Association called attention to the need for a college to which they could send their sons and daughters. Dr. E.S. Moss, a prominent physician, had been approached by R.C. Medaris about the need. The first public mention of this Institution was only a thumbnail sketch recorded on the front page of the 28 June 1888 edition of the *Western Recorder* which stated, "At Williamsburg $6,000 has been raised for a school which will open next winter."

[2] Williamsburg Institute *Catalogue,* 1892-1893, p. 24.

There were only two classes of people: the learned and the unlearned; those who knew and those who knew they knew nothing. Greatness is never found among those who know everything. As was true then, so it is today. No one can tell the proud and haughty much of anything.

[3] Mount Zion Association, Record Book No. 1, pp. 9-10. The Mount Zion Association, meeting at the Williamsburg Church on Saturday, 11 September 1886, heard this report from the Committee on Education. "Your Committee would further call your attention to the great need of founding a Baptist college in the county for the education of our sons and daughters." The Committee consisted of W. R. Denham, W. H. Brummitt, and W. R. Smith.

Ibid., pp. 23-24, 28. At the Association's meeting in September, 1887, the group heard and passed the following recommendation. "We call your attention to the urgent necessity of founding a Baptist school in our county, and we think Williamsburg is the proper place for said school, and we further recommend that this body appoint a financial agent to collect funds and secure a lot at once and report to our next Association." The Committee appointed consisted of R. C. Medaris, Jesse B. Lewis, and J. H. Hart. At this same meeting R. C. Medaris was appointed Financial Agent on Education.

FAITH AND A PROMISE

Like Abraham of Old they began their journey with precious little more than faith and a promise. During the first years gifts came from across the nation, the East in particular. Little did the founders know that their vision would shortly catch the eye of men like John D. Rockefeller and Andrew Carnegie, both of whom would initially support the effort through their philanthropy.[4] In fact, this College was only one of many institutions they supported initially; yet, the support was most meaningful to the institution at a critical time.

John D. Rockefeller gave through the American Baptist Education Society and later through the General Education Board. Rockefeller supported several colleges. Remember there were no community colleges or multi-conglomerate state universities in those days.

IN THE MOUNTAINS, OF THE MOUNTAINS, AND BY THE MOUNTAINS

Nonetheless, Rockefeller was one of the original contributors to the endowment, giving $4,500 in 1891. Mr. Wallace Buttrick, Rockefeller's personal representative, when asked why the support was given, responded that the gift "was justified by the fact that this is a mountain school, in the mountains, of the mountains, and by the mountains."[5]

Andrew Carnegie also saw the enduring good being done and pledged $18,000 during the College's early years.

ROCKEFELLER, CARNEGIE, AND JAY GOULD

[4] Mr. Rockefeller and Mr. Carnegie probably gave because of their direct and indirect interest in the lumber, coal, and railway businesses but also because of their genuine philanthropic motivation. The College has been intimately related to the coal business from the beginning and even today offers an Associate Degree in Mining Technology. It was Jay Gould looking down from his New York office who decided to put the railroad through Williamsburg, thus changing mountain life tremendously.

According to Gene Siler, Sr., "Heads or Tails," *The Whitley Republican*, 19 March 1981, Andrew Carnegie had only four years of schooling but "gave away $60 million to public libraries, including one at Corbin . . . . This man who was not a member of any church gave away more than seven thousand pipe organs to churches, including one at Williamsburg."

ROCKEFELLER

[5] Wallace Buttrick, "Memorandum Regarding Cumberland College," 23 June 1921, New York, New York: Rockefeller Archive Center.

Claire Collier, personal correspondence, 6 June 1985, New York: Rockefeller Archive Center.

"Mr. Rockefeller made a series of gifts to the Institute through the American Baptist Education Society between 1891 and 1906, totaling $23,508.42. Most of the money seems to have been used for the endowment fund. There is no record of any subsequent donations to either Williamsburg Institute or Cumberland College. The General Education Board made a pledge of $50,000 for the Institute's endowment in 1908, which was paid in 1913. While the money came from the John D. Rockefeller Foundation for Higher Education, the fund was the property of the General Education Board. There is no indication that Mr. Rockefeller influenced the grant in any way. In 1920, the General Education Board pledged $50,000 toward the endowment, which was paid in 1924. A three-year grant for teachers' salaries was also made in 1920, . . . giving $5,000 in 1920-21; $4,500 in 1921-22; and $4,000 in 1922-23 . . . ."

Moreover, William Jennings Bryan, the silver-tongued orator, visited the campus,[6] thanks to the efforts of Professor Gorman Jones. Bryan was a contributor to the College's endowment[7] and today a scholarship fund still bears his name.

This was but the beginning of famous names associated with Cumberland College including Mr. and Mrs. Grover Hermann, Mr. and Mrs. O. Wayne Rollins, Mr. and Mrs. Fred C. Andersen, Mr. Bing Crosby, The J. Howard Pew Trusts, The James Graham Brown Foundation, Mr. and Mrs. Foster G. McGaw, Mr. and Mrs. Jim Rose, The Andrew W. Mellon Foundation, The William Randolph Hearst Foundation, Mr. William Jennings Bryan, The Honorable John Sherman Cooper, Mr. John Fox, Jr., Colonel Harland Sanders, Mrs. Duncan Hines, Mr. Henry Clay Frick, Mrs. Alfred Harcourt and the list goes on and on.

BETTER TO HAVE TRIED AND FAILED THAN NOT TO HAVE TRIED AT ALL

When the author found out about the relationship between Mr. Rockefeller and Cumberland College, an attempt was made to rekindle the family's interest, but to no avail. The author feels, however, that it is better to have tried and failed than not to have tried at all. Here is the letter received by the author from David Rockefeller on 23 June 1986, and it is understandable why the foundation must "pick and choose."

"Dear Dr. Taylor:

"Thank you for your letter of June 10 regarding Cumberland College. Senator John Sherman Cooper had also written in Cumberland's behalf, and thus I was anticipating hearing from you. I was also glad to receive the enclosed long-range plan and videotape, which gave a full picture of the quality of Cumberland and of your hopes for the future. Knowing of my grandfather's early and formative support for this fine institution, these materials were of special interest. It is rewarding to learn in greater detail about the result and success of Grandfather's generosity.

"Unfortunately, while proud of that result, my brothers and I have over several years simply had to decline special support for many of the initiatives my grandfather and father took on. The reason for this position is that they taught us well the importance of philanthropy and of being engaged in those institutions where one offers support. As I have followed that course, my commitments have become extensive and now make it necessary for me to be quite firm in resisting adding to them — no matter how tempting and worthwhile other opportunities might be.

"I hope I may count on your friendly understanding of the necessity of this decision."

WILLIAM JENNINGS BRYAN

[6] When Bryan came to speak at the College's lyceum series in 1905, Dr. Ancil Gatliff met his train at Corbin and drove Bryan to Williamsburg to be a guest at Dr. Gatliff's home. The story was told by Dr. Gatliff's daughter Una Gatliff Mahan of how she, after Mr. Bryan left the room, as a childish prank slipped on Bryan's coat and paraded around the room to the delight of a neighbor girl who was present.

[7] Listed in Appendix V are the names of those who gave to begin the College's endowment fund.

HENRY CLAY FRICK

The McGraw-Hill Encyclopedia of World Biography, 1973 ed., vol. 4, s.v. "Henry Clay Frick." Cited by permission of Heraty Associates, Encyclopedia Division, Palatine, Illinois. Henry Clay Frick was an outstanding American industrialist, financier, art collector, and philanthropist.

Frick entered into a partnership with Andrew Carnegie in expanding the Carnegie Steel Company into the largest such industry in the world, forming the United States Steel Company. For this large enterprise, Frick needed extensive coal deposits, and he acquired local acreage from the Faraday Coal and Coke Company in 1911. This acquisition included several acres of land in Whitley County. Six years after Frick's death, his heirs deeded this Whitley County land to Princeton, Harvard, and the Massachusetts Institute of Technology. In 1933 these three institutions deeded the land to Cumberland College, but they retained the oil and gas rights. The coal rights, however, were included in the deed to Cumberland College. The Board of Trustees gave

LOOKING BACK

The Cumberland College story began to unfold long ago as the Cumberland River went lapping along the outskirts of a little mountain town named Williamsburg in Whitley County, Kentucky.[8]

The sawmills were humming, the mules were pulling the bull-tongued plows, and the people were migrating on horseback and by covered wagon over the Cumberland Gap, across the Cumberland mountains, through the Cumberland forest

---

much of the credit for securing this coal land to Mr. A.T. Siler, attorney and trustee. It was several years, however, before the College began to reap any benefits from the investment of this one man, Henry Clay Frick.

[8] "History and Profile of the Cumberland Valley Area," *1985 Cumberland Valley Phone Directory and Guide* (Security Publishing Group: Lexington, Kentucky, 1985), p.2. In 1792 Kentucky was the fifteenth state admitted to the Union. There were originally nine counties in Kentucky. By 1800 most of the area now known as Clay, Knox, Laurel, Rockcastle and Whitley Counties were known as Knox County, named for General Henry Knox. Clay County was formed in 1906 and was named for Green Clay, an early settler and landowner. In 1810 Rockcastle County was formed; in 1818 Whitley County was formed; and in 1825 Laurel County was formed. Rockcastle County was named for the Rockcastle River and Laurel County for the laurel shrubbery growing there.

COLONEL WILLIAM WHITLEY

Jones, "Legend and Lore," 23 November 1983. In 1818 John Parsons introduced an Act into the House providing for the division of Knox County. Joseph Eve introduced the same Act to the Senate. The Act passed both bodies by "an overwhelming vote." According to Eve the new county would be named Whitley, . . . " 'in commemoration of the valuable services rendered our section by Colonel William Whitley . . . .' " Whitley had protected the area from Indian attacks before his death at the " 'Battle of Thames, in October 1813, at the age of 65 . . . .' " The Act was approved on 17 January 1818, and Whitley County became the fifty-ninth county in Kentucky.

Whitley, a native of Augusta County, Virginia, first came to Kentucky in 1775 by way of Cumberland Gap. The William Whitley house, constructed by Whitley, still stands today about two miles west of Crab Orchard, Kentucky.

SAMUEL COX

Jones, "Legend and Lore," 8 December 1983. The first Whitley County court convened at the home of Samuel Cox on 20 April 1818. The primary topic for discussion was safety for the county's citizens from Indian attacks. John Berry called for the strengthening of the county's newly formed militia, relating the following account of a Cherokee attack at the Joseph Johnson home on Lynn Camp.

" 'They entered his house about dusk, and killed him with their knives and tomahawks. His wife was milking and was not aware of what happened until she came in and saw Joe lying on the floor, bleeding to death. She saw the Cherokee plundering the house, and ran as fast as she could to Elder Johnson's house (Joseph's Pap). The Cherokees were after her, but she got to the elder Johnson's house just in time. Yes siree, they're plunderin' and stealin' all over the county. What we need is strengthen the militia.' "

TECUMSEH

Jones, "Legend and Lore," 22 December 1983. On 21 April 1818, the Court met to continue their discussions. The Chairman of the group, Ambrose Arthur, moved that the county's "seat of justice" be named for Colonel William Whitley.

" '. . . We're so much indebted to him for protection from those . . . Indians. Neither will we forget his bravery at the Battle of the Thames. I'll bet my last shilling that it was he who killed old Tecumseh. I was there when the main engagement took place . . . . Tecumseh was shot through the chest with two balls and . . . only Whitley and David King were the only ones that loaded their muskets in that fashion. I move, Gentlemen, that we call the town Williamsburgh (Williamsburg) in commemoration of the escencial [sic] services of the memoriable [sic] services of Colonel William Whitley.' The motion was unanimously passed."

Jones, "Legend and Lore," 5 January 1984.
"On June 15, 1818, trustees were appointed by the court to lay off the town of Williamsburgh . . . .
'Beginning on the river below Samuel Cox's at a stake; thence S 45 East 57 poles to a stake above Samuel Cox's dwelling house on the river; thence South 54 West 57 poles to a stake; thence N 45 W 57 poles to a stake; thence

and meadows, navigating down the Cumberland River to nearby Cumberland Falls as pioneers in the westward expansion.[9]

THIS IS DANIEL BOONE COUNTRY
Williamsburg has a special attraction because of its river, its timber, its natural

---

North 54 East 57 poles to the Beginning, according to a plot made by Joseph Gillis, hereunto annexed . . . .'
. . . Thus, there were 45 lots and approximately one acre where the courthouse and grounds are now located.
The county, town, public buildings etc. were laid out in what is now referred to as the lower part of 'Downtown' Williamsburg.''

PITTSBURG

Jones, ''Legend and Lore'' 19 January 1984. In February, 1819, the court ordered the name of the town changed from Williamsburgh to Pittsburg. ''However, there is nothing to show in any other court record, act of legislature, or news item that 'this town' was ever called Pittsburg, as ordered by the court.''

A SNAIL'S PACE

[9] On 3 May 1984, Jones wrote in ''Legend and Lore,'' on the early settlers and the growth of Whitley County and Williamsburg.

''The growth of Williamsburg and Whitley County for the first fifty years was at a snail's pace. The population of Williamsburg in the first fifty years of its existence had grown from 20 persons in the 1820 Census to 139 persons in the Census of 1870.

Perhaps of interest is the population growth of Williamsburg and Whitley County. In 1820 in Whitley County there were 2,340; 1830 — 3,804; 1850 — 7,222; 1860 — 7,522; 1870 — 8,140. There were 146 slaves in 1840, 201 in 1850, and 183 in 1860. Williamsburg population in 1820 was 20; in 1830, 50; in 1840, 75; in 1850, 93; in 1860, 125 and in 1870, 139.

Lewis Collins in his 'Historical Sketches of Kentucky,' first published in 1848, contains one of the earliest descriptions of Whitley County. Quoting in part, 'Corn is the staple product, and hogs the principal export of the county . . . valuation of the taxable property of Whitley County in 1846 was $388,332.00; the number of acres of land in the county, 167,967; the average value of land per acre, $1.42. Williamsburg, the seat of Justice . . . is situated on the right bank of the Cumberland River . . . and contains two lawyers, four stores and groceries, one tavern, and several mechanic shops.' ''

EARLY SETTLERS

Jones, ''Legend and Lore,'' 2 February 1984.

''After Williamsburg and Whitley County were established, the town lots laid off, the courthouse built, events moved slowly. Samuel Cox continued to operate his ferry and tavern. Benjamin Parsons ran his small grocery. 'Whitley Court House' continued as the post office until the 1880's. The population of Williamsburg was sparce. According to the first decennial census taken in 1820, after the establishment of Williamsburg and Whitley County, the population of Williamsburg was 20 souls. Fifty years later, in 1870, the population of the 'seat of Justice' was 139 souls.

Thus, most of the people who lived in what is now Whitley and McCreary County lived in the various settlements in the county. The citizens were busy eking out a bare living by farming, rearing children, and ever alert for hostile Indians that still roamed the county.

[HE CROSSED THE DELAWARE AND FOUGHT WITH WASHINGTON AT VALLEY FORGE]

The early settlers of Whitley County prior to the establishment of the county and the seat of justice were:

Poplar Creek settlers, John Rose, Samuel Rose, Tobias Harp, Joseph Peace, Jesse Peace, Isaiah Jones, Andrew Lee, Charles Cleghorn, John Mahan, William Wells, John Tye [Revolutionary soldier], George Tye, Elizabeth Tye, Joshua Tye, William Matthews, James Matthews, William Mays, Andrew Evans, William Evans, Sr., William Evans, Jr., Thomas Foley, Isaac Johnson, Jesse Sears, Stephen Golden and Pierce Dant Hamlin (a very distinguished Revolutionary War soldier, with an impressive record of crossing the Delaware and fighting with General George Washington at Valley Forge, Pa.).

Laurel Fork early settlers (Frakes), Shelt Partin, Venison Partin, James Brummett and William Lambdin.

Early settlers of Meadow Creek, Isaac Martin (Revolutionary soldier), W. C. Martin, Aaron Freeman, Nathan Freeman, Solomon Perkins, Jonathan McNeil, Andrew Craig, Robert Craig (Revolutionary soldier), John Berry, James Coffee, John Hart, Jesse Rapier, John Sharp, Thomas Sharp, Joel Watkins, William Mackey, Augusta Hill, Will Sharp,

beauty, but most importantly because of King Coal. What's more, this is an historic area in the study of migration patterns[10] and westward movement. After all, the

John Brown, John Johnson, William Dryden and Robert Craig, Jr.

Cumberland River below Mulberry, John Sutton (pre-Revolutionary), Joseph Wilson (pre-Revolutionary), John Sutton (pre-Revolutionary), John Rains and Reece Gatliff.

Cumberland River (Loudon to mouth of Poplar Creek) Aries Witt, William Witt, Nicholas Wilson, John Wilson, James Wilson, William Logan, David Wilson, Jr., Michael Wilson, William Vonay, Jonathan Vonay, John Farris, James Finley [Revolutionary soldier], James Freeman and James Mahan [Revolutionary soldier]. Cumberland River (near Loudon), John Cummins, William Cummins, Hugh Cummins, Charles Gatliff [Revolutionary soldier], William Johnson, Thomas Mahan, William Pennington, John Sears, John Sears, Jr., Nathan Cox, Isaac Taylor and John Hamblin.

Mulberry and Cumberland River, William Monhollen, Amos Veach and Isaac Veach.

Patterson Creek, John Bennett, Robert Blakley, Alex Bryant, William Patterson, William Powers, James Jones, William Bodkin, John Polley, Benjamin Hamblin, Richard Bodkin, George Bunch and Benjamin Rose.

Whitley Court House, Samuel Cox, Nathan Cox, Benjamin Parsons, Milton Eve, Joseph Eve and Andrew Craig.

Bosstown or Lot, Francis Faulkner [Jones, "Legend and Lore" 26 January 1984. Francis Faulkner was one of Whitley County's first Gentlemen Justices. John W. Faulkner who lived in Williamsburg with his wife, Mrs. Debbie Faulkner, until his death was related to Francis Faulkner.], Boss Faulkner, Evan Siler, John Wesley Siler, Lucinda Evans Siler, Jacob Nicholson and Elisha Siler.

The Cross Roads, Nathan Shelley, Reuben Meadors, Henry Porch [Revolutionary soldier], Robert Creekmore, Ballantine Creekmore, Uriah Parks and Simon Peter Jones.

Redbird and Sanders Creek, Nathaniel Smith, Elijah Prewitt, Henry Sanders, John White, William Troy Meadors, Pleasant Winkler Meadors and Abraham Smith.

[Other Revolutionary soldiers from Whitley County were: Thomas Adkins, John Anderson, Joseph Gillis, John Hood, Thomas Laughlin, Joseph Moore, Joseph Moses, James Rogers, William Rose, William Sexton, Darley Smitheart, Michael Stephens, James Sullivan, Daniel Twigg and Anes Witt.]

Of course, there were other settlers, but we are not able to list them all because the early census records only the name of the head of the household.

About one-half of these early settlers migrated from North Carolina, the other half from Virginia.

The settlers traveled in companies consisting of sometimes more than a dozen families. Traveling together, settling in the same communities as neighbors was for purposes of security. Through the years the county has existed, the early pioneers referred to a particular region of the county as a 'settlement.'

There was an abundance of fruit: wild cherries, plums, crabapples, grapes, persimmons, paw-paw, walnuts, chestnuts, hickory nuts, hazelnuts, beechnuts, chincapins, muscadines, blackberries, raspberries and blueberries. Thus, the early settlers had a varied diet. Also, they planted corn, beans, potatoes, cabbage, various greens and the like.

The forest was a vast storehouse of supplies. It was a veritable land that flowed with 'milk and honey.' Wild honey was in abundance, poke-sallet, watercress, fat turkeys, deer, bear and all sorts of small game. The woods contained plenty of herbs, may-apple root, snake root, yellow-root, sassafras, mullin and ginseng. The settlers used some of these for tea and some for medicinal purposes.

The Cumberland and its tributaries were a fisherman's paradise. All kinds of game fish, catfish and other species thrived in the fresh, untainted streams.

The Indians apparently inhabited a great portion of the county on several occasions. There was evidence of the remnants of several old Indian towns. Around these were several acres of cleared land on which there was an abundance of grass. Some of these old settlements were found at Rockholds, Meadow Creek, Redbird, Pleasant View and Boston (Lot)."

[10] "History and Profile of the Cumberland Valley Area," pp. 1-2.

Arnold Payne, a graduate of Cumberland College, wrote the following to the Editor of *The Daily Sentinel*, Nacogdoches, Texas, on 11 October 1986: "I attended Cumberland College, Williamsburg, Kentucky. This college is within a few miles of Cumberland Gap and serves primarily the mountain youth. Among these students are those with family histories back to the days of Daniel Boone, David Crockett, James Bowie, and Sam Houston."

Dr. Payne is also a graduate of Texas A&M University and works as an educational consultant in Nacogdoches, Texas.

COMMUNITY NAMES

Most of the names of the communities in and around Williamsburg have interesting origins. Siler, "Heads or Tales,"

region was initially explored and the first cabin in the area was built in 1750 by

---

8 December 1977, relates the following.

"Corbin was named for a Christian Church minister . . . .

Woodbine was named for the honeysuckle vine, which is also called Woodbine.

Rockhold was named for Thomas Rockhold, merchant and legislator at that locality.

Three places were named for women — Packard for Miss Amelia Packard, a longtime teacher; Sally Gap for Mrs. Sally Lawson; Emlyn for the daughter of a coal developer at that place.

Two localities were named for beautiful surroundings — Pleasant View and Pleasant Run, a small creek. Both were and are very pleasant spots.

Three places were named after trees — Mt. Ash, Red Ash and Black Oak.

Savoy was named for an area in Southeast France.

Three additional spots were named for men — Gatliff was named for Dr. Ancil Gatliff . . . and Siler was named for Preacher Wiltz Siler, father of L.O. Siler and Ben Siler, and Boston was named for Boss Faulkner, ancestor of many, many Faulkners in this area.

Keswick was named for an urbanized district in England.

Jellico was named for a herb called Angelica root . . . .

Julip was named by Rosa Sullivan, the first postmistress at that place. Rosa loved a popular song of that period, 'You wore a tulip, sweeter than Julip' and so forth.

Carpenter was named for a Dr. Carpenter of bygone days . . . ."

On 24 July 1980, Siler in "Heads or Tales," wrote of the twin cities of Lot and Boston, located in the south end of Whitley County.

"Boston has been a little town more than a hundred years. In its heyday it had a church, high school, Masonic Lodge, one doctor, one lawyer, one store where they sold stick candy, a post office and a map showing the town laid off in lots.

Boston was named for Boss Faulkner and the populace was made up of Faulkners, Silers, Lawsons, Perkinses and a few others. One prominent citizen was Hubert Faulkner, who wrote a book called 'Plowman's Folly.'

Lot was named by the railroad company which built a station and put up a sign on it that said, 'LOT.' The land in and near the Lot Depot was fertile as the plains of Lot mentioned in the *Bible* and so the name seemed to fit like a kid glove. It's been Lot ever since.

No one could ever tell when he left Lot and went over to Boston, but when you walked 100 yards away from the depot and over toward the postoffice you could be sure you were in Boston. There was a great big open ditch near the depot that had two crossties over it for a foot bridge. You could almost hear that Boston hospitality saying 'Welcome stranger — and don't ever leave us. If you do leave us, it will be worse folly than "Plowman's Folly." ' "

On 10 November 1977, Siler wrote in "Heads or Tales," of several other local communities, two of which have changed their names in this century.

"The little towns that changed names are Woodbine, formerly Joefield and Wofford, formerly Mahan.

Places now completely gone are Coalmont, which means mountains of coal, and Peerless, which means without an equal. Both of these were little coal mining towns . . . .

The underpass is at Faber, while the other railroad crossings are at Rockholds and Wofford.

. . . At Woodbine, you will see the only brick-making factory in the county.

Then you will enter Faber, home of that underpass, ...

Next you will come to Rockholds, the biggest town between Woodbine and Williamsburg. Got its name from Thomas Rockhold, who once served in the state legislature and who, I believe, had a country store at this important crossroads community. At Rockholds, you can turn eastward and land on Meadow Creek or Westward and arrive at Buffalo, ...

You can continue your journey and pass Jack's Fork and then go past that ghostly spot I mentioned, once called Coalmont . . . .

And now you may have some good luck. You will come to Wofford, the only place in the county which was once a health resort. It had a mineral spring. Its water was said to be good for your health. Nearby they had a combination boarding house, store and post office, all in one building . . . .

After you pass Wofford, you will encounter another ghostly place once called Peerless. It had miners' houses on the hillside and a company store down by the railroad track."

In his 16 December 1965, "Heads or Tails" column, Siler wrote of two Perry County towns named for Whitley County men.

Dr. Thomas Walker,[11] and later Daniel Boone himself pioneered or ventured into this area. Long before Walker and Boone, tribal Indians inhabited this land.[12]

Bulan was named for Bulan Cheeley, and "Jeff, for Jeff Roberts. These men were engaged in the coal business up in that county, and the little places they helped to establish were named for them."

TOM SILER

Tom Siler, *Tennessee Towns: From Adams to Yorkville* (Knoxville, Tennessee: East Tennessee Historical Society, 1985), p. 44.

(An interesting coincidence is that Mr. Tom Siler is an alumnus of Cumberland College and is an avid supporter of the College. Several years ago Mr. Jack Howard of Scripps-Howard newspapers responded when asked, "Why do you give to Cumberland College?" that he had received a letter from the College asking for money. He picked up the telephone and called the sports editor at *The Knoxville News Sentinel.* He asked Tom Siler if he knew anything about the College, and Tom responded that he did indeed, he had even attended the College. Since that time Mr. Howard has supported the College.)

Until 1883, the town now known as Jellico was called Smithburg. It was renamed Jellico, according to Siler, "from the angelica root used in brewing an exhilerating drink called Jelka." With the coming of the railroad, Jellico was the center for coal shipping since both the L&N line and the Southern line passed through the town. "Jellico Coal" was "known throughout Appalachia."

In September 1906, the town of Jellico was struck by one of the worst disasters in its history when a train car loaded with dynamite exploded.

DISASTER IN JELLICO

The following account, "Jellico Wrecked by Dynamite Explosion," appeared in the *Advance Sentinel,* 28 December 1906.

"The appalling disaster caused by the explosion of dynamite in our town, Friday, September 21st is so great and so far reaching that our people can not begin to grasp the magnitude of it. Everywhere one turns he faces wreck and ruin. Not a single residence in the town escaped damage; some of course are worse than others. It would be impossible to give in detail all the damage done to each residence, many are so badly damaged that they can never be replaced in their former condition . . . . It is utterly impossible to describe the awful destruction to residence property, especially in the territory bounded by a line running east with the corporation line and with the corporation line to the state line and with the state line to the railroad . . . .

The day may come when the city of Jellico will have outlived financially the calamity whose dire results now hang like a pall over all the community . . . .

Over all the scene men and women appear with blanched faces and trembling hearts realizing that they have passed through the very jaws of death.

Such is but a suggestion of the awful picture that presented itself in Jellico on the morning of the explosion. None who saw it can forget it."

DR. THOMAS WALKER

[11] According to Jones, "Legend and Lore," 26 January 1984, Dr. Thomas Walker was the first white man to record being in Whitley County. Walker, an explorer from Virginia, kept a diary on his travels. He noted on April 24 that he had come upon " 'fresh tracks of seven or eight Indian.' " On 27 April 1750, Walker reported finding " 'the remains of several Indian cabbins [sic] and amongst them a round hill . . . 20 feet high and 60 feet over the top.' " These "Indian mounds [are] located near Tye's Ferry about 20 miles from Williamsburg."

According to "History and Profile of the Cumberland Valley Area," pp. 1-2, Walker made the following notation in his diary concerning the area: " 'Nature has gathered here her richest blessing of all things which add to men's comfort and happiness, and I can think of no better place to found a settlement for our people than this beautiful valley.' "

THE DUKE OF CUMBERLAND

Walker was also credited with naming the region Cumberland Valley for the Duke of Cumberland, Commander-in-Chief of the British Armed Forces.

[12] According to "History and Profile of the Cumberland Valley Area," p.1, the earliest known white visitors explored the area in 1674, but it was nearly a century before pioneers began to settle in the area.

DR. EPHRAIM McDOWELL

By 1777, according to Siler, "Heads or Tales," 14 July 1977, settlers were coming into the area, but there were few doctors to see to their needs. In fact, it was only a few years later that Dr. Ephraim McDowell of Danville without the use of any anesthesia "successfully performed abdominal surgery on a woman." There was no such thing as anesthesia in existence. So the patient used

By 1883, however, Scotch-Irish had streamed through Cumberland Gap, and the railroad was on its way to Williamsburg.[13]

---

the 23rd Psalm, repeating it over and over until the surgery was finished.''

In "Legend and Lore," 26 January 1984, Jones wrote: "John Tye, Jr., 1794, was the first white man in Whitley County (still Lincoln County) killed by the Indians at the mouth of Dulin Branch, above the late Joe Lark Bennett's.

The second white man killed by the Indians in Whitley County was Joseph Johnson, son of Michael, about where the brick plant used to be located near Woodbine . . . .''

This accounting was reported in greater detail to Mrs. Harold Browning, editor of *The Whitley Republican,* on 5 February 1948, by Verna Wilder Denham. In a letter to Mrs. Browning, Mrs. Denham quoted Lewis Collins, ''Historical Sketches of Kentucky,'' first published in 1848: '' 'Shortly before settlements were formed in what is now Whitley County, John Tye, his son, and some two or three other men, having encamped on the Head of Big Poplar Creek, were attacked after night by a party of Cherokee Indians. Tye's son was killed, and the old man wounded. The other men fled after the first fire of the Indians, and made their escape.' ''

In his 5 April 1984, "Legend and Lore" Jones wrote of Verna Wilder Denham.

"In the opinion of the author, the late Verna Denham was the only historian of Williamsburg, during the days of her life, and those that lived in her days and years.

Mrs. Denham was born in 1857 and died at the age of 96, in 1953. She was one of Williamsburg's most beloved citizens. She was the wife of the late illustrious attorney, L. D. Denham. Both Mr. and Mrs. Denham were from study (sic) pioneer families, who were cultural influences in the early history of the county. She remained alert and energetic almost to the end. With unfailing memory, accurate records kept, and ardent research, her records present these facts:

Back in 1869 there were no speedy highways or lightening railroad express to bring merchandise to your front door; no Sears-Roebuck over night delivery by parcel post. In 1869, the Rev. Joel Wilder, father of Mrs. Denham, opened the first drug store in Williamsburg. He had to go to Livingston (that is as far as the Louisville and Nashville Railroad extended) by way of horseback and ox-cart, to collect his goods sent from Louisville. Or, if he ordered them from Knoxville, by the same conveyance, he had to meet the train at Caryville, Tenn., the nearest railroad terminus to the south of Williamsburg.

Mrs. Denham's father was the son of Solomon Wilder and the grandson of Sampson Wilder who purchased 200 acres of land near the present Red Bird Church in 1809. Sampson Wilder and four other men helped survey and supervise the building of the road from Williamsburg to Barbourville in 1818.

Note: Mrs. Verna Denham was the grandmother of Dr. Ralph Denham, a prominent cardiologist in Louisville, and Honorable Glenn Denham, a prominent Middlesboro attorney.''

In the 24 October 1985, "Legend and Lore," Jones relates an accounting of Edward Arthur, 1830-1920. The information was provided Jones by the late Mr. Hugh C. Steely. Edward Arthur was a pioneer who fought in the Mexican War as well as the Civil War. He traveled all over the country and even sailed from California to New York by way of the Isthmus of Panama. On one of his trips on a wagon train, Arthur watched as Indians skinned a man alive. Arthur was the father of three sons and three daughters. One daughter, Susan, married Dr. E. S. Moss.

INDIANS PASS THROUGH WILLIAMSBURG

In his 17 January 1985, "Legend and Lore," Jones recalls a story told by James O. White of Rockhold. White described a scene from his early childhood days in Williamsburg in 1895, when as a boy of 11, "he watched a tribe, or tribes of Indians pass through Williamsburg. They were on foot from their Reservation in the South to Washington to receive a supply of clothing from the Federal Government.''

[13] Harry M. Caudill, *Theirs Be The Power* (University of Illinois Press: Urbana and Chicago, 1983), p. 9.

THE L&N RAILROAD: A FORERUNNER TO I-75

On 17 May 1984, Jones wrote in "Legend and Lore" on the coming of the railroad to Whitley County and on the coal industry in the area.

"With the advent of the railroad, both Williamsburg and Whitley County began to flourish like a 'Green Bay

This, then, was a time in our nation's history when people moved more slowly and time passed less swiftly.[14]

There were, of course, no radio or television, few if any automobiles, and pre-

---

Tree.' Out in the settlements there was plenty of white oak for crossties, and staves. This was a good cash crop.

Corbin was born about that time also, and soon was to become one of the largest railroad centers in the South.

Another boon to Williamsburg, Corbin and the whole of Whitley County was the development and mining of vast deposits of coal underlying most of the mountain areas of the county. Coal mining began as soon as the Louisville and Nashville Railroad was completed to Smithburg (now Jellico), and the Southern was completed from Knoxville to Smithburg.''

By 1914, according to Jones, ''Legend and Lore,'' 5 December 1985,

''. . . the Williamsburg depot was about the busiest place in town.

The L&N Train schedule for 1914 was: 'Local Time Table, Williamsburg, Kentucky:

NORTH BOUND

No. 34 Through 1:34 a.m.

No. 38 Local 10:20 a.m.

No. 32 Through 2:49 p.m.

No. 26 Local 8:00 p.m.

SOUTH BOUND

No. 31 Through 3:00 p.m.

No. 25 Local 6:59 a.m.

No. 33 Through 1:57 p.m.

Numbers 25 and 37 connect with trains at Savoy for the Pine Mountain Branch (Packard and Gatliff).

Number 32 stops on flag for Louisville and Cincinnati and beyond. Numbers 25, 26, 37 and 38 run via Jellico and make all local stops between Corbin and Knoxville.' ''

Siler in ''Heads or Tales,'' 5 June 1975, reminisced of the

''. . . romance and friendly atmosphere of trains . . . . School children would look at the train's fleeting glory and dream of something almost unimaginable at the end of the line — a circus, a street car, a big ice cream soda, pink or chocolate brown, way out yonder somewhere.

People on the train were friendly and often asked where you were going and 'where you from?'

If the conductor had time he would sit down with you, talk a little and make you feel at home on his train.''

P. T. BARNUM

Many people recall the excitement each time the train went through town, but special excitement was brought when the circus would pass through town on the railroad. Children would line the tracks to watch as the P. T. Barnum Circus would pass. The following information ''P.T. Barnum was Showman,'' appeared in the *Lexington Herald-Leader,* Lexington, Kentucky, 17 July 1986, p. C11.

''Phineas Taylor Barnum (1810 - 1891) was born in Bethel, Conn. He worked at his father's country store and later was a bartender, newspaper publisher and theater ticket seller.

In 1835 he entered show business by exhibiting a black woman who was said to have been George Washington's nurse and to be more than 160 years old. Later he bought two museums in New York and combined them into Barnum's Museum. Among the exhibitions was Tom-Thumb, the famous midget.

Because the lines of people did not move fast enough through the museum, Barnum had a sign put up directing people to the 'egress.' Many visitors who didn't know that the word meant 'exit' thought they were going to see some strange monster, but they found themselves suddenly on the outside.

Thumb became so famous that Barnum took him to Europe and exhibited him before Queen Victoria and the French court. He later induced Jenny Lind, 'the Swedish nightingale,' to come to America by contracting to pay for 150 concerts at $1,000 a night. It was a great success.

In 1871 Barnum organized a circus and menagerie that required 500 men and horses to move it from place to place. In the next few years this exhibition was seen by several million people. It was called 'The Greatest Show on Earth.'

Later Barnum combined his circus with that of his rival, James Bailey. In 1882, he brought to the United States the huge African elephant Jumbo. It became one of the greatest exhibitions of the time.''

[14] ''The Cumberland College Story,'' Pamphlet for Prospective Students, 1960.

cious few newspapers or magazines. The greatest social events of the day were weddings and burials and all day church meetings with "dinner on the ground." And like any other community, one generation followed another as time marched on.

COLLEGE FEVER

By the beginning of the Civil War,[15] "scores of colleges" many of which lacked the "resources necessary for permanent survival" had been founded. No limitation, Indian attack, poor facility or inclement weather could slow down the college founding movement which continued even after the war. Seemingly every community

---

LIFE FOR OUR FOREFATHERS

In "Legend and Lore," 26 September 1985, Jones reminds us that our forefathers "carved out the wilderness, braved the dangers of Indian attacks, built log cabins, and raised products to sustain them . . . . So, be proud you are the descendant of mountaineers."

In his 24 May 1984, "Legend and Lore," Jones described the food of the early settlers. They ate mostly wild meat: hogs, turkeys, venison, lamb, and fresh fish. During the summers vegetables were grown and dried or stored for winter. Corn and wheat were also an annual crop. Herbs were grown for seasoning and sugar came from maple trees, wild honey, and molasses. Salt came from "salt mines near Mount Vernon, Kentucky."

THE RAILROAD AND PROGRESS: LUMBER AND COAL

On 25 June 1985, in "Legend and Lore," Jones wrote of the conditions in Whitley County during the 1880's. "Prior to 1880, there were no telephones, electricity, railroads, or hard surfaced highways in this country . . . . Progress in this area was very slow." With the coming of the L&N Railroad came progress.

"Various companies in the East brought in sawmills, stave mills, tanneries, and industry began a rapid growth . . . . The main industrial growth however was the development of the coal industry . . . . Perhaps the first coal mine in Whitley County of significance was the Birdeye Coal Company on Cane Creek, near Jellico. It was followed by Kensee Mines and the Proctor Coal Company . . . .

In 1908, Dr. A. Gatliff, a pioneer in the coal mining industry, organized the mines at Gatliff. In 1910-1911, the Mahan-Jellico Coal Company, under the management of T.B. Mahan, was organized. The coal camp was named Packard, after a brilliant student and faculty member of the Williamsburg Institute, Amelia Packard."

Siler in "Heads or Tales," 30 April 1981, reminds us that coal mining was different then. "In other days they used compressed air punchers instead of electric cutting machinery. And they used dinky steam locomotives or mules to pull out the mining cars loaded with coal."

LORETTA LYNN: A COAL MINER'S DAUGHTER

In his 31 July 1980, "Heads or Tales," Siler recalls that Loretta Lynn was a coal miner's daughter from Butcher Hollow in eastern Kentucky and that the movie, "Coal Miner's Daughter," fairly accurately portrays life as it was in a mining camp.

"Miners go into the long, black, damp corridors that reach a mile or more under the mountain and then after working 7 or 8 hours in semidarkness they come out, mostly laughing and 'joshing' each other.

Miners have a good sense of humor. They call a new man on the job a 'greenhorn.' And if he is wearing pretty good clothes they say, 'He is wearing store clothes . . . .'

Often an older miner will send a young greenhorn out to get a left-handed monkey wrench or a pair of rib shears."

THE CIVIL WAR

[15] Jones wrote the following account of the Civil War in his "Legend and Lore," 8 March 1984, and 15 March 1984: "The Civil War years were sorrowful ones for the citizens of not only the Commonwealth, but for Whitley County as well." Both the North and the South sought Kentucky's support. Kentucky, however, was divided. "Ironically, the leaders of both the North and South were born in Kentucky:" Lincoln in 1809 "on Nolin's Creek, near Hodgenville" and Davis "at Fairview, between Elkton and Hopkinsville in 1808."

"Most of Whitley County's citizens were pro-union." Of the 580 volunteers, only eight went with the Confederacy.

"*The Louisville Journal* of Dec. 17, 1862, relates in some detail depredations committed by the Rebels coming into Whitley County, up Clear Fork, to Williamsburg, then west to Jellico Creek and Marsh Creek and back to Tennessee

in the country wanted a college to call its own. A hometown college was a status symbol, brought money to the town, gave local folk an opportunity to broaden

---

by way of Buffalo Creek.

The article recited that the Rebels burned houses and drove away with horses and cattle. Larkin Cross and Ranson Conover was [sic] hanged in an apple tree belonging to the widow Angel. Four of the rebels were killed and several were wounded.

On July 25, 1863, Colonel John S. Scott came up from Tennessee with 1600 soldiers to destroy communications and obtain cattle, mules and arms.

At Williamsburg he was met by 100 pickets from the 44th Ohio Infantry. Scott's brigade drove the outnumbered pickets toward London, and he was able to get to Winchester where he retreated back to Tennessee with heavy losses.

On April 23, 1863, a small Confederate detachment was defeated at Rockholds with four being killed, and nine taken prisoner.

In June, 1863, a contingent of John Hunt Morgan's raiders were camped on the River Road (now 6th Street) in the bottoms near where Will Buhl used to live.''

ULYSSES S. GRANT

According to "History and Profile of the Cumberland Valley Area," p. 3,

"The first battle in Kentucky is believed to have been fought in 1861 at Barbourville . . . . Many of the battles in the area, though not well known, were pivotal in the war's outcome. By controlling the Cumberland area, the Union was able to keep the Confederates from advancing and disrupting the flow of men and goods on the Ohio River, which fed into the Mississippi and the heart of the South. General Ulysses S. Grant was once stationed in Barbourville, and the region was often the site of many of the famous raids by the Confederacy's General John Hunt Morgan.''

AUNT JULIA MARCUM

On 8 November 1984, Jones' "Legend and Lore" contained a copy of "the handwritten account of Ms. Julia Marcum's experiences during the Civil War . . . .'' The original handwritten account is the property of Dr. Ralph Denham of Louisville and reads as follows:

"In Scott County, Tennessee (Huntsville, the County Seat), I was born in the year of 1844, the 7th day of November. My father and mother, Hiram C. Marcum and Permelia Huff Marcum, lived and owned a farm on the Waters Buffalo Creek four miles east of Huntsville, the county seat of Scott County.

Hiram C. Marcum was a son of Arthur Marcum and Ann Marcum. She was Ann Bransgrove. Father had four brothers: Joseph, John, William, and George and three sisters: Polly, Tabitha, and Luvina. My mother (Permelia Huff Marcum) was a daughter of John and Prudence Christian Huff. The Huffs were decendents of England and Ireland, the Marcums of England.

Hiram and Permelia Marcum had five children, one son, Clayburn; four daughters: Didama, Minerva, Julia Ann and Martha Ellen.

He was a farmer, lived on his farm made a living and was a happy, law abiding Christian man and also his family. He stood for the flag and freedom of America and its perfect laws.

In the year 1861, the south seceded against the North for slaves and bondage of slaves. Hiram Marcum was for freedom of our nation and its liberties for the people. In the year 1861, the secedants declared war against the North. Father stood for the Union and its Principles. Then, the Presydent [sic] declared war on the Southern States. The Confederates elected for themselves a president, then divided the nation and called out their army to fight the Northern people. Marcum stood for the Union. Then they mustered their armies and their people became enraged toward each other, tried to kill and destroy each other and the Rebels invaded our County as there were but few Rebels in the County. They sent their armies there to kill and destroy our men, women and property. They came to our home and hunted for Marcum, watched night and day to kill him because he was a union man for the Federal side and threatened his family with death if we did not tell where he was. Then, on the 7th night of September at 2 o'clock in the morning, 1861, they came to our house, broke the door open with bayonets on their guns and said there was 36 men around who had come to kill Marcum and would kill all the women and burn us all in the house. We began to holler and scream for help.

Just one soldier stayed in the house. We burned tallow candles at that day and time. There was but a small piece of candle and sister Didama got hold of a match and lighted it. He picked out at us with the bayonet on his gun and choked Mother. Didama ran upstairs to get another candle, he ran upstairs, grabbed hold of her and said he would cut her throat and burn us all in the house. She screamed for help. Father was hid out on the farm. He heard us calling for help. All the weapons that we had in the house were two chopping axes. Minerva got one and I the other one. Two men ran from the door just as I started upstairs. Minerva threw her ax down. I went on up. He struck at me

their horizons, and provided renewal and hope for the future.[16] In the mountain region several institutions were founded, four of which were in Whitley County.

First was Boston Academy at Lot in the 1870's. Professor William H. Nesbit who has been called the "Father of Whitley County Education" came from Pennsylvania and founded this school.

Cora College (Cora Institute) with its charter approved 30 April 1888, was located at Pleasant View. Professor Nesbit was apparently one of the founders of this school, also. There is the claim that the college even took its name from that of Nesbit's wife, Cora.[17]

Williamsburg Academy (later to be given the name of Highland College) was

---

with the bayonet on his gun, I ran under the gun and chopped him in the face and breast with an ax, cut him to the hollow and split his chin open with the ax, getting the best of him. I knocked his gun from his hands. He staggered around and around and said 'don't chop me any more.' But I did not stop. He got hold of the gun and stuck the bayonet in my forehead, burst my skull, knocked my brains out, put out my left eye and shot my third finger off my right hand. Father came up the stairs just as the gun fell out of his hands. Father shot him in the shoulder, he fell dead.

The light was knocked out. All was in darkness. I was knocked unconscious and didn't come to for some time. They got a light and brought me back to life. Father brought me downstairs, laid me on the bed, took his gun and went out of the house, but all the rest of the Rebels had run off. Then I asked Father to leave for they would come back and kill him and he went away from home. Then, Brother Clayburn went out to get somebody to come to our assistance. As he went, he found the horse the Rebel had ridden there in the lane. He got on it and rode to several houses and begged for help. He got one woman, Mrs. Taylor to come with him.

He turned the horse loose. It went back to camp a mile and a half from our home. Colonel Raines' regiment was camped there. When daylight came, Mother sent Mrs. Taylor to tell the Colonel of it and to come and take the old dead Rebel away from her house. Captain Gordon came with a company of soldiers, when he saw me, he sent back to the regiment for their doctors. They dressed my wounds and took the dead man away. We were left in a terrible fix to the mercy of the Rebels but they went away."

Jones began the story of Ms. Marcum on 17 November 1983, in "Legend and Lore," by noting that Julia Marcum who lived in Williamsburg until her death was the

". . . only woman in the United States ever to get a Federal Civil War Pension without the bother of being married or in some way of tying herself up with a man . . . .

On May 10, 1936, she was given a military funeral.

. . . Aunt Julia spent most of her life in patriotic and religious work. On patriotic anniversaries she always had her house and lawn . . . decorated with flags.

There is a historical marker located on the courthouse lawn that decribes briefly her exploits as a 16-year-old girl . . . ."

[16] John S. Brubacher and Willis Rudy, *Higher Education in Transition* (Harper and Row, Publishers, 1976), pp. 59-60.

BOSTON ACADEMY

[17] James Hayden Siler, *A History of Jellico, Tennessee; Containing Historical Information on Campbell County, Tennessee, and Whitley County, Kentucky.* From articles by Siler appearing in the Jellico *Advance-Sentinel,* Summer and Fall, 1938, p.24. James Hayden Siler gave a good account of the Boston Academy's founding saying the most important subscription school of the 1870's was the Boston Academy (sometimes referred to as Boston High School). Professor Nesbit "was a brilliant scholar, and fine teacher, and many prominent Whitley Countians 'went to' him." Siler continues his description of the Boston Academy by telling of another of its teachers, Professor Napoleon Bonaparte Hays who later became Attorney General for the Commonwealth of Kentucky. Hays had taught at Pineville, Barbourville, and Flat Lick before coming to Lot with his wife who was an accomplished pianist. They brought with them a piano, the first ever seen by many of the folks at Lot.

According to Siler "the Boston Academy was probably equivalent to the first two years of high school" with courses in algebra, geometry, and French. "The school was well-known" throughout the region. In fact, former Governor James D. Black attended the Boston Academy.

Professor Nesbit died on February 26, 1890, and his remains lie buried in the Highland Cemetery, Williamsburg. The inscription on his stone reads, "In memory of Professor William A. Nesbit, the pioneer and most efficient instructor of the mountains

founded by Reverend A.A. Myers. The Academy opened its doors in the fall of 1882.[18]

Williamsburg Institute (later named Cumberland College and hereinafter referred to as Cumberland College) opened for classes on 7 January 1889.

Other colleges in the area but not in Whitley County were Berea College founded in 1855[19] to the north and Union College founded in 1879[20] to the east. Lincoln Memorial University was founded later in 1897,[21] also to the east.

Because of the rigorous mountain terrain, each of these higher education institutions provided a needed service. Those familiar with Appalachia know that when the College was being brought into existence — and even today — there was, and is, a genuine need for higher education opportunities for deserving mountain youth. Clearly the need for educational opportunities existed in Williamsburg in the late 1800's since there were few roads and fewer elementary and secondary schools.[22]

The Civil War had been over for no more than a few decades when the movement to found Cumberland College took place. This College would weather the Spanish

---

of Kentucky. Born in Pa. Sept. 12, 1835. Died Pleasant View, Ky. Feb. 26, 1890. Erected by his mountain students.''

Nesbit was also one of the co-founders of Cora College, Pleasant View, along with James Stillman, M.E. Mahan, Benjamin Sharp, H.S. Jones, R. Bird, H.F. Rose, H.C. King, H.S. Sullivan, and W.C. Bryant. Robert Boone Bird donated the land for the school. Cora College ceased to exist in the early 1890's.

[18] Verna Wilder Denham, ''Historical Record of the Williamsburg Academy, 1878, 1907'' (Typed MS, Cumberland College Library), p.2.

CASSIUS M. CLAY

[19] According to Berea College's *Catalogue,* Berea owes its beginning to the reform movements of the last century. The founders were men and women of apostolic faith and courage. The Reverend John G. Fee, ardently supporting the cause of freedom through his preaching against slavery, attracted the attention of Cassius M. Clay, a leader in the movement of gradual emancipation. Mr. Clay had noticed that the people in the mountains were the natural supporters of freedom because they owned land but did not own slaves, and he invited Mr. Fee in 1853 to establish a settlement on the edge of the mountains where free speech could be maintained.

Cassius Marcellus Clay was, incidentally, the uncle of Green Clay Smith, one of Cumberland College's founders.

[20] Union College, *Catalogue.*

[21] Lincoln Memorial University, *Catalogue.*

[22] Jones, in his ''Legend and Lore,'' 7 November 1985, reminds us that ''Public schools were late in reaching Whitley County and her neighbors.'' In fact, the 1870 Census showed only five percent of the County's adults able to read and write. The North had its private schools, village schools, and church schools, but it was only with the movement to establish free schools by the Masons in the early 1800's that the South began its move toward education. However, the Appalachian area still lagged behind.

The primary text of the 1870's in Whitley County schools was ''Noah Webster's 'Blue Back Speller,' '' and by the 1880's ''McGuffey Readers'' were used.

The recess games included '' 'London Bridge is Falling Down,' 'Ring Around the Roses,' 'Hide -n- Seek,' 'Fox and Hounds,' 'Antey Over' . . . .''

American War, two World Wars, the Korean and Vietnam conflicts,[23] several

---

PATRIOTISM

[23] The subject of patriotism comes as no surprise to anyone in this geographical area. After all, this is the area which gave rise to Sergeant York, the Hatfields and the McCoys, Daisy Mae and 'Lil Abner, the Beverly Hillbillies, and the Dukes of Hazzard.

Today an American flag flies on Cumberland's property adjacent to Interstate Highway 75 where approximately twelve million people pass by annually. The flag is flown in a spirit of patriotism for this great country and respect for all of the college's alumni and professors who have gallantly served this nation. Cumberland has played a part in our nation's history, sending staff and students alike off to defend this country.

One professor Dr. J.T. Vallandingham took leaves of absence to fight in both World War I and World War II. President emeritus James M. Boswell served as a Lieutenant Commander in World War II during which time he wrote a text on damage control which is still used by the United States Navy, I'm told.

Several alumni and other Whitley Countians have served as military officers, some becoming Generals and one becoming an Admiral, not to mention an array of other officers who have distinguished themselves through honor and duty to God and country.

ADMIRAL CHARLES BLAKELY

Siler in "Heads or Tales," 10 February 1977, wrote of Charles Blakely.

"Admiral Charles A. Blakely was once a barefoot boy from Briar Creek but later he became the highest ranking Naval Officer whoever emerged from the state of Kentucky, so far as I have learned from any available source.

After graduating from the United States Naval Academy in the early years of this century, Charles served in many places all around the world. He qualified himself both as a plane pilot and as a submarine commander and had been the 'old man' in charge of numerous naval units all the way from the Hall of Montezuma to the Shores of Tripoli.

. . . Charley was a very personable and brilliant man and when he would return to Williamburg, he was socialized and respected by everyone all over town. They would say, 'Charley is back on leave and he's looking like a real big man of the navy.' Up and down the streets people talked about Charley Blakely."

[SEEING THEIR CHILDREN OBTAIN ADVANTAGES THEY THEMSELVES NEVER HAD]

Charles A. Blakely was the son of Sue Blakely Slaughter and John W. Siler. He was born at Briar Creek and educated at Williamsburg Academy, graduating in the class of 1897.

According to Simon L. Renfro, *Renfro Revelations,* Vol. III, No. 4, April 1946, p.87, Blakely received the Distinguished Service Medal from the United States and the Distinguished Service Order from Great Britain for his service in World War I. Among the ships he commanded were the U.S.S. Denver, the U.S.S. Michigan, and the U.S.S. O'Brien.

Not only was he a naval officer but a soldier and aviator as well. He served as an Infantry volunteer during the Spanish American War and was later appointed to the Naval Military Academy. In 1932 he enrolled in an observer's aviation course at Pensacola Naval Air Station. In 1935 he enrolled as a student aviator, completing his training in 1936. He was the first man to have experience in submarines, surface vessels, and aerial flight.

Blakely then served as commanding officer of the Naval Air Station at Pensacola and of the Scouting Force Aircraft Squadrons. In 1936 he was one of only three Vice Admirals in the Navy and he took command of the Battle Force Aircraft Squadrons. Following this command, he served as Commandant of the 11th Naval District and the Naval Operating Base, San Diego. He retired as Vice Admiral in 1942.

Blakely is said to have always had a love for Whitley County and its people.

" 'All through my wanderings in the past forty-seven years I have not forgotten Whitley County and the relatives and friends who, in my youth, helped me when the going was rough. Nor have I forgotten the wise precepts and advice instilled into the mountain youth by the rugged citizenry of Whitley County in their desire to see their children obtain advantages they themselves never had, which resulted in Williamsburg becoming an early education center that would be a credit to any community. Williamsburg, and its people — my people — laid the foundation for what success I may have had.' "

[ALWAYS TELL PEOPLE WHERE YOU'RE FROM AND BE PROUD OF IT]

". . . The Admiral had a deep and abiding love for his native land. He tells of meeting Grace Moore in Washington, and asked her where she was from. She replied, 'Near Knoxville.' He said, 'Well, I am from Williamsburg.' 'Oh,' she cried, 'I am from Jellico.' 'I told her to come out boldly and say she came from Jellico, that she owed it to her home and that no one in Knoxville cared where she came from.' He claimed that it was good advice for any young person who came from a small place. 'And,' he concluded, 'The good Lord knows I have scattered the name

economic depressions and recessions, and other cataclysmic changes while remaining

of Briar Creek (where I was born) to the four corners of the globe.' ''

CAPTAIN DWIGHT L. MOODY

Dwight Lyman Moody, a native of Packard, attended Cumberland College before entering the United States Naval Academy in 1931. After being graduated from the Academy, Moody served various naval assignments from Assistant Navigator to Commanding Officer.

During his career Moody earned several commendations including the American Defense Service Medal with Star and the World War II Victory Medal.

After having survived the rigors of war, Moody's death occurred several years later as a result of an extreme reaction to the sting of a bumblebee.

MAJOR GENERAL CHARLES G. CALLOWAY

Charles G. Calloway, Resume'. Major General Charles G. Calloway was reared in Whitley County and attended Cumberland College from the eighth grade through one year of college.

In 1925 Calloway received an appointment to the United States Military Academy and was graduated in 1929.

General Calloway served with McArthur in Australia, New Guinea, and the Philippine Islands and with the Army General Staff in Washington, D.C., during World War II.

In 1954 Calloway was promoted to the rank of Brigadier General and given command of the New Research and Development Command. In 1957 he received the rank of Major General.

In 1960 Calloway was moved to the Army General Staff, Washington, D.C., where he remained until his retirement in 1961. Calloway married Marian Dalrymple in 1930. She was a graduate of Cumberland College.

Siler in his ''Heads or Tales,'' 26 August 1985, described Calloway ''as a red headed boy . . . whose father was a humble working man.''

MAJOR GENERAL FLOYD L. PARKS

''Major General Floyd Parks, Army Chief of Information, Washington, will be the 1951 Honor Guest at Laurel County Homecoming.'' *The Whitley Republican*, 31 May 1951. Parks was born in Louisville but his family moved to Lily shortly after his birth when his father Lyman Lewis Parks purchased the Lily Mining and Manufacturing Company. Later the family moved to Williamsburg so the children could attend school at the Williamsburg Institute. Parks' mother Lizzie Pratt Manly Parks was the daughter of one of the founders of the Southern Baptist Theological Seminary.

Parks went from Cumberland College to Clemson College in South Carolina where he was graduated with a bachelor's degree. He enlisted as a private in the Army in 1918. While continuing his Army career, Parks attended Yale Univesity and was graduated in 1924 with a master's degree in mechanical engineering.

Parks served as an instructor at Camp Meade for one year before being sent to Hawaii. In 1941 as a Lieutenant Colonel he became Secretary, General Staff of the General Headquarters. He then served as Chief of Staff of Army Headquarters, Ground Forces in Washington, D.C.; Assistant Division Commander 9th Infantry Division; Chief of Staff, Headquarters, First Allied Airborne Army in Europe. As Commander of the First Airborne Army, Parks participated in the crossing of the Rhine at Wesel in March 1945 in what is said to have been the largest airborne force lifted in one day during the war.

Parks was also responsible for leading the U.S. troops into Berlin on 1 July 1945, and he made the arrangements for the U.S. personnel at the Potsdam Conference and was commended by President Truman for his preparations.

General Parks was Chief Commander of the Allied Kommandantantura, the military governing body of Berlin, and he was responsible for the inauguration of policies and procedures to improve the relationships among the occupation forces.

Parks returned to Washington in 1946 as Chief of the Public Information Division, War Department, later designated as Chief of Information. He held this position except for one year when he served as Deputy Commander of the United States Army in the Pacific.

In March 1955, Congressman Eugene Siler along with other congressmen were guests of the President at the White House. General Parks was present at this meeting. In the article, ''Eisenhower and Siler Reminisce on Arbuckle Coffee Coupons.'' *The Whitley Republican*, 17 March 1955, p. 1, Siler recollected that Parks had been a member of his father's Sunday School class at the First Baptist Church, Williamsburg.

In his 26 August 1965, ''Heads or Tales,'' Siler further recalled that Parks as a child often wore patched clothes and that

true to the founding purpose: "To provide a first class education at rates that are compatible within the means of mountain people."[24]

CAN ONE MAN CHANGE THE WORLD?

The question is often asked in today's cynical world, "Can one man change the world?" Clearly the answer is "yes" today even as it was when the College was getting underway. So often when God decides to do something great He uses just one person, be it an Abraham, a Moses, a Martha, a Mary, a Paul, or a Timothy. One

---

"he worked at every odd job he could get to help pay his school expenses and support his family budget."

BRIGADIER GENERAL ROY W. EASLEY

The following information on General Easley was provided by Mrs. Homer Davis of Williamsburg, Kentucky. Mrs. Davis is the sister of General Easley.

Brigadier General Easley was born in Frankfort and was graduated from Williamsburg Institute. He joined the Army's First Officers' Training Camp in 1917 and by June 1918 was commissioned a First Lieutenant. In 1921 he made the rank of Captain and organized and commanded Company "D" of the Kentucky National Guard. In 1931 he was promoted to Major and then to Lieutenant Colonel, Kentucky National Guard; and in 1936 to Colonel, Kentucky National Guard.

During World War II, Easley was assistant division commander of the 38th "Cyclone" Division in the Philippines. He received the bronze star and other honors.

Following his retirement, he served as Executive Director of the Kentucky Disabled Ex-Serviceman's Board and as Director of the Department of Welfare's Correction Department.

Easley passed away in 1985 at the age of 94.

COLONEL RONALD B. STEWART

Ronald B. Stewart, Resume'. Colonel Ronald B. Stewart was graduated from Cumberland College in 1953 and from the University of Kentucky School of Law in 1959.

In 1954 Stewart enlisted in the Army where his interest in law was heightened. He served various posts as counsel. In 1969 Colonel Stewart began his military judicial service which lasted until 1985. He holds the record of the longest period of continuous judicial service in U.S. Army history serving not only here in the States but also in Vietnam, Europe, the Middle East, and Panama.

VETERANS

A large number of veterans are buried in Whitley County. What's more, Congressman Hal Rogers recently reported there are more veterans coming from this section of our nation than any other section of the nation.

COLONEL HARLAND SANDERS

Our town to the north, Corbin, is the home of Colonel Harland Sanders and Kentucky Fried Chicken who bring international credit to these hills and hollows. Colonel Sanders had a nephew who attended Cumberland College.

FAST HORSES AND BEAUTIFUL WOMEN

This is a land of fast horses and beautiful women. Is it any wonder Cumberland College is proud of its College campus and boasted for a number of years of the only ROTC unit on a private college campus in Kentucky?

DUNCAN HINES

Cumberland also records as an alumnae Duncan Hines' wife Clara Wright whose father Arkley Wright served as Academic Dean at Cumberland College. Unfortunately, Cumberland attracted the significant support of neither Kentucky Fried Chicken nor Duncan Hines.

BOY SCOUT COUNTRY

In 1908 the Boy Scouts of America were founded just to the west of Williamsburg in Burnside, Kentucky.

[24] Williamsburg Institute, *Catalogue*, 1889.

man can make the difference, all the difference in the world. Great movements always begin with just one person.

PERSISTENCE

The vision for a college in Williamsburg was originally held by R.C. Medaris and shared by Green Clay Smith. The impetus for the College founding clearly came about largely as a result of individual efforts. The persistence of these two men, in particular, must be recognized.

GREEN CLAY SMITH:
MILITARY GENERAL AND GOVERNOR

Green Clay Smith (1832-1895) was a presidential candidate for the Prohibitionist Party in 1876, Governor of the Territory of Montana, and a Civil War military General. Green Clay Smith began his career by studying law as his father had done. Following a time of serving in the Kentucky legislature, Smith joined the Union Army where he became a Major General. While serving as a member of Congress, Smith was appointed Governor of the Territory of Montana. In 1876 Smith was nominated as the presidential candidate of the Prohibitionist Party. Shortly thereafter, Smith entered the Baptist ministry and left politics.[25]

(Smith was one of three Governors closely related to Cumberland College: Mr. Edwin P. Morrow,[26] a Republican Governor of Kentucky from 1919 to 1923, attended Williamsburg Institute from 1895-1897; and Mr. Bert T. Combs, the Democratic Governor of Kentucky from 1959-1963, attended Cumberland College from 1929-1931. Two other Cumberland alumni came very close to being elected governor in subsequent years, Congressman Eugene Siler and Mr. Edwin Denney.)

---

[25] *A History of the First Baptist Church, Somerset, Kentucky,* 1799-1974, comp. and ed. History Committee of the First Baptist Church (Wolfe City, Texas: Southern Baptist Press, 1974), p. 27.

Young, *"To Win the Prize,"* p. 3. Young describes Smith as follows:

"Green Clay Smith (1832-1895) was a grandson of Green Clay (1757-1828), of Madison County, Kentucky, and a nephew of the fiery abolitionist, Cassius Marcellus Clay. His mother, Elizabeth Lewis Clay, married John Speed Smith, a lawyer who settled in Richmond . . . .

. . . Endowed with unusual abilities, he [Green Clay Smith] served pastorates at a number of Baptist churches in Kentucky, including a successful tenure at the Somerset Church.

The clothing Smith wore gave no indication that he was a preacher. On his chest he carried a diamond of 'remarkable purity' set in an old-fashioned pin. He used a colored pipe which he smoked upon the streets whenever he pleased. He was of medium stature, his eyes dark and keen, his hair and beard long. Such was the dynamic pulpiteer who came to Williamsburg to proclaim the gospel and to organize a church."

GOVERNOR EDWIN P. MORROW

[26] Edwin P. Morrow graduated from Williamsburg Institute in 1897. He became the 40th governor of Kentucky on December 9, 1919, and served until December 11, 1923.

The following account of Mr. Morrow's visit to Williamsburg on October 28, 1915, is taken from *The Cumberland College*

Nonetheless, during General Smith's pastorate in Washington, a local newspaper had this to say about him: "He is known throughout the country, and it is seldom a church has a pastor who was once a general, a congressman, a Governor of a Territory, and a presidential candidate."[27]

WHAT ALMOST WAS, WASN'T
Green Clay Smith almost became president of the United States. Had he received

---

Monthly, November 1915.

"From the depot the gentlemen were conducted to the Court House in a procession led by the local band. There President Wood [the president of Cumberland College] presided.

Mr. Morrow . . . [was] fittingly introduced by Mr. A.T. Siler, and addressed the people upon state and national issues.

We welcomed Mr. Morrow with special pleasure, because he was for several years a student here in Cumberland College (then Williamsburg Institute), and has always shown himself a most loyal alumnus.

. . . Mr. Morrow spoke with genuine emotion of the "golden days" he spent in the halls of Cumberland College, and of the strength and inspiration he received there."

"BE GENTLE WITH THE PEOPLE — ALWAYS BE GENTLE WITH THE PEOPLE"
Siler in "Heads or Tales," 12 January 1984, reminds us that Morrow was from Somerset as is John Sherman Cooper. Cooper had once talked with Morrow about a political career and Morrow gave Cooper this advice, " 'Be gentle with the people — always be gentle with the people.' "

Siler further recalls his father A.T. Siler writing a letter of condolence to Morrow after he was defeated in 1915. Morrow replied, " 'Every man, whether king or clown, must some day go to Trouble Town.' "

Charles Morrow, brother of Edwin, also attended Cumberland College.

[27] *A History of First Baptist Church, Somerset, Kentucky,* p. 27; "Metropolitan Baptist Church: A Wide-Awake and Pulsing Organization on Capitol Hill," *The Washington Times,* Sunday, 9 September 1894. General Smith was pastor of the Metropolitan Baptist Church (now Capital Hill Metropolitan Baptist Church), Washington, D.C., from 1890 to his death in 1895.

"He is a Kentuckian by birth, and his father fought with and was a friend of William Henry Harrison, and was afterward a Congressman. Mr. Smith served in the war with Mexico as a volunteer and was commissioned lieutenant for gallant services. After this he finished his education, studied law, and at the outbreak of the Civil War, was a member of the Kentucky legislature. He was an uncompromising Union man and raised a regiment of cavalry, going to the front in command. In 1862 he was made a brigadier general and was sent to Congress in 1863.

. . . He was a member of the Republican convention which nominated Lincoln and Johnson, and came very near being placed on the ticket as a candidate for Vice President instead of Andrew Johnson.

In 1866 he was appointed Governor of Montana Territory and took charge when it required a man of nerve to fill the position. Shortly after he entered the ministry, and in 1876 he was the Prohibitionist candidate for President. He was a most engaging speaker and took high rank as an orator in a crowd, and at a meeting in New York held during the war he captured a great crowd, following Governor Morton, of Indiana, and Henry Ward Beecher. As a preacher he is eloquent, and as a pastor scarcely equaled in the city. He is kept busy visiting the members of his congregation, and is the life of all social gathering. Called 'General' by most of his flock, he is respected by young and old. He is greatly interested in the work of the young people of his church, and believes in doing all he can to further it. In this connection he says: 'I believe in all means used to elevate the standard of thought among the young. They are the hope of the future. If good papers and good books can be placed in the hands of the boys and girls, outside the influences of a church, much good can be done. In the church one must keep them busy.' "

Siler relates in his 9 September 1965, "Heads or Tales," that Smith's daughter Mrs. J.L. Whitehead lived in Williamsburg for several years and that her father visited in her home and preached in the County. In fact, "several Whitley County people were named for him."

POCAHONTAS AND WOODROW WILSON
Siler goes on to recall that another person who eventually did live in the White House also visited Williamsburg. Mrs. Edith Galt Wilson, the wife of Woodrow Wilson, visited her sister who lived here. Siler recalls that Mrs. Wilson "had dark hair and

one more vote he, rather than Johnson, would have followed Lincoln as President. When President Lincoln was nominated for his second term in 1864, General Smith was one vote short in the preliminary caucus of being chosen as the Vice Presidential candidate. "Had Smith attained this position instead of Johnson, the course of history might have been altered considerably."[28]

As General Smith was being laid to rest in Arlington National Cemetery, no one could possibly have known the impact this one single, solitary life would have on the people in the hills and hollows of Appalachia and indeed throughout the nation and the world.

General Green Clay Smith was so instrumental in the founding of the College that in August of 1895 his obituary read:

His zeal and wisdom and sympathy enabled the struggling men who are trustees of Williamsburg Institute to bring this noble institution into being. We honor him because he was a General and Governor and Moderator of the General Association of Kentucky, the successful pastor, evangelist, and lecturer; and then we love him because he was our friend and brother and helper. No military honors, no towering shaft of marble we could build for him would ever equal the monument already erected in the Williamsburg Institute. After several weeks of sickness he passed over the river without fear and went home to the Father. His body was borne from his late residence in Washington City to the beautiful Arlington Cemetery and laid to rest beneath the shade of great forest trees. We cannot but wish that his tired body had found its resting place among the mountains he loved so well and where the people who loved him much could comfort their hearts by keeping the air above it fragrant with the breath of fresh flowers.[29]

R.C. MEDARIS:
LITERARY EXEMPLAR, 'SINEWY AND LANK'

Not only was Smith instrumental in the College's founding, but R.C. Medaris

---

fair skin and was descended from Pocahontas, the famous Indian girl from Virginia who saved the life of Captain John Smith when the country was not even in its swaddling clothes."

[28] David Leigh Colvin, *Prohibition in the United States* (New York), pp. 111-112 as cited in *A History of First Baptist Church, Somerset, Kentucky*, p. 27; "Metropolitan Baptist Church," Sunday, 9 September 1894.

According to Siler, "Heads or Tales," 9 September 1965, Smith came even closer to winning the caucus. Siler reports that Smith came within "a half vote of being named as running mate of Lincoln. Andrew Johnson of Tennessee beat Green Clay Smith by only half a vote for the nomination."

[29] *Baptist Evangelist,* "Smith's Obituary." A copy of this original article is contained in the official records of the College's Board of Trustees, 1895.

(1858-1942) also provided the impetus for the College's beginning. Rarely does a man like Medaris come down the stage of history.[30]

A native of Anderson County, Tennessee, Medaris was born in a log cabin on the Clinch River. At the age of seventeen he experienced a profound religious conversion. On the same day he reported he received God's call to preach the Gospel. His ordination did not come, however, until nine years later. At the time he moved to Whitley County he was living at Newcomb, in Campbell County, Tennessee. While there he served the churches in that community, at Jellico, and at Lot, Kentucky.

What manner of man was Medaris? A member of the church described him as 'full of the Spirit of God and (of) zeal for his cause . . . .' When John Fox, Jr., was casting about for an exemplar of the fearless, dynamic mountain preacher, his choice fell on Medaris, whom he had probably first met at Jellico.[31]

R.C. Medaris worked to bring the College into existence. At the 1887 session

---

[30] Young, *"To Win the Prize,"* p. 13.

JOHN FOX, JR.

[31] *Ibid.*, pp. 13-14.
''After the preacher's tenure at Williamsburg had ended, their [Fox and Medaris] paths crossed again to the east, deeper in the mountains of Kentucky. Knowing Medaris as an energetic man of God, Fox portrays him in three of his novels as Sherd Raines, the 'circuit-rider.' This fictionalized Medaris is painted as smooth of face, full of figure, yet 'sinewy and lank, though not awkward; his movements were too quick and decisive for that.' His long black hair often hid a white scar across his square brow. His eyes were steady, his head poised, his mouth and chin strong. His whole face showed that the struggle for self-mastery had won over the animal-like forces within him.

The novelist describes the 'circuit-rider's' preaching as a 'stirring up (of) the people, it was said, ''as though Satan was atter them.'' One mountain man was made to remark that he could 'jus' draw the heart out'n a holler log!' He began a sermon, the man commented, by 'callin' 'em his brethren 'n' sisteren, 'n' folks seed mighty soon that he meant it, too . . . .' ''

John Fox, Jr., is the author of the following books: *A Mountain Europa* (written primarily about Proctor Coal Company, the very coal company from which funds would be used in the College's early years to get it underway), *Hell-fer-Sartin and Other Stories*, *A Cumberland Vendetta*, *The Kentuckians*, *Crittenden*, *Blue Grass and Rhododendron*, *The Little Shepherd of Kingdom Come*, *Christmas Eve on Lonesome and Other Stories*, *Following the Sun-Flag-A Vain Pursuit Through Machurria*, *A Knight of the Cumberland*, *The Trail of the Lonesome Pine*, and *The Heart of the Hills*.

John Ed Pearce, *The Courier Journal Magazine*, Sunday, 25 August 1985, pp. 10-11, copyright (c) 1985. *Courier Journal Sunday Magazine*. Reprinted with permission. John Fox, Jr., was born near Paris, Kentucky, and he is buried there. He was one of ten children. Fox was educated at Stony Point Academy, Transylvania University, and Harvard University, being graduated from Harvard at the age of 19.

Following graduation Fox became a reporter for the New York *Sun* and then for *The New York Times*.

Eventually Fox returned to Paris to teach at Stony Point. After a few months he decided to join his father and two brothers in the coal mining business at Jellico. He enjoyed roaming the area and getting to know the people.

''Here he met and talked with the mountain people, descendants of the English and Scots-Irish settlers who had come to the Cumberlands in the late 1700's and had lodged there while the rest of America's westward migration swept past. Their Anglo-Saxon speech, songs, habits and customs, already forgotten in most of the country, intrigued Fox.''

It was the exposure to these people which prompted Fox's, *A Mountain Europa*. He received $262 for the story; a photograph of the check hangs on the wall in his Memorial Library in Paris, Kentucky.

From Jellico, Fox's father and brothers moved to Big Stone Gap, Virginia, where they continued their coal speculation. Fox

of the Association, the Committee on Education requested the Board of Trustees of the Institute to retain Medaris as the financial agent. He continued in this work until the opening of the Institute the following January.[32]

Medaris was the first of a series of pastors of First Baptist Church, Williamsburg, who would be associated with and supportive of the College. The Williamsburg Church and the College have been intwined, interwoven, and interrelated since the beginning.[33]

A POOR MAN'S COLLEGE

But looking back to that September day in 1887, one can imagine the men of meager means gathered at that little weatherbeaten church house solemnly passing a resolution looking toward the College's founding. R.C. Medaris was appointed financial agent to receive funds and later in the same year at a special session of the Association in Williamsburg, the College would officially get underway. General Green Clay Smith clearly provided inspiration while R.C. Medaris provided the needed leadership.[34]

General Green Clay Smith gave such encouragement to the movement, meeting at the Williamsburg church on 31 December 1887, that $4,005 was subscribed. Simultaneously, Articles of Incorporation were drafted and a Charter drawn, and these were approved by the Legislature on 6 April 1888.[35] The Institute was given the authority to award the Bachelor of Science degree, the Bachelor of Arts degree, and the Master of Arts degree.[36]

---

went with them and made this town his home. Here he wrote more stories including *The Trail of the Lonesome Pine,* a story of a mountain girl and city boy who fall in love, but whose cultural differences come between them. The boy sends the girl off to get educated and when she returns she finds that he has taken on the mountain ways while she is now graceful and refined. Their problems are eventually resolved and the story turns out well.

This, however, was not the case for Fox, who married Fritzi Scheff, "a beautiful and high-spirited Austrian opera singer." After being married they lived in Big Stone Gap, but Mrs. Fox was not happy there, and they eventually separated.

Fox was an excellent story teller and "became a great hit on the lecture circuit."

[32] Young, *"To Win the Prize,"* p. 178. "When he [Medaris] left the state to return to Tennessee in 1891, the Church passed 'Resolution of Respect' for its 'Dearly and Much Beloved Brother.' The establishment of the Institute was listed among his vast accomplishments during the six years he had labored in Kentucky . . . ."

[33] Other pastors of the First Baptist Church, Williamsburg, to support Cumberland College were: Mr. William James Johnson, Mr. John Newton Prestridge, Mr. Henry H. Hibbs, Dr. Elijah Floyd Wright, Sr., Mr. Condie Collins Pugh, Mr. Robert G. Bowers, Mr. Louis Shoup Gaines, Mr. Alfred Paul Bagby, Sr., Dr. Thomas Eugene Hunnicut West, Dr. Herbert Conway Gabhart, Dr. Clyde H. Freed, Sr., Dr. Robert Leland Palmer, Dr. James William Highland, Dr. David William Perkins, and Dr. Harold Steely Mauney. Three pastors served the church before the Institute was begun: Mr. Levi Jackson Steely, Mr. William Henderson Brummett, and Mr. Robert Cummings Medaris.

[34] Mount Zion Association, Record Book No. 1, p. 28; "The Cumberland College Monthly," Vol. 2, No. 1, October 1913, p. 1.

[35] Mount Zion Association, Record Book No. 1, pp. 51-53.

[36] Williamsburg Institute, "Articles of Incorporation," 8 April 1888.

A temporary board was elected consisting of Dr. E.S. Moss, chairman; Mr. H.C. Harmon, secretary; and Mr. J.W. Siler, treasurer.

A building committee composed of Dr. Ancil Gatliff, Dr. E.S. Moss, Mr. J.P. Mahan, Mr. J.E. Sampson, and Mr. H. C. Harmon selected the site and bought the Smith land below Sproule's house on May 7, 1888, for $800.[37] The building was begun[38] with Mr. J.A. Cooley as the contractor.[39] This building, then known as the Institute and later known as the Old Recitation Building, is now known as Roburn Hall.[40] The building was to accommodate 200 pupils and the estimated cost was $12,500.[41]

A SPECIAL PURPOSE FOR A SPECIAL GROUP

From the beginning Cumberland has been a special purpose College serving a particularly deserving group of students. A review of Cumberland's catalogues bears witness to its commitment to students primarily from Appalachia. The statement from one of the earliest catalogues is: "It is the purpose of Williamsburg Institute to furnish thorough instruction and to give an opportunity for a first-class education at rates that are compatible with the means of mountain people."[42]

Although General Green Clay Smith and Mr. R.C. Medaris must be given much credit for the College's founding, men like Dr. Ancil Gatliff, Dr. E.S. Moss, Mr.

---

[37] Mount Zion Association, Record Book No. 1; Board of Trustees, Williamsburg Institute, *Minutes*, 1888. Traditionally the College has expanded its campus base by buying and clearing the property. Today the campus contains 36 acres of land, all of which began with the initial purchase of Sproule's house. Appendix VI lists the land and property acquisitions of the College.

[38] *Western Recorder*, 8 November 1888. The following advertisement appeared: "The walls of the Williamsburg Institute are going up rapidly, and if the weather is fair the building will be ready to teach in January 1, 1889. If young men and women desire to attend a good school on little money let them write to Dr. E.S. Moss . . . for full particulars."

[39] Board of Trustees, Williamsburg Institute, *Minutes*, 1888.

[40] *Cumberland College Monthly*, 2 January 1914. Dr. E.E. Wood explained that Roburn was a shortened form of a Latin word meaning "oaken" or "pertaining to oak." According to Wood, the word Roburn has the "two advantages of a good sound and a good meaning . . . for the elevations on which stand our 'halls of learning;' elevations once covered with oak . . . ."

[41] Mount Zion Association, Record Book No. 1, p. 51-53. The College's financial agent Reverend R.C. Medaris along with the trustees secured $5,850 in cash and pledges toward the opening of the Institute and had collected and spent $1,555.25. It was reported that Medaris traveled 2,500 miles seeking funds, no small distance in that day.

[42] Williamsburg Institute, *Catalogue*, 1892-1893, p. 24.

BRAINS COUNT MORE THAN DOLLARS
Ironically enough an article had appeared in the *Western Recorder* on 29 September 1887, pointing out the native drive of bright but deserving students: "Every college needs the leaven of poor but earnest students who force their way to the front and compel the wealthy idler to recognize that brains count far more than dollars, and the capacity to grasp truth is somewhat better than a fine coat or a patent leather boot."

James P. Mahan, Mr. Thomas Breckenridge Mahan, and others[43] would soon capture the vision and carry the torch of educational opportunity for mountain youth, illuminating the night with the light of hope.

The College's founders and all those who carried on to make the College what it is today truly captured the vision as expressed by Bernard Shaw: "You see things; and you say 'Why?' But I dream things that never were; and I say 'Why not?' "[44]

---

[43] Other notables in the College's early history are John Wesley Siler, J.W. Johnson, H.H. Hibbs, E.E. Wood, A.R. Evans, Gorman Jones, and A.T. Siler.

[44] Bernard Shaw, "Back to Methuselah," Part 1, Act 1, 1921, in John Bartlett, *Familiar Quotations* (Boston: Little, Brown and Company, Inc., 1882; 15th and 125th Anniversary edition, Emily Beck and the Editorial Staff of Little Brown and Company, ed.). Quoted by permission of the Society of Authors on behalf of the Bernard Shaw Estate.

JOHN D. ROCKEFELLER
1839-1937
(Photograph courtesy of the Rockefeller Archives Center)

ANDREW CARNEGIE
1835-1919
(Photograph courtesy of the Carnegie Corporation of New York)

HENRY CLAY FRICK
1849-1919
(Photograph courtesy of the Department of Library Services,
American Museum of Natural History)

WILLIAM JENNINGS BRYAN
1860-1925
(Photograph courtesy of Bryan College, Dayton, Tennessee)

DANIEL BOONE
1734-1820
(Photograph courtesy of Kentucky Department of Travel
Development)

WILLIAM WHITLEY
1749-1813
(Photograph courtesy of Commonwealth of Kentucky,
Department of Parks)

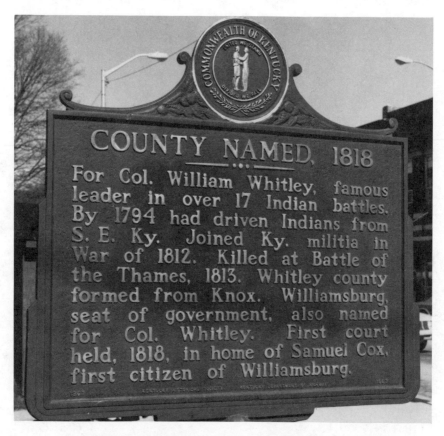

HISTORICAL MARKER ON THE COURTHOUSE SQUARE
Williamsburg, Kentucky
(Photograph by Housman Photography)

RED ASH MINING CAMP
Whitley County, Kentucky
These pictures were taken around 1922.
(Photographs courtesy of Alice Lloyd College Archives.)

MOUNT MORGAN COAL COMPANY
Williamsburg, Kentucky
This mine operated from 1906 to 1913 and employed approximately 200 men.
(Photograph from the Cumberland College Collection, undated).

PACKARD

The Mahan Jellico Coal Company began operation at Packard in 1908. The mining camp took the name Packard, it is thought, from Amelia Packard, a student and then teacher at Cumberland College who taught reading, writing, and music. The town is now non-existent.

(Source of photograph unknown).

RAILROAD STATION AT WILLIAMSBURG

(Photograph by Lay and Gatliff, undated)

HOLE CAUSED BY THE EXPLOSION IN JELLICO
SEPTEMBER 21, 1906

(Photograph courtesy of Jellico Printing Company, Jellico, Tennessee)

JULIA MARCUM

(Source of photograph unknown)

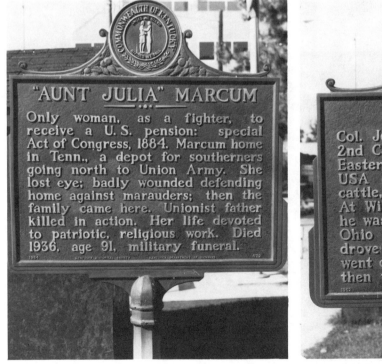

"AUNT JULIA" MARCUM

Only woman, as a fighter, to receive a U.S. pension: special Act of Congress, 1884. Marcum home in Tenn., a depot for southerners going north to Union Army. She lost eye; badly wounded defending home against marauders; then the family came here. Unionist father killed in action. Her life devoted to patriotic, religious work. Died 1936, age 91, military funeral.

SCOTT'S RAID

Col. John S. Scott with 1,600 of 2nd Cav. Brig. CSA came up from Eastern Tenn. on raid to destroy USA communications and obtain cattle, horses, mules and arms. At Williamsburg on July 25, 1863 he was met by 100 pickets of 44th Ohio Inf. After a skirmish, he drove them toward London. Scott went on to Winchester, retreating then to Tenn. with heavy losses.

HISTORICAL MARKERS LOCATED IN WILLIAMSBURG, KENTUCKY

(Photographs by Housman Photography)

**A WAGON TRAIL THROUGH THE
APPALACHIAN MOUNTAINS**

(Photograph from the 1911-1912 *Catalogue.*)

**APPALACHIAN MOUNTAIN
WOMAN AT THE WELL**

(Photograph from *Promises to Keep*)

THE OLD WATER MILL

A corn-grinding mill, known as King's Mill, was located a little distance up Cumberland River from what is now known as the "new bridge" in Williamsburg.

(Photograph from *The Eglantine,* 1908)

**EARLY PHOTOGRAPH OF WILLIAMSBURG
LOOKING EAST ON MAIN STREET**

(Photograph from an early post card, undated, Cumberland College Collection)

**THE BRIDGE ACROSS THE CUMBERLAND RIVER AT WILLIAMSBURG
PROBABLY CONSTRUCTED AROUND 1892**

(Photograph from *The Eglantine,* 1908)

DORMITORY AT CORA INSTITUTE
Pleasant View, Kentucky
(Photograph from *Renfro Revelations* by Simon L. Renfro, April 1944)

PROFESSOR WILLIAM A. NESBIT
"Father of Whitley County Education"
1835-1890
(Photograph from *Renfro Revelations* by
Simon L. Renfro, April 1944)

REVEREND AND MRS. A.A. MYERS
(Photograph courtesy of *Phoenix of the Mountains;
A History of Lincoln Memorial University*)

TEACHERS INSTITUTE OF WHITLEY COUNTY, WILLIAMSBURG ACADEMIC SCHOOL, 1890

(Photograph courtesy of the Filson Club, Louisville, Kentucky)
Used here by their permission and by permission of Stuart Sprague, *Eastern Kentucky: A Pictoral History* (Norfolk: The Donning Company Publishers).

BLACK SCHOOL NEAR MAHAN
Whitley County, Kentucky, n.d.

(Photograph courtesy of the Filson Club, Louisville, Kentucky)
Used here by their permission and by permission of Stuart Sprague, *Eastern Kentucky: A Pictoral History* (Norfolk: The Donning Company Publishers).

ADMIRAL CHARLES A. BLAKELY
(Photograph from *Renfro Revelations* by
Simon Renfro, April 1946)

MAJOR GENERAL CHARLES CALLOWAY
(Photograph courtesy of Charles
Calloway)

BRIGADIER GENERAL ROY W. EASLEY
(Photograph courtesy of Mrs. Homer
Davis)

MAJOR GENERAL FLOYD L. PARKS
(Photograph from *The Whitley Republican*,
May 31, 1951)

THE AMERICAN FLAG GREETS
TRAVELERS ALONG I-75
(Photograph by Housman Photography)

COLONEL RONALD B. STEWART
(Photograph courtesy of Ronald B.
Stewart)

LIEUTENANT COLONEL E.T. MACKEY
(Photograph from *Renfro Revelations* by
Simon Renfro, May 1947)

CAPTAIN WILLARD HAMBLIN
(Photograph from *Renfro Revelations* by
Simon Renfro, July 1945)

CAPTAIN DWIGHT LYMAN MOODY
(Photograph courtesy of the United States
Navy)

COLONEL HARLAND SANDERS
1890-1980

In 1956 Harland Sanders was 66 years old, out of work, and drawing $105 a month on Social Security. Within a few years he became a millionaire, and the business he started became known around the world as "Kentucky Fried Chicken." It all began in nearby Corbin, Kentucky. Colonel Sanders helped his nephew to attend Cumberland College by assisting with his expenses.

(Photograph courtesy of Kentucky Fried Chicken)

JAMES CASH PENNEY
1875-1971

On 17 September 1950, J.C. Penney gave the address at the commemoration of the seventy-eighth anniversary of Williamsburg's first Sunday School. Services were held in the auditorium of the First Baptist Church with one thousand people in attendance.

In 1902 at the age of 26, Mr. Penney opened his first retail store in the small mining town of Kemmerer in the hills of southwestern Wyoming. Sales for the first day totaled $466.59. At the time of Mr. Penney's death in 1971, annual sales totaled around $5 billion in more than 2,000 retail units.

Mr. Penney's credo was based on his much-loved concept of the Golden Rule. It has been stated concerning Mr. Penney that: "An abiding faith in God, the Christian ethic of the Golden Rule, self-reliance, self-discipline, and honor formed the foundation on which he built his entire life."

(Photograph courtesy of J.C. Penney Archives)

DUNCAN AND CLARA WRIGHT HINES

Clara Wright Hines (1904-1983) graduated from Cumberland College in the class of 1923. She was the daughter of Cumberland's first Academic Dean, Arkley Wright. Mrs. Hines was a fine lady as is evidenced by these lines from a letter she wrote in response to a request from the author for a picture of her father on 18 November 1982.

"Dear Dr. Taylor:
"I am trying to find the few photos of my Father; nice of you to wish to hang his portrait in the gallery.
"You needn't speak of me as being 'famous.' I suppose I am after a fashion. It is my husband who was and still is famous. I just made it to that on his coat tails . . . ."

Mr. and Mrs. Hines were married in March 1946. Duncan Hines (1880-1959) was known internationally as a food critic. He gained acclaim by writing three guidebooks for travelers recommending restaurants, hotels, motels, and vacation places along America's highways.

In 1949 Hines formed Hines-Park Foods and the Duncan Hines Institute which published guidebooks and cookbooks, conducted food research, and supervised the licensing of foods which bore his name.

(Photograph courtesy of Jane Morningstar)

GREEN CLAY SMITH
1832-1895
(Photograph courtesy of First Baptist Church
Williamsburg, Kentucky)

ROBERT CUMMINGS MEDARIS
1858-1942
(Photograph from Young, *"To Win the
Prize"*)

**MONUMENT OF GREEN CLAY SMITH
ARLINGTON NATIONAL CEMETERY**
(Photograph by
(Ankers Capitol Photographers, Washington, D.C.)

GRAVE STONE OF JOHN FOX, JR.
PARIS CEMETERY,
PARIS, KENTUCKY

BOOK SHELF OF MEMENTOES
BROUGHT FROM NEW YORK BY
JOHN FOX, JR. IN DUNCAN TAVERN,
PARIS, KENTUCKY

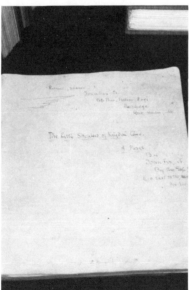

HANDWRITTEN MANUSCRIPT AND TYPED MANUSCRIPT OF
Little Shepherd of Kingdom Come
by John Fox, Jr.

WRITING DESK OF JOHN FOX, JR.
IN DUNCAN TAVERN,
PARIS, KENTUCKY

(Photographs by Tom Frazier)

CHAPTER 2
STRUGGLES

THROUGH HARDSHIPS AND DIFFICULTIES

The College's administration and trustees have had to struggle from the beginning, but struggle gives meaning and purpose to life today as it did then. Local men, many of whom were trustees, paid tuition and board for the students and salaries for the faculty until every dollar, for some of them, went to the Institution after other obligations were met, reported Dr. Moss, the first chairman of the Institution's board. Moss went on to say, "There must be an endowment, for the Institution cannot run without it."[1]

Two months later the *Western Recorder* reported, "Those in charge . . . felt sure that so noble an enterprise would be upheld by 'grace divine,' and trusting in God, started it, and through hardships and difficulties known to God alone, have established the fact that it may be made a grand success."[2]

DR. ANCIL GATLIFF

Dr. Ancil Gatliff (1850-1918), a physician, had traveled back into the hills and hollows of the mountains, had seen the poverty, had visited the sick children, the elderly, the infirmed, the lonely. He had seen the people trying to eke out a living on the rocky soil called home. He had tended to the needs of the helpless, birthing babies, tending to the sick, and burying the dead. Gatliff, no doubt, dreamed of a school where these mountain youngsters could have a good diet, a clean and warm bed, and a good educational opportunity.

Born 3 January 1850, Dr. Ancil Gatliff was the son of John Speed Gatliff and Luvisa Jones Gatliff. He was reared on the farm on the Cumberland River near Watt's Creek. Gatliff attended the county school and afterward taught at Liberty School House.

---

[1] *Western Recorder,* 20 February 1890.

Pleas Jones, Williamsburg, Kentucky, interview, 22 June 1960. In this interview, Jones recalled that this was a poor man's school. It was not uncommon for students to ride mules great distances from their homes to day school. The staff and students had a feeling of belonging and purpose which gives life meaning. There was a sense of community; no one was disinherited or estranged. There was caring and sharing which gives meaning and purpose. Even as late as the 1920's people still rode mules. Judge Jones recalled his own experience of riding mules back and forth to Cumberland College.

[2] *Western Recorder,* 17 April 1890.

He received his medical training at Louisville, Kentucky.[3]

Dr. Gatliff early became interested in the founding of Williamsburg Institute[4] and continued to support it liberally all his life. He served as the president of the Institute's Board from 1889 until his death in 1918.

GATLIFF'S VISION

During the early years of the College's history, few individuals gave as did Dr. Ancil Gatliff. It was an extremely cold December day in 1887 when the Mount Zion Association met in a called session with the Williamsburg Church. Prior to the church meeting, Green Clay Smith held a meeting at the home of John Wesley Siler with Gatliff and others in attendance. General Smith was in town to give Reverend R. C. Medaris a hand with the raising of a budget of money for the projected school. Smith urged upon Gatliff the importance of his beginning the subscription with $1,000. Considering his own circumstances and the state of the economy, the doctor remonstrated that he would be unable to do so. When the conference closed, the visitor said, "We are going to have that thousand." Gatliff told General Smith not to count on his making such a subscription. That evening when the Association convened in the meeting house, Dr. Gatliff, when called on, made the requested pledge and

---

[3]Young, *"To Win the Prize,"* pp. 150, 182.

Jones, "Legend and Lore," 21 November 1985. Jones wrote of Gatliff's invention, a medicine called "Havis' iron bitters." According to Jones, "those who were puny, run down, couldn't eat and the like, could after taking a few doses of Dr. Gatliff's Havis' iron bitters; they felt good again, and some were reported to have sung like a lark."

Siler, "Heads or Tales," 17 June 1965. Writing on Dr. Ancil Gatliff, Siler remarked:
"One of the 'heads' or personalities I knew around town when I was a boy was Dr. Ancil Gatliff. He died of Spanish influenza in 1918 when he was about 68 years old. This man was quiet, dignified and retiring and yet was firm and strong as steel. Starting out in life as a country doctor and poor as a church mouse ready for bankruptcy, Dr. Gatliff set up housekeeping, they say, with a dry goods box for a dining room table. Seeing the rich deposits of coal in Whitley County and elsewhere that needed to be opened up with the prevailing manpower that was ready to work, Dr. Gatliff organized several coal companies, borrowed money, bought land and finally witnessed the sight of hundreds of coal miners going into the hills to shatter down the rich, black fuel to feed the hungry appetites of grates, stoves and industrial furnaces in all the country around about. The good doctor became so engrossed in industrial development and business affairs that he eventually closed up his pill bottles and medicine case and referred all his patients to other doctors of the county.
. . . Dr. Gatliff was also very public spirited in his attitude and outlook. He poured something like a quarter of a million dollars into Cumberland College, started Williamsburg's present water and sewer systems and took the lead in any worthwhile activity for the betterment of his people. Besides all this, he was always ready, willing and able to help most any poor boy or girl get an education. Some of these he kept in his home and treated as if they were members of his own family.
Two towns were named for him, Gatliff, Ky., and Gatliff, Tenn. Many persons were named in his honor as well as the main building and athletic field of Cumberland College.
. . . Two times this man was elected president or moderator of the Kentucky Baptist Convention, these occasions having been way back in 1915 and 1916. Of course, this was quite an honor for any layman, the preachers ordinarily being singled out to receive such outstanding recognition."

[4] Mount Zion Association, Record Book No. 1, p. 52; Board of Trustees, Williamsburg Institute, *Minutes,* 1888.

sparked the raising of $4,500 there on the spot.[5]

Gatliff had long had a dream about the establishment of an educational institution in Williamsburg.[6] He seemed now to realize that the time to begin was at hand. And without regarding his better judgment and his financial condition, he subscribed $1,000, thus encouraging others to give. At that time his gift was the largest donation that had ever been made to any cause in this section of Kentucky, and in proportion to his resources at the time, it was the largest gift he ever would make.[7]

SHE HAD TEARS IN HER EYES

T. E. Mahan, son-in-law of Dr. Ancil Gatliff, later recalled the story told that Mrs. Gatliff had tears in her eyes because neither she nor her husband knew where they would get the $1,000 with which to pay the pledge.

Mrs. Gatliff herself sacrificed through the years, foregoing personal items she wanted in order to help the College.[8]

A BURNING EMBER ON THE GRATE

Shortly afterward when the coal business was just beginning, Dr. Gatliff and a neighbor Jim Mahan were watching a big piece of coal burn on the grate. Gatliff said to Mahan, "If that turns out alright, [sic] we can build that College, can't we?" From that time on Gatliff's one concern was the College, according to his daughter, Mrs. N.A. Archer.[9]

---

[5] Young, *"To Win the Prize"* p. 182.

[6] Siler, "Heads or Tales," 9 February 1978. "And the Doctor had still other visions. Of all the impossible things! He dreamed of a college in a place where they didn't even have a high school. 'Put it on the hill overlooking Cumberland River and the county seat,' someone said. And so they did."

[7] Young, *"To Win the Prize,"* p. 182.

[8] Dr. and Mrs. Gatliff had five children: Mrs. Ruby (N. A.) Archer, Mrs. Pearl (N. B.) Perkins, Mrs. Una (T. E.) Mahan, Mr. J. B. Gatliff, and Mr. E. M. Gatliff.

Florida Ellen Moss Gatliff was the daughter of W. T. and Mary Moss of Bell County, Kentucky. She and Dr. Gatliff were married in 1876. Their home was the first on the river side of the courthouse square in Williamsburg. In 1879, Dr. and Mrs. Gatliff moved to their new home near the corner of Fifth and Main Streets where they lived the remainder of their lives.

Mrs. Gatliff joined her husband in donating to the College, at times giving sacrificially. She was also generous in her giving to the First Baptist Church of Williamsburg. At one time she purchased a house to serve as a home for her pastor. This gift was to be a memorial to her husband. At her death her Will provided a bequest for the church's endowment. A ladies' Sunday School class in the First Baptist Church of Williamsburg bears the name of Florida Moss Gatliff. Mrs. Gatliff passed away in 1932.

[9] Hall, "Cumberland College," p.14.

Hibbs, "Tender Memories," in *Doctor Ancil Gatliff,* pp. 21-22. Gatliff was a generous giver to his church in Williamsburg,

Gatliff had already had experience in organizing successful enterprises. He largely gave up his medical practice because he was extensively connected with coal companies and mining in southeastern Kentucky and northern Tennessee.[10]

In May 1884 Gatliff had helped to organize the Bank of Williamsburg and served as its president from May 1891 until his death. Later, he was the founder, first president, and largest contributor to the Kentucky Baptist Educational Society.[11]

Dr. Gatliff was a warm, caring, affable, and personable man. Very few times does a man of this stature appear on the pages of history. With his feet astride these valleys, his vision was lifted above these mountains.

FAITH, HARD WORK, SACRIFICE, AND STRUGGLE

As one looks back to the College's beginning, the odds against the venture, of course, were all but overwhelming. But by faith, hard work, sacrifice, and struggle,

---

and he also gave ten dollars each month, a considerable sum in those days, to Pastor Hibbs to give to the poor. When Hibbs took this money to the homes of the poor, he noted: ". . . It was not uncommon for me to catch him sitting by their sick beds nursing them with his own hands. While he said nothing about it, when he left I think he invariably left a good bill [of paper money] in their hands . . . ."

Hibbs went on to say, "How many love letters he must have received from young men whom he had helped over the rough places in their school life with his money! There are hundreds of them who will now rise up and call him blessed." [Remember this was a day before social welfare or almost any other kind of subsidy.]

[10] Siler, "Heads or Tales," 9 February 1978, wrote the following concerning Gatliff: "But getting back to all those coal dreams. These dreams impelled him to go down close to the Tennessee line and open what later became Proctor Coal company. Then he crossed the state line and organized a mine over at Cotula. Next, another Gatliff enterprise began hauling coal out at a place called Westbourne. And pretty soon the Doctor was leading forth in setting up a coal mine in the very shadows of Williamsburg. This one was called Mount Morgan Coal Company."

Siler goes on to tell about Gatliff's trip to Louisville to talk with Milton Smith, President of the L & N Railroad: "They looked at maps and geographical surveys. When they came out of the seclusion of President Smith's office, you could almost feel the effervescence of success and hear the work train constructing Pine Mountain Railroad up Cumberland River, across Clear Fork and past Sutton's Mill. And so Gatliff Hollow was opened up and Gatliff Coal Company soon boomed from cornfields into a railroad station and a big department store larger than anything between Lexington and Knoxville. A new town was born, and they called it Gatliff."

[11] Hibbs, "Tender Memories," in *Doctor Ancil Gatliff,* p. 19. Dr. Gatliff was mentioned several times for the office of governor and other high political positions, but he declined, preferring to " 'dwell among his own people.' "

Gatliff served for two years as Moderator of the General Association of Baptists, that being the chief place of honor and leadership of the denomination. F.D. Perkins, "Words From a Friend," in *Doctor Ancil Gatliff,* p. 26, reported that upon assuming the moderatorship of the General Association, Dr. Gatliff said with evident feeling: " 'Brethren, I am not worthy of the honor you have conferred upon me . . . . By the grace of God, I am what I am.' "

Concerning Dr. Gatliff, Dr. E.Y. Mullins of Southern Seminary declared in "A Great Man Gone," in *Doctor Ancil Gatliff,* p. 29: "As a presiding officer he was eminently fair and always conciliatory and despised any petty political maneuvering and sought always to promote the great ends for which the General Association stands."

Gatliff was the founder of the waterworks, an entrepreneur, a coal magnate, a banker, a medical doctor, and an educator.

the vision became a reality, and the College opened its doors on 7 January 1889.

ALL NIGHT LONG

Men worked all night long to ensure the Institute was ready for occupancy.[12] R.C. Medaris, who was there on the opening day, recalled:

> On Saturday before the school was to open the next Monday, we worked till midnight, and then we arose at midnight, Sunday night and went to the school building and began getting everything ready for the opening. About seven o'clock the good ladies brought us our breakfast and we ate heartily of it. When the 200 happy boys and girls were coming in at the front door, we were sweeping the rubbish out at the back. We were dirty and tired but we stayed on the grounds until about noon.[13]

THIS SCHOOL WILL NEVER DIE

As Williamsburg Institute opened its doors for students that morning on 7 January 1889, Mr. John Wesley Siler, one of the College's first trustees, was present. He was there sponsoring, encouraging, and pushing forward:[14] four young men: A.J. Meadors, A.J. Parker, A.S. Petrey, and E.L. Stephens, all of whom were in the first graduating class in 1893.[15] Siler said, "Go forward young men, this

---

[12] Hall, "Cumberland College," p. 15. Miss Besse Rose, a long-time professor at Cumberland College related this story: " 'It was feared that the building would not be ready because the plaster was not dry. The trustees wanted the building ready, but did not want to break the Sabbath. They stayed and kept the fires in the stoves until midnight on Saturday and came back at midnight Sunday to keep the fires until time for school.' "

[13] Robert Cummin[g]s Medaris, *Blazing the Gospel Trail,* 2nd ed. (Williamsburg, Ky., 1920), p. 99.

[14] *Western Recorder,* 17 January 1889.

[15] Williamsburg Institute, *Catalogue,* 1893.

The first four graduates had rather remarkable careers. A. J. Meadors entered the field of education. He taught in the elementary grades of the Institute one year. He became principal of a high school in Arkansas and later president of Conway Female College in Arkansas. E. L. Stephens taught for some years in the Institute. He became a prominent attorney. A. J. Parker became a minister and was at one time supply pastor of the Williamsburg Baptist Church. A. S. Petrey became a minister and taught for a while in the Institute. He did missionary work in Hazard and Perry County, organizing twelve churches in the area including the First Missionary Baptist Church of Hazard in 1898. His interest in educational work led him to found and become president of the Hazard Baptist Institute in 1902. These first four graduates were typical of many of the graduates of the Institute and of the College.

Harold E. Dye, *The Prophet of Little Cane Creek* (Atlanta, Georgia: Home Mission Board, Southern Baptist Convention, 1949), pp. 61-62. All Rights Reserved. Used by Permission.

IT TAKES A WOMAN TO GET SOMETHING DONE

Harold E. Dye relates the following story as told by A.S. Petrey, one of the first four graduates of the Institute.

" 'I was editor of a weekly newspaper . . . [and] I launched an editorial against HOGS . . . . I took the editorial

school will never die. We will pass on, but the college itself will live.''[16]

SERENDIPITY — A GREAT CELEBRATION

After a curriculum had been adopted, a faculty hired, and a building constructed, one found serendipity on that opening day. To catch the thrill and excitement of the opening day and the days that followed, one must look to R. C. Medaris' words:

> We had present many of the citizens of the county and town, and warm and enthusiastic speeches were made by Dr. A. Gatliff, Dr. E. S. Moss, Judge J. R. Sampson, Rev. W. H. Brummitt, O. B. Davis, Professor Milford White, Professor C. G. Garlow, and T. B. Mahan . . . . Students are coming in daily. We have only three rooms ready, but we need several hundred dollars more. I trust all those who have subscribed and have not paid will remit to the undersigned at once. We are not in debt, nor do we intend to be.[17]

THEY CAME BY HORSEBACK, WAGON, AND ON FOOT

Reflecting on the early student enrollment, it was said that ''the College attracted students who came on horseback, wagon, and on foot.'' With the inflow of students, the Institute's founders could feel success in their bones as the enrollment grew rapidly. Remember there were no public schools in the area in that day. The *Western Recorder* reported that students came from the counties of Whitley, Laurel, Knox, Bell, Harlan,

---

position that hogs are all right in their place, but that place is not on Main Street or in my wife's flower beds. We got a law passed against owning and keeping hogs in town. But getting the ordinance enforced was another matter.

Our town marshal almost lost his life trying to carry out the will of the town councilmen. He had an old sow by the ear and was leading her toward the stray pen which he had built at the edge of town. The old sow was squealing. I was behind, urging her litter of pigs along, when suddenly a man appeared by my side and yelled at the marshal. He had a heavy revolver lined up against the back of the officer. I managed to convince him that the law would go hard with him if he shot and that we were not afraid of his gun. Jim Davidson was the marshal and a good one. Ignoring the heavy revolver he continued urging the hogs along until they were safely in the stray pen. That stray pen, though, had a sort of up and down experience. Every time the marshal got it built out of slabs, irate citizens swooped down upon it, released its grunting prisoners and burned it to the ground. We did not have enough money in our treasury to keep on building the pens.

Then one day it happened. The wife of one of the leading businessmen of the town came tripping down the street in her pretty dress. She knew that all eyes were upon her as she made her way along the board walk. She clutched at her rustling skirt now and then to keep it from dragging in the mud. Suddenly a big shoat came out from under the walk. He was dripping with mud. Just as the fair lady tried to step by, the hog shook himself violently and the mud flew. She screamed, but her nice dress was ruined. Maybe you think she didn't get immediate action. What the marshal's guns could not effect, one angry and determined woman accomplished in the matter of hours. Hogs disappeared from our streets.' ''

[16] *Western Recorder,* 17 January 1889, p.5.

[17] *Ibid.*

Clay, Jackson, Owsley, Leslie, and other mountain counties.[18]

Little did the founders know that the College would produce two governors, a congressman, several generals, a significant number of medical doctors, college and university presidents, and the list could go on and on.[19]

Dr. Ancil Gatliff said the school was started so that the boys and girls of the mountains could get an education in a Christian atmosphere at a price they could afford.[20] This statement appeared in the 1889 *Catalogue:* "It is and shall be the one aim of the Trustees and faculty to build, fashion, and develop young men and women in the most approved way possible, intellectually and morally, for a higher and nobler walk in life. Every possible resource and effort will be employed in the futherance of this end."[21]

---

[18] *Western Recorder,* 17 April 1890, p.5.

The College's catalogues for the years 1889 through 1906 indicate some students came from New York, Virginia, Ohio, and Alabama now and then, but primarily the students came from Appalachia.

Western Recorder, 12 June 1890, p. 4, reports that there were 350 students enrolled at the Institute.

One writing in the *Western Recorder* 17 April 1890, and signed by J. R. S. Middlesborough refers to the Institute:
"It is located in a beautiful, healthy, mountain town on the banks of the Cumberland River — a town which for peace, quiet and morals, and religious culture of its people, is unequaled by few and surpassed by none; a town where the moral sentiment of the people is so strong as to demonstrate that 'prohibition does prohibit' when backed by a courageous people, determined to drive out the evil; for such truth is Williamsburg, by the grace of God and the unceasing efforts in the right direction of its good people."

MAKE THEM BRIGHT AND SHINING LIGHTS
The writer, after asking the question as to why interest should be taken in this College, said, "Because you can thereby have a part in the great work of giving to noble young men and women the moral and intellectual training which will make them bright and shining lights in the social and religious world and which without this help, they must be deprived of."

A SHINING EDUCATIONAL JEWEL IN ITS MOUNTAIN SETTING
John L. Crawford writing in the *Corbin Times Tribune,* "Ravelings," 20 May 1984, p.4., had this to say about Cumberland College:
". . . This Williamsburg educational center is one of the most successful private colleges in Kentucky. It is unique in several ways, one of which is that it has one of the highest percentages of students on scholarship in the country. No worthy student is turned away because of lack of money. This policy has imposed a hardship on the College, but liberal support and frugal management of available funds make the program possible.
. . . It is a shining educational jewel in its mountain setting, and its long rays of light reach far beyond its boundaries."

MOUNTAIN BRAINS
[19] Ironically enough, about the time the College was getting started, articles appeared about the native intelligence of the mountain youngsters. The following appeared in the *Western Recorder,* 25 April 1889, p. 5:
"Produced within this mountainous district is the highest quality of natural brain power . . . . Mountain brains, when thoroughly trained, are . . . in the lead in many departments of professional, commercial, and industrial pursuits. Knowing this fact, why not educate our mountain boys and girls to the fullest extent? The moral atmosphere of the community in which this college is located is of such a standard of excellence that any kind of wrong doing consigns the party to disgrace and degradation to such an extent as to have the effect to prevent local bad conduct. The water, air, and food for excellence, purity and wholesomeness are unsurpassed."

[20] Pleas Jones, Interview.
[21] Williamsburg Institute, *Catalogue,* 1889-1890, p. 18. A copy of that first *Catalogue* can be found in Appendix VII.

STEWARDSHIP, NOT OWNERSHIP

The bedrock of any higher education institution is its trustees and administration who hold the institution in public trust as stewards, not owners. No institution will long have vigor, enthusiasm, or motivation without trustee support and encouragement. Cumberland College's trustees and administration have continually demonstrated their concern through contributions of time, talent, money, love, prayer, and by selecting strong chief executive officers who undergird the College.[22]

THE GATLIFF CONNECTION

Dr. and Mrs. Gatliff's two sons James Blaine Gatliff and Edward Moss Gatliff; one daughter Pearl Gatliff Perkins; one grandson James Blaine Gatliff, Jr.; and one granddaughter Norma Perkins Hagan served on the College's Board of Trustees.

The three sons-in-law of Dr. and Mrs. Gatliff served on the College's Board of Trustees: Norman B. Perkins, N. Ancil Archer, and Thomas Elmer Mahan.

While Dr. E. S. Moss was elected the first temporary chairman of the Board of Trustees, shortly after the legislature granted the Charter for the Williamsburg Institute, the Mt. Zion Association elected Dr. Ancil Gatliff the president of the Board, James Perry Mahan the vice-president, John Wesley Siler the treasurer, and Dr. E.S. Moss the secretary.[23]

In the early decades of the school the roster of trustees read like a list of prominent leaders of the community. James Perry Mahan served as a trustee until 1906

---

[22] Even today the Board, working in informal and friendly fashion, makes policy through six committees: the executive committee which acts in the absence of the full Board; the building and grounds committee; the academic affairs committee; the finance, budget, and investment committee; the honorary degree committee; and the student affairs committee. While broad policy is set by the Board, the College carries on the day-to-day operations under the direction of the president who is the chief executive officer of the Corporation and who implements policy.

Looking back all the way to the beginning one can see the Board involved in fund raising campaigns, the lifeblood for an institution's sustenance. The first challenge came from Rockefeller's American Baptist Education Society with the condition that $15,000 must be raised. Several financial agents would serve the College initially, including Green Clay Smith, R. C. Medaris, William James Johnson, H. T. Daniels, and H. H. Hibbs.

[23] Hall, "Cumberland College," pp. 11-12.

The *Minutes* of the meeting of the Mt. Zion Association, 8 September 1888, reflect this action. The trustees or Board of Directors approved by the Mount Zion Association were all prominent citizens and were men who genuinely cared for others. Those trustees, as listed in the Institute's 1889 *Catalogue*, were A. Gatliff, president, Williamsburg; J. P. Mahan, vice-president, Williamsburg; E. S. Moss, secretary, Williamsburg; J. W. Siler, treasurer, Williamsburg; J. R. Sampson, auditor, Williamsburg; William Ellison, Williamsburg; John A. Black, Barbourville; Gilbert Garrard, Manchester; J. Q. Pearce, Pineville; N. M. Scales, London; and H. C. Gentry, Mt. Vernon. Gatliff and three men who belonged to other congregations made up a portion of this first Board of Trustees. Gatliff was not a member of the Baptist Church until two years after the College was founded. Moreover,

when he died. John Wesley Siler served until his death in 1912. J.M. Ellison, who became a trustee in 1895, served until his death in 1942. Dr. C.G. Ellison, who became a trustee in 1898, served until his death in 1939. Another long term member of the Board T.B. Mahan served from 1896 until his death in 1930. In 1918 when Dr. Gatliff passed away, Mahan was elected its president of the Board, a position he held until his death. In 1901 Adam Troy Siler took his place on the Board and served for fifty-two years. His son Congressman Eugene Siler, Sr., has also served on the College's Board as has his grandson Federal Judge Eugene Siler, Jr. In fact, Judge Siler has served as chairman of the Board since 1984.

The early trustees, even as today, were men of stature. They were unassuming and unpretentious. They were more concerned about "doing something significant" than in being recognized.

EDWIN SMITH MOSS

The first chairman of the Board Dr. Edwin Smith Moss (1859-1943) was a graduate of the Hospital College of Medicine at Louisville. Reared at Pineville and at Tazewell, Tennessee, Moss came to Williamsburg in 1877 and studied medicine under Dr. Ancil Gatliff before entering medical school in Louisville. Following his graduation, Moss returned to Williamsburg to establish his own practice. In 1882 Dr. Moss married Belinda Jane Arthur, the daughter of Ed Arthur.

Dr. Moss worked as a pioneer surgeon in this section and in adjoining parts of Virginia and Tennessee.[24] He built and operated for fifteen years the first private hospital in southeastern Kentucky. It is said that Moss performed four of the first successful appendectomies in Kentucky.

In 1883 Dr. Moss and eleven others organized the Williamsburg Baptist Church, and in 1884 he helped organize the Bank of Williamsburg. In 1904 Moss organized the First National Bank of Williamsburg and served as its president for 31 years. Moss was also very active in politics and the Republican Party. He was a member "of the Commission that built the old bridge across the Cumberland River."[25]

Dr. E. S. Moss "was a pleasant gentleman, who knew and respected everyone on the street, and always had a pleasant smile for everyone."[26]

---

the College continues to serve an array of students. Since the beginning the college has encouraged its students to attend church, if not a Baptist church, then the church of their choice.

[24] Jones, "Legend and Lore," 21 November 1985.

[25] Young, "*To Win the Prize*," p. 4.

[26] Jones, "Legend and Lore," 21 November 1985.

"DOCK MOSSING"

Siler in his "Heads or Tales," 5 March 1970, claims that "politics was his [Dr. Moss's] avocation in all seasons." Dr. Moss

THE GREAT NEED

It was in 1886 that Reverend R.C. Medaris spoke to Moss of the great need for a school in this part of the state. Moss agreed. He and Medaris, along with General Green Clay Smith, Dr. Ancil Gatliff, and a few others made subscriptions to secure the land to build the Institute. Dr. Moss was one of the first six trustees of the Institute appointed by the Mount Zion Association on 31 December 1887.[27] Shortly thereafter he was elected the temporary chairman. Dr. Moss continued as a member of the Board for the next fifteen years,[28] but his interest in the College continued until his death in 1943.[29]

YOU'RE TALKING TO THE RIGHT MAN

As the pages of history turned, the following story was commonly told by Dr. Moss' son Dr. C.A. Moss. A stranger was getting off the train in Williamsburg and struck up a conversation with Dr. Moss. This young man asked several questions and each time Moss responded by saying, "You are talking with the right man." The young man asked if Moss knew of a nice hotel? Moss responded, "You are talking to the right man." The young man asked if Moss knew of a good doctor and hospital because his wife was expecting? Moss responded, "You are talking to the right man." The man asked if Moss knew of a good eye doctor as he was having trouble with his glasses? Moss responded, "You are talking to the right man."

Dr. Moss was correct; he was the right man. He owned the Central Hotel; he founded the First National Bank; he founded the local hospital; he was a medical doctor; and he was an opthalmologist. Indeed, the young stranger had found the right man![30]

---

would whisper in peoples' ear about politics, and this became known around town as "Dock Mossing." If you wanted to tell someone something in confidence, you would just say, "Come here, I want to Dock Moss you."

[27] Mount Zion Association, Record Book No. 1, pp. 52-53; Young, *"To Win the Prize,"* p. 178.

[28] Williamsburg Institute, *Catalogue.*

[29] Dr. Moss is buried in Highland Cemetery in Williamsburg alongside his wife Belinda Arthur Moss and his son Edwin Arthur Moss.

[30] Jones, "Legend and Lore," 21 November 1985. Dr. E.S. Moss was succeeded as president of the First National Bank by his son Dr. C.A. Moss, a medical doctor and opthalmologist.

According to Dr. C.A. Moss' "Obituary," in *The Whitley Republican,* 3 October 1968, he was quite an accomplished man, being not only a doctor but a businessman, historian, and civic and political leader. His interests included "photography, collecting historic items, making dulcimers, compiling local history, tracing and recording geneology, and grafting and raising nut trees."

Dr. C.A. Moss was married to Lillian Stanfell who passed away in 1922, and then to Lucy Paisley, and he was the father of three sons and two daughters: Clive Arthur Moss, Jr., Dr. James Paisley Moss, William Edward Moss, Mrs. David Slight, and Belinda Moss.

WILLIAM JAMES JOHNSON: PRINCIPAL AND FUND RAISER

One of the first significant acts of the Board,[31] other than acquiring the Charter, purchasing the land, adopting the name, building the first building, and getting the endowment underway, was the employment of William James Johnson (1864-1894) as the Institute's first president, then called a principal, in the fall of 1889.

Johnson came to Williamsburg in 1889 with his wife Ora to become pastor of the Baptist Church.[32] In addition to serving as pastor of the Church and principal of the Institute, Johnson also served as an instructor of Latin, Greek, rhetoric, and English literature at the Institute.[33]

In the spring of 1890 Johnson became so involved in raising money for the Institute that he gave up the principalship to Professor E. E. Wood. Johnson continued as pastor of the church until 1894 even though he was away from the church for extended periods on Institute business.

When the Rockefeller and Gatliff matching gift offer for a $15,000 endowment came, the trustees decided ''to put a man in the field right away to raise the matching funds.''[34] Johnson was the man. Johnson was successful and the College did receive the money from Rockefeller and Gatliff. Later Johnson was employed to raise funds for a boarding hall,[35] and he was successful in this campaign, also.

---

[31] Hall, ''Cumberland College,'' pp. 9-10.

The Institute fell under the purview of the Mount Zion Association. The Association was authorized to elect a Board of Trustees or change the Board as it saw fit at annual meetings or provide replacement during the interim period. As spelled out in the Charter, the trustees numbered fifteen and had the power to do any and everything necessary for the management of the school and its property. The type of school established, the term of admission of pupils, and the course of study were all left to the discretion of the trustees. The trustees could adopt a seal and change it as it wished.

[32] According to Young, ''*To Win the Prize*,'' pp. 15-17, Johnson was a native of an isolated area in Alabama. He was self taught as a child in the subjects of Latin, Greek, German, theology, grammar, rhetoric, logic, history, mathematics, and philosophy. In 1883 Johnson entered Southern Seminary in Louisville and graduated with a B. D. degree. Following graduation he served as evangelist and pastor in the Kentucky counties of Scott, Grant, Owen, and Carroll.

[33] Williamsburg Institute, *Catalogue*, 1889 - 1890, p. 3.

[34] *Western Recorder*, 25 September 1890, p. 8.

A HOLSTEIN COW

Looking back, people and churches gave liberally to help meet the Rockefeller challenge. For instance, a gentleman named T. J. Stackhouse of Lexington gave a Holstein cow worth $162.00. The cow was sold and the proceeds added to the fund to meet the challenge. In Frankfort, the church where Green Clay Smith had pastored gave $150.00 and challenged other churches to do likewise. Ironically, Frankfort's First Baptist Church, in 1982, created a $10,000 endowment in honor of their pastor Dr. Billy Hurt, alumnus and trustee of Cumberland College. This is the very church previously pastored by Green Clay Smith. Another Cumberland trustee Dr. Robert Browning pastors the First Baptist Church in Somerset, also once pastored by General Green Clay Smith.

[35] *Williamsburg Times*, 14 August 1891.

In January 1892 Johnson was again allowed by the Baptist Church to travel and seek funds on behalf of the Institute. The Church continued to pay Johnson's salary.

Johnson collected many gifts for the Institute. The debt on the Institute was paid, the building completed and enlarged, a boarding hall was added, and nearly $50,000 was secured for the endowment.

But Johnson's travels and his rigorous routine began to take their toll on his health,[36] and he was forced to leave the Institute and the Church.[37] He asked those who had made pledges to the Institute to pay them as quickly as possible and for those who hadn't given yet, he pled that they would.[38]

COPPER PENNIES

One can imagine Johnson on horseback, wading streams, crossing turbulent rivers, climbing mountains in the rain, snow, and sleet, raising money, and begging for the Institute. Johnson reported: "My heart swells with gratitude when I think of those little boys and girls all over the state who gave me their last copper or made pledges and are now doing little jobs to pay them."[39]

Johnson wanted to make life better for the mountain youngsters by providing educational opportunities. He lived his motto: "Nothing can happen to a person so bad as to have done wrong, nothing so good as to have done right."[40]

STUDENTS WORK TO MAKE ENDS MEET

Early in the history of the school, pleas were made for assistance to help meet the needs of the students. These youngsters wanted to work but funds were insufficient to meet all the needs. History reflects Cumberland's work ethic in William James Johnson's words:

> Think of the sacrifice our students are making to come here. We have some who are living on forty cents a week and are dependent on working nights and mornings to make it, and, if they fail, they have either to beg, starve, or leave. Most of them leave. Several are doing their own cooking

------

[36] *Western Recorder*, 21 July 1892, p. 8. "The work has been hard and fatiguing, and almost completely prostrated me. I have gone several days without getting but one meal and no sleep at all. I never stopped for the weather, but took it as came; but the Lord was with me, and, upon the whole, I enjoyed it. I feel that I have many friends wherever I have gone whom I shall remember with the greatest pleasure."

[37] Jones, "Legend and Lore," 3 November 1983, Jones mentions that Professor "Evans said that Johnson 'poured out his soul unto death, pleading with Kentucky Baptists for help.' " Jones goes on to say that it is likely that Johnson's illness and subsequent death were probably a direct result of his work to raise funds for the Institute.

[38] *Western Recorder*, 25 May 1893, p. 5. Johnson died 13 January 1894 in Scott County, Kentucky, of tuberculosis.

[39] *Western Recorder*, 21 July 1892, p. 8.

[40] Young, *"To Win the Prize,"* p.17.

and washing while working and studying. Many are working around people's houses for their board, girls cooking, washing, etc. Yet this year over fifty have been turned away because no accommodations could be furnished them . . . . They are now turning their imploring eyes to you saying, 'Help us.' Will you not do it? How my heart has bled within me as bright boys and girls from their distant mountain homes have come to me and said, 'Can't you find some place for us to stay and work our way through school?' I had to answer 'No' and see them turn sad and pale, leave for their poor, lonely homes, perhaps never to be heard of again, if so to be outlaws or desperados, lost to their country.[41]

A HIGHER CALLING THAN A MERE TITLE;
A NOBLER CALLING THAN A MERE PROFESSION

R. C. Medaris, Green Clay Smith, E. S. Moss, and Ancil Gatliff then were the first men to raise money for the College and William James Johnson soon followed, giving his life. In 1891 H. T. Daniel was named financial agent for the Institute. He worked long, tireless hours and died at an early age while soliciting funds in Shelbyville.[42] Neither Medaris, Smith, Moss, Gatliff, Johnson, nor Daniel had worked in vain. They had worked for a higher calling than a mere title; a nobler calling than a mere profession.

THEY JUST WOULDN'T LET IT DIE

Those who built and sustained the College through the early years faced and overcame almost insurmountable odds. "The early trustees just would not let it die."[43] Professors served for meager salaries, at times almost without pay. These professors were rewarded with inner strength which makes life rich, rewarding, and worthwhile. Many of the students came to campus without funds (even as it is today) and many paid at least part, if not all, of their fees by working (even as they do today).

THEY BECAME MULISH

These were hard and difficult times for the early trustees and administration.

Inspired by their own zeal, fired and ever urged on by the grandest of men, General Green Clay Smith, they determined to build a college, asked for help from the Baptists of Kentucky, and could not get it. Instead of

---

[41] *Western Recorder,* 12 May 1892, p. 4.

[42] *Western Recorder,* 1 January 1891.

[43] Pleas Jones, interview.

giving up they became 'mulish,' and regardless of everything, contracted for the building and went on with it.[44]

Men of modest means gave what was great sums of money for those days. Dr. E. S. Moss, reflecting on the struggle to make ends meet as the Institute got underway, reported: "Our expenses are heavy, and our people have been paying from their own pockets what has been necessary for the last two years, but we do need a permanent fund, and when that is done I am sure that in a few years all Kentucky will feel the school is an advantage to all."[45]

FAR-REACHING INFLUENCE

In the ranks of Cumberland College's alumni are found the names of many Kentucky mountain people who have become prominent doctors, judges, legislators, governors, generals, attorneys, a congressman, clergymen, missionaries, business leaders, teachers, and other professionals including being good mothers and fathers and outstanding members of the community. Without Cumberland College many folks would never have had a college experience to start them on their way to successful careers. The faith of the founding fathers is clearly vindicated as alumni have chosen to serve in rural communities and elsewhere, laboring daily to build a better and stronger nation.

From the beginning, the graduates gave promise of far-reaching influence. According to the 1909 *Eglantine,* among the graduates of the classes between 1893 and 1908, two were graduates of the University of Kentucky, two from Brown University, one from Harvard, and one from Denison. Thirty-three of these graduates served as teachers, principals or superintendents, seven as lawyers, five as medical doctors, three as businessmen, three as ministers, and one as a foreign missionary.[46]

---

[44] *Western Recorder,* 20 February 1890.

Brubacher and Rudy, *Higher Education in Transition,* p. 59. At this time colleges and universities were cropping up all over the country, many of which wanted help and sought it through denominational affiliation.

At one time or another, some fifty different type schools would be established locally in the state by Baptist ministers, Baptist churches, or associations. These would flourish for a while and then pass out of existence. This is probably why the Baptists would not give their help to build the College. Today, however, under Baptist auspices, there exists in the state, three liberal arts colleges, one four-year minister training school, two children's homes, one boarding high school, plus five hospitals. Cumberland College is the largest of the colleges with an annual enrollment of around 2,000 students.

The following appeared in the *Western Recorder,* 30 May 1889: "They have succeeded in putting up a substantial brick building and getting it in condition to be occupied, which, when completed will constitute a fair beginning of a work that will do great good . . . . The school has a very warm place in the hearts of the people."

[45] *Western Recorder,* 12 August 1889.

[46] According to Hall, "Cumberland College," p. 35, the first woman graduated from Williamsburg Institute was Grace Pope in the class of 1898. Miss Pope was from Williamsburg.

THE FACULTY, THE FIRST YEAR

From the beginning the faculty has been chosen on the basis of sound scholarship, superior teaching, high academic standing, character, integrity, as well as, and most importantly, a moral, personal, and professional commitment to values. A personal commitment to the individual student has always been important.

When the Institute opened its doors, there were two teachers: Carl D. Garlough and Milford White.[47] Others were soon added.

Carl D. Garlough (sometimes spelled Garlow) was instructor of mathematics. He held a Bachelor of Arts and a Bachelor of Philosophy degree. Milford White was instructor in arithmetic, English grammar, and civil government.

Other teachers during the first years were: Miss Maggie A. Hackley, teacher of English and penmanship; Mrs. Roxie Buchannan, teacher of primary department; Miss Bettie Lewis, teacher of music and elocution; and Mr. J. H. Criscillis, assistant tutor of English.[48]

THE DENISON CONNECTION

After the first few years most of the teachers had either a Bachelor of Arts or a Bachelor of Science degree and came primarily from the north, Ohio in particular. The early teachers came primarily, but not exclusively, from Denison University. These were Phi Beta Kappas who manned the College's classrooms and who played a major role in the College's development.[49]

The Denison connection had a profound and lasting impact on Cumberland College with three of the longtime teachers and administrators coming from Denison including Dr. E.E. Wood, president; Gorman Jones, professor of French and history; and P.R. Jones, professor of chemistry. Two other Denison graduates, F.D. Perkins

---

In 1907 there were at least four students enrolled at the Institute whose names are recognized even today: E.M. Gatliff, president of the senior class, became a distinguished legislator; James Lloyd Creech, who was to become president of Cumberland College eighteen years later, served as treasurer of the junior class; Besse Rose, president of the sophomore class, joined the faculty in 1912, remaining a member until 1962; Rose Marlowe, who became a missionary to China, was a member of the preparatory class.

[47] Hall, "Cumberland College," p. 15.

[48] Williamsburg Institute, *Catalogue*, 1889.

KENTUCKY'S POET LAUREATE

James Thomas Cotton Noe served as an instructor of English at the Williamsburg Institute in the 1890's. He wrote about the Williamsburg and Corbin people, and especially about, "Tip Sams had twins and a razor back sow, five swayback mules, and an old roan cow."

After leaving the Institute, Noe taught at the University of Kentucky. In 1928, by a joint resolution of the legislature, Noe was named Poet Laureate of Kentucky for life.

[49] Young, *"To Win the Prize,"* pp. 186-189.

and Laurence C. Irwin, joined the faculty in 1902 and 1906, respectively, but did not remain for many years.[50]

STAY ON STRANGER

When Professor P. R. Jones came to Williamsburg to teach at the Institute, he did so at the request of Denison's president. ". . . You see, I really came down here by accident. . . . The President of Denison said to me, 'I have already accepted a place for you in a small college at Williamsburg, Kentucky, where the president and another leading teacher are Denison graduates.' "

Jones came with the thought of staying a year, but he ended up staying fifty-eight years.[51]

TRIVIUM, QUADRIVIUM, AND DISCIPLINARIUM RHETORIC

The earliest colleges were small in size and were designated to train the clergy, doctors, and lawyers. Colleges were grounded in "trivium" (grammar, rhetoric, and logic), "quadrivium" (arithmetic, music, astronomy, and geometry), and "disciplinarium rhetoric" (liberal arts).[52] The Institute's curriculum was no different.

THE EARLY CURRICULUM

Although there was a small faculty and student body in the early days of the Institute, the curriculum was broad in its offerings and a real attempt was made to

---

[50] Williamsburg Institute, *Catalogue.*

On 29 June 1978, Siler in "Heads or Tales," wrote concerning the College's three hills prior to the recent purchase of the fourth hill on which sits the old city school property.

THE MAKING OF GIANTS

" . . . There have always been giants up on Cumberland College's three hills — Mahan Hall Hill, Roburn Hall Hill, Gatliff Auditorium Hill. Rome was built on seven hills, but Cumberland was built on only three.

These giants I mentioned are not the kind Joshua found when he went over Jordan to spy out the promised land. Neither are they the type of giants that play baseball at the Polo Grounds in New York City.

But the Cumberland College giants I knew were of the mind and spirit. At one time Cumberland with just a small faculty had four Phi Beta Kappas — Wood, Jones, Fitzgerald and Evans. Still other teachers were such giants of the spirit that they would always go the twain mile to give an extra push to a few denser pupils that might need help.

Such great helpers were Professor Val, Professor PR, who sometimes scared the liver out of a few of the more timid ones, and Miss Bess Rose who would rather see a student succeed than to receive a free ticket to the World Series.

Those folks were all Cumberland College giants."

[51] Siler, "Heads or Tales," 27 February 1969.

[52] Class notes of James H. Taylor, student, Vanderbilt University in class lecture, Education 3800, "Nature and Function of Higher Education," Professor Thomas A. Stovall, Fall, 1981.

meet the needs of the young people of the area. A copy of the first *Catalogue* can be found in Appendix VII.

The college department had a four-year course with eight schools offering classes in English language and literature, Latin, Greek, political science, philosophy, the modern languages of German and French, mathematics, physics, and other natural sciences.

The Bachelor of Science degree was conferred on those who completed the scientific course; the Bachelor of Arts degree was conferred on those who completed the classical course. The Master of Arts degree was conferred on all who completed with "marked success" the full course prescribed for the Bachelor of Arts degree with French and German.[53]

The normal department offered a two-year course to prepare for teaching in the grades. The preparatory department at that time included grades one through three.[54]

With the advent of the railroad coming to Williamsburg and with the industrial and population shifts, there came a need for more variety in the curriculum.

In March 1909 the Trustees voted to offer elementary work in the Institute the next year. Some elementary work had been offered before, but this act allowed all eight grades to be taught.[55]

Beginning in 1911 a course in telegraphy was offered.[56] A commercial department and a home economics course were added in 1913, and in 1915 a banking course was added.[57]

THE THREAD WHICH RUNS SO TRUE

From the beginning until the present day, the thread which runs so true through the College's history is that of the student work program and the unapologetic value orientation of the curriculum.

At Cumberland the privilege of a college education has always been based upon ability and character, not upon the amount of money a student or his parents might have.

Even today more than 600 students work on campus an average of twelve hours a week, washing dishes, carrying out the garbage, doing clerical work, mowing the

---

[53] Hall, "Cumberland College," pp. 16, 35.

[54] Williamsburg Institute, *Catalogue,* 1889, p. 21. A review of the catalogues of those early years reveals very few changes in the courses offered the first twenty years or so.

[55] Board of Trustees, Williamsburg Institute, *Minutes,* 6 March 1909.

[56] Williamsburg Institute, *Catalogue,* 1909-1910, p. 12.

[57] Cumberland College, *Catalogue,* 1914-1915.

grass in the summer, shoveling the snow in the winter, raking the leaves in the fall, preparing the flower beds in the spring, or doing whatever else needs to be done. At Cumberland work is never degraded or demeaned. Rather, work is seen as virtuous since work teaches the values of promptness, dependability, and accuracy, and work develops qualities of thrift, self-reliance, integrity, and pride in a job well done.

A good bit of financial assistance at Cumberland College has always been awarded in the form of work. The work program is optional and the amount depends on ability and need. Students work in the buildings, in the library, in the cafeteria, on maintenance crews, as assistants in our laboratories, and in other capacities. Since there are hundreds of mountain students who possess high intelligence but have little money, the work program is essential.

Work is an education in itself even today, as it was also in the beginning for the College.

WILLIAMSBURG INSTITUTE
(Now known as Roburn Hall)

(Photograph from the 1893-1894 *Catalogue*)

PICTURE OF ROBURN BELL

"The old bell, bigger than most church bells, says 1892. So that's the year it first rang in the little tower high above the front door of Roburn Hall . . . ." Jones, "Legend and Lore," 13 May 1976. [The bell actually is inscribed 1895.]

(Photograph by Housman Photography)

THE JOHN WESLEY SILER HOME

The John Wesley Siler home was located at Fifth and Sycamore Streets. Business affecting the beginning and growth of the Institute was often carried on at this residence.

(Photograph by Housman Photography)

FIRST FOUR GRADUATES OF WILLIAMSBURG INSTITUTE

In 1893 the Institute graduated four young men: (bottom row, left to right) A.S. Petrey, E.L. Stephens, A.J. Meadors, and (standing) A.J. Parker.

(Photograph from the Cumberland College Collection)

THE ANCIL GATLIFF HOME

THE J.B. GATLIFF HOME

(Photographs by Housman Photography)

PEARL GATLIFF PERKINS
1884-1964
Trustee, 1957-1964
(Photograph from *Renfro Revelations*
by Simon Renfro, March 1945)

JAMES BLAINE GATLIFF
1882-1970
Trustee, 1918-1964
Chairman of the Board, 1931-1964
(Photograph courtesy of Mrs. J.B.
Gatliff, Jr.)

EDWARD MOSS GATLIFF
1887-1949
Trustee, 1949
(Photograph from the
Cumberland College Collection)

JAMES BLAINE GATLIFF, JR.
1908-
Trustee 1946-1965
(Photograph courtesy of Mrs. J.B.
Gatliff, Jr.)

N. ANCIL ARCHER
1874-1946
Trustee, 1911-1946
(Photograph from the Cumberland
College Collection)

NORMAN B. PERKINS
1877-1955
Trustee, 1917-1955
(Photograph from the Cumberland
College Collection)

THOMAS ELMER MAHAN
1891-1976
Trustee 1950-1970
(Photograph from Young, *"To Win
the Prize"*)

THE GATLIFF CONNECTION

Dr. and Mrs. Gatliff's two sons, James Blaine Gatliff and Edward Moss Gatliff; one daughter Pearl Gatliff Perkins; one grandson James Blaine Gatliff, Jr.; one granddaughter Norma Jeanne Perkins Hagan; and three sons-in-law, Norman B. Perkins, N. Ancil Archer, and Thomas Elmer Mahan served on the College's Board of Trustees.

ANCIL GATLIFF
1850-1918

Trustee, 1889-1918
Chairman of the Board, 1888-1918
The students dedicated the 1908 yearbook "To
Dr. Ancil Gatliff, the man whose untiring generosity
has made possible our hopes for an education."
(Photograph from the
Cumberland College Collection)

FLORIDA ELLEN MOSS GATLIFF
1854-1932

(Photograph courtesy of the
First Baptist Church,
Williamsburg, Kentucky)

JAMES PERRY MAHAN
1859-1906

JOIE B. MAHAN

James Perry Mahan is one of the men responsible for Cumberland's early founding. He was one of the three delegates to the special meeting of the Mount Zion Association in 1887 when the trustees were appointed and the Charter petitioned. Mahan served the College as a trustee from that time until 1906. He also served as vice president of the Board from 1893 until his death in 1906.

Mahan, the son of Milton E. Mahan and Jane Arthur Mahan, was reared on Wolf Creek along with his brother, Thomas Breckenridge. James married Joie Buchanan.

Active in business, James Perry Mahan served as president of the First National Bank, Jellico, as well as president of Mount Morgan Coal Company. Mahan was also active in his church, Williamsburg First Church, where he served as deacon and treasurer.

On 6 March 1906, James Perry Mahan died. He is buried in Highland Cemetery. The College's Trustees paid tribute to Mahan with the following resolution: "We bear witness to the great worth of our deceased brother, and to his wise counsels, his charity, his loving sympathy . . . ." Mahan supported the college not only through his work but also financially. This financial support continued through his widow who, in 1912, donate $10,000 to help the college pay off its debt.

In 1907, *The Eglantine* was dedicated to Mahan, "A man who, without early advantages, climbed to a place of honorable distinction and developed a strong, generous, noble character."

Young, *"To Win the Prize,"* passim; Cumberland College, *The Eglantine,* 1907; *Minutes,* Board of Trustees, Williamsburg Institute, 31 March 1906; Mount Zion Association, Record Book No. 1, pp. 23-24.

(Photographs from the Cumberland College Collection)

THOMAS BRECKENRIDGE MAHAN
1856-1930

"Those Who Made the Investment in the
Institution Never Had Cause to Regret It"

Thomas Breckenridge Mahan was born at Wolf Creek and was the older brother of James Perry Mahan. Like his brother, Thomas Breckenridge Mahan served as a trustee of Cumberland College, first taking office in 1896. In 1918 when Dr. Ancil Gatliff died, Mahan became president of the Board, a position he held until his death in 1930.

Mahan was the principal owner of Mahan Jellico Coal Company. This mine was opened in 1908, and the camp surrounding it was named Packard. In all, Mahan served as president of six coal companies and vice-president of two others.

A deacon at the First Church, Williamsburg, Mahan served also on the executive board of the Mount Zion Association. He financially supported both of these causes as well as the College.

While addressing the students at the College, Mahan once remarked on the "large investment of life and money that had been made in Cumberland." He went on to say "that those who had made the investment had never had any reason to regret it." Thomas Breckenridge Mahan was one of those investors.

Hall, *A History of Cumberland College,* p. 86; Young, *"To Win the Prize,"* *passim;* Jones, "Legend and Lore," 27 November 1985.

(Photograph from the Cumberland College Collection)

COLONEL GARROD ELLISON, M.D.
1861-1939

How Colonel Garrod Ellison came to be named is an interesting story. "He was born during the Civil War. One day some Northern soldiers stopped at Grandmother Ellison's farm. They demanded to have her cow, her chickens, and her horse, plus food. She loudly told them they couldn't because she needed them for her children as her husband was in the army and away from home. About this time Colonel Garrod came into the house and Grandmother explained her situation and the Colonel assured her they would *not* take her food needed for her children. She named my father for the Colonel, hence C.G. Ellison means Colonel Garrod Ellison."

Dr. C.G. Ellison was the younger brother of James Madison Ellison, and like his brother, Dr. Ellison served as a trustee of the College. Appointed to the Board in 1898, Dr. Ellison served the College for the remainder of his life. He was elected secretary to the Board in 1900 and retained this office until his death in 1939.

Dr. Ellison and his wife Rachel were the parents of five daughters and two sons: Lois, Jane, Maude, Dorcas, Josephine, Arthur, and Ancil.

Ellison served as a deacon at the First Church where he was a member. He also acted as treasurer for the church for eleven years. In 1914 Dr. Ellison was elected Mayor of the City of Williamsburg, and he held this office for three terms.

Dr. C.G. Ellison, a physician, was a caring man. He treated the rich and poor alike, never failing to go where he was needed and accepting as payment for his services whatever the people could give. He was loved by the people in return.

Dr. Ellison was a cheerful man, and his patients were quoted as saying, "I always felt better the moment he came into my room." He never refused to see a patient, even when he knew they had no money with which to pay. One family across Jellico Mountain paid their doctor bills in maple sugar.

Young, *"To Win the Prize,"* p. 120; *Minutes,* Board of Trustees, Williamsburg Institute, 26 May 1898; *Ibid.,* 17 May 1900; Eugene Lovett, *The History of Williamsburg, Kentucky, 1818-1978,* (Williamsburg, Kentucky, 1981), p. 12; Lois Ellison Goldsmith, personal correspondence, 8 June 1986, and 1 July 1984; Josephine Ellison Quarles, personal correspondence, 9 June 1986; Jane Ellison Hall, personal correspondence, n.d.

(Photograph from the Cumberland College Collection)

JAMES MADISON ELLISON
1858-1942

James Madison Ellison began his tenure as a trustee of Cumberland College in 1895, and he served until his death in 1942. From 1910 until his death, he also served as treasurer of the Board.

Ellison was reared at Savoy along with seven brothers. He married Nannie Coffee, and one child Myrtle Ellison Dishman was born to the union. Ellison later married Maude England, and they had eight children: Raymond, Mabel, Lillian, William, Jeanette, James, Dorothy, and Mildred.

James Madison Ellison was a member of the First Baptist Church of Williamsburg where he served as a deacon.

Minutes, Board of Trustees, Williamsburg Institute, 12 February 1895.

(Photograph from the Cumberland College Collection)

ADAM TROY SILER
1870-1953
"Be Somebody"

Adam Troy Siler was born at Tackett Creek and was reared in Whitley County. In 1897 he married Minnie Chandler. Three children were born to this union: Lillian, Eugene E., and Irma. In 1926 he married Minnie Murphy.

In 1901 Siler was appointed a trustee of Cumberland College. He remained a trustee until his death in 1953.

Mr. Siler was a leader. "He was twice County School Superintendent, twice a Kentucky Railroad Commissioner, twice 11th Congressional District Chairman, 35 years a bank president, twice president of Kentucky Baptists, 50 years a practicing lawyer."

When elected moderator of the General Association of Kentucky Baptists, Siler was the first layman elected to that position in more than 40 years.

Siler's creed and motto was, "Be Somebody," a lesson he tried to impress upon his college girls' Sunday School class at First Baptist Church.

Young, *"To Win the Prize,"* passim; Siler, "Heads or Tales," 12 February 1976; Jones "Legend and Lore," 27 November 1985.

(Photograph from the Cumberland College Collection)

JOHN WESLEY SILER
1843-1912
"A Friend of the Institute: Staunch and Untiring"

John Wesley Siler was another of the three delegates to the special meeting of the Mount Zion Association in 1887 when he was appointed trustee and treasurer of the Institute. He held these posts until his death in 1912.

Siler was the son of Burgess and Mary Siler of Cane Creek and the husband of Debbie Buchanan Siler.

John Wesley Siler has been described as a "lively politician who just had to hug all the women, slap all the men on the back and hand out nickles to all the children." He was actively involved in the community and its business. He organized the Bank of Williamsburg; he was the County Court Clerk; he was a collector for the Internal Revenue Service; and he was president of Imperial Coal Company. Additionally, Siler was an active member of the Williamsburg First Church where he served as trustee and clerk.

The Eglantine in 1908 had the following to say concerning John Wesley Siler: ". . . He has been from its establishment a friend of the Institute, staunch and untiring, an adviser, keensighted and wise . . . ."

When Siler died in 1912, his entire estate of $50,000 was left to the College for the endowment with a portion to be set aside each year to purchase a gold medal as a prize to the woman student who won the essay contest.

Young, *"To Win the Prize,"* passim; *The Eglantine,* Cumberland College, 1908; *Minutes,* Board of Trustees, Williamsburg Institute, 6 March 1909; Mount Zion Association, Record Book No. 1, p. 53; Siler, "Heads or Tales," 10 February 1977.

(Photograph from the Cumberland College Collection)

EDWIN SMITH MOSS

First Chairman of the Board of Williamsburg Institute
(Photograph from the Cumberland College Collection)

WILLIAM JAMES JOHNSON
Principal 1889-1890

(Photograph courtesy of First Baptist Church, Williamsburg, Kentucky)

JOHNSON HALL

On 11 February 1894, Johnson Hall was dedicated in memory of William James Johnson. According to the *Minutes,* Board of Trustees, 11 February 1894, the College's treasurer John W. Siler announced that even though the upper floor of the building was not furnished, the building was ready for use and free of debt. In 1895, according to the Board of Trustees, *Minutes,* 5 December, the building was insured for $6,000.

This boarding hall was occupied that first year by girls, but the next year by boys. Those who lived here paid only the actual cost of running the building. In 1913, after the construction of Felix Hall for boys, Johnson Hall was enlarged at a cost of $20,000 (a considerable sum in those days), and girls again occupied its rooms.

The Board of Trustees met in a called meeting on 6 March 1894, and passed the following regulations for Johnson Hall:

(1) No one may leave the Hall without permission of the Matron.

(2) No permission can be given to shop or visit during school hours.

(3) The Matron shall make such regulations regarding conduct in the halls, rooms, and meal hours, etc., and these regulations are to be given respectful obedience.

(4) The young ladies in going out at night are to be chaperoned by the Matron, or someone designated by her. On such occasions they are to sit near each other, and to leave the place together, and to yield to the wishes of the chaperone.

(5) When the bell taps for chapel exercises all are expected to go to the school building, and to wait until the first stroke of each hour bell, which calls them to recitations.

(6) Board is to be paid monthly in advance.

(Photograph from the 1896-1897 *Catalogue.*)

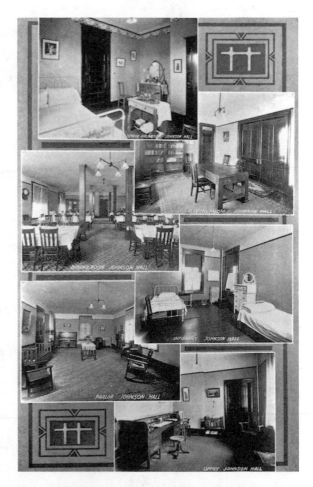

JOHNSON HALL - INTERIOR VIEWS

The first matron of Johnson Hall was Julia Webster. She was employed at a salary of $25 a month for five months. For the month of January, 1894, the total expenses (including food, utilities, and Mrs. Webster's salary) for the Boarding Hall were $168.80.

(Photograph from the 1916-1917 *Catalogue*)

JOHNSON HALL DINING ROOM

From the time of its construction until the construction of the T.J. Roberts Memorial Cafeteria in 1958, Johnson Hall served as the dining room for students. It was a place of eloquent dining with tablecloths, china, and silver accompanied by the proper dress, fine manners, and appropriate demeanor. Nonetheless, students never liked to sit at the end of the table for fear the plate would be emptied before it was passed to them.

(Photograph from the 1916-1917 *Catalogue*)

ETHEL REBECCA HARMON

A member of the graduating class of 1932, Miss Ethel Rebecca Harmon served as a teacher and missionary to Nigeria beginning in 1938.

After graduating from Cumberland College, Miss Harmon attended Georgetown College. In 1938 she was graduated from Women's Missionary Training School in Louisville and was chosen by the Foreign Mission Board for service in Nigeria.

Miss Harmon retired in 1971 and currently resides in Corbin, Kentucky.

(Photograph courtesy of Miss Harmon)

BENJAMIN PLEASANT ROACH
1872-1961

Benjamin Pleasant Roach was graduated in 1899 from the Williamsburg Institute and from Southern Baptist Theological Seminary in 1903. In 1904 Roach was appointed as a missionary to China, and he and his bride Laureola Lloyd Roach went to China where he served for fifteen years. Mrs. Roach died in 1918 and shortly thereafter Roach retired.

After returning to the United States, Roach pastored several churches. In 1948 he married Virginia Cox and took over the family business, the Bank and Trust Company of Jonesboro, Tennessee.

Mr. Roach passed away in 1961.

(Photograph courtesy of Roger L. Roach)

ROSE MARLOWE
1890 - 1980

Rose Marlowe, a graduate of the class of 1912, was appointed as a missionary to China in 1921. After the Communist takeover of China, Miss Marlowe was transferred to Japan where she lived until her retirement in 1956. During World War II, Miss Marlowe spent several months in an internment camp and a month on a prison ship.

After her return to the United States, Miss Marlowe lived in Louisville where she continued her missionary work though retired. She passed away in 1980.

(Photograph courtesy of Mrs. Dorothy Ashley)

E.E. Wood, President: A.B. Denison University '90; A.M. Denison University '93; Instructor in Latin, English and Philosophy.

Gorman Jones: A.B. Denison University '90; A.M. Denison University '93; Instructor in Greek, History, and Political Economy.

F.D. Perkins: Principal High School, Plain City, Ohio, 1898: Superintendent Public Schools, Ostrander, Ohio, 1898-90); A.B. Denison University '92; Principal, Amboy Academy, Amboy, Ind. 1902; Instructor in Mathematics and Logic.

Elmere Johnson: B.S. Baylor University '05; Instructor in German and Natural Sciences.

Miss Georgia Kirtley: Normal Training School of Cincinnati, O. '86; Summer Work at University of Chicago 1900; Instructor at Clinton College 1891-95; Instructor in B Grammar Department.

Miss Nannie Moore: A. B. Williamsburg Institute '05; C. Grammar.

Miss Roxye Caddell: B.S. Williamsburg Institute '06; D. Grammar.

Miss Mary Bettie Brock: Primary.

J.T. Fitzgerald: A.B. Richmond College, '06; Instructor in Latin and Algebra.

Lawrence C. Irvin: Ph.D. Denison University '06; Instructor in Latin and Teachers' Department.

Miss Grace Truman Ogg: A.B. Kentucky State College '05; Instructor in Mathematics and Science.

Mrs. Mary M. Brownie: Instructor in Telegraphy.

Miss Ella Ruckel Mellwaine: Crane Normal Institute of Music 1901; Instructor in Crane Normal Institute 1901-06; Supervisor of Music, Potsdam High School, N.Y. 1905-06; Instructor in Music.

Miss Pauline Kirtley: Art School of Cincinnati; Instructor in Art.

J.W. Jordan: Manager Boys' Dormitory.

Miss Sallie Ward: Graduate Sayre Institute, Lexington, Ky.; Matron of Girls' Hall.

THE EARLY FACULTY

By 1907 there were fourteen teachers listed in *The Eglantine*. Also listed were the matron and manager of the dormitories.

(Photographs from *The Eglantine,* 1907)

Here are pictures of early athletic teams and other organizations including pictures of early academic and vocational programs. The College through the years has taken on an array of shapes, sizes, and directions as depicted by the pictures on this and the following pages. Some folks may look at the pictures and laugh while others may look at the words and scratch their head(s). I guess I'll do both when I read the history again.

VARSITY BASKETBALL TEAM

By 1909 the men's varsity basketball team had been organized as had the pygmies basketball team.

Women's basketball was ahead of the sport for men and in 1907 the women had three teams. In 1908 four additional teams were added, and in 1909 one additional team was added.

(Photograph from *The Eglantine*, 1909)

1907 BASEBALL TEAM

Baseball was in full swing by 1907.

(Photograph from *The Eglantine*, 1907)

PYGMIES

(Photograph from *The Eglantine*, 1909)

1905 FOOTBALL TEAM

A football team was put on the field in 1905, but in 1907, football was disbanded until the 1920's.

(Photograph from the 1906 *Catalogue*)

GATLIFFIAN SOCIETY
(Photograph from *The Eglantine*, 1907)

GLEE CLUB
The Glee Club had four members: D. H. Howard, first tenor; E. H. Faulkner, second tenor; C. P. Estes, first bass; and James Lloyd Creech, second tenor.

(Photograph from *The Eglantine*, 1907)

HYPERION SOCIETY
(Photograph from *The Eglantine*, 1907)

PHILOSOPHIAN LITERARY SOCIETY
There were two literary societies for men, the Gatliffian and the Hyperion, and one for women, the Philosophian.

(Photograph from *The Eglantine*, 1907)

PIONEER LAWN TENNIS CLUB
The most mysterious club on campus, the Amalgamated Order of Resperators, was composed of five members. Little is known of the club except references to their pranks such as letting a goat loose in Johnson Hall.

Other clubs on campus were the United Sons of Rest, the Jack and Pony Club, the Philisiphian Glee Club, the Star Tennis Club, the Smith-Jones Club, the Bell County Club, and the Pioneer Lawn Tennis Club.

(Photograph from *The Eglantine*, 1909)

PHI LAMBDA TAU SORORITY
(Photograph from *The Eglantine,* 1907)

SIGMA PHI SORORITY
(Photograph from *The Eglantine,* 1907)

MAY DAY

Activities included such annual events as May Day celebration.

Another annual event was an automobile ride for seniors. The following item appeared in *The Cumberland College Monthly,* June, 1913.

"Dr. and Mrs. N.A. Archer gave the Senior Class their annual automobile ride Tuesday morning May 20th. Five cars decorated in college pennants and banners carried our party over all the streets of Williamsburg. Then we were arranged in a line back of court house square where we 'posed' for a picture. Finally we gathered at Dr. and Mrs. Archer's home where a delightful luncheon was served."

(Photograph from *The Eglantine,* 1914)

DELTA KAPPA FRATERNITY

There were two sororities for women, Phi Lambda Tau and Sigma Phi, and one fraternity for men, Delta Kappa.

(Photograph from *The Eglantine,* 1907)

Domestic Science offered courses in cooking and sewing. Classes were held in Dixie Hall.
(Photographs from the 1915-1916 *Catalogue*)

PHYSICS LABORATORY

According to the 1914-1915 *Catalogue,* science classes were "taught mainly on a laboratory basis. Students work alone or in pairs, doing two hours' work in the laboratory as an equivalent of one hours' recitation. The laboratory is well equipped at present for the courses offered."
(Photograph from the 1914-1915 *Catalogue*)

The Commercial Department offered classes in bookkeeping, shorthand and typewriting.
(Photograph from the 1915-1916 *Catalogue*)

CORNER IN ART ROOM
Drawing and painting were taught.
(Photograph from the 1914-1915 *Catalogue*)

MANUAL TRAINING BENCHWORK

MANUAL TRAINING SAW AND LATHES

The courses in manual training included benchwork, wood turning, mechanical drawing, cabinet making, house building, and a course in simple blacksmith work.
(Photographs from the 1915-1916 *Catalogue*)

CHAPTER 3
THEY BUILT MIGHTIER THAN THEY KNEW

AN EVER-PRESSING NEED

Because of the ever-pressing need for funds and since the College was small, had no endowment, and only one building, William James Johnson saw clearly the need to undergird the College in its initial years. Johnson at the age of 27 decided to devote his full time to fund raising for the Institute in 1890. After all, what good would the Institution do if it couldn't exist? The principalship of the Institute was then thrust upon a twenty-eight-year-old man Edwin Ellsworth Wood, who served for twenty-two years as principal, vice-president, and then president of Williamsburg Institute.

EDWIN ELLSWORTH WOOD

President Edwin Ellsworth Wood (1863-1940) has been described as a man "of rare intelligence and excellent education whose intelligence and education were combined with genius for teaching," and as having the power to make a person "love the good and right and true."[1]

Born in Indiana in 1863, Wood was educated at Denison University where in 1890, he received the A.B. degree and was graduated Phi Beta Kappa.[2] In 1890 Wood came to Williamsburg and was appointed principal of the Institute following Johnson's resignation.[3] For reasons remaining obscure, Wood resigned as principal

---

[1] Hall, "Cumberland College," p. 20.

[2] Wood also received from Denison University the Master of Arts degree in 1893 and the Doctor of Laws degree in 1922. He was a member of the International Philosophic Society and a fellow of the Royal Society of Arts in London. Dr. Wood had a very broad education for the time. He found time to correspond with professors at Yale on different subjects. After he left the presidency he spent part of the year at Yale. He spent some time at the University of California, Los Angeles, as a kind of adjunct member, and he audited classes of professors he knew. In 1922 when Wood was awarded the honorary Doctor of Laws degree from Denison University, the following proclamation was read:

"Mr. President: I have the pleasure and the honor to present for an honorary degree one of our alumni, who during his college course reflected the finest Denison spirit, and since his graduation has devoted himself with rare consistency to the cause of Christian education. By his wise administration and unceasing efforts, an institution which was struggling for existence when he found it, has been lifted to the rank of a junior college, has greatly widened the scope of its work and influence, and has placed on a substantial financial basis. In his public addresses and writings he has constantly promoted the cause of higher learning. As a teacher he exemplifies the highest ideals of leadership and inspires his students with love of learning . . . ."

[3] Jones, "Legend and Lore," 25 October 1984. In this article, Mr. Jones quotes from an article which appeared in *The Louisville Post,* 7 December 1922, by Ralph Coghlan.

" '. . . Tell me what you are proud of and I'll tell you what you are. If you go in Williamsburg and ask any man on the street what is the main attraction, what is the focal point of its life, he will say 'Cumberland College.'

in 1893,[4] returning later to the Institute as its vice-president.

In Chicago, it's the Stockyards, typifying industry; in New York, it's Fifth Avenue, meaning fashion, or Wall Street, meaning wealth; in Paris, it's the Louvre, meaning beauty, or Montmart, meaning wine, women and song. In Williamsburg, the alurements of industry, wealth, fashion and beauty are subordinated to a passion for religion, religious education and old time living.

. . . Curiously enough, the religious spirit seems not at all affected by the sudden wave of prosperity, except in a beautiful way. When Dr. Wood came here as head of the Williamsburg Institute (forerunner of Cumberland College) he found such of the citizens as the Gatliffs, the Sampsons, the Moses, the Silers, the Mahans and the Ellisons, at that time, poor men giving until it hurt to build and keep the young college growing. Often, Dr. Wood relates, these men actually handicapped their businesses in their zeal to make Williamsburg the Religious Center of the mountains. Now, happily funds to maintain the work are forthcoming in abundance, and the fears of those early days have long since been displaced.

The situation on that fateful Monday morning, January 1, [It is assumed that this was a typographical error; the date should have been January 7] 1889, when the New Institute was dedicated, is vividly described by Dr. Wood. "The undertaking to them (the citizens of Williamsburg) at that time was gigantic," says he. They feared lest after all their effort, the whole thing might prove a failure. But, when money was lacking, they drew it from their own pockets and as the end of the year drew nigh, they saw the house steadily nearing completion. On Saturday night before the opening, men and women worked in the building until midnight, cleaning it up. They were there again to begin work as soon as the clock in the courthouse tower should strike the hour of midnight, and all of them broke down and wept in pure joy at the realization of their hopes.

Dr. Wood, after all these years, knows the mountain folk to the marrow. He is not one of them, . . . [but he] has been able to study them objectively to get a perspective on them. "They possess," says he, "a sense of honor, a purity of motive that makes them human beings, the salt of the earth."

Particularly did he emphasize their religious zeal and their fine native intelligence. "It is totally absurd the way the Kentucky mountaineers have been maligned by fiction writers." Says he, "We have our bad men, just as great cities have their thieves and harlots. But they are outnumbered by the good mountaineers all through the country (waving their hands towards the hills that encircle Williamsburg). You will find little churches everywhere, where mountain people go frequently to worship. All through here, you will find some of the finest physical and mental specimens of the human race."

I say the people of the mountains are the hope of America. My reason for saying this is not only that they themselves are inherently right and sound in their attitude toward God and country, but they are bringing up lots of children. Families of six, eight, ten and twelve children are common — and they are fine, lusty youngsters too. This is a sign of health, vigor and power of the race. The mountains, of course, do not hold them all. They are spread throughout America, and wherever they are, they form a bulwark against the crazy fanaticism of some of our foreign population.

As to their charm, their kindliness, their neighborliness, their warm hospitality, their pride and intelligence, Dr. Wood is full of tribute. He wants to correct the false notions that exist. Even in the case of the bad man, he wants to explain that after all there is great good in him. Long isolation and quickness to resent inquiry or insult have made many to stray from the right path, while retaining good instincts.' "

THE GOEBEL ASSASINATION

[4] Williamsburg Institute, Board of Trustees, *Minutes.* 1893. The reason thought behind the resignation of Wood was that he resigned to go to Frankfort to work for his brother-in-law Charles Finley in state government.

The following story is told by Siler, "Heads or Tales," 14 April 1966, concerning Charles Finley.

"On the morning of January 30, 1900, around 11 o'clock on a Tuesday, one very prominent and well-known state senator from Covington, Kentucky, was fatally shot from ambush in front of the State Capitol in Frankfort. Four days later he died. His name was William Goebel or Bill Goebel, as many called him. He had been the Democratic nominee for governor at the preceding November election. But upon the face of the election returns Goebel had been defeated and another Bill, a Republican, one William S. Taylor, had been declared by the election commission to be governor by majority vote of the people.

. . . Senator Goebel had filed an election contest before the legislature. And on that very day of January 30 or possibly the next day, Senator Goebel was to have been declared by the legislature to be the winner of the previous election for governor. Goebel on this occasion was walking to his official duties in the Capitol. He was accompanied

JOHN NEWTON PRESTRIDGE

In September, 1893, forty-year-old John Newton Prestridge (1853-1913) joined the Institute's faculty as Instructor of Bible.[5] When Wood resigned as president, Prestridge was elected to fill his post, serving in this capacity from September 1893 to October 1897.

Prestridge, a graduate of Howard College, also attended The Southern Baptist Theological Seminary. He was called to the Williamsburg First Baptist Church in 1893. His wife Frances accompanied him.[6]

During his tenure as president of the Institute, Prestridge also served as secretary of the Board of Trustees.[7]

The 11 June 1896 edition of the *Western Recorder* reported that "the whole section [of southeastern Kentucky] is feeling the influence of President Prestridge and his teachers which send out about a hundred teachers each year."

In 1897 Prestridge resigned the presidency and his pastorate and went to Louisville to edit a weekly paper called the *Baptist Argus*. At the turn of the century Prestridge began a movement to form a worldwide congress for the Baptist denomination, and by 1905 the Baptist World Alliance was functioning with Prestridge being dubbed, "Father of the World Congress."[8]

---

by a man named Jack Chinn. Then a rifle was projected out of a nearby, partially opened window which had the blind pulled down. The rifle fired and Goebel fell while clutching a small, pearl handle pistol that he carried. He was moved to a neighboring hotel and on his death bed, on January 31, 1900, just after the legislature had declared him to be the winner . . . Senator Goebel was sworn in as governor of Kentucky. Within three days he was dead.

. . . Two young Whitley County men were accused of complicity in all of this tragedy. Their names also were printed in all the newspapers. These men were Charles Finley, age 34, born and raised on Main Street in Williamsburg, and Caleb Powers, age 30, born and raised in a log cabin near Nevisdale. Finley always lived in Williamsburg. But Powers had moved over to Barbourville and been elected County Superintendent of Schools in Knox County before Goebel was slain. Both Finley and Powers were, either because of this Goebel trouble or in spite of it, elected to Congress by the people of Southeastern Kentucky in later years . . . .

. . . That rifle was fired out of the office of the Secretary of State located close to the State Capitol. Finley had been Secretary of State up until the Goebel-Taylor election. The very place of ambush had been his former office. Powers had succeeded Finley and had taken over as Secretary of State and had occupied this same office before Goebel was slain. Both Finley and Powers and various others were indicted and charged with the Goebel slaying. Finley crossed the river into Republican Indiana and remained there for about eight years until Republican Augustus Wilson was elected Governor of Kentucky and had signed pardons for the two secretaries of state, who later became congressmen from Southeastern Kentucky . . . ."

[5] Hall, "Cumberland College," p. 20; Williamsburg Institute, *Catalogue*, 1893-1894, p.4.

[6] Young, *"To Win the Prize,"* p. 18.

[7] Williamsburg Institute, *Catalogue*, 1893-1894, 1895-1896, 1896-1897.

[8] Young, *"To Win the Prize,"* p. 19.

WOOD: ADMINISTRATOR AND TEACHER

Following Prestridge's resignation, Edwin Ellsworth Wood, who was vice-president, became president in 1898.[9] While serving as administrator at the Institute, Wood also served as a classroom teacher of English, Latin, and occasionally mathematics, metaphysics, intellectual science, philosophy, and German.[10] Additionally, while at the Institute, Wood married Margaret Finley, a native Whitley Countian, and fathered three children: Katherine, Margaret, and Charles.[11]

Under the Wood administration the Institute grew and prospered.[12] Wood reported in 1899, "I have never seen so many young people eager for an education."[13] In fact, in 1900, the General Association in Kentucky reported that the Institute had experienced a year of "signal prosperity," and that Dr. Wood had "abundantly vindicated the wisdom of calling him to his important position."[14]

---

[9] Williamsburg Institute, Board of Trustees, *Minutes*, 1898.

[10] It was Dr. Wood's belief that students needed foreign language to aid them in furthering their education. When World War I broke out, Wood went on a crusade to persuade other colleges and universities to keep German in their curriculum.

[11] In an interview by Gary I. Blanton on 31 July 1984 with Dr. Wood's son-in-law, Edward Sheils (a former English teacher and registrar at Cumberland College), the following account of Sheils' remembrance of Dr. Wood in an English composition class was related: "Almost immediately I was aware that Dr. Wood was quite different from the other English teachers I had in high school. He could get the most out of us. We didn't feel it was an assignment, it was something we wanted to do right. He was not critical of our writing in the beginning but let us know how it should have been done. You could not be in his class and not come out quite changed."

Wood was a very prolific and thought-provoking writer. *The Cumberland College Monthly* from 1914-1919 contained many articles written by Dr. Wood: "The Price of Peace," "The Moral Obligation to be Intelligent," "The Best Reason for Going to War," "The Passion for Perfection," "Wonders of the Human Brain," and others.

[12] As early as 1902 comparisons and contrasts were being drawn between Berea College and Cumberland College. The following information appeared in the *Western Recorder,* 13 February 1902:
". . . Berea, with its forty-seven year history, thirty-seven teachers and million dollar endowment and plant, reached about four hundred mountain boys and girls last year . . . .
Williamsburg Institute, with its twelve-year history, twelve teachers, small endowment and buildings, reaches about 500 mountain boys and girls every year.
Berea sends her agents and literature all over the country and offers every inducement, while Williamsburg Institute has never made a special effort to get patronage because she has always had more than she could successfully teach."

Today the endowment of Berea, according to Richard Wilson's "Officials Don't Rest on Laurels of Endowment," *The Courier Journal,* 5 October 1986, pp. 1, 20, reprinted with permission, is valued at well over one hundred ninety million dollars. Unfortunately, Cumberland College's endowment is less than ten million dollars. One could only wish that Cumberland had also sent agents and literature all over as did Berea.

According to the *Minutes* of the 22 April 1906 Board of Trustees meeting, Dr. Wood was named to the Board of Trustees despite some of the Trustees' opposition of electing a Trustee from the faculty. The Trustees in electing Wood stated that they did so because of his long service to the Institute and because of his knowledge of the affairs of the school.

[13] *Western Recorder,* 23 March 1899.

[14] *The Sixty-Third Anniversary of the General Association of Baptists in Kentucky* (Louisville: Baptist Book Concern, 1900), p. 24.

"Education in the Mountains," *Western Recorder,* 18 June 1908.
"President E.E. Wood, of the Williamsburg Institute, presented a paper on 'The History and Results of Baptist

The Wood administration was marked by extensive expansion. The College purchased the Highland College property; Johnson Hall and Felix Hall were built; and the College's debt, incurred during the early years, was decreased.

H. H. HIBBS

Following Prestridge as pastor of the First Baptist Church was H. H. Hibbs (1862-1936), a graduate of Southern Seminary.[15] Hibbs also agreed to work for the Institute two months a year as a fund raiser.

AN UNSUNG HERO IN A LABOR OF LOVE

As one reads the College's official records and articles from the *Western Recorder,* it is easy to see that H. H. Hibbs was an unsung hero who gave his strength, time, talent, and almost every waking moment to enhancing the Institute's financial position. It was a labor of love, and he succeeded in raising some $200,000 through his efforts, a considerable sum today and even more so then.[16]

Education to the Mountains of Kentucky.' He sketched the progress that has been made in our educational work in Eastern Kentucky during the past twenty years. This work began with the Williamsburg Institute under most discouraging circumstances. President Wood sketched the dreams and struggles of its early friends and mentioned the interest and efforts of the late Green Clay Smith. He referred to some of the noble Baptist men of Williamsburg, who devoted their hearts and means to the building up of this school, such as Dr. A. Gatliff and others, who have first and last given large sums to our institute . . . . Williamsburg Institute has become a power in Eastern Kentucky. It had last year an enrollment of nearly 1,000 pupils, with a constantly growing endowment and equipment. The speaker sketched the growth of other mountain Baptist schools . . . . These schools are slowly and surely elevating the mountain people from darkness to a brighter and more intelligent life. This paper was heard with profound interest."

[15] Young, *"To Win the Prize,"* p. 19. Hibbs stayed at the First Baptist Church for thirteen years, the longest time of any of the church's eighteen pastors.

Mr. Hibbs was, indeed, a remarkable man. The following story, "A Remarkable Story of Richmond's Henry Hibbs," appeared in *The Whitley Republican,* 14 January 1960. The information for the story was taken from the Brown University Alumni Monthly.

"In 1917, Dr. Hibbs was invited to Richmond to organize a professional and vocational college in social work. In 1920 the school became affiliated with the College of William and Mary, and in 1925 it became a definite part of the College, and its name changed to the Richmond Professional Institute of the College of William and Mary. In 1936 the original school of social work became a graduate school.

The Board of Visitors of the College of William and Mary, in a resolution dated May 23, recalled Dr. Hibbs' service as organizer of the Institution and resident adminstrative head after 1925 when it became a part of the College of William and Mary. The Board stated that 'it may be said with more than ordinary justification that the Richmond Professional Institute as an institution represents "the lengthened shadow of one man." ' "

[16] Young, *"To Win the Prize,"* p. 180.

H. H. Hibbs, Letter, *Western Recorder,* 23 April 1908. In writing of the dedication of the new church building for the First Baptist Church, Hibbs remarked:

"Did any man ever serve a more generous, enthusiastic and God-fearing people? God is leading us into great things here and the wonderful liberality of these mountain people in their struggle to uplift their own section, coupled with the good work the college itself is doing, is the secret of the success the pastor has as their agent in securing the

One of Hibbs' first assignments was to add $10,000 to the endowment in order to create a special fund to help youngsters who were unable to pay their own expenses. The Trustees pledged to raise $1,000, and Hibbs was to raise the remaining amount elsewhere.[17]

AN AMBASSADOR FOR THE KING OF KINGS

Looking back one can just imagine Dr. Gatliff talking to Mr. Hibbs: "Brother Hibbs, I know there are wealthy folks like Mr. Rockefeller and Mr. Carnegie who are giving money away for legitimate causes up there in New York. Wonder if they could help us build this College for our mountain folks?" Hibbs, of course, was willing to give it his best effort; he never felt like a beggar but rather like an ambassador for the King of Kings, and he was willing to try his best to get that help, because, after all, his heavenly Father owned the cattle on a thousand hills.

THE MAGNIFICENT OBSESSION

Gatliff and Hibbs then became partners in soliciting funds and shared a magnificent obsession for building a college for mountain youth. Looking back one finds that Hibbs received a pass from Mr. M. J. Smith, President of the L&N Railroad, in May of 1898 for the purpose of soliciting funds for the Institute, and he was on his way to the North to solicit gifts. Hibbs, of course, accepted the pass with the pledge that he would use it for the interest of the Institute only.[18]

In 1900 the Trustees authorized Hibbs to raise $1,000 a year for five years for an emergency fund for a faculty salary increase.[19] In 1901 the Trustees sent Hibbs out to raise money for a girls' dormitory, for repairing and adding to the College's buildings, and for increasing the endowment.[20]

---

late $50,000 from the General Education Board and also other large gifts from the rich men of the North . . . .
   Our own Dr. William H. Felix, under whose evangelistic efforts Dr. Gatliff and others of our brethren were converted, was invited to be with us. Sickness prevented his attendance, but he wrote us a letter of much tenderness and love expressing the fact that he was with us in spirit if not in body."

[17] Hall, "Cumberland College," p. 22; Williamsburg Institute, Board of Trustees, *Minutes,* 25 June 1898. Hibbs was authorized to correspond with John D. Rockefeller, and a month later, Dr. W. C. Buttrick, Rockefeller's representative, was invited to visit the institute. Buttrick made the trip to Williamsburg, and by 1906 Rockefeller's Education Society had sent $23,508.42 to the Institute, most of which was used for the endowment on a matching gift basis.

[18] Williamsburg Institute, Board of Trustees, *Minutes,* 14 May 1898. Hibbs, no doubt, reasoned he would rather ride in a caboose than on horseback across streams in sleet, ice, and snow. Besides when Johnson was president, the railroad wasn't really an option. After all, when it comes to raising funds, neither Gatliff nor Hibbs had to manufacture a need for soliciting funds; they had one.

[19] Williamsburg Institute, Board of Trustees, *Minutes,* 2 April 1900; 21 June 1900; 6 September 1900. According to the *Minutes* of the Board of Trustees, 24 August 1899, Hibbs was given a salary of $150.00 per month during the months he was raising money for the Institute.

[20] Williamsburg Institute, Board of Trustees, *Minutes,* 14 March 1901.

While Hibbs was busy at this task, Dr. Ancil Gatliff offered the Institute $15,000, provided $45,000 more could be acquired. Gatliff's money was used for a new building.[21]

THEY PUT THEIR MONEY WHERE THEIR MOUTH WAS

The Trustees not only sent Hibbs out to raise money but generously gave of their own personal resources until it hurt. In 1903 when faced with a need to remove the Institute's debt and a need to finish a dormitory and to repair Johnson Hall for the girls, the Trustees simply put their names down on paper for a total pledge of $18,000 to be paid over three years.[22]

By 1906 the money had been raised for a new dormitory, and Felix Hall was built to accommodate about ninety men.[23] The building was named in honor of Dr. W.H. Felix, "a friend and honored member of the Board, a wise counselor, a generous contributor to the endowment, and a loyal supporter of the cause."[24] Today a plaque is prominently displayed in the foyer of the building in honor of Dr. Felix even though the building is now called Mahan Hall, honoring E.C. Mahan of Knoxville, Tennessee.

THE L&N RAILROAD

Dr. Gatliff's clear love for the college can be illustrated in connection with his visit to the president of the L&N Railroad Mr. Smith whose company had stopped the building of a railroad to one of Dr. Gatliff's mines. Mr. Hibbs related the details of this incident:

. . . About 1907 he came to me one day and said: 'Brother Hibbs, Mr. Smith has moved his construction company away and ceased the building of the road up to my new mine, and I do not know what I will do. I have just got to have that mine opened up, for I cannot give to the Institute unless

---

[21] *Western Recorder,* 27 July 1899. In 1900 the *Minutes* of the Board of Trustee meeting of 6 September show that Gatliff renovated the chapel in the Institute's building at his own expense.

[22] According to the Williamsburg Institute, Board of Trustees, *Minutes,* 26 January 1901 and 25 August 1903, Johnson Hall, originally occupied by girls, was used as a men's residence hall until Felix Hall was built. At one time the Central Hotel owned by Dr. E. S. Moss was used as a residence for the girls.

[23] Williamsburg Institute, Board of Trustees, *Minutes,* 20 December 1904, 17 June 1906.

[24] Williamsburg Institute, Board of Trustees, *Minutes,* 21 May 1902, 23 March 1912.

Dr. Ancil Gatliff was converted under the preaching of Reverend W.H. Felix in 1890 according to Young, *"To Win the Prize,"* p. 79.

I can make money. Well, I will just go down to Louisville and talk with Mr. Smith.' He went, and when he returned he told me of the conversation he had with Mr. Smith . . . . 'I told Mr. Smith that I had to have that road built, panic or no panic, for the mountain boys and girls must have a chance for an education and he and his railroad needed the mountains to be educated more than anybody else. Unless I can get that coal mine opened up I cannot give money to the Institute.' Mr. Smith replied: 'Well, Doctor, I reckon I will have to do what you say,' and he sent the construction company back and finished this road, and, as I recollect, built no other during the panic.[25]

Thanks to the L&N Railroad, Dr. Gatliff did get his mines opened and shortly thereafter a young barefoot boy of eight recalls meeting Dr. Gatliff as recorded in the youngster's diary at that early age. That youngster William McCall recounts this diary entry in his book, *I Thunk Me a Thaut:*

[WORMS]

A MINER PULLING STUMPS DIDN'T GET OUT fast enuf. Mountain fell on him. Mashed him flat as pancake. Doctur Gatliff rich mine owner come to funeral on Sunday. Teacher was with him. Hooked finger at me. Sayd Doctur Gatliff wanted to go fishing next day in Clear Fork river. Sayd he would pay me penny for airy wurm I digged for him. Thunk me a thaut.

Took him 2 buckits full on Monday. *Mercy* he sayd. Asked how many. I sayd 2947 counted 2 times. Stopped me when I started to count them for him. Sayd they looked like a milyun to him. Paid me 3 ten dollars and wouldn't let me go home and get 53 cents. Asked how I digged so many. Told him I hired tuther boys in camp. Asked how much did I pay them. I sayd haf. He asked what I would do iffen he didnt pay. Told him I had enuf money home. He asked what I was going to do with the thurty dollars. I told him I was saving mony to go to Cumburland Collij in Williamsburg Kentucky. Sayd he lived thar and iffen Id tell him when I come he would help by giving me a job — but not diggin wurms.

---

[25] Hibbs, ''Tender Memories,'' in *Doctor Ancil Gatliff,* p. 20.

These acts of kindness by the L&N Railroad (extending the railroad to Dr. Gatliff's mine and providing the pass for Mr. Hibbs) were two of a series of favors the Company performed for the College. The Railroad Company also provided transportation for students, visitors, and faculty alike to and from Williamsburg as well as giving land and gifts to the College. (Interstate 75 performs a similar function today as the railroad did one hundred years ago by providing access to and from the campus.)

The College's relationship with the railroad company exists even today. On 9 August 1986, Richard D. Sanborn, President and Chief Executive Officer of CSX Railway, was awarded an honorary doctorate from Cumberland College in appreciation for all the railroad company has done for the College since its inception.

Dr. Gatliff didn't forget his promise and Will McCall did go to Cumberland College and then on to Columbia Teachers College where he became a distinguished professor of education.

The story of Dr. McCall emphasizes the transforming power Gatliff's vision for a college had on people from the hills and hollows.[26]

THE EDUCATION SOCIETY OF KENTUCKY

By 1907 the endowment had reached $55,000,[27] but a goal of $200,000, then $500,000 was set by the Board. In light of the goal, Dr. Gatliff gave 4,000 acres of coal land estimated to be worth $100,000 to the Education Society he had helped to found with the understanding that the Institute should receive $75,000 from the Society.[28]

---

[26] Cumberland College, *Vita Abundantior,* "McCall: Mountain Boy to Educator," Summer Edition, 1975, p. 13. "Dr. McCall became a member of the faculty at Teachers College at twenty-four years of age; he remained there for forty-one years. During the time he was at the college, Dr. E. L. Thorndike and Dr. John Dewey were also there."

William McCall, *I Thunk Me a Thaut,* (New York: Teachers College Press, Columbia University, 1975) pp. 37-42. "A decade after he came to Columbia, McCall was an established figure in education, his accomplishments so distinguished that he was the third scholar — after Thorndike and Dewey — to be invited to China to help modernize its educational system."

FROM COAL DIGGER TO COLLEGE PROFESSOR
Cumberland College, *Promises to Keep,* p. 3. McCall wrote: ". . . I began to work in the coal mines of Kentucky when I was nine years of age and continued in that work for about half of each year until age twenty. Due to the financial and educational help of Cumberland College, I was enabled to shift from coal digger to college professor."

[27] Cumberland College, *Catalogue,* 1928-1929, p. 9. When James P. Mahan died in 1906, he left his property to the school and the church, with the Institute receiving the largest share.

Dr. Wood, at Mahan's funeral, said of Mahan, "Having no children of his own he richly endowed all mountain children . . . ." "James P. Mahan," in *A Great Quartette,* p. 4.

[28] *Western Recorder,* 5 July 1906. Because of the gift to the Baptist Education Society, the *Western Recorder* cited Gatliff as a man whose "generosity is equaled only by his wisdom."

The directors of the Education Society, as recorded in the 27 September 1907 edition of the *Western Recorder,* were H. H. Hibbs, W. H. Felix, and Ancil Gatliff.

According to the *Minutes* of the Board of Trustees, Cumberland College, 5 June 1908, the trustees voted for the school to affiliate with the Baptist Education Society of Kentucky. In order to make this affiliation possible the trustees substituted an article for an article in the original Charter. This new article provided that the trustees of the school be elected by the Society from nominations made by the school. In this way Kentucky Baptists came to exercise control over the school.

E. Y. Mullins, P. T. Hale, and A. Y. Ford, "Statement to the Denomination from the Baptist Education Society of

A. A. MYERS

Another man and woman who must not be overlooked are the Reverend and Mrs. A. A. Myers. Reverend Myers (1838-1924) was a Trustee at Berea, a founder of Williamsburg Academy, later known as Highland College which became a part of Cumberland College, and one of the people who gave impetus to the founding of Lincoln Memorial University.

The Reverend and Mrs. Myers, both graduates of Hillsdale College, Michigan, came into the area about 1875 under the auspices of the American Missionary Association to devote themselves to religious and to educational work in the mountains.[29] In 1882, Myers had raised enough money with the help of the American Missionary Association and the Congregational Church to begin the Academy.[30]

Kentucky,'' *Western Recorder,* 10 April 1908.

". . . As you have doubtless seen, through the papers, the General Education Board of New York has offered to give Williamsburg Institute $50,000, upon conditions which are reasonable, one of which is that the Williamsburg Baptist Church and Special Education Society of Kentucky give to Williamsburg Institute $75,000. When the Baptist Education Society of Kentucky turns over to Williamsburg Institute $75,000, Dr. A. Gatliff will immediately deed to the Society his 4,000 acres of valuable mineral and timber lands. From this property, the Board hopes to assist all schools that are affiliated with it.

The Board, therefore, earnestly recommends and lovingly urges our churches to rally promptly to this work, and hopes that every Kentucky Baptist who is interested in progress and enlightenment will make as liberal a contribution as he feels able to give.''

[29] According to Brubacher and Rudy in *Higher Education in Transition,* p. 75, after the Civil War northern church groups, the United States Army, and the Freedman's Bureau were active in helping to get education for blacks started.

One such group was the American Missionary Association which founded Williamsburg Academy (Highland College).

Among the outstanding alumni was Charlie Blakely who went on to become an admiral in the United States Navy. Both the Gray Brick and the frame building (now the Student Health Center) stand today on the Cumberland campus as a reminder of the service and sacrifice of the Congregationalists to bring educational opportunities to this mountain region. One can only surmise that the reason the Congregationalists' College didn't survive was because of their unwillingness to ordain uneducated ministers.

SHOT FROM AMBUSH

[30] According to Verna Wilder Denham's, *Historical Record of Williamsburg Academy, 1878-1907,* Myers right away bought the land and the building was started for the Academy. Mrs. Denham goes on to say that of the Myers there are not enough words in any language, and none of a descriptive power shining enough, to tell the many deeds of love and sacrifice. From the time they entered Williamsburg to the day they left, he fought whiskey and all forms of vice. Getting rid of saloons and sellers of alcohol was largely due to his heroic efforts. His life was often threatened. In fact, he carried a bullet in his body to his grave after being shot by a saloonkeeper from ambush.

Myers never at any time received a salary for his work. He lived on private income and an occasional gift from a church or personal friend. By 1890 the Myers had left their field of labor in Williamsburg and settled at Cumberland Gap to continue their work where they were instrumental in the founding of Lincoln Memorial University, an institution whose purpose was similar to that of Cumberland College in that it was founded to provide education for the children of the humble people of America, among whom Lincoln was born.

Jones, "Legend and Lore," 5 April 1984, gives the following account written from Mrs. Denham's record.

" . . . 'In January, 1878, the Rev. A. A. Myers conducted a ten day revival in Williamsburg, following the suggestions of Professor Dodge, his brother-in-law. Immediately after the revival, 'The Union Gospel Association' was organized, with prominent men and women from various denominations as members. The Rev. Horace Meadors, a Baptist Minister, was appointed the first chairman. J.W. Sullivan was chairman of the Building Committee

The Academy had well-qualified teachers

. . . coming from the best colleges in the North and East and some from the West: Oberlin, Wellesley, Smith, Mt. Holyoke, and various other colleges equally as good.

The aim and purpose of the Academy was the education of all who would attend, especially the boys and girls from the mountains and isolated sections in and around Williamsburg. None were turned away; some way was found for all who wanted to attend. Often the teachers gave scholarships, either paying themselves or through friends.[31]

---

and J. M. Blakley, Clerk of the Reorganization Committee. R. D. Hill was the first Sunday School Superintendent.'

In December, 1881, Rev. Myers returned with his wife and immediately set out to further organize not only the church, but a school which was called forthwith, 'The Williamsburg Academy.'

In 1884 the first church in Williamsburg was dedicated. It was located on the present Main Street, near the site of the Gentry Hotel. After careful study of the covenants of various churches, the Chairman decided on the 'Congregational,' because as Mrs. Denham says, 'he thought this church would best suit the largest number to worship as a Union Church.'

Mr. Myers made frequent trips north to various large churches soliciting funds for the infant church and school. He also visited the office of the Louisville and Nashville Railroad to urge the completion of the railroad, already surveyed. With the building of the railroad the real progress of Williamsburg began. Soon the Kentucky Lumber Company, the Phares Lumber Company and many others were established in Williamsburg.

The new industrial managers of these mills gave liberally to the school as did the Congregational Churches in the large cities.

'The American Missionary Association prided themselves on being pioneers. There were always new friends waiting for their help. In 1907 the Academy (then called Highland Normal) was sold to The Williamsburg Institute, and later in 1916 [actually it was 1913] called Cumberland College. Some of the Williamsburg Academy were: '(In the first class of 1891) Miss Nora E. Hill (Mrs. H. C. Gillis) and J. K. Watkins, 1892: Frank Blakley, Charles Gregg, and E. E. Nelson. Others: Willard Ames, Berea, Fannie B. Hill, Nellie Farris Francisco, James K. Higginbotham, Hattie P. Jones, Frank Jones, Rebecca Reid, Sherman Chambers, Ava Parker Freeman, Henry A. Baker, B. F. Snyder, Ben Watkins, G. S. Gillis, Charles A. Blakely, Benjamin Noe, Miss Jessie Jones, Miss Leila Watkins, William Wilder, John B. Carter, Anna K. Reid, Laura Gillis Day, Miss Flora Sullivan, Miss Hattie Sullivan, Mrs. Ethel Denham Henry, Mrs. Mattie Adkins Lovett, Miss Mima Snyder, Ernest Denham, Clarence Denham, Mrs. G. C. Butts, Keith Lester, Carlo Cawood, Burgess Bethurum, Dr. Will Arthur, Miss Theo Hill Terry, Mrs. Minnie Sutton Patrick, and Claiborne Arthur.

. . . After the Congregational Church located at Fifth and Main Streets burned in 1914, a small chapel was built for the Congregational worshipers. By mutual consent in 1930, the church disbanded.' ''

In his 21 November 1985, ''Legend and Lore,'' Jones wrote of Reuben Douglas Hill, another leader in the founding of the Williamsburg Academy.

''Reuben Douglas Hill was a native of Campbell County, Tenn. In 1854, his parents moved to Williamsburg. He received his education in the public schools of Whitley County and at home supplemented by four months attendance at Madison Academy, Rutledge, Tenn.

From the age of sixteen to twenty one, he taught in the public schools. From 1869 through 1872, he was in the drug business in Williamsburg. On March 28, 1872, he was licensed to practice law and was a very successful lawyer.

On May 3, 1871, he married Nancy Elizabeth Wilder, daughter of Joel and Sarah Wilder. To their union, four children were born: Theodosia Ernest, Nora Edith, Fannie Blanche and Arthur Myers. He was a leader in founding the Williamsburg Academy. He was the first Sunday School Superintendent in Williamsburg, and an active leader of the first Church established in Williamsburg, the Congregational Church.''

[31] Verna Wilder Denham, *Historical Record of Williamsburg Academy,* 1878-1907, pp. 5-8. People from all classes of life

Due to financial constraints in 1907, Williamsburg Academy, then known as Highland College, was sold to Williamsburg Institute, soon to be known as Cumberland College. This purchase gave the Institute three additional buildings: a "modern" recitation building, a girls' dormitory, and another frame building.[32]

With the purchase of Highland College came the need for a way to cross from the hill on which Highland College had been located to the hill on which Williamsburg Institute was located, and several years later, in 1920, a viaduct was constructed to join the two hills.

PLEDGES FROM ROCKEFELLER AND CARNEGIE

Upon the basis of Gatliff's gift to the Education Society, Hibbs was able to secure in 1908 conditional pledges of $50,000 from Rockefeller's General Education Board of New York and $18,000 from Mr. Andrew Carnegie. By 1912 the Kentucky pledges were paid and the Institute's Board was ready to collect the pledges from Rockefeller and Carnegie. But the Institute's debt of $41,000 barred the way to the Rockefeller and Carnegie gifts because neither would give to schools in debt.[33]

This embarrassment was largely due to the panic of 1907.[34] Mr. Ezra Stephens of Hartford, Connecticut, a member of the Institute's Board of Trustees,[35] had pledged

---

attended the school, especially many of the poorer class who wanted an education bad enough to work and sacrifice for it. They came from all the mountain counties working their way through school. Some even paid their way with farm supplies.

WHY WAS WILLIAMSBURG ACADEMY SOLD?

[32] According to Mrs. Denham in her *Historical Record of the Williamsburg Academy, 1878-1907,* the American Missionary Society prided itself on being pioneers. It was their policy to get a work well started and then sell it or turn it over to any church or school organization that would finance it and carry on the work, thus releasing their money to be used in some other needy field. So it was with the Williamsburg Academy and it was turned over to the Congregational Church. Reverend Myers came from a Free Will Baptist Church, and when he began his work here it was generally thought that he would turn the Academy over to the Baptists. When the Academy went instead to the Congregationalists, the Baptists began planning for their own school, Williamsburg Institute.

At the time of the sale of the Academy to Williamsburg Institute in 1907, the local Trustees of the Academy were mostly new and young men. An article entitled *Northern Mission in Southern Mountains* had appeared concerning the Academy which some people said was slanderous. This made the acquisition of the Congregationalist College more appealing. As is so often the case when enough patience and time are given, adversity turns into triumph. While abrasive relationships existed for a time and although some had their feelings hurt, the great healer called time soon turned problems into possibilities.

A few years later Mrs. Denham reported that Williamsburg Academy is now part of Cumberland College and "They are doing good work."

[33] Hall, "Cumberland College," p. 41.

[34] Cumberland College, *Catalogue,* 1928-1929, p.9.

[35] Williamsburg Institute, Board of Trustees, *Minutes,* 28 January 1905.

$40,000 to construct the Stephens' Building.[36] On the basis of this pledge the Trustees bought the property of Highland College for $40,000. Stephens paid $10,000 on his pledge but then failed in business during the panic.[37] This left a $30,000 debt. By 1912 the debt with accrued interest amounted to $41,000.[38]

No avenue of aid from the outside seemed open. The Trustees and friends arose to the emergency and the entire indebtedness was raised without leaving Williamsburg.[39] With the debt lifted the funds from Rockefeller and Carnegie were collected and the endowment rose to $275,000 by 1912.[40]

GORMAN JONES

In 1910 Dr. Wood asked the Board for an extended vacation to end 1 January 1911. The Board responded by appointing Professor Gorman Jones (1867-1936) as acting president in Wood's absence.[41]

Professor Jones first came to Cumberland College in 1891 from Ohio at the request of Dr. Wood. A graduate of Denison University, Jones was a member of Phi Beta Kappa. When Professor Jones was asked to come to the Institute, he accepted the position and remained at the College[42] until his death in 1936 as professor of French, Greek, and history.[43]

---

[36] Williamsburg Institute, Board of Trustees, *Minutes,* 1 December 1906.

[37] Stephens should not be condemned for his inability to pay. After all, through no fault of his own the economy turned sour. Stephens should rather be praised, for he taught the local trustees to attempt great things for God and to expect great things from God. Without Stephens, the Institute may never have acquired the Highland College property or the endowment. Stephens, then, must be viewed as a saint, not a sinner.

[38] Cumberland College, *Catalogue,* 1928-1929, p. 9.

[39] *Ibid.* Dr. Gatliff gave $16,000 and Mrs. J. P. Mahan $10,000, and others as they were able.

[40] *Ibid.* In 1912 J. W. Siler, the Institute's Treasurer since its beginning, passed away, leaving his entire estate amounting to $50,000 to the school.

[41] Hall, "Cumberland College," p. 57.

[42] *Ibid.,* p. 56.

While actively involved in his duties at the College, Professor Jones also took an active part in the community and his church. According to the 6 February 1936 edition of *The Whitley Republican,* Professor Jones was honored by the citizens of Williamsburg with a silver loving cup for "his efforts to uplift ideals." Jones was a member of the Williamsburg First Baptist Church where he served as Sunday School teacher, Sunday School superintendent, and for thirty years as organist. He also served as a director of the Bank of Williamsburg and a director of Mahan Jellico Coal Company.

[43] *Ibid.* Professor Jones received his Bachelor of Arts and his Master of Arts degree from Denison in 1890 and 1893, respectively. In 1894 and 1895 he did further work at the University of Chicago and in 1898 at the University of Wisconsin.

In 1892 Professor Jones married Olive Lowell Miller, also of Ohio. Four daughters were born to this union before Mrs. Jones passed away in 1910.[44] In 1915 Professor Jones married Mary Allen Fullerton of Chicago.

It was in August of 1910 that the Board of Trustees requested Professor Jones to serve as acting president.[45] Then in December of that year Dr. Wood asked for an extension of his leave because of medical reasons, so Professor Jones was asked to remain as acting president until Dr. Wood was well enough to return.[46] Professor Jones served in this post one more year.

THE LYCEUM SERIES

Perhaps Professor Jones' greatest contributions to the College were as a teacher and director of the lyceum series.[47] Through this series Professor Jones brought well-known speakers and musicians to the campus to add to the cultural opportunities available for the young people.[48]

---

[44] Professor Jones and Olive Lowell Miller Jones were the parents of Dorothy (Mrs. T. J. Roberts), Virginia (Mrs. J. T. Vallandingham), Lowell (Mrs. E. E. Siler, Sr.), and Nettie (Mrs. Wallace Boyd).

[45] Williamsburg Institute, Board of Trustees, *Minutes,* 27 August 1910.

[46] Williamsburg Institute, Board of Trustees, *Minutes,* 17 December 1910.

[47] Hall, "Cumberland College," p. 57.

YOU'RE SITTING IN THE GOVERNOR'S CHAIR

Former students of Professor Jones recall many incidents involving Jones. One of these incidents has been repeated by Judge Pleas Jones.

It was the beginning of the term and each student stood and stated his name and where he was from. It was one such student's turn. 'I am Hershell Sutton and I am from Woodbine.' 'Mr. Sutton,' Jones said as he gestured with his umbrella, 'You are sitting in the seat of a former governor of this state and you should do well to reflect credit on that Governor.' Jones was referring to Governor Edwin P. Morrow. Sutton did well and did reflect credit by becoming a prominent attorney."

The following recollection of Professor Gorman Jones is provided by Dr. Ralph Denham, Letter, 30 June 1986.

"The croquet court that was in the wooded area just above where the Norma Jeanne Perkins Hagan library is now located enjoyed a very democratic and competitive group on most afternoons starting about four o'clock. The participants from the College were Gorman Jones, P. R. Jones, A. R. Evans, J. T. Vallandingham, and occasionally J. L. Creech. From the town were W. R. 'Bud' Mounce (L & N section foreman), Steve Estes, Tip Estes, Samp Mahan, Dr. C. G. Ellison, occasionally Dr. N. A. Archer (and Dr. A. Paul Bagby when he was not golfing), and a few others whose names I do not recall. I can still hear the 'Jimmy Connors' grunt' that Professor Gorman Jones would emit as he would roque the ball of an opponent to a distant corner. They each had their favorite mallets carefully protected when not in use. Periodically a match with a group from Barbourville took place. As I recall, Bud Mounce and Gorman Jones were the stars of the Williamsburg group."

Others recall that Professor Jones was always an immaculate dresser.

[48] *The Cumberland College Monthly,* February 1915, stated: "There is perhaps no town in Kentucky that has a better Lyceum course than Williamsburg has. There are other towns that have a larger number of attractions but none that have better ones.

WOOD RETURNS

In 1912 Dr. Wood whose health had improved resumed his post at the Institute, and Professor Jones again devoted the bulk of his time to his classroom duties. For a short time in 1915, Jones again stepped in for Dr. Wood because of illness.[49]

Our annual course consists of five or six of the best lectures, concerts, and entertainments that are to be heard from the Lyceum platform.''

QUOTABLE NOTABLES

Such notable orators as William Jennings Bryan, Senator Robert Taylor, Senator J. P. Bolliver, Captain R. P. Hobson, Senator Ben Tillman, Frank Gunsaulus, Robert Burdette, Len G. Broughton, Russell Conwell, Thomas Dixon, Frank Dixon, Thomas E. Greene, Edward Amherst Ott, and Thomas Brooks Fletcher were brought to campus by Professor Jones.

Additionally, musicians such as the Leiter Opera Company, Orpheus Four, the Sam Lewis Company, and the Tooley Opera Company performed.

In fact, numerous other well-known individuals have spoken or performed in Williamsburg or on the College campus including Wilma Dykeman; Jessie Stuart; Senator Everett Dirkson with his son-in-law Senator Howard Baker; Homer Rhodehaver, choir leader for evangelist Billy Sunday; Sergeant Alvin York; James Cash Penny; G. Gordon Liddy; and Jean Ritchie.

In 1985, the children of Lowell Jones Siler (Professor Gorman Jones' daughter) and Eugene E. Siler,Sr. (Adam Troy Siler's son) began the Jones-Siler Arts and Lecture Series at Cumberland College. Through this Series the lyceum series begun by Professor Jones has been continued with such performers as Lee Luvisi, pianist; and Charles H. Webb and Wallace Hornibrook, duo-pianists.

JELLICO'S FAMOUS MUSICIANS

According to Siler, ''Heads or Tales,'' 18 December 1980, 14 May 1981, Jellico has produced a number of talented musicians, among them being Grace Moore and Homer Rhodehaver.

The Cumberland Echo, 24 February 1923; Siler, ''Heads or Tales,'' 14 May 1981. Homer Rhodehaver, owner of the hymn ''Brighten the Corner Where You Are,'' was raised near Jellico at Newcomb. He served as the director of the choir for the Methodist Church before joining Billy Sunday's team as song leader and trombonist. Billy Sunday, a revivalist, traveled the country preaching against the evils of alcohol. He was also a professional baseball player and was said to have been faster at running the bases ''than any man in the big leagues.''

Tom Siler, *Tennessee Towns,* p. 44; Grace Moore Parera, *You're Only Human Once* (Garden City, N.Y., The County Life Press, 1944; reprinted., Garden City, N.Y.: Garden City Publishing Company, 1946); Rowena Rutherford Farrar, *Grace Moore and Her Many Worlds,* (London England: Cornwall Books, 1981). Grace Moore, a world famous lyric soprano, though born in Cocke County, Tennessee, moved to Jellico at the age of five with her family and called that town her home. Miss Moore's first solo ''Rock of Ages'' was sung at the First Baptist Church in Jellico. Mr. Rhodehaver tried to persuade Miss Moore to join Billy Sunday's singing team but she had other plans. She studied in Nashville, Washington, D.C., and New York City, and became a world-famous opera star performing with the Metropolitan Opera more than ninety times. Additionally, she sang with the Chicago Opera, the Cincinnati Opera, the San Antonio Opera, the San Francisco Opera, and with several European and South American Operas. She also made at least three movies in Hollywood. In 1947 Miss Moore was killed when the plane she was in went down shortly after take off from Copenhagen.

Miss Moore's brother R. L. Moore many years later became a very loyal supporter of Cumberland College, contributing thousands of dollars to the College before his death in 1985.

[49] Cumberland College, Board of Trustees, *Minutes,* April 1915, p. 2; *The Cumberland College Monthly,* Vol. 3, No. 7, April 1915.

GATLIFF'S PHILANTHROPY CONTINUES

During these transitions Gatliff gave to the school gifts totaling more than $100,000. In 1911 he donated the money to build the first gymnasium at a cost of $5,000. In 1913 he paid the cost of $20,000 to enlarge Johnson Hall. Four years later he gave the school the water works that he had developed for the town.[50]

---

[50] Cumberland College, Board of Trustees, *Minutes,* 15 September 1917.

On 6 January 1921, the trustees decided to sell the water works system to E. C. Disel. Mr. Disel agreed to provide 3,600,000 gallons of water each year free to the College. The College kept a lien on the property.

Cumberland College, *Catalogue,* 1928-1929, p. 9. By 1911 the College's plant value was estimated at $200,000; by 1928 it was approximately half a million dollars and the endowment was nearly half a million dollars.

CITY OF BROTHERLY ACTIVITY

While the College was developing, so was the town and surrounding area. Siler in "Heads or Tales," 11 May 1967, recalls downtown Williamsburg.

"Perkins Brothers was a store run by Will, Wesley and Pleasant. They sold everything from coffee to horse collars. They were noted for salesmanship. Will Perkins could sell you a pair of shoes even when you would rather go barefooted.

Williams Brothers sold groceries and notions. They were kind, good men. They always had one extra cane bottomed chair for you if you would come in and talk a while. Paris Williams, the older brother, used to talk to himself as he walked around town. Someone asked him why. He said he just liked to hear what he had to say.

Nelson Brothers used to run a drug store. They were Emerson and Arvalee. They could fix you a sarsaparilla that would make you feel like a young colt getting ready for Derby Day.

Two Siler Brothers, Bill and Scott, were not in business together but had places side by side. Bill was in a general store at Third and Main. Scott was cashier in the Bank of Williamsburg next door. If you bought a suit of clothes from Bill, the money would be in the hands of Scott before sunset, deposited in the bank.

The Ellison brothers were here but were not partners. Jim Ellison was a real estate man and treasurer of Cumberland College. C. G. Ellison was a physician. These highly respected men both lived and operated on Main Street. They were noted church men. When the church doors opened they would be walking in the door every service. And they didn't sit on the back seats either.

The Renfro Brothers were Cy and Simon. One was a Baptist, one a Methodist. Both were active in their churches. Once I heard a man say that Cy Renfro would get up before daybreak to go out and pay any of his obligations, even when he was only a surety for the other fellow.

The Mahan Brothers were Breck, Samp and Crit. They were in the coal, banking, and merchandise business. But they were not partners. These men came from Wolf Creek. They were known for their rugged honesty and dependability.

The Steely Brothers were Bart, the lawyer; Arthur, the dentist; and Lee, the merchant. These were happy and popular men. Main Street looked well decorated and very stable when they walked up and down the thoroughfare.

The Gatliff Brothers were here, too. They were Ancil, the coal man who was a great builder and developer, and Curns, the hardware merchant, a deeply religious business man whose citizenship made a better county because he lived here.

The Finley Brothers were Charles, a one-time congressman and a full-time politician, and Wolford, a doctor and automobile dealer. These men were both very active in their church, the First Christian Church, and when they took a stand it was for what they thought was best for the community. They were solid like the Rock of Gibraltar.

All these brothers, now deceased, made a good town. I was deeply impressed by these brothers along Main Street.''

THE TOWN DOCTORS

In his 6 December 1967, "Heads or Tales," Siler wrote of the doctors in town including Dr. J. D. Adkins, Dr. L. R. Croley, Dr. C. G. Ellison, Dr. E. S. Moss, Dr. A. A. Richardson, Dr. W. J. Smith, Dr. E. B. Stonecipher, and Dr. E. H. West. Siler went on to write that "Dr. Richardson would often go forth to help some poor family without a dime to pay him. Later he would

On 14 October 1918 after a brief illness, Dr. Gatliff passed away. Dr. E. F. Wright, Gatliff's pastor, described the funeral service: "Tears blinded all eyes as we at last turned away, going back to take up our work, to be brave of heart and true in all things, for thus can we best honor him whom we love and have lost awhile."[51]

After Gatliff's death men, women, and children with tears in their eyes gave pennies to help erect a monument in his honor and memory. The monument which stands across from the First Baptist Church is appropriately inscribed: "Write me as one who loved his fellow man." Dr. Ancil Gatliff was truly an unselfish and remarkable man.[52]

---

come back home laughing just like he had made a hundred dollars fee out of his trip."

HENRY BOND: LAWYER AND TEACHER

Another person whom Siler recalls from the early part of this century in Williamsburg is Henry W. Bond, a lawyer and teacher. In his 14 December 1968, "Heads or Tales," Siler reminisces:

"Henry W. Bond did not practice many lawsuits. Neither did he lecture as a teacher in any great university. Henry was a Briar Creek lawyer, a Williamsburg attorney and teacher . . . .

Dr. Horace Bond's son or Henry's grandnephew is Julian Bond, a member of the Georgia Legislature. He was proposed at the recent Democratic convention in Chicago for Vice President. He was too young, he said. And, of course, he was. But he will blow some horns and turn some wheels as the future unfolds. You just watch!"

ROBERT BOONE BIRD

The Whitley Republican, 20 August 1970, p. 1. Robert Boone Bird (1901-1970), a native of Williamsburg and a graduate of Cumberland College, attended the University of Kentucky's College of Law. From 1957 to 1965 he held the distinction of being the only Republican on the Kentucky Court of Appeals. He served as Chief Justice in 1960-1961.

HOTELS AND TAVERNS

In his 5 November 1981, "Heads or Tales," Siler recalled the hotels and taverns in and around Williamsburg.

"Up in Lexington, I noticed the wreckers and wrecking ball were in process of completely razing the old historic Phoenix Hotel.

The Phoenix is more than 150 years old and was visited by several U.S. Presidents and famous people from stagecoach days up to this jet plane era of 1981.

. . . Wilbur Hotel in Corbin was impressive when it flourished there for many years . . . .

The Gentry Hotel in Williamsburg under the management of Mrs. Sullivan brought out steaks frying and popping and this caused comments among drummers all over this territory.

The Glanmorgan in Jellico fed you well and then turned you in the big chairs in the lobby where you could watch the flames dance over the famous Jellico coal until curfew (bank-the-fire) time when you jumped in bed upstairs.

Over in Pineville was the Continental Hotel with its large porch or open veranda where you could sit and feel prosperous while you looked at the 'Chained Rock' up on the mountain. Pearl White, the famous movie actress, stayed at Continental while she acted in a moving picture requiring a mountain background.

Once I was in the newly constructed hotel at Lynch when that big operation began up there. It seemed half rustic and half modernistic but it would open up your country-bred eyes as you looked upon such a place far up in the Harlan hills . . . .

The Stearns Hotel used to put out some cuisine that would please your palate. One specialty I remember was the demitasse or small cup of black coffee to open your eyes at breakfast in the mornings. This was never heard of before in our Kentucky mountains so far as I know . . . ."

[51] E. F. Wright. "In Memoriam, the Pastor's Tribute," in *Doctor Ancil Gatliff,* p.9.

[52] *The Cumberland Echo,* 1 May 1925. This paper told of Cumberland's first real homecoming celebration and of the dedication

NAME CHANGED

On 15 March 1913 Williamsburg Institute's name was officially changed to Cumberland College when it was fully understood that Mr. Rockefeller's representative had no objections to this change. Representing Mr. Rockefeller at this meeting was Mr. Buttrick. The *Minutes* record the action as follows: "A motion was made by J.M. Ellison and seconded by J.M. Mahan that the name of the Williamsburg Institute be changed to Cumberland College after the question has been settled with Mr. Buttrick."[53]

The name Cumberland was probably chosen because of the College's close proximity to Cumberland Gap and Cumberland Falls and its location on the Cumberland River in the Cumberland Mountains. Gatliff probably had no real desire to have the College named for him even though the College was his primary concern.

SENIOR COLLEGE TO JUNIOR COLLEGE

These were hard times in our nation's economy, and in April 1916 the Board of Trustees appointed a committee to look into the possibility of changing the College's status from a senior college to a junior college.[54]

---

of the Gatliff Memorial Fountain. The Fountain was dedicated on 26 May 1925.

"Let every alumnus of Cumberland College have a part in the Gatliff Memorial Fountain, for among the beneficiaries of the late Dr. Gatliff, the Cumberland alumni stand out as generous contributors to his Memorial. If you have not already contributed, do so now and send your gift to Miss Minnie Murphy, treasurer, Gatliff Memorial Fund.

Why not observe Gatliff Memorial Day in Cumberland College, when every student from primary to senior departments will bring his gift of pennies, dimes, and upward to be applied on the cost of the Fountain."

When the ceremony was held, the statue, sculpted in Italy, was unveiled by J.B. Gatliff, Jr., grandson of Dr. Ancil Gatliff.

DR. GATLIFF AND THE COOPERATIVE PROGRAM

The seventy-eighth session of the General Association of Kentucky Baptists (now the Kentucky Baptist Convention) met in opening session on 16 November 1915 at the Baptist Church at Jellico, Tennessee, located on the line of Whitley County, Kentucky, and some ten miles south of Williamsburg. Dr. Ancil Gatliff was moderator of the General Association that year. Before adjournment, the body, composed of one hundred and ninety-four messengers, adopted its "budget plan for the collection of funds." This was a very significant decision on the part of Kentucky Baptists, for it was a precursor of the establishment of the Southern Baptists' unified world mission budget plan, the Cooperative Program, in 1925. The effects of this decision, no doubt, far exceeded the vision of those present, for it would ultimately help to provide much needed resources to all agencies on the state denominational level, especially to the educational institutions who at that time, and for several years, were struggling to survive.

[53] Cumberland College, Board of Trustees, *Minutes,* 18 January 1913.

The name Cumberland was and is a good name because it reflects the area's traits and characteristics. Cumberland Gap is a natural pass through the Appalachians and is the meeting point of the states of Virginia, Tennessee, and Kentucky. The Gap is a narrow passage with steep sides rising to 500 feet and covered with laurel and rhododendron. Cumberland Falls is a natural falls on the Cumberland River dropping 68 feet. The Cumberland River is an important branch of the Ohio River which begins in the Cumberland Mountains of eastern Kentucky and empties into the Ohio River in northwestern Kentucky. The river is 720 miles long. The Cumberland Mountains are a part of the Appalachian Mountain system extending across eastern Kentucky and Tennessee rising 2,000 to 3,000 feet in some areas. The mountains are known for their rich coal fields.

[54] Cumberland College, Board of Trustees, *Minutes,* 8 April 1916. The committee was to work with Dr. H.B. Adams from

The findings of the committee were accepted, and in 1916 it was decided to phase out the junior and senior classes. In 1918 Cumberland College became a junior college, a feeder school for the senior colleges in the state, especially Georgetown College.[55] On 3 May 1919 the trustees voted, upon the recommendation of the faculty, to award only the Associate of Arts degree. Thus, Cumberland College became a junior college and remained a junior college until 1959 when it again assumed senior college status by adding a junior class. The senior class was added in 1960.

DR. WOOD RESIGNS

In March 1919 because of poor health Dr. Wood asked to be released of his duties as president as soon as a replacement could be found.[56] He did, however, agree to remain as a teacher.[57]

As soon as a replacement was found, the Board relieved Wood of his duties as president and also gave him a paid leave of absence from his teaching duties until his health improved.[58]

On 23 January 1940 Dr. Edwin Ellsworth Wood passed away. He is buried in Highland Cemetery, Williamsburg. Mrs. Wood who died on 5 April 1942 was laid to rest alongside Dr. Wood.

NAMES INDELIBLY WRITTEN INTO THE COLLEGE'S HISTORY

The founders of Cumberland College were inspired by a need for an educational institution and a vision of a bright shining city set on a hill ''devoted to illumination, consecrated to enlightenment,'' with ''boys and girls from humble homes filling its halls and coming forth from its shining portals, their faces radiant with the light of learning.''[59]

Georgetown College and to make a recommendation to the Board. Obviously, as a junior college Cumberland would be a constant source of supply of students for Georgetown.

[55] Cumberland College, *Catalogue*, 1916-1917, p. 6. The semester system was adopted and the courses were correlated with those of Georgetown.

[56] Cumberland College, Board of Trustees, *Minutes*, 29 March 1919.

[57] Hall, ''Cumberland College,'' p. 58. Wood remained as a teacher until the end of the 1936-1937 school year when he resigned.

[58] *Ibid.*, p. 57. At the same time the alumni honored Dr. Wood by presenting to ''him a loving cup as a token of appreciation for his faithful service.''

[59] Wood, ''Dr. Gatliff's Vision,'' in *Doctor Ancil Gatliff*, pp. 13-14.

The following tribute to Dr. E. E. Wood was quoted by Pleas Jones in his ''Legend and Lore,'' 1 November 1984. The article was originally written by Ralph Coghlan and appeared in the *Louisville Post,* 7 December 1922.
''Cumberland College's function, in Dr. Wood's mind, is to direct and guide this individualism.
'The school has taught,' says he, 'the great Christian lesson of working together for the common good.' The story

It would be impossible to pay too much tribute to those who have devoted their lives to building the foundation for Cumberland College. Their names are indelibly written into the College's history. From modest beginnings came a College recognized today far beyond the confines of Appalachia.

FROM DARKNESS TO LIGHT

The 1908 *The Eglantine,* the College's yearbook, reported:

Is it any wonder that this our beloved Alma Mater, situated as it is in the heart of the mountains, has sent out to lives of usefulness and service such a band of noble young men and women who courageously fight for truth? Always ambitious, wherever found, they reach a high plane of excellence as teachers, preachers, missionaries, lawyers, doctors, farmers, and housekeepers. Inspired by the sacrificing lives of teachers and trustees who make this pillar of light, our Alma Mater, possible, their influence in the State is powerful and ennobling.

The students were also aware of the lasting and enduring good which was being accomplished even in those early years. They knew that an investment in the lives of young people is a contribution that will live forever.

The 18 June 1908 edition of the *Western Recorder* reported: "the schools are slowly and surely elevating the mountain people from darkness to a brighter and more intelligent life."

The founders visualized buildings adequate for instruction and administration. They envisioned exemplary and inspired teaching by men and women of the highest scholarship and the highest ideals. They envisioned serving young men and women of limited means. Thousands of men and women have come

---

of this school is one of united struggle.

The power flowing from the mountaineer's sense of honor; from his unending resolution; from his fine fearlessness and courage and from his surging emotions — this power is religious education in attempting to hitch to a star, a star of conquering ideas. The Divine ideal of self sacrifice and of cooperation, the School is holding up.

The teachers, the trustees and supporters of the school are unveiling the glory of the Christian life. They are demonstrating that God's ways are not man's ways, but better. These men are justifying the ways of God by living them, and this unselfish life, this spirit of altruistic endeavor, is grappling the untamed forces of the mountains and yoking them to the work of God.

Cumberland College is now a thriving school with an enrollment of around 500 students annually. After serving as president for many years, Dr. Wood retired because of bad health and was succeeded by the able and well-liked Dr. C. W. Elsey. Dr. Wood, however, retains the Chair of English and Philosophy. Its stirring history, one of united struggle with its lofty standards, make it one of Kentucky's most interesting and useful schools."

and gone on out to a more abundant life because they made that vision a reality.[60]

People have been touched by the College and genuinely love this College. As Daniel Webster is reported to have said about Dartmouth: "It is, sir . . . [only] a small college, and yet there are those who love it [dearly]."[61]

---

[60] Cumberland College, "A Vision or a Reality," Capital Campaign Brochure, 1959.

[61] Daniel Webster, "Dartmouth College Case [1818]," in John Bartlett, *Familiar Quotations* (Boston: Little, Brown and Company, Inc., 1882; 14th Edition, Emily Morrison Beck, ed. 1968), p. 546.

EDWIN ELLSWORTH WOOD
President 1890-1893; 1898-1910; 1912-1919

(Photograph from *The Eglantine,* 1907)

JOHN NEWTON PRESTRIDGE
President 1893-1897

(Photograph courtesy of the First Baptist Church, Williamsburg, Kentucky)

H.H. HIBBS, SR.
1862-1936

"An Unsung Hero"

H.H. Hibbs served as pastor of Williamsburg Baptist Church for thirteen years beginning in 1897. During that time he also served at times as financial agent for the Institute.

The Eglantine, 1909, had these words of praise for Hibbs: "Pastor of the First Baptist Church and Financial Agent for the Institute. To his living faith and fervent preaching this church and community are most deeply indebted. Through his tireless efforts and convincing appeals, his power to move men in a good cause, he has added to the funds of the Institute about $200,000, which makes possible the large work and the actual prospective development of this school."

(Photograph from *The Eglantine*, 1909)

REVEREND W. H. FELIX

Reverend Felix was pastor of the First Baptist Church, Lexington, from 1863-1869 and again from 1887-1898. He also served as moderator of the General Association of Baptists in Kentucky in 1894, 1897, 1898, 1900, 1903, and 1904.

(Photograph from the Cumberland College Collection)

FELIX HALL - FOR BOYS

In 1906 this brick dormitory to accommodate about ninety boys was built and was called Felix Hall in honor of Dr. W.H. Felix of Lexington, Kentucky. Dr. Felix had been elected to the Board of Trustees in 1902 and served until his death in 1912.

The name of the dormitory was later changed to Mahan Hall, honoring Mr. E.C. Mahan of Knoxville.

(Photograph from the 1914-1915 *Catalogue*)

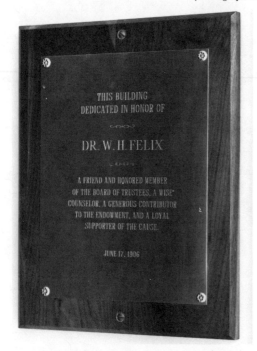

PLAQUE HONORING DR. FELIX

(Photograph from the Cumberland College Collection)

FELIX HALL - INTERIOR VIEWS

(Photograph from the 1914-1915 *Catalogue*)

FELIX HALL
Architect's Drawing

The building was constructed by Sam Easley and an Italian brick mason, John Begalletti.
(Photograph from the 1904-1905 *Catalogue*)

VIEW FROM FELIX HALL
(Photograph from the Cumberland College Collection, undated)

DIXIE HALL

Dixie Hall was constructed in the 1880's for use by Williamsburg Academy (Highland College) and was one of the buildings purchased from the Academy by Williamsburg Institute in 1907.

Dixie Hall was located just in front of where the Gatliff Memorial Chapel now stands.

The building was razed in 1955 to make way for the Gatliff Chapel.

(Photograph from the 1911-1912 *Catalogue*)

MANUAL TRAINING BUILDING

The third building acquired through the purchase of Highland College was the Manual Training Building. This was a two-story frame structure which stood east of the Gray Brick Building.

Dr. Ralph Denham recalls from his childhood days in a letter dated 21 July 1986: "I remember wondering what those huge machines were for. We spent many hours exploring beneath the building in the crawl space. We also made many unauthorized trips to the nether region of Dixie Hall and to the attic and belfry and roof top of the Gray Brick Building. Dr. J.L. Creech personally escorted us out of these areas on numerous occasions."

(Photograph from the Cumberland College Collection, undated)

THE NEW RECITATION BUILDING

The "new" recitation building was acquired in 1907 with the purchase of Highland College. Constructed at a cost of $20,000 in June 1906 as the Reuben D. Hill Building, its name was changed to the Gray Brick Building when it became a part of the Institute's properties.

In addition to serving as the recitation building, prior to the construction of the Gatliff building in 1955, this building housed the administrative offices of the College.

An amusing story is told about the Gray Brick Building by Siler, "Heads or Tales," 3 November 1966: "Years ago some Cumberland College pranksters took Professor Jones' milk cow and pushed or pulled her up the steps of the administration building and left her in the chapel throughout Halloween night and into the next school day. Professor Jones' only reaction was that he was sorry for the cow and the way she had been treated."

(Photograph from the 1908-1909 *Catalogue*)

THE INSTITUTE'S THREE BUILDINGS PRIOR TO 1907

Prior to the acquisition of Highland Cemetery, the Williamsburg Institute consisted of three buildings: the Recitation Hall (now named Roburn Hall), the boarding hall named Johnson Hall, and the boarding hall named Felix Hall (now named Mahan Hall).

(Photograph from *The Eglantine,* 1907).

THE VIADUCT:
AN ENGINEERING FEAT FOR ITS DAY

The following inscription appears on an end of the Viaduct.

Erected A.D. 1920
A.T. Siler

T.B. Mahan   *J.M. Ellison*
Committee

Manley & Young   *Engineer*
L.W. Handcock   *Contractors*

(Drawing by Manley and Young, Knoxville, Tennessee, taken from the 1919-1920 *Catalogue*)

THE VIADUCT

The Viaduct, constructed in 1920, joined the two hills on which the Cumberland College campus was constructed. The hill to the left of the Viaduct was the site of what was formerly known as Highland College and the hill to the right, Williamsburg Institute. From the time the Institute purchased Highland College until the Viaduct was constructed, access to one side of the campus from the other side was gained by crossing the ravine.

The old water tower, donated to the College by Dr. Gatliff, can be seen in the background.

(Photograph from the 1920-1921 *Catalogue*)

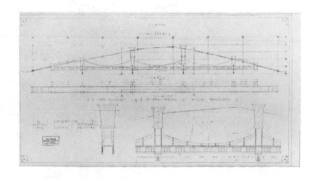

EDGAR C. MAHAN

Mr. Edgar C. Mahan (1879-1948) gave the land to the College which connects the College's campus with the property bought from Highland College.

Mr. Mahan served on the Board of Trustees from 1915 to his death in 1948. In 1949 in honor of Mahan and out of respect for all he had done for Cumberland College, the name of Felix Hall was changed to Mahan Hall although a plaque remains prominently displayed in the hallway in honor of Dr. Felix.

The College is a contingent beneficiary of the Edgar C. Mahan estate.

(Photograph from the Cumberland College Collection)

106

THE BUILDING THAT WAS NEVER BUILT

Mr. Ezra Stephens of Hartford, Connecticut, served as a member of the College's Board of Trustees from 1905-1912. Mr. Stephens subscribed $40,000 from which the Stephens' College Building would be constructed. Because of business failure, however, the building was never constructed. Nevertheless, much credit must be given to Stephens who raised the sights of the local trustees and administration to attempt great things for God and to expect great things from God. Without Mr. Stephens, much of the money would never have been raised.

(Photographs from the 1906 *Catalogue*)

EZRA STEPHENS

107

GORMAN JONES
Acting President 1910-1912

(Photograph from the Cumberland College Collection)

108

GYMNASIUM

The gymnasium built in 1911 by Sam Easley was paid for by Dr. Ancil Gatliff. This building served as the College gym until a new gym was erected in 1928. The old gym then served as the library until 1960. From 1960 until 1967 this was the Music Building. On 23 February 1967 the building was destroyed by fire.

According to Siler, "Heads or Tales," 26 August 1976, Easley also built the Dr. N.A. Archer and Ruby Gatliff Archer home as a replica of an exhibited house at the 1904 World's Fair. This house now serves as the home of the President of Cumberland College. Easley is credited with constructing also the J.B. Gatliff residence, the N.B. Perkins residence, and the S.E. Mahan residence.

(Photograph from the 1911-1912 *Catalogue*)

GIRLS' GYMNASIUM CLASS
(Photograph from the 1912-1913 *Catalogue*)

INTERIOR GATLIFF GYMNASIUM
(Photograph from the 1920-1921 *Catalogue*)

JOHNSON HALL

Johnson Hall was enlarged by Dr. Ancil Gatliff in 1913 at a cost of $20,000.

(Photograph from the 1914 *Catalogue*)

JOHNSON HALL

This architect's sketch for remodeled Johnson Hall which appeared in the 1912 *Catalogue* bears a remarkable resemblence to how the building appears today.

FOUNTAIN AND STATUE DEDICATED TO THE MEMORY OF DR. ANCIL GATLIFF

(Photograph by Housman Photography)

110

WILLIAMSBURG, KENTUCKY, AND THE CUMBERLAND RIVER

(Photograph from *The Eglantine*, 1908)

CUMBERLAND FALLS

(Photograph from *The Eglantine*, 1907)

CUMBERLAND GAP

CUMBERLAND RIVER

CUMBERLAND MOUNTAINS

CUMBERLAND FALLS

(Photographs from *Promises to Keep*)

CHAPTER 4
A NEW DAY DAWNING

A TIME OF TRANSITION

Albert Robinson Evans was asked to serve as acting president following the resignation of Dr. Wood on 29 March 1919. Evans was promised a salary of $1,800 per year for his services.[1]

ALBERT ROBINSON EVANS

Professor Albert Robinson Evans (1880-1957) was another of Cumberland's Phi Beta Kappa scholars. The son of James George and Sarah Miracle Evans, he was raised in Knox County, Kentucky, and attended the Williamsburg Institute, being graduated from the Collegiate Department in 1905.[2] Evans then taught at the Institute for a few months before entering Brown University.[3] In 1908 he was graduated from Brown University,[4] and returned to the Williamsburg Institute where he remained except for a few years until his retirement in 1955.[5] Evans did additional work at the University of Chicago and received his Master of Arts degree from the University of Kentucky.

Professor Evans at times taught Latin and philosophy, but his main interests were in the area of education and social science. He was considered an excellent teacher.[6]

---

[1] Cumberland College, Board of Trustees, *Minutes,* 29 March 1919.

[2] Evans was one of three Cumberland College alumni to become president of the College, the other two being James Lloyd Creech and the author. Other graduates who became presidents are A. S. Petrey, President of Hazard Baptist Institute; A. J. Meadors, President of Conway Female College; Arliss Roaden, President of Tennessee Technological Institute; Betty Siegel, President of Kennesaw College (incidentally, Dr. Siegel is the niece of President Creech); Vivian Blevins, former Director of the University of Kentucky's Southeast Community College and now President of Lee College in Baytown, Texas; and Michael Colegrove, President of Hargrave Military Academy.

[3] Actually Evans began his teaching career long before being graduated from the Williamburg Institute. From 1897 to 1906 Evans taught at seven different schools in the county.

[4] While at Brown University Evans was a member of Phi Beta Kappa, a scholastic honor society, as well as Phi Sigma Kappa, a social fraternity, and the Sphinx Club.

[5] From 1924 to 1928 Evans served as superintendent of the city schools of Corbin.

[6] Sometime in the early part of 1914, Evans was approached about considering the principalship of the Jellico, Tennessee, high school. The trustees of the College got word concerning this offer and called a meeting of the Board because the "inducements being offered were rather attractive." According to the Board's *Minutes,* 11 May 1914, the trustees acted immediately "to affect an agreement whereby he remains as teacher in the Cumberland College." The agreement was reached and the *Cumberland College*

Evans, however, did not confine himself to the College. He was active at the First Baptist Church, teaching the Florida Moss Gatliff Sunday School class and serving as chairman of the Deacons. He was also a member of the Williamsburg City Council.

A. R. Evans and his wife Mabel Carrie Gatliff were the parents of two daughters, Helen and Virginia.

Professor Evans served as acting president from 29 March 1919 until 26 May 1921, but he continued to serve the College as a teacher until his retirement in June 1955. He passed away on 28 September 1957.[7]

THE CAMPUS JOINED

In 1920 E. C. Mahan bought for $3,350 two lots of land connecting the new Recitation Building (the Reuben Hall Building now named the Gray Brick Building) obtained by the purchase of the Highland College property with the old Recitation Building (Roburn Hall) and gave these to the School.[8]

LIBRARY REPAIRED, COLLECTION EXPANDED

The only library the school had was one room. President Evans drew up a plan for repairing this room and presented this plan along with a proposition from one of the trustees, N.B. Perkins, to the Board in December 1920. Perkins offered to give $3,000 for books if the trustees would have the necessary repairs made in the library. The trustees accepted the offer and instructed Evans to have the changes made in the library.[9]

A DEFEAT FOR THE RECORD BOOKS

It was around this time in the College's history that Cumberland's basketball team defeated the University of Kentucky's basketball team in a game played in the Gatliff Gymnasium. Cumberland's team was composed of Eugene Siler, Sr., guard;

Monthly, June 1914, reported "Professor Evans has been offered the principalship of the Jellico High School at a salary of $1,600 a year, but has decided to remain with us. Everyone here is highly gratified at his decision."

Dr. Ralph Denham, in his letter dated July 1986, has the following recollection of Mr. Evans as a teacher:

"Professor A.R. Evans ran a tight ship as far as his sociology class was concerned. His pronouncements at times were seared into the memory, such as: 'The characteristics of the proletariat is not its poverty but its insecurity.'

Most of his chapel meditations centered on the book of Job, but his major theme seemed to be: 'Be sure your sins will find you out.'

A hapless student caught looking at his pocket watch during a class would become the center of a mini-lecture: 'I don't mind your looking at your watch but do object to your shaking it and holding it to your ear to find out if it is still running.' "

[7] As a memorial to Mr. Evans, the College's chapter of the Student National Education Association was named the A. R. Evans Chapter.

[8] Cumberland College, Board of Trustees, *Minutes,* 10 April 1920.

[9] Cumberland College, Board of Trustees, *Minutes,* 6 December 1920.

Red Davies, guard; Jerome Perkins, forward; Asberry Siler, forward; and Paul Adkins, center. Since that defeat, the University's varsity basketball team has never again played a Cumberland basketball team.[10]

DEANS

The first mention of the word "Dean" is in the College's *Catalogue*, 1920-1921. Arkley Wright, Latin instructor, was academic dean;[11] J.L. Creech was dean of the teachers' department and superintendent of the grades; Miss Virginia McConnell

---

[10] Siler, "Heads or Tales," 11 December 1975.

The following account of the game is given by Eugene Siler Sr., a member of the winning team, in his "Heads or Tales," 11 December 1975.

"We were all pretty good shots, only I was not supposed to shoot but merely get the rebound and scramble it out for a trip down to the other end of the court.

So the Wildcats swaggered out on the court. They looked like champions and were the best team in the state. For them this was considered to be a practice game to get ready for the University of Tennessee the following night. Besides, they would pick up an easy $100 or so between trains before leaving for Knoxville on the Midnight Choo-Choo.

Cousin Paul got the tip-off at center. He was not tall compared to present day centers, but he was a real good jumper and quick as lightening. His toss was often death for the opponents.

Cousin Asberry received the tip and then passed the ball to Cousin Paul as he crossed over and pushed the ball up into the net. Bingo! The game had started auspiciously for us.

It was nip and tuck for the first half and the game came out just about even-stephen when we staggered out to rest a few minutes and listen to Coach P. R. Jones tell us we were probably going to beat the Wildcats, best team in the state.

Then our team of cousins and friends rolled out for the final fracas. We knew we were gonna win — don't ask me how we knew. Sometimes you know but you don't know how you know. It's a mysterious gift of the mind. The Lord writes a message on the blackboard of your cerebellum and his message says, 'You are going to win.' And so win we did.

Strange part was that one of the scrambler guards, hardly ever known to throw a goal, slipped down the floor, received a pass, dribbled a time or two and plopped the ball through the hoop. In a few minutes he repeated this miracle. The final whistle blew and the game was all history.

I was that scrambler — Gene Siler you lucky dog! This was about the greatest day of my life up to that time."

[11] The following information concerning Arkley Wright was contributed by his sons, John G. Wright and Robert G. Wright.

Arkley Wright was born 1 May 1878 on a farm south of English in Carroll County, Kentucky. He was the eldest of five surviving children. Wright attended Georgetown College and majored in Greek.

In 1903 Arkley Wright married Annie Mattick, and in 1904 a child Clara was born. Annie Wright died in 1907. In 1910 Wright married Anna Mae Greene of Erlanger. To this union five sons were born: William, Arkley Jackson, Robert G., Richard O., and John G.

Wright first came to Cumberland in 1911 as a faculty member to teach Latin and history. From 1914-1920 he was employed elsewhere, but returned to Cumberland in 1920 as academic dean. In 1924 at his own request he was relieved of his duties as dean but remained as a member of the history faculty. He resumed the deanship for the 1925-1926 year, but resigned at the end of that year to seek other employment.

Prior to coming to Cumberland, he taught at Lincoln Memorial University, and after leaving Cumberland he served as Superintendent of Schools in Hopkinsville. In 1934 he returned to Williamsburg as City School Superintendent for one year.

Mr. Wright died in 1951.

"Looking back, Father is very intriguing. His background was not strong on education but from somewhere he had the drive to pursue knowledge. He did all his life. I remember at Hopkinsville that he studied the negro poets of America, not the most politic subject for that time or place. He was always associated with the church and studied the scriptures and related material. In his last years he worked with Clara on a couple of papers about Job and about King David."

was dean of women,[12] and J.T. Vallandingham, mathematics instructor, was dean of men.[13]

ENROLLMENT INCREASES

During this period the enrollment increased. In 1907-1908 the college department enrolled thirty-one students, and enrollment increased steadily until 1917-1918 when it dropped to ten students. This decrease was probably due to World War I. In 1920-1921 there were again thirty-one students, but by the 1921-1922 school year, the enrollment more than doubled the previous year. In the preparatory department

---

[12] On 26 January 1921, the following item appeared in the student newspaper, *The Cumberland College Echo.*
"McConnell's Ten Commandments
  I. Thou shalt not call out the window to the boys as they pass.
 II. Thou shall not leave thy room during study hours nor stay up after ten o'clock; for I, the matron, am a jealous matron, visiting the iniquity of the offenders with campus, but showing mercy unto the many who keep my commandments.
III. Thou shalt not use profane language except under extraordinary circumstances, such as when it is thine honor to fill thy lamp.
 IV. Thou shalt remember the school week consists of seven days: Five days shalt thou labor and keep up thy notebook, and on the sixth day thou shalt clean thy room; but the seventh day thou shalt report for Church twice.
  V. Honor Professor Evans and Professor Wright; refrain from chewing gum and whistling when within thy hall, that thy days may be long in Cumberland College.
 VI. Thou shalt not steal spoons from the table.
VII. Thou shalt not kill time.
VIII. Thou shalt report baths on Wednesdays and Saturdays.
 IX. Thou shalt pay for thine own ice cream when in town in order that thou mightest not see a boy.
  X. Thou shalt love thy beau with all thine heart, but not without a chaperone."

[13] Dr. Vallandingham was a beloved and respected man; so much so his Obituary in *The Whitley Republican,* 24 July 1980, mentioned that while at Cumberland College Dr. Vallandingham held numerous positions: chairman of the mathematics department; chairman emeritus of the mathematics department; girls' basketball coach; tutor for West Point appointees; keeper and collector of student accounts; and dean of men.
Among the many courses Dr. Vallandingham taught at Cumberland were Latin, algebra, geometry, and trigonometry.

Incidentally, the grandson of Dr. Vallandingham, Walter Blaine Early, now serves as a biology professor and head of the biology department at the College.

In 1969 Dr. Vallandingham was awarded an honorary Doctor of Laws degree from Cumberland College. Here is a portion of the text read by Dr. J.M. Boswell, President, at that service.
". . . Recognized even from his first days of teaching as an outstanding instructor, he has been able to get the maximum effort from his students and has dealt with each one personally in light of his background. He has been both tireless and successful in his efforts to challenge his students: the good, the average, and the poor student. If he had students who were inadequately prepared, he would meet with them in groups or individually outside of class in order to get them to the point that they could do satisfactory work.
Several years ago, Dr. White, then Dean of the College of Arts and Sciences at the University of Kentucky, told me of a study that had been made at the University of Kentucky of the students who had transferred from other schools into the engineering program of the University. He said the study revealed that a certain segment of transfer students in the engineering program were invariably without the grades of 'F' and 'D' in their engineering requirements. He

the enrollment steadily increased from fifty-one in 1907-1908 to two hundred four by 1921-1922.[14]

Requirements for entrance to the college department could be met by a certificate from an accredited high school, by examination, or by taking the preparatory course at Cumberland.[15] Sixty semester hours were required for graduation.[16] Candidates for the Bachelor of Arts degree had to take twelve hours in Latin or its equivalent in Greek.[17] All students were required to attend chapel exercises[18] and to take English I and English II, mathematics I, Bible I, and philosophy II. The remaining subjects were chosen from a field of electives.[19]

---

said that further investigation revealed that these students were from Cumberland College and that each of them has had his pre-engineering mathematics under Professor Vallandingham.

Engineers who have studied under him are now in places of responsibility in many states in the Union and some in foreign countries. Some who have studied under him are doing research in industry. Several students who have studied under him in the four-year program have attended graduate school . . . . Other students of Prof. Vallandingham are working on their doctors' degrees. His students and former students pay him the highest tribute as a teacher. Some emphasize his patience, others praise him for his ability to simplify and develop appreciation for a subject which is a puzzle to many people, but all give him highest praise as a Christian gentleman, an outstanding teacher, and a source of inspiration to all who know him . . . ."

Dr. Ralph Denham in his letter of 21 July 1986, has this remembrance of Dr. Vallandingham.

"Professor J. T. Vallandingham was a particular favorite of mine. His classes in mathematics and trigonometry seemed to always go smoothly with that twinkle in his eye and infinite patience with all students.

In the summer of 1940 while I was attending Vanderbilt Medical School I was in Williamsburg visiting my mother who lived at 710 Walnut Street immediately across the street from the old Gray Brick Building. I was sitting in the porch swing visiting with my mother when Prof. Val came by. He stopped for a friendly chat, took a few steps to leave and returned to ask, 'Ralph, would you do me a favor? Would you conduct my trigonometry class on Thursday and Friday since I need to make a trip to Cynthiana?' Protesting as vigorously as possible about my lack of expertise in the subject did not overcome his pleasant persuasion so I found myself as Professor of Mathematics (pro tem) for two days. All of us survived until Prof. Val could correct my mistakes when he returned."

[14] Hall, "Cumberland College," p. 55.

[15] Cumberland College, *Catalogue*, 1919-1920.

[16] The following appeared in *The Cumberland Echo*, 10 March 1923: "At a senior class meeting concerning arrangements for commencement, it was decided that instead of the usual childish white dresses, the Seniors would appear in dignified caps and gowns. This will give a more academic atmosphere to the services during commencement and it is hoped the decision will meet with the approval of all."

[17] Cumberland College. *Catalogue*, 1922-1923.

EDUCATED BEYOND THEIR INTELLIGENCE

[18] Local citizens would often appear in the chapel exercises of the College. *The Cumberland Echo*, 17 May 1924, reports one such visit.

"Judge H. H. Tye, Nestor of the Whitley County Bar Association and local supporter of Cumberland College, addressed the College at the chapel exercises Monday, April 29. The main theme of his talk was 'Making Education Practical,' and he dealt with the subject in his usual humorous, yet logical, manner. He warned us against using big words just for the effect and said there were too many high brows in the world who were educated beyond their intelligence. The Judge showed us the necessity of Latin in the law profession, and I think, convinced many of us that Latin was not as dead as we might think, although there are many of Prof. Evans' students who wish that the language had died in early infancy."

[19] Cumberland College. *Catalogue*, 1922-1923.

A NEW PRESIDENT IS NAMED

At the 26 May 1921 meeting of the Board of Trustees, Charles William Elsey was elected president of Cumberland College, and Professor Evans was relieved of his duties as acting president to return to the classroom.

CHARLES WILLIAM ELSEY

Charles William Elsey (1880-1964) was born in Laurel County, Kentucky, and grew up in Lexington. He was a graduate of Southern Seminary.[20] He held pastorates in Lexington and Cynthiana before coming to Williamsburg in 1921 with his wife Birdie Gibson Young Elsey.

While at Cumberland one of Elsey's main concerns was financing the student work program. Elsey reported to the Board on 11 December 1922 that approximately $5,000 would be needed for the year in order to pay the twenty-two girls and fifteen boys for their services. With only $1,000 available for this expenditure,[21] Elsey sought the trustees' assistance. Again on 30 April 1923 Elsey pointed out to the Board that ''this outlay is a drain on the resources of the college for which no provision has been made.'' The Board then authorized an appropriation of $2,000 for student work. Elsey still found the funding of the student work program a problem. On 19 December 1923 he told the Board that ''only such help as is necessary to the proper care of the buildings and doings of the work in the dining rooms and kitchens is employed.'' And although only the minimum number of workers were employed, the cost was still above the appropriation. This problem continued to exist throughout Elsey's term and has continued to even today. Throughout the College's history, there has been more

---

[20] According to the College's *Catalogue,* 1921-1922, Dr. Elsey had a Bachelor of Arts degree from Georgetown College and a Theology degree from The Southern Baptist Theological Seminary.

A FUND FOR POOR MOUNTAIN GIRLS

[21] In 1916 Mr. John T. Burgess established a $7,000 endowed fund, the interest from which was to be used for the education of poor mountain girls. Except for this income of approximately $1,000, Elsey did not have the needed funds to pay for the student work program.

A FUND FOR POOR MOUNTAIN BOYS

According to the College's Board of Trustee *Minutes,* 23 October 1919, another scholarship fund was begun in 1919 by Mr. and Mrs. S. W. McComb who gave the College $10,000 in U. S. Government Bonds to start the S. Jameson McComb Fund. The McCombs hoped to add to the Fund another $15,000 within three years. The Fund was to remain intact with the interest loaned or invested to worthy young men who needed assistance in order to obtain an education. The loans were to be repaid whenever it was possible to do so. Preference was to be given to boys and young men from Harlan and Whitley Counties, but not confined to such. When the loans were repaid, the money was to be added to the principle until such time that it reached $50,000. After that time both the interest and the repayments could be used to assist needy boys. If, however, the money were not needed for loans, then the surplus could be used according to the need as seen by the College's trustees.

Over the years friends and supporters of the College have helped to provide the needed financial assistance for Cumberland's students by the establishing of scholarship and/or loan funds. For a complete listing of these funds, see Appendix VIII.

118

work to be done and more students wanting to do the work[22] than there has been money to pay for the labor.

A TIME FOR CHANGE

At their 12 December 1921 meeting, the Board of Trustees voted to make the grade department a model school as required by the new school law of Kentucky which was to come into effect on 1 July 1922. This model school was to be a school of demonstration and was to cover the eight grades of the elementary school.[23] Students who completed this course of study could get certificates to teach without having to take an examination.

On 1 February 1923 the State Department of Education approved the College's Normal School.[24]

---

[22] Dr. Leroy Voris, a member of the 1923-1925 classes, had the job of fireman and firemaker for Felix Hall for which he was paid a monthly sum of $15.00. Dr. Voris recalled his experiences in a letter. "I fired the furnace in Felix Hall with the soft coal and lots of clinkers." Dr. Voris went on from Cumberland to earn his bachelor's degree from Georgetown College, his master's degree from Pennsylvania State College, and his doctor's degree from Cornell. He served as a member of the Pennsylvania State College's faculty and the Cornell faculty before appointment as Executive Secretary, Food and Nutrition Board, National Academy of Science. Dr. Voris retired in 1971.

A student who attended Cumberland College in the late 1940's related how she and another student washed dishes in the kitchen in the old dining hall, then located in Johnson Hall, seven days a week, for twenty-five cents a day. But even this small amount, applied to their college expenses, afforded them the opportunity to remain in school and to graduate. Inspired and encouraged by this achievement, both obtained higher degrees; one later to join the staff of a state department of education; the other to become a college professor.

These three mountain students, representative of hundreds of their fellow alumni, who, when given the opportunity to earn their own way, were on their way to achieve their cherished goal of an education.

[23] The College's *Catalogue*, 1921-1922, contained the following description of a Standard Model School.
"It is our purpose that this Model School shall be, in every respect, Standard.
To make clear what is meant by Standard, we quote from the report of the Kentucky Education Commission on Public Education in Kentucky. 'On the basis of the foregoing tests, it appears that the city elementary schools are below the standard reached in other states, in some cases as much as a year. The showing of the rural elementary schools, especially of the one-room schools, is wretchedly poor; they are generally two or three years below standard.' This means that we intend that our eighth grade graduates shall measure from about one to three years above commonly accepted standards in Kentucky.
In order to reach this standard the College must maintain a grade faculty of superior academic and professional training, and the teachers must have favorable conditions under which to work."

[24] President Elsey in his annual report to the Board of Trustees, 30 April 1923, read the following letter dated 1 February 1923, from George Colvin, Superintendent of Public Instruction in Kentucky.
"Permit me to advise you that by unanimous action of the Board of Regents for Normal School Inspection, Cumberland College has been given the privilege of issuing elementary certificates, upon the same conditions prescribed by and for the two state normal schools.
I congratulate you upon this deserved recognition of your work and am particularly appreciative of the assistance that you can render the cause of education in helping the state to prepare teachers."

RELIGIOUS CULTURE

By 1920 courses were being offered in what was termed religious culture. These courses were aimed at preparing the students with intelligent and sympathetic understanding for leadership in the local churches and in their life's work.[25]

ELSEY RESIGNS

C. W. Elsey resigned the presidency of the College effective 1 June 1925. James Lloyd Creech was chosen to succeed Elsey and was given the title of Dean. On

---

[25] The 1919-1920 College *Catalogue* lists the following courses as religious culture courses: Old Testament History, New Testament History, Biblical Introduction, Biblical Interpretation, Sunday School Training, Missions, Religious Pedagogy, and Religious Organizations and Efficiency.

According to the *Minutes* of the 1922 meeting of the General Association of Baptists, p. 59, the Baptists of Kentucky decided to take a stand against teaching the theory of evolution in their colleges by adopting a resolution to withhold all financial support from the schools which taught the theory of evolution contradictory to the Scriptures.

The College's Board of Trustees, *Minutes,* of 8 April 1924 and 6 December 1924, record that a questionnaire was sent to the College's teachers by the Kentucky Baptist Society. Mr. A. T. Siler was asked to prepare in writing the Board's position on the subject of evolution. The document prepared clearly stated that the College's Board took complete responsibility for the teaching at the College.

The issue, however, was not laid to rest. According to Kenneth Bailey's, *Southern White Protestantism in the Twentieth Century* (New York: Harper & Row, Publishers, 1964), p. 64, the Fundamentalists were strong in Kentucky, and in 1925 Cumberland College was dismissed from the Kentucky Baptist Society when "officials declined to dismiss a professor who was accused of pro-Darwinian tendencies."

According to the 1926 *Annual* of the Southern Baptist Convention, pp. 18, 98, the Convention by unanimous vote accepted "Genesis as teaching that man was the special creation of God." They further rejected "every theory, evolution or other, which teaches that man originated in, or came by way of, a lower animal ancestry." The agencies of the Convention were asked to accept "said action of the Convention to the end that the great cause of our present unrest and agitation over the evolution question may be effectively and finally removed in the minds of the constituency of the Convention and all others concerned."

Shortly thereafter on 1 December 1926 President Creech gave the following report to the Board of Trustees:

THE STONE THE BUILDER REJECTED
IS TO BECOME THE HEAD OF THE FOUNDATION

"In my judgement, you now have the most highly trained and efficient faculty in the history of the school. While many of the private schools of the state are unable to maintain with the accrediting agencies a rating of 'B' grade and some of them have fallen below any fixed standards and are not accredited at all, your college stands at the top, both in its high school and college departments, accredited as class 'A'.

Those of you who were in attendance at the General Association meeting held recently at Lebanon, Kentucky, and those who have been reading the *Western Recorder* the last sixty days are aware of the distressing situation with reference to the schools, generally, of the State. They are running hopelessly in debt, and are finding the greatest difficulty in maintaining educational standings for accredited relationships with the higher institutions of learning. I have made a careful study of the whole situation, and unless I am much mistaken, a considerable number of the schools in this State will close in from two to five years; and in my judgement, the closing will come nearer the two years than the five. Further, it is my opinion that the Baptists of the State, though under the circumstances they are rather non-committal, are looking more today than ever before to Cumberland College to play a leading part in the educational program. It seems to me certain that 'the stone which the builders rejected is to become the head of the foundation.' "

31 October 1925 Creech assumed the title of president of Cumberland College.[26]

JAMES LLOYD CREECH:
A GENTLEMAN AND A SCHOLAR

James Lloyd Creech (1884-1955) was a native of Poor Fork in Harlan County, Kentucky. He was graduated from the Williamsburg Institute in 1908 and attended the University of Michigan[27] Law School. He was admitted to the Kentucky Bar in 1912. Creech also earned his Bachelor of Science degree from Columbia University and did further work at the Harvard Graduate School of Education and Columbia University. He received an honorary doctorate from Georgetown College in 1938.

Creech served as a teacher in rural schools of Kentucky and also as a teacher in the Barbourville Institute. In 1913, after having been president of Barbourville Institute for one year, he became a member of the faculty of Cumberland College.

While a student at the Williamsburg Institute, Creech had been involved in the School's activities. He served as treasurer of the class of 1907; vice-president of his graduating class; member of the Gatliffian Literary Society, glee club, and the oratorical association. After joining the College's faculty he directed a large mixed chorus while serving as an instructor in the teacher's department. He later served as dean of the teachers' department and as superintendent of the grades. After becoming president he was listed among the education and psychology faculty.[28]

The years served by Dr. Creech as president of Cumberland College were difficult years, for it was during the time that this great nation faced an economic depression and the Second World War. It was only through the tight-fisted integrity of President Creech that the College was kept alive.

---

[26] Cumberland College, Board of Trustees, *Minutes*, 20 April 1925, 31 October 1925.

Ironically, James M. Boswell who followed Creech as president several years later was also given the title of dean before being named president of Cumberland College.

THE MICHIGAN CONNECTION
[27] While Creech studied at the University of Michigan, James M. Boswell, the man who succeeded Creech, studied at Michigan State University. The man who succeeded Boswell was raised in Michigan though his family was from Beaver Dam, Kentucky. Also, A. A. Myers, the founder of Highland College which was acquired by Cumberland College, was from Hillsdale College in Hillsdale, Michigan. A good deal of private support has come from Michigan, the "Land of the Lakes."

MORE AFRAID OF YOU THAN OF THAT SNAKE
[28] The following story is told by Nancy Marie White Jones, the wife of Judge Pleas Jones and a student in one of Dr. Creech's classes. Mrs. Jones was graduated with the class of 1932.
   '' 'The snake is as afraid of you as you are of it. If you will hold the snake correctly, you will never fear snakes again.' said Dr. Creech to a group of terrified students in his class. To demonstrate his point, he called on one of the more frightened girls, Nancy Marie White. She looked at the snake and looked at the Professor and then reached her hands out toward the snake. He complimented her on her courage. Nancy replied, 'If I had not been more afraid of you than that snake, I could never have held it.' ''

A NEW GYMNASIUM

One of the first objectives of President Creech was to build a new gymnasium. At the 4 May 1926 meeting of the Board of Trustees, a committee was appointed to study the feasibility and cost of adding to the current gymnasium.

After consideration of the committee's finding, the Board, on 1 December 1926, voted to build a new gymnasium. A sum of $35,000 was to be raised over a five-year period for this new construction, to repair the old recitation building (Roburn Hall),[29] except the first floor, and to pay for one or two extra teachers, if needed.

Two days later at a called meeting of the Board, a committee was appointed to locate the site for the new gymnasium. The site as described in the Board of Trustee *Minutes,* 29 June 1927, was "on the campus, west of the Gray Recitation Building, on the south side of Walnut Street, just above the entrance to the Viaduct."

ACCREDITATION BY
THE SOUTHERN ASSOCIATION OF COLLEGES

Cumberland College's high school and college departments were rated by the state accrediting agencies as Class A, and all work completed at Cumberland was accepted hour for hour by the University of Kentucky because of this rating. However, in 1930 the University of Kentucky decided to accept as accredited colleges only those colleges who were accredited through the Association of Colleges and Secondary Schools of the Southern States. Since Cumberland was only a two-year College and had a large number of students planning to enter the University, the Board took action to make adjustments to bring the College "up to standards set for membership in the Association . . . ."[30] At the 3-4 December 1931 meeting of the Association, Cumberland College was admitted to membership. From that time to the present the College has maintained continuous accreditation by the Southern Association of Colleges and Schools.[31]

FINANCIALLY SOUND FOR ITS DAY

At the 29 June 1927 meeting of the Board of Trustees, President Creech reported that he expected the College to have a surplus of $6,000 the coming year and that although the College did have a small debt that it was amply provided for.

---

[29] At the 29 June 1927, meeting of the Board of Trustees, it was decided that only the second floor of Roburn Hall would be repaired. The estimated cost of the repairs was $6,000.

[30] Cumberland College, Board of Trustees, *Minutes,* 17 February 1931.

[31] Upon assuming the status of a senior college in 1961, it was necessary to graduate three classes before being considered for senior-college accreditation. Initial accreditation was granted in December 1964 and reaffirmed in 1974 and 1985.

122

Later President Creech recommended that a portion of the surplus be used to employ a physical education director "who would also take active leadership in providing for our student body that social life which has so long been needed in our college."[32]

THE RECREATIONAL PLAN

Dr. Creech was disturbed that the recreational and social life of the students at Cumberland was lacking. With the College's financial problems largely solved, at least temporarily, and the academic program accredited, Creech turned his attention to the recreational and social life of the student body.[33]

---

[32] Cumberland College, Board of Trustees, *Minutes,* 12 May 1928.

A JOLLY GOOD TIME FOR THE ENTIRE STUDENT BODY

[33] Cumberland College, Board of Trustees, *Minutes,* 12 May 1928. President Creech made these comments to the Board:

"The recreational life has been too much limited to ten or fifteen pupils who engage in specialized athletics to the neglect of the hundreds who need recreation but do not get it. A few of the more aggressive couples of boys and girls, probably not over a half dozen couples in all, go in for some social life and frequently carry things to excess, while the hundreds of students come to the college and go away carrying such a timidity and feeling of awkwardness as frequently to handicap them in later years in mixing and mingling with people. With our financial problems largely solved, with our attendance built up to where we want it, and with our accredited relationships with the higher institutions of learning firmly fixed at the top, we are now ready to turn to the next most important thing, the recreational and social life of the student body.

Our rules of discipline must always continue strict so the parents will have no uneasiness when their children are in our charge. What we need is a jolly good time for the entire student body in group activities under supervision."

Hall, "Cumberland College," pp. 139-141. In its early years the College had a football team, but it had been discontinued. In 1920 football was again added to the list of sport activities. Other sports included basketball, baseball, tennis and golf. The last reference to football was in the College's 1929-1930 *Catalogue.* It is not certain why football was discontinued, but at the 17 May 1930 meeting of the Board of Trustees, President Creech and the faculty recommended "that as far as athletics were concerned, the college concentrate on basketball."

It would not be until the fall of 1985 that the College would again have an organized football program. It is a non-scholarship program; the players pay to play, and their payments help carry the load. Moreover, the program provides a fall activity, increases the ratio of males to females on campus, and provides a focal point around which to rally for school spirit.

A CASE OF MISTAKEN IDENTITY

Over the years there have been many stories told of how Cumberland's football team was defeated by Georgia Tech's team, 222-0, some time around 1916. This, however, was a case of mistaken identity brought on by two colleges bearing the same name. In an article by the New York Times News Service, "Mr. Georgia Tech Recalls Rout," *Lexington Herald-Leader,* 8 October 1986, D7, the team which was defeated 222-0 was from Lebanon, Tennessee's, Cumberland College (not Cumberland College of Williamburg, Kentucky).

A LONG WAY TO FALL

An amusing story is told by Ethel Sears Crook, class of 1939, concerning President Creech and Johnson Hall.

"While making his nightly rounds, President Creech noticed a rope hanging from a second story window in Johnson Hall. Since the purpose of the rope could only mean trouble, the President gave the rope a firm tug. Instead of falling, the rope began to be pulled upward with the President attached. As his head cleared the window, the two young ladies pulling the rope shrieked . . . and let go of the rope. The bruised and slightly battered President decided punishment would be unnecessary, for the girls had had a lesson they would not soon forget."

Rules were adopted for playing on varsity athletic teams,[34] an athletic director was employed,[35] and a program of health education was adopted.[36] Creech's concern that the recreational and social life of the students should be filled with fun and enjoyment continued throughout his tenure.[37]

---

[34] Cumberland College, Board of Trustees, *Minutes,* 11 May 1929. The eligibility rules for playing on a varsity athletic team were as follows:

"1. He must have made passing grades on at least twelve semester hours of college work or one and one-half units of high school work in the last semester he was enrolled in this or other school.

2. He must not have enrolled in this or other school and withdrawn without completing the semester's work.

3. His deportment record must be clear for his last semester's work in this school or other school.

4. He must maintain standards of scholarship and deportment in this school in keeping with the requirements above mentioned."

[35] The first athletic director hired was Wilson Evans of Pennington Gap, Virginia. He began his work with the 1930-31 academic year.

Dr. Ralph Denham, in his letter of 21 July 1986, recalled Wilson Evans' tenure at Cumberland College as physical education director.

"Wilson Evans, a graduate of Berea College, arrived at Cumberland College about the same time that Dr. Jim Boswell did. He was in charge of physical education and he was also a very good all-around athlete at tennis, basketball, baseball, and track. I was pitching for one of the local softball teams when Wilson came to bat. We were playing at the old Gatliff field where rightfield sloped downhill. With a mighty swing he hit the softball what seemed to me to be a world record for distance as it sailed over the right fielder's head to end what up to then had been a very close game. Wilson returned to coach at Berea about 1934."

For a complete listing of Cumberland's athletic directors, see Appendix IX.

[36] Cumberland College, Board of Trustees, *Minutes,* 15 May 1930. Creech gave the following report:

"With the beginning of the present semester, the faculty decided to make physical education compulsory for all students of the high school and college departments except such as might be exempted by a physician's certificate of disability. This program has been successfully put into effect, and its results for good have been outstanding; the students have been healthier and happier.

This sort of program includes, as well physical education more technically defined, also games and plays, and intramural sports of various kinds. Thus the entire student body profits from the investment in the gymnasium. It would be hard to justify the outlay of so large a sum of money if the only purpose served by the building were for the training of a varsity basketball team of ten or fifteen members; but our gymnasium was planned to provide for classes in physical education as well as for basketball and it serves admirably the double purpose."

BETTER TO HAVE FIFTY BOYS FROM HEADS OF HOLLOWS PLAYING BASKETBALL THAN FIVE MOST EXPERT PLAYERS WINNING OVER THE BIG BLUE FRESHMEN

[37] Cumberland College, Board of Trustees, *Minutes,* 27 May 1939. Creech gave the following report:

"From the beginning the college has been animated by a loyalty and devotion growing out of high and noble aims and objectives on the part of its founders. Vision in keeping the college so related to the problems of the people it serves, and the spirit growing out of worthy aims and objectives consciously conceived, can not fail to appeal to a willing and generous people to give assurance that the great work so courageously and nobly begun may continue.

. . . I give it to you as my candid opinion that it is better for the college to have fifty boys from the heads of the hollows who have never had on a basketball uniform, playing basketball for the fun, than to have five most expert players win over the Kentucky freshmen.

. . . Many girls in the mountains have carried heavy burdens in the home; they have worked in the fields and have had the care of younger brothers and sisters, carried them in their arms. Many of these girls come to us with awkward stride, with hollow chests, humped backs, round shoulders, and such physical defects. Many of the boys,

SUMMER SCHOOL PROGRAM BEGUN
AND CURRICULUM EXPANDED

President Creech felt the College could render a service to the area by maintaining a summer school, and he made this recommendation to the Board of Trustees during their 19 March 1932 meeting. Records are not clear exactly when the first summer school session was held, but the first summer session under the Cooperative Teacher-Training Curriculum was held in the summer of 1939. This program was primarily for students qualifying for the Provisional Elementary Certificate, but a wide range of courses were offered so that other students could also attend.[38]

By 1935 courses were being offered for vocational, preprofessional, and professional careers. The vocational courses included home economics, typing, shorthand, cooking, and sewing. The preprofessional courses were for lawyers or engineers, and the professional courses were for those interested in a career in education.[39]

GRADE SCHOOL DISCONTINUED

In 1926 President Creech recommended to the Board that the College's grade and high school departments be phased out. The primary reason for this recommendation was the building and adequately staffing of the Williamsburg City School.[40] The Board's decision to this recommendation was to adopt a Model One Teacher Graded School for first through eighth grades with a maximum of 35 youngsters enrolled.[41]

In 1934 Creech again recommended that the elementary school be discontinued.

---

too, have many very damaging bodily defects that could be remedied.

I heartily favor an athletic program that will let up on the emphasis of winning of intercollegiate contests and will place more emphasis on health education, and on plays and games engaged in by all the students for the fun and enjoyment they have in the playing."

The College's emphasis on physical education and athletics has brought recognition to the teams, their coaches, and players. Awards have been earned in basketball, baseball, track, judo, and tennis. A more detailed history of the College's athletic program is currently being written by Dr. James Key of the College's physical education department.

An interesting note, Charles Cooper, III, the son of Charles Cooper, Jr., played basketball for Cumberland College in 1981. Charles Cooper, Jr., was the first black man to play in the National Basketball Association. He made his debut in 1950 with the Boston Celtics.

[38] Cumberland College, *Catalogue,* 1940-1941, p. 41.

By 1932, according to that year's *Catalogue,* the college offered courses leading to the Provisional Elementary Teaching Certificate, the Standard Elementary Teaching Certificate, and the Provisional High School Teaching Certificate.

[39] Cumberland College, *Catalogue,* 1935-1936.

[40] Cumberland College, Board of Trustees, *Minutes,* 1 December 1926.

[41] Cumberland College, Board of Trustees, *Minutes,* 3 December 1926.

The Board agreed with this recommendation, and the elementary school was closed at the end of the 1934 school year.[42]

HIGH SCHOOL DISCONTINUED

In 1940 the faculty recommended that the high school department be discontinued after the class of 1941 graduated, and the Board approved this action.[43]

STUDENT LABOR PROGRAM

President Creech had a personal concern for the students and a conservative fiscal policy for the College. The Student Labor Program as refined by President Creech exemplified his feelings and ideas.

Students were employed to perform janitorial and housekeeping duties that had previously been performed by hired help. This policy saved the school hundreds of dollars while at the same time provided a means for the youngsters to secure an education.[44]

The program was well-supervised,[45] and students were required to meet certain scholastic requirements before being employed.[46] Because of the high scholastic

---

[42] Cumberland College, Board of Trustees, *Minutes,* 19 May 1934.

[43] Cumberland College, Board of Trustees, *Minutes,* 25 May 1940. The teachers in the high school department were transferred to the college department.

[44] Cumberland College, Board of Trustees, *Minutes,* 1 December 1926. At this meeting Creech commented:
"Now the young men are doing the work for which a janitor was formerly paid more than a thousand dollars a year, and in our combination dining hall plan, work for which hundreds of dollars had heretofore been paid to outside help is now done by the girls boarding at that dormitory. Last year forty-three boys and girls worked for all or for a considerable part of their boarding costs.
. . . It is thus evident that this plan of student help under proper supervision works in both directions. It brings a big savings in dollars to the school, and at the same time, it affords an opportunity for the very best of the boys and girls of the mountain section to secure an education and enter into the realms of knowledge the doors of which, without such opportunities, would have been forever closed to them because of their lack of funds to defray regular school expenses."

CRATIS WILLIAMS
Cratis Williams, a graduate in the class of 1930, attended the College with assistance from the student work program. Williams, known as "Mr. Appalachia," spent a great portion of his life interpreting the heritage of the Appalachians. He received his doctorate from New York University where he wrote a three-volume dissertation, *The Southern Mountaineer in Fact and Fiction.* In 1942 Williams joined the faculty of Appalachian State University where he remained until his retirement in 1976. Dr. Williams passed away in 1985.

[45] Cumberland College, Board of Trustees, *Minutes,* 28 April 1926.

[46] Cumberland College, Board of Trustees, *Minutes,* 15 May 1930. Creech reported:
"Student help is utilized rather effectively . . . . When Cumberland College combined its boarding departments and provided for student labor, it set up certain requirements as prerequisite for students who wished to get working positions, as well as loans from the student loan fund, one of which is that no student may be considered for a working

requirements set for the youngsters in this program, the College earned an "enviable reputation . . . in higher institutions of learning to which they [the College's graduates] transfer[ed] after graduating here."[47] In fact, the 21 March 1929 issue of the *Western Recorder* reported that Cumberland's "student body will compare favorably with any student body anywhere." They are "intelligent and tractable and many of them are from the homes of the elite, while others are from the homes of the poor."[48]

Of the work program Creech said, "If I were in the field to raise money, I had rather this single fact than any other feature of the school."[49]

RURAL DEVELOPMENT PROGRAM

Creech was interested in improving Whitley County; he had a genuine concern for the area and its people. In fact, it has been told that he liked to sit on a bench in front of the Courthouse and talk with the people.

In an effort to help the area's farmers, Creech and several of the College's faculty offered their services to assist in terrace farming, crop rotation, soil building, and contour plowing.[50]

In 1940 President Creech presented to the Board of Trustees a Rural Betterment Plan. Under this Plan students would be employed "to grow crops, with assistance from the College, and under the supervision of the College, to defray necessary expenses of tuition, registration fees, books, etc." Students working under this plan were advanced money for seeds and fertilizer to grow the crops after signing a promissory note. The students could then grow, harvest, and sell their crops. The promissory note was forgiven when the students attended the College for one year and paid the normal tuition costs.[51]

NOTEWORTHY GRADUATES

Hundreds upon hundreds of men and women have passed through the halls of Cumberland College with the assistance of the Student Labor Program, Rural Development Program, scholarships, or loans, and a good number of these graduates have gone on to careers of the highest stature. It would be impossible to recognize each of these people although some have been mentioned.

---

position or a loan until he has furnished a statement from the Principal or Superintendent of the school last attended showing that in scholarship he stood in the upper 50% of his class.

[47] *Ibid.*

[48] *Western Recorder,* 21 March 1929, p. 6.

[49] Cumberland College, Board of Trustees, *Minutes,* 28 April 1926.

[50] Hall, "Cumberland College," p. 78.

[51] Cumberland College, Board of Trustees, *Minutes,* 25 May 1940.

Little did President Creech know that he was helping youngsters who would one day become medical doctors, attorneys, judges, and other professionals, even a Governor, and the list could go on and on.

Here is what a few of these graduates have to say about the College.

BERT T. COMBS

Bert T. Combs, former Governor of Kentucky, was graduated from Cumberland College in 1930. Here are some of his thoughts as expressed in an interview in 1980, when he was recognized as an outstanding alumnus at Homecoming.

I learned about Cumberland College fifty years ago. I was seventeen at the time. I lived in Manchester in Clay County. I had finished high school at Manchester. I had absolutely no prospects for a job or going to college. There were seven in my family, seven children. My father managed to feed and house us and that was about it. So my mother and a friend of hers, who taught business school, shorthand and typing and so on, got me to take shorthand and typing from this lady. And so then they decided they would send me to college. They didn't know where, but Mrs. Benge knew about Cumberland, and she said, 'You need to go to Cumberland College, it's a good school, and it won't cost very much, and that's where you need to go.' But I said, 'It will cost something, and I don't have anything.' She said, 'I am gonna get you a job. I can get you a job in Williamsburg with a coal mine.' She knew somebody in one of the coal companies. And so a little later she said, 'You have a job waiting for you.' My mother and her friend pushed me on a bus and said, 'You are going to Cumberland College.'

So I got on the bus in Manchester with a blue serge suit and a long bill cap (the kids wore long bill caps in those days). I came to Williamsburg and came up and enrolled. This was the second semester 1929, and this was January. The next day I went to the office of this coal company. I have forgotten the name of it, but they didn't know anything about Bert Combs, of course, or they didn't know anything about a job for anybody like me. So here I was. I was enrolled and had been assigned in classes. I hadn't attended any classes, but I had absolutely no money.

Dr. J. L. Creech was president at the time and somebody said to me, 'There is a little money in a fund for emergency purposes and why don't you see Dr. Creech.' Creech said, 'Well, I don't know. I want you to write something for me.' He gave me two pieces of paper and told me to write two or three sentences on each piece of paper. He said, 'Come back in three days.'

I went back in three days, and he loaned me $100. So I stayed in

Cumberland. This is, of course, a personal story; but the point is at that time and through the years there have been hundreds and even thousands of young people in this part of Kentucky in the Appalachian region that couldn't have gone to College except that Cumberland was here and Cumberland cooperated to make it possible for those kids to stay in college. I remember Dr. Creech said in one of the specimens he wanted me to write, 'Cumberland College educates the youth of the mountains.' That's exactly the truth, and I'm certain except for Cumberland I would have never gone to college.

I think Cumberland has done an outstanding job in making it possible for the youth of this region to obtain a college education. Of course, when I was here it was a two-year college, but with what I got at Cumberland that enabled me to go to another institution and also taught me that education was important; that without knowledge you cannot compete. It's just that simple, and I think a practical example is that from the early 30's until the middle 60's, it may be the early 70's, the youth of this region, and that means the leaders, the potential leaders, were leaving this part of Kentucky. For the last ten years, since 1970, they have been coming back, and the trend is very definitely now in a return to this region of the country, and I think the educational institutions are largely responsible for that. Without educational facilities these people would not come back to eastern Kentucky. They would leave, and they would stay.

When I was here we had a dedicated and fortunately educated group of faculty members that I think would measure up to any faculty anywhere. They were men and women of dedication, and more importantly, of vision, and they had the ability to transmit that dedication and a desire in their students to continue their education. And those faculty members had this philosophy in mind: Some people look at things as they are and say so what, and others dream of what might be and say, why not. And those ladies and gentlemen dreamed of what might be and were not ashamed of it, and they said, why not. They were idealists. Ideas, of course, are like stars. You don't reach them with your hands, but they knew that although they couldn't reach the stars, like a sailor in the ocean if they set their course on those stars and dedicated themselves with their vision and their energy, they would reach the proper destination.

When I was here I fired the furnace in Felix Hall. Dr. Creech was a bachelor and he lived in that Hall, first door on the right when you went in. We didn't need any thermometer; he was the thermometer. He was a good thermometer, and if I let that heat vary five degrees, up or down, I immediately heard about it from Dr. Creech.

To me Cumberland College is unique in that if a young person has average ability to learn, a desire to learn, and is willing to work, he or she can go to Cumberland College, at least I found it that way, and I'm certain it is still that way.

In addition to making it possible for hundreds, perhaps thousands of young people to go to college, students received at Cumberland a solid foundation in art, sciences, history, and literature, and the kind of training that is so important, if not absolutely necessary, for a person who is going to be competitive in whatever area, industry, or profession he takes up. The teachers here taught the importance of patriotism and religion, but they didn't do it to the extent that it caused reaction. Students, I think, were encouraged to practice high morals and high ethics.

I see a very great future for Cumberland College. It is now the biggest private institution of higher learning in Kentucky. It, of course, has been a four-year institution for several years now. It is still dedicated to the principles on which it was founded, but it has kept up with changes in the world. It has increased greatly, of course, in its enrollment. They have a very imaginative, a very capable, a very progressive president, President Taylor. They have an excellent supporting staff, and I have kept up with it enough to know that they still have a faculty of dedication and vision, many of whom, in particular, have the ability to instill in young people the feeling that the pursuit of knowledge is important in itself, is an end in itself for that matter. And so I see with that combination and with the dedication and the desire to continue to educate many young people of Appalachia on the same basis that the College has followed since its founding, I believe Cumberland College will perform a great role in the future, not only for students of Appalachia, but across Kentucky and across this country.

Cumberland has a dedicated, imaginative, capable President, a fine supporting staff, and perhaps more importantly, a faculty dedicated to instilling in young people a desire to learn and to become good citizens. But we still have a lot of work to do. I know Cumberland College, although successful, has problems and will always have problems because that's part of life, but the problems today ought to be the progress of tomorrow, and from tomorrow's progress each of us ought to be in a position to say, 'I had a part, even though perhaps a small part, in building a bigger and better Cumberland College.'[52]

EUGENE E. SILER, SR.

Eugene E. Siler Sr., United States Congressman and attorney, was a graduate of the class of 1920. A life-long resident of Williamsburg, Siler had these thoughts

---

[52] Bert T. Combs, Address and interview at Homecoming, 22 November 1980.

Judge Combs has had an active career serving as Commonwealth Attorney, 31st Judicial District, Kentucky, 1950-1951; Judge,

concerning Cumberland College.

What Harvard is to Cambridge, what Yale is to New Haven, what Brown is to Providence, that's what Cumberland College is to Williamsburg.

Just as most people would not want to live in a town without a church, many people would not want to live in a town without a college.

Cumberland brings to Williamsburg three circulations. The jingling circulation of money, the enlightened circulation of culture, the exuberant circulation of youth. And all these circulations are good. Without these Williamsburg would be in the throngs of deprivation and depression.

Around 1880 Williamsburg was a struggling village without a railroad or church or college. Some local poet expressed the situation with these lines:

'Williamsburg without a steeple,

poor folks and common people,

Cox's Tavern, Adams store,

a blacksmith shop and nothing more.'

Can you imagine the monotony of life in Williamsburg without a college or college people? Those were the Dark Ages of local history when citizens blundered without a lamp.

But in 1889 the lamp arrived and was lit. And the flame is still burning today. This was the year of Cumberland College which began as Williamsburg Institute. The lamp was put upon the college seal. Look for the lamp on the seal. It is still there. You will see it. This lamp has continued to burn for 82 years. And certainly Williamsburg is a brighter, happier community because of the lamp.

With 1800 students and 100 college teachers in town daily, business people are glad to see all the extra commerce generated by Cumberland College. Other people are happy to see the elevation of cultural values. Literature, art and music are handmaidens, you know, of every college in the land. And still other segments of our people would like to stay perpetually young. This is possible whenever the college band comes marching down Main Street, whenever college cheerleaders are turning flips on the basketball court, whenever distant runners on the track team go flying past as some elderly lady plods her weary way toward her home around dusk.

'O, we climb our college's hills by day

And we sing our songs by night.'[53]

Court of Appeals, Kentucky, 1951-1955; Governor, Commonwealth of Kentucky, 1959-1963; and Judge, United States Court of Appeals, 6th District, 1967-1970. He currently practices law with the firm Wyatt, Tarrant, and Combs, Louisville, Kentucky.

[53] Eugene E. Siler, Sr., "What Cumberland College is to Williamsburg," *The Cumberland College Magazine,* Spring edition, 1972.

PLEAS JONES

Pleas Jones was a member of the 1934 graduating class. Here are his thoughts.

Cumberland College to me is an oasis in a desert of misunderstanding and ignorance. To me it is like a city set on a hill whose lights could not be hid. Had it not been for Cumberland College many of the young men of Appalachia would have been truck drivers, maybe coal miners, or at least menial laborers, but Cumberland College has never closed its doors to any deserving, qualified student who seeks to enter Cumberland in pursuit of an academic record.

Now I was born of poor, humble parents and they were not able to send me to college, although I had their good wishes, it just seemed an impossibility. But through a compassionate president and an understanding friend who was a member of the Board of Trustees, I was able to receive a loan, and I attended Cumberland College.

Cumberland College had a great faculty and still has a great faculty. I felt like the Apostle Paul must have felt because it opened doors to me that never could have been opened. Cumberland College has had a great influence on my life. All that I have accomplished, all that I have done, I think I owe it to the institution and the training that I received here at the college. I feel that through the influence of those great teachers that I learned to open a door, turn a leaf, and lift a stone, and Cumberland has meant so much to me, and so much to many who have gone out from this institution.

Now there have been thousands from all parts of Appalachia and other regions all over the United States, and even in Africa, and from some of the other foreign countries, and the Mid-East who have been here in school. There have been lawyers, teachers, doctors, nurses, dentists, and we have even had two governors, one congressman, and three appellate judges that have graduated from this institution. So I want to say to you that Cumberland College is like an oasis in a desert of misunderstanding and ignorance. But it is a great institution for learning, and it has provided the educational facilities for people to find a better station and a better way of life.[54]

MERIEL D. HARRIS

Meriel D. Harris, a practicing attorney in Somerset, Kentucky, was a member of the 1933 graduating class.

---

[54] Pleas Jones, Interview.

My class was one of the depression era and in those days almost everyone required financial assistance. This the college provided. I like to think of Cumberland as President Taylor does, as a city, a shining city, set upon a hill with the light of learning and opportunity streaming into the hollows and upon the hills of Appalachia. Cumberland provides the more abundant life. Its influence will continue to grow and will be felt for years and years to come. To paraphrase Tennyson, its echoes will grow from soul to soul and grow forever and forever. It richly deserves the wholehearted support of us all.

Historically, Cumberland College has created a great group of teachers or instructors for the public schools of its service area, and since its emergence as a four-year college it is now graduating people who are entering the professions, who are becoming leaders in corporations, who are becoming outstanding judges, physicians, and college professors, and who are in a much better position to lend financial support and leadership in many other ways to the College.

Cumberland College is unique in my opinion because it truly offers a student the opportunity to develop his talents to the very maximum. If you do not have financial support, Cumberland seems to find a way to provide that for you, and I think we might say that a greater percentage of Cumberland's students require financial assistance than those of probably any other college in the Commonwealth. But it's unique because it provides that. In addition to that, I like to think that Cumberland really turns no one away who is deserving. Cumberland affords that atmosphere and an opportunity for every deserving student who is ambitious to go as far as his talents and abilities will permit. I think in that way it is very unique. They have a personal interest in the student, too. They seem to watch over their lives in many facets. In that way it is a sort of family atmosphere.

In my opinion, the major accomplishment of Cumberland College is to provide, as it has, and still is, an oasis of culture and learning in the area that it serves. Overall, I would have to say that Cumberland has provided a great and real core of leadership for southeastern Kentucky and for many parts of the State and the nation as well.

I see that Cumberland in the future will continue to grow and expand. Its growth has been nothing short of dramatic in the last several years and I expect that Cumberland will continue to attract students because of its curriculum and because of a need and because of its fine history. I feel that Cumberland will continue to grow and expand and attract the kind of faculty which will meet the needs of students in a changing world, and I think that the role which Cumberland will play in the future will simply dwarf its accomplishments of the past which have not been inconsiderable, to say the least.[55]

JAMES CHEELY

James Cheely was a member of the 1932 graduating class. Here are his comments.

I entered the Cumberland College elementary school in 1919, completing eight years of elementary school in what is now Roburn Hall, four years of high school, and two years of college. I received my A.A. degree in 1932. I have most pleasant memories of those years in school with an excellent group of teachers, all of whom were dedicated and efficient.

My grandfather, T. B. Mahan, was president of the trustees, and I cherish my diploma from the school with his signature. I fear that I was a little cocky with this family connection, but I have discovered since then that the only thing that counts is your life and not your connections.[56]

FACULTY AND STUDENTS

When Dr. Creech became president in 1925, there were fourteen teachers at the school.[57] This number grew to eighteen in 1933 with the majority of the teachers holding a minimum of a master's degree.[58]

In 1945 the number of teachers had shrunk to thirteen, largely because of World War II. Several of the faculty, including J.M. Boswell and J.T. Vallandingham,[59] joined the armed services to help defend our country.

The War also affected the enrollment. In 1925 there were eighty-seven students enrolled in the college program.[60] This number grew to 245 students in the academic year 1934-1935[61] and remained fairly stable for several years. By 1943, however, the

---

[55] Meriel D. Harris, Interview.

[56] James Cheely, Letter.

[57] Cumberland College, *Catalogue,* 1925-1926.

[58] Cumberland College, *Catalogue,* 1933.

[59] Cumberland College, *Catalogue,* 1945-1946.

This story is commonly told of Dr. Vallandingham that when Pearl Harbor was bombed he picked up his books and announced, "Come, young men, we must join the Army." And he did just that!

[60] Cumberland College, *Catalogue,* 1925-1926.

[61] Cumberland College, *Catalogue,* 1934-1935.

enrollment had dropped to 143 students with only nineteen of these being men.[62]

---

[62] Cumberland College, *Catalogue,* 1943-1944.

The following stories are told by former students as recollections of their days at or around Cumberland College.

DOZING IN CLASS

Liz Young Krause wrote the following in a letter.

"My most memorable happening at Cumberland occurred with Professor P. R. Jones the first day of the semester, 1943, having spent the night on the train coming up from Detroit to begin classes. My cousin (Georgia Mae Bunch) and I were sharing the same seat in Professor Jones' class (shortage of seats that first day). Being very tired, I dozed off (imagine) during Professor Jones' introduction to the chemistry class.

After class was over, Professor Jones motioned for Georgia Mae to come to his desk. He then told her, 'Miss Bunch, if you let your cousin, Miss Young, go to sleep in one of my classes again, I'll throw you out!' He made quite an impression on both of us! I never dozed again. Two of my sisters-in-law, upon hearing what had happened, assured me that once he 'started kidding a student that this meant the student was somewhat in his good graces!' This somewhat assured me as I felt that my first class entry would ruin me.

Anyway this prediction proved true. I eventually got a 'scholarship' in chemistry (which I think came out of his pocket) which paid my tuition for the second year.

Also Professor Jones, I'm sure, was the moving force for getting me into the BSN (nursing program) at Johns Hopkins University, Baltimore.

What a great fellow he was."

In his 30 June 1986, letter, Dr. Ralph Denham recalled those early days:

"My childhood recollections include being chased off of the campus innumerable times by Dr. J.L. Creech, then President of Cumberland College. We boys of the neighborhood chased lightening bugs, June bugs, baseballs, footballs, and each other in and around the Gray Brick and old Dixie Hall. We personally got in the way of many workmen, blasters, bricklayers, steel erectors, and others as the present gymnasium was built. It is a wonder that we survived without injury as we built tunnels and platforms with the large stacks of brick, stood by as they blasted out the foundation with dynamite ('fire-in-the-hole'), climbed scaffolds and ladders, crawled across girders high in the sky before the roof went on, and were in the way far more than we should have been.

P.R. Jones, in his basement chemistry lab, had a unique way of dispersing our gang if we were disturbing his class. He would call us over to the window of the lab and allow us to take a good whiff of hydrogen sulfide or some equally malodorous substance.

Later, as we were a bit older we frequently would tag along as the professors took their afternoon walk in pleasant weather. The walk was along the L&N Railroad right of way heading north from the footbridge along the double track, across the Cumberland River via the railroad trestle, by the cemetery, and on to Sunshine Valley near Watts Creek trestle, then return. I cannot recall any great bits of philosophy that spilled off on us but I do remember the participants: Professor A.R. Evans, Gorman Jones, P.R. Jones, J.T. Vallandingham were always present. Dr. E.E. Wood was not that active at the time and the young turks, Jim Boswell, Wyatt Wood, and Wilson Evans, were either too busy elsewhere or uninvited."

In the Fall, 1967, Issue of *Now,* the alumni magazine, the following tribute was given to Professor P. R. Jones.

"Professor Jones has been recognized as a master teacher. Having a unique way of illustrating his lectures, those who studied under him were never bored and came to appreciate his unusual effectiveness as a teacher. Possessing an unusual sense of humor, he was able to maintain the interest of his students during lectures and demonstrations covering the most difficult topics.

Under him have studied doctors, dentists, laboratory technicians, nurses, military leaders, public school teachers, public administrators, college teachers, farmers, ministers, and missionaries. Since he taught both biological science and physical science for many years, and since some courses in both these fields were required of all students, he taught for a long period of time just about every person who graduated from the college."

Dr. Ralph Denham in his letter of July, 1986, had this remembrance of Professor Jones: "I recall a game we played against Hiwassee College. It was very close and late in the game. My man got away for an easy lay up. A very loud voice from the stands called out, 'Denham, that was your man!' Professor P. R. Jones really got involved as all could plainly hear."

Another story told by Dr. Denham concerning Professor Jones is that during the nation's economic depression, President Creech

CREECH INCAPACITATED

In the latter part of 1945 President Creech suffered a stroke and was unable to perform his duties as president. James M. Boswell, a member of the College's faculty who had served 39 months of active duty in the United States Navy as a commissioned officer, was contacted and asked to seek an early discharge so he could assume the position of dean of administration and help run the College during Creech's recuperation. Boswell complied.

On 22 January 1946 the Board of Trustees met and heard a report from Creech's physician that Dr. Creech was still unable to see to the work of the College. The trustees voted Boswell as acting president to serve until June 30 of that year.[63] His salary was set at $300 per month.[64]

President Creech's health did not improve quickly,[65] and he decided to resign as president and as a member of the faculty effective 31 May 1946.[66]

At a meeting of the Board of Trustees on 1 June 1946, Creech was elected president emeritus with a salary of $100 a month.[67] At that same meeting a committee was appointed to contact "Professor J.T. Vallandingham to ascertain his attitude and wishes relative to accepting the position of president of Cumberland College."[68]

At the 31 May 1947 meeting of the Board, the committee reported that "Mr.

---

allowed the campus to go through deferred maintenance. Some of the community's citizens decided to ask Professor Jones if he could get Creech to maintain better the campus. Jones responded, "I'm a resident, not the president."

FROM THE HILLS TO HARVARD

John Paul Maggard attended Cumberland College in 1941 and began teaching at Grassy Gap, Kentucky, the next year. Following military service during World War II, he attended Harvard Graduate School of Business. Maggard earned his Doctor of Philosophy degree from the University of North Carolina. He served as a professor of Miami University in Ohio from 1956 until his recent retirement. A room in the School of Business Administration at Miami University is named in his honor.

Maggard's areas of expertise are in advertising. In 1976 he received the Western Electric Award for Innovation in Undergraduate Education. He and his wife Melva currently reside in Asheville, North Carolina, and he is considering becoming involved in real estate sales.

[63] Cumberland College, Board of Trustees, *Minutes*, 22 January 1946.

[64] Cumberland College, Board of Trustees, *Minutes*, 25 January 1946.

[65] James M. Boswell, "An Evaluation of the Contribution of J. L. Creech to Cumberland College While Serving as President of the Institution," *The Kentucky Baptist Heritage*, Vol. X, No. 2, November 1983, p. 29.

". . . Following his stroke in the early fall of 1945, he was somewhat crippled and his physical activities were limited. As time went on, he recovered from the effects of his stroke to some extent and became almost independent of others. He was able to walk well again and his physical condition improved to the point he could drive his car to his farms. Before he was able to drive a car I used to take him to visit his farms and other places to which he wanted to go. After he was able to drive again, he would invite me to go with him to visit his enterprises.

In the last year or so of his life, he spent a good deal of time in the hospital. However, he would leave the hospital for short periods as his condition permitted. He passed away in August of 1955, some ten years after his stroke."

[66] Cumberland College, Board of Trustees, *Minutes*, 1 June 1946.

[67] *Ibid.* The position, President Emeritus, was "to carry no authority whatsoever in the management of the school."

[68] *Ibid.*

Vallandingham was not a candidate for this position." James Malcolm Boswell was then elected president of Cumberland College at an annual salary of $4,000, plus living quarters in Mahan Hall.[69]

THE MAN WITH A GOLDEN HEART

In 1929 the following was said of President Creech, "If it were possible for a golden heart to beat, his would be a heart of gold."[70]

Creech's presidency was marked as a period of stability and growth. There was an increase in enrollment; two new buildings were added (a gymnasium and a home economics building); the College became a member of the Southern Association of Colleges and Secondary Schools; the College became free of debt and operated on a balanced budget; a highly skilled and competent faculty was employed; an emphasis remained on moral and religious values; the Student Labor Program was refined; and the Rural Betterment Program was begun.

These accomplishments were seen during a period of depression when many colleges faced difficult times. President Creech, however, provided sound leadership, and Cumberland College "became an institution with a broader and stronger base academically and financially."[71]

---

[69] Cumberland College, Board of Trustees, *Minutes,* 31 May 1947. Actually, the appointment of Boswell was for one year from 31 May 1947 to 31 May 1948.

Ironically enough, history would repeat itself. Since Boswell had to wait several months before being named president, one can well imagine that these were sensitive, delicate, and trying times. Years later when the writer was asked to become president, he would also be asked to wait a similar number of months before being named president.

[70] *Western Recorder,* 21 March 1929, p.6.

[71] Boswell, "An Evaluation of the Contribution of J.L. Creech to Cumberland College While Serving as President of the Institution." p. 29.

ALBERT ROBINSON EVANS
Acting President 1919-1921

(Photograph from the *Lamp,* 1948)

PARRY RAYMOND JONES
Faculty Member 1909-1967

Professor P.R. Jones (1888-1973) came to Cumberland College immediately after receiving his bachelor's degree from Denison University, and he remained in the College's employment until his retirement in 1967, except for one year. He earned his master's degree in chemistry from Ohio State University and had additional work at the University of Kentucky.

Professor Jones taught a multitude of subjects while at Cumberland, including geography, mathematics, zoology, botany, physics, physical science, and chemistry. He also served as head of the chemistry department.

In 1927 Professor Jones took on the added responsibilities of Academic Dean, a position he held until 30 September 1961.

Professor Jones was also involved in the College's athletic program. He coached the football team; he served as the basketball coach from 1910 to 1927; and he was the baseball coach for five years.

Professor Jones and his wife Nancy Eleanor (Nellie) Starett Jones lived in a house located on Main Street, just up the street from Johnson Hall. Because of their home's closeness to the campus, Professor and Mrs. Jones often entertained students in their home.

In 1967 Professor Jones was awarded the honorary Doctor of Laws degree by Cumberland College in recognition of his years of service, and in 1968 the chemistry wing of the new science building was named in his honor.

As an active member of the First Baptist Church, Professor Jones served as a deacon, and he taught a Sunday School class for thirty years.

In 1971 Professor and Mrs. Jones gave their Main Street home to the College with the only stipulation being that the College make repairs, pay the insurance, and allow the Joneses to live in the home until their deaths.

Cumberland College, Board of Trustees, *Minutes,* 26 August 1967; Cumberland College, Alumni Office, *Now,* Fall, 1967, vol. 1, no. 3, p. 2.

(Photograph from the *Lamp,* 1956)

BESSE MAHAN ROSE
Faculty Member 1912-1962

Besse Mahan Rose (1889-1963), the daughter of Ben and Margaret Early Rose of Williamsburg, was graduated from the Williamsburg Institute in 1909 and from Georgetown College in 1912.

Her first teaching assignment at the Institute was in the grade school. She later taught in the high school, then in the College. She served as principal of the grade school and of the high school and also held the titles of registrar and head of the English department during her tenure.

After coming to the Institute, Miss Rose earned her Master's degree from Columbia University and did further work at the University of Wisconsin and George Peabody College.

In 1956 the yearbook was dedicated to Miss Rose with these words: "During her years here, she has patiently taught the fundamentals of English, given us a clearer understanding of literature, guided us in our dramatic club productions and conversed with us about the colorful background of Cumberland."

In 1959 Miss Rose was honored in a chapel service and presented with a large silver tray.

(Photograph from the *Lamp,* 1956)

JOHN THOMPSON VALLANDINGHAM
Faculty Member 1913-1980

John Thompson Vallandingham (1887-1980) was born in Owen County, Kentucky. At an early age he was stricken with a disease, probably polio, and he had to wear a brace for many years.

Dr. Vallandingham was graduated in 1911 from Georgetown College with a major in mathematics, and in 1912-1913 he served as teacher and principal of the Brookville High School. In 1913 Dr. Vallandingham came to Cumberland College to teach for one semester, but he stayed in the College's employment for the remainder of his life. He took graduate studies at Ypsilanti State College in Michigan, the University of Chicago, and the University of Kentucky. In 1956 he received the honorary Doctor of Laws degree from Georgetown College, and in 1969 he received an honorary degree from Cumberland College.

Dr. Vallandingham served in both World War I and World War II. As soon as the first war broke out he urged the young men to "sign up," and he did likewise, becoming a First Lieutenant of the Field Artillery. During World War II he served as a Major.

In 1919 Professor Vallandingham returned to the College, and in 1928 he married one of his former students Virginia Jones, the daughter of Professor and Mrs. Gorman Jones. One daughter Virginia was born to this union.

Dr. Vallandingham was a quiet, dignified man who was said to be patient and thorough. Over the years he spent many extra hours with students trying to help them both academically and personally. In 1964 he was honored by having the Scholastic Honor Society at Cumberland College named for him. In 1974 the Alumni Association hosted a banquet in his honor.

Dr. Vallandingham was an active member of the First Baptist Church of Williamsburg where he taught Sunday School and served as a deacon and deacon emeritus. He also held a 29-year perfect attendance record at the Williamsburg Rotary Club.

The Cumberland College Monthly, Vol. 5, No. 9, June 1917, and Vol. 6, No. 3, December 1917; *The Whitley Republican,* "Obituary," 24 July 1980; Virginia Vallandingham Early, Interview, 25 July 1984; Eugene E. Lovett, Interview, 9 October 1986.

(Photograph from the *Lamp,* 1958)

DR. NELL MOORE
Faculty Member 1922-1972

Dr. Nell Moore (1891-1980) taught music at Cumberland College for fifty years. She served as head of the music department and was head emeritus at the time of her retirement.

Dr. Moore, a native of Smith's Grove, Kentucky, was a graduate of the Louisville Conservatory. She received her master's degree and her doctor's degree from the Institute of Musical Art, Detroit, Michigan.

Dr. Moore was known for her love of teaching and her demands of her students. The 1957 yearbook was dedicated to Dr. Moore with these words: "Her love of music radiates her whole personality and awakens an interest for music in all who know her. Every member of the music department learns that she has infinite patience but is a believer in hard work.

"Miss Nell is more than a music teacher. Her zeal for continuous study and her tolerance toward others is an inspiration and guide to our campus."

On the occasion of Dr. Moore's retirement in 1972, a banquet was given by her colleagues and associates honoring her fifty years of service. A gigantic cake weighing 350 pounds and shaped as a piano was baked for Dr. Moore by the head chef of General Mills Company, Minneapolis, Minnesota.

In 1979 Dr. Moore was again honored when the recital hall of the Mary W. McGaw Music Building was named in her honor.

(Photograph from the *Lamp,* 1956)

141

MISS MARY THOMAS
Faculty Member 1929-1965

Miss Mary Thomas joined Cumberland's faculty in 1929. During her tenure she served as Dean of Women and as a member of the history department faculty.

Miss Thomas received both her bachelor's and her master's degrees from Indiana University. Additionally, she took further work at the University of Indiana and the University of Wisconsin.

In 1950 the yearbook of Cumberland College was dedicated to Miss Thomas with these words:

"One of the best-known and most-beloved professors on the Cumberland College campus is Miss Thomas, who for the past twenty years has been professor of history. With her cheerful smile, her glowing enthusiasm, and her unique sense of humor, she has won her way into the hearts of all.

"With a genuine love for history, Miss Thomas has worked untiringly to instill a wider interest in history among her students.

"Especially have her efforts as faculty adviser of the International Relations Club proved effective. She has made it one of the most outstanding organizations on the campus through her inspiration and guidance."

(Photograph from the *Lamp*, 1950)

SEVEN LONG-TIME FACULTY MEMBERS

Pictured left to right are: James Lloyd Creech; Albert Robinson Evans; John T. Vallandingham; Parry Raymond Jones; Besse Mahan Rose; Nell Moore; and Mary Thomas. The picture was taken at the Homecoming of the First Baptist Church, 1952.

(Photograph courtesy of Ann Renfro Shelley)

THE COLLEGE LIBRARY
(circa 1915 or 1916)
(Photograph from the 1918 *Catalogue*)

ARKLEY WRIGHT
Cumberland College's
first Academic Dean
(Photograph courtesy of John G. Wright,
son of Arkley Wright)

CHARLES WILLIAM ELSEY
President 1921-1925

(Photograph courtesy of the First Baptist Church, Shelbyville, Kentucky)

WILLIAMSBURG'S FIRST BAPTIST CHURCH

The building pictured above was dedicated 5 April 1908 and was destroyed by fire in 1924. The building below was erected in 1926.

(Photographs courtesy of the First Baptist Church, Williamsburg, Kentucky)

JAMES LLOYD CREECH
President 1925-1946

(Photograph from the *Lamp*)

THE GYMNASIUM

The gymnasium was completed in 1928 at a cost of $56,000. William Rutherford, Jr., was the architect. The building was never officially named the Gatliff Gymnasium but simply assumed the name since the old gymnasium was named in honor of Dr. Ancil Gatliff.

Cumberland College, Board of Trustees, *Minutes,* 3 December 1926.

(Photograph by Housman Photography)

THE STUDENT HEALTH BUILDING

This building served originally as the meeting-house of the Williamsburg Congregational Church. Sometime after the church disbanded in the 1930's the building came into use by the College.

Currently, this building houses the Student Health Center. It is staffed by a registered nurse and is open to students, faculty, and staff.

(Photograph by Housman Photography)

HOME ECONOMICS BUILDING

In 1929 the Home Economics Building was completed as an annex to Johnson Hall. Mrs. Florida Moss Gatliff, the widow of Dr. Ancil Gatliff, paid for the building.

(Photograph by Housman Photography)

FIFTIETH ANNIVERSARY

President Creech observed in his report to the Board of Trustees on 29 May 1939:

"On this, the fiftieth anniversary of the founding, the friends of the College are pleased to pay tribute to the foresight and wisdom, to the loyalty and devotion of those who have wrought so wondrously in the founding and building of the College, and to bring it to its present enviable position as an institution of learning. May this rich heritage that has come through the great personalities identified with the College in the past be handed on to succeeding generations, each generation being conscious of the sacred obligations passed on to it."

THEY BUILDED BETTER THAN THEY KNEW

In 1939 the College's fiftieth anniversary was celebrated, and a plaque was erected to four of the men who helped to build this college: Dr. Ancil Gatliff: James P. Mahan; Thomas B. Mahan; and John W. Siler with the inscription: "They builded better than they knew." This was surely true, for the contributions of the College's founders have magnified and multiplied many times and in many ways.

Dr. Ancil Gatliff's granddaughter, Norma Jeanne Perkins, and Mr. Thomas Breckenridge's grandson, Edgar Cheely, unveiled the monument.

(Photographs by Housman Photography)

148

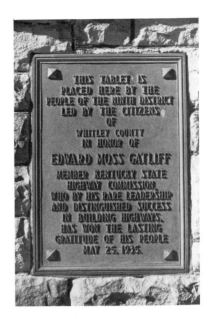

Monument and tablet erected to Edward Moss Gatliff on the Courthouse Square, Williamsburg, Kentucky, 25 May 1935.

(Photograph by Housman Photography)

EDWIN PORCH MORROW
1877-1935
Fortieth Governor
Commonwealth of Kentucky
1919-1923

(Photograph by Cusick Studio, undated)

BERT T. COMBS

Forty-Sixth Governor
Commonwealth of Kentucky
1959-1963

(Photograph courtesy of Wyatt, Tarrant, and Combs,
Louisville, Kentucky)

EUGENE E. SILER, SR.

The Honorable Eugene E. Siler, Sr., the son of A.T. Siler, was graduated from Cumberland College in 1920 and from the University of Kentucky in 1922. He studied law at Columbia University. He was a judge of the Court of Appeals of Kentucky, 1945-1949, and a United States Congressman, representing the Fifth District in Kentucky, 1955-1965. He was elected as Moderator of the General Association of Baptists in Kentucky in 1952 and served two years. Siler served as a member of Cumberland College's Board of Trustees from 1946 to 1965 and as a Deacon and Sunday School teacher at Williamsburg's First Baptist Church. He is now a practicing attorney in Williamsburg.

According to Congressman Carroll Hubbard, addressing the graduating class of Cumberland College in May, 1984, it was Eugene Siler, Sr., who led this nation's Congress to place the words, "One Nation Under God," in our pledge to the flag of the United States.

Congressman Siler can also be credited as the first Congressman to speak out against the Vietnam conflict, calling it a "great mistake," and, as a Congressman, he voted against the sending of troops to Vietnam in 1964.

Siler, "Heads or Tales," 13 March 1975; 17 July 1980.

(Photograph from the Cumberland College Collection)

THE HONORABLE PLEAS JONES

The Honorable Pleas Jones was graduated from Cumberland College in 1934. He then attended the University of Kentucky Law School. He was a veteran of World War II.

Judge Jones served this area and its people in a host of positions: school teacher, circuit court clerk, county judge, commonwealth attorney, and circuit judge. In 1973, Judge Jones was appointed to the state Court of Appeals, then Kentucky's highest court, and in 1976, when the court system was reorganized, he was appointed Supreme Court Justice from the Third Appellate District, a post he held until 1979.

Judge Jones was an active member of Williamsburg's Main Street Baptist Church where he served as Sunday School teacher, church treasurer, and chairman of the Building and Finance Committee. He also served as Commander of Williamsburg's American Legion post, president of Williamsburg's Lions Club, president of the Kentucky Society of the Sons of the American Revolution, and member of the Rotary Club, Masons, and Shriners.

Judge Jones passed away on 19 September 1986, following a long illness. He was a faithful supporter of Cumberland College and was well versed in the history of the College and the area. He is missed.

(Photograph from the Cumberland College Collection)

150

MERIEL D. HARRIS

Meriel D. Harris, a native of Somerset, Kentucky, was graduated from Cumberland College in 1933. He later attended Western Kentucky University, the University of Kentucky, and Northwestern University where he earned his Juris Doctor Degree in law. Mr. Harris has served as a practicing attorney in Somerset from 1951 to the present.

(Photograph from the Cumberland College Collection)

H.H. FUSON

H.H. Fuson served as a trustee of Cumberland College from 1923 to 1964, excluding a four-year period during World War II.

(Photograph from the Cumberland College Collection)

JEAN RITCHIE

Jean Ritchie, a native of Viper, Perry County, Kentucky, is a 1944 graduate of Cumberland College. She then attended the University of Kentucky where she studied social work, graduating with honors and a Phi Beta Kappa key. Friends helped her find a job in New York where she met the man she later married.

Jean Ritchie, who usually accompanies herself on the hammered dulcimer, is regarded as one of the country's authentic folk artists of song and a member of one of folk music's oldest families.

Miss Ritchie spends three months every year in Perry County living in a log cabin which is located close to where she was born. She spends three to four months touring and performing. The remainder of the time, Miss Ritchie lives in Port Washington, a community on Long Island, New York, with her photographer husband George Pickow.

(Photograph from *Promises to Keep.*)

DONALD A. SWANSON

Donald A. Swanson attended Cumberland College in 1943. He later attended Columbia University and the University of Virginia. Mr. Swanson is currently serving as Vice President, Sales, Parke-Davis, Morris Plains, New Jersey.

(Photograph from the Cumberland College Collection)

CHAPTER 5
COMING OF AGE

THE GOLDEN DAYS

When James Malcolm Boswell assumed the presidency, there were approximately 200 students enrolled in the College. When he stepped down from the presidency in 1980, the enrollment exceeded 2,000 students.

The 1950's, 1960's, and 1970's were undoubtedly a "hey-day" for colleges with the G.I. Bill, educational and technical advancements after Sputnik in 1957, and vastly expanded federal and state student aid programs, culminating in the Middle Income Assistance Act and subsequent programs. Remember these were the days following World War II and during and after the Korean Conflict with post-World War II and post-Korean Conflict baby booms. You will recall that the 1960's saw the election of Kennedy, the Bay of Pigs invasion, and college kids being sent to Vietnam. From our mountains we watched or participated in the "War on Poverty," the "New Frontier," the "Peace Corps," the U.S. and Soviet missile crisis. We watched the assassinations of Kennedy and King on national television and witnessed the attempt by President Lyndon Johnson to settle a nation of unrest.

Yet, all the while Cumberland College, like other colleges, provided an educational opportunity for those who had the ability and who sought the opportunity.

BOSWELL AT THE HELM

With President Creech incapacitated because of the stroke, Boswell was called back from service by the College's Board, and he assumed the helm of the College in October 1945, although he was not given the title of president for almost two years. Having been associated with the College since 1931, Boswell had an advantage of familiarity with the College's operation and an acquaintance with the community and region. He soon launched into the tasks of college administrator, with emphasis on promoting the College and recruiting students.[1]

---

[1] Because a car was not always available to Boswell during the early years of his administration, he did a great deal of traveling on behalf of the college by train or bus.

A RECRUIT BECAME A COLLEGE PRESIDENT
Dr. Betty Siegel, class of 1950, now president of Kennesaw College in Georgia, writes:
"When I was considering which college to attend I had two major choices. I had a scholarship from Stephens

JAMES MALCOLM BOSWELL

James Malcolm Boswell (1906 -   ) was initially attracted to Cumberland because it provided him an opportunity to teach. He came to teach mathematics in 1931 but didn't intend to stay. As time passed he was able to see the good the College was doing in affording a quality education for every student who seemed capable of going to college regardless of his or her financial background.[2] The College's general practice of not turning away a student, regardless of his or her ability to pay, has proved no little hardship through the years. Yet the philosophy is rewarding, so rewarding that Boswell became one of its most influential exponents.

James Malcolm Boswell, or ''Dr. B'' as he has become affectionately known, was born near Leesburg, Kentucky, in Harrison County. One of three children, he grew up on a farm and was up before daybreak milking six or eight cows before going to school. His elementary school days were spent in a rustic grade school in Harrison County; he was graduated from high school in Cynthiana.

In 1924 Boswell entered Georgetown College and majored in mathematics and minored in physics and Latin. His interest in sports continued from his high school days, and he was actively involved with the athletic program at Georgetown. In 1928 Boswell was graduated Magna Cum Laude from Georgetown College. On his graduation he was given the Charles Dudley Adams Athletic Cup, an award made to a male graduate on the basis of athletic achievement and academic performance.

Boswell took graduate studies at the University of Michigan and the University of Kentucky, and he has received honorary degrees from Georgetown College, Cumberland College, and Eastern Kentucky University.[3]

College in Missouri, or I could attend Cumberland. Dr. Boswell personally came to see me and sat in my living room telling me about Cumberland. The fact that the college president was interested in me as an individual was the major influence that caused me to reject my scholarship and attend Cumberland.''

STAY ON STRANGER

[2] James M. Boswell, Interview, 11 November 1980.

''I came here to teach and at that time I didn't see the value of an institution like Cumberland College. When I came here in 1931, I didn't intend to stay at the institution. I thought it was just another institution which offered an opportunity to teach, but after I had been here a short while I was able to see the service the College rendered to this community in which it is and was able to see it was unique in that the College had a great philosophy of trying to afford an education regardless of financial background.''

''I WAS SELDOM BEATEN''

[3] *Ibid.* In speaking of his college days, Boswell recalls: ''I was seldom beaten in the shot, and when I was able to high-jump again I didn't lose that one either. During my junior and senior years in college, I usually won both the high-jump and the shot-put, and our competition was not only against other small colleges but also was against some of the larger universities as well.''

Along with track, Boswell competed and lettered in basketball, football and baseball. When asked as to when he studied, Boswell

After being graduated from Georgetown College, Boswell joined their faculty as mathematics instructor and freshman basketball coach. But by 1931, because of the Depression, Boswell, with several other instructors, was told that he should seek employment elsewhere because the College was unable to pay the teachers' salaries. He spent the summer of 1931 at Campbellsville College teaching mathematics, and it was during that summer that President Creech contacted Boswell about coming to Cumberland College. He came in the fall of 1931 as the College's physics teacher and the high school mathematics teacher.

In January 1932 Boswell married Mary Susan Dudley, an instructor of French and German at Georgetown College. In fact, she had been one of Boswell's teachers while he was a student at Georgetown.

The Boswells are the parents of two children: Jim Boswell and Louise Boswell Tipton.[4]

COACH OF ALL SPORTS

In 1932 Boswell was named coach of all Cumberland College sports. He recalls that the Gatliff Gymnasium, completed in 1928, was at that time a showplace for college basketball. "Compared to some of the other gyms in Kentucky and Tennessee in which we played, it was a palace," says Boswell.[5] According to reliable sources President Creech drew the plans and specifications for the building on the back of a matchbox.

---

proudly replied, "I was graduated second in my class at Georgetown College with a major in math and minors in physics and Latin. I didn't take easy courses."

One of Boswell's teammates at Georgetown was Blanton Collier. Collier went on to become a coach at the University of Kentucky and later for the Cleveland Browns.

[4] *Ibid.*

Mrs. Boswell grew up in Chicago. She received her bachelor's degree from Georgetown College and her master's degree from the University of Tennessee. Mrs. Boswell joined Cumberland's faculty in 1945 as instructor in modern language, a position she held until 1984.

Dr. Boswell admitted that he and his wife "wanted to get married sooner, but the finances were quite a bit tighter then." They dated for three years before being married, and it has been said that from the time Boswell came to Cumberland to the time of the marriage, he spent every weekend, when possible, in Georgetown. The first home of the Boswells was the upper floor of the old Marsh Mahan home (now the site of the Everett Buhl home). The Boswells later, however, moved to Felix Hall.

Speaking of Mrs. Boswell, Dr. Boswell noted, "She has been a consistently stabilizing force in my life. She is my partner, my love, and my very best friend."

[5] *Ibid.*

A MAN AND HIS HAT

Anyone who reminisces about those days always turns to a certain brown hat Boswell wore to the games. "The late Coach Diddle of Western had his towel; the late Coach Rupp had his omnipresent brown suit; and Dr. Boswell had his floppy brown hat." He would twist it, stomp on it, throw it in the air, and then stomp on it again. One day Boswell wore his Sunday Stetson to a basketball game by mistake. Cumberland played badly that evening and by the end of the game Boswell was so frustrated that "he ran his fist through his Stetson." The hat was declared completely terminal at the local hattery.[6]

POACHED EGGS, TOAST, AND TEA

Boswell was an advocate of allowing his players only a light meal before a game. The following story is told by Dr. Ralph Denham, one of Boswell's varsity basketball players, 1934-1936.

When we had a home game Coach Boswell had us to report to Johnson Hall dining room for a pregame meal consisting of two poached eggs, toast, and tea. We were then to return to the dorm or to our homes to rest for an hour or two before the game. Several of us would go to my home adjacent to the campus and my mother, who was not a sports fan, insisted that we eat a full meal so that we would have "the strength" to play. Needless to say it was an offer we could not refuse.[7]

Dr. Boswell's excitement and enthusiasm was also displayed in his classroom. He tells the following story concerning his teaching:

YOU CAN'T ARGUE WITH SUCCESS

During the early days of my teaching experience at Cumberland it seems that President Creech paid more attention to me than he did to any other instructor on the staff . . . .

. . . Dr. Creech would come to my high school classes and sit for a period

---

[6] Pleas Jones, "The Life & Times: Dr. Boswell," *Cumberland Today,* Vol. 1, No. 2, Winter Edition, p. 5.

[7] Ralph Denham, Letter, July 1986. Denham also recalls the time his team was traveling to Athens, Tennessee, to play Tennessee Wesleyan. "Coach Boswell misjudged an icy patch in the road, and we ended up through a fence and in some farmer's pasture." Denham goes on to report that the team "managed to push and shove until the car was back on the road, shored up the fence to some extent, and then went on to Athens."

of time. Then one day, he called me into his office and told me what I might do to make my teaching more effective. He said I talked too much, that I did too much explaining, and that I talked too loudly. He said I did not even walk as I should, that is, that I created too much disturbance as I walked on the wooden floors in the hallway of the Gray Brick. He then told me what I should do to become a better teacher.

I tried to modify my teaching methods to comply with his suggestions and recommendations. Nevertheless, I was convinced that what I was doing was effective, and I was confident that I was a competent teacher. He continued to visit my high school mathematics classes and subsequently would call me into his office for interviews. Apparently I did not change my teaching methods sufficiently to suit him since he pursued his pattern of classroom visitation and interviews.

However, at that particular time, there was in the State of Kentucky a program by which high school students in certain fields, if selected by the staff of the high school, went to a regional testing center and took a statewide standardized test on any of several academic subjects. These statewide tests were given in such courses as Algebra I, Algebra II, Plane Geometry, Physics, French, Latin, English I, II, III, and IV, American History, and Ancient History.

Every year the high school mathematics students I selected to go to the regional center did well, ranking among the best in the state in their particular fields . . . . One day he [Creech] called me to his office and said, 'Boswell, since your students have done so well on statewide tests, it is evident that you are effective in your teaching. I don't agree with your teaching methods but I can't argue with success, even if your methods are wrong.' He said, 'I will never bother you again in this respect.' and he didn't.[8]

Not only were Boswell's efforts as a teacher and as a coach rewarded, but so were his efforts as president. Little did he know, however, that his efforts along with those of a dedicated faculty, staff, Board of Trustees, and others would cause literally thousands, over the years, to better themselves.

For many, Boswell's administration would make life unalterably different from what it possibly would have been otherwise. Boswell was now at the forefront, standing on the shoulders of Presidents Johnson, Wood, Prestridge, Jones, Evans, Elsey, Creech, and a host of unseen guests.

---

[8] James M. Boswell, "An Evaluation of the Contribution of J. L. Creech to Cumberland College While Serving as President of the Institution," *The Kentucky Baptist Heritage*, p. 24.

BUILDINGS

During Boswell's years as president several buildings were constructed or acquired including the Gatliff Building, the Norma Jeanne Perkins Hagan Library, the Sophomore Dormitory (now known as the Nicholson-Jones Residence Hall), the T. J. Roberts Cafeteria, North Hall (now known as E. O. Robinson Hall), West Hall (which remains unnamed), the biology wing of the Science Building (which remains unnamed), the chemistry wing of the Science Building which was appropriately named for Professor P. R. Jones, the Ruby Gatliff Archer Home, the Ruby Gatliff Archer Hall, the Boswell Campus Center which was named in honor of Dr. and Mrs. Boswell, the George M. Asher Memorial Hall, and the Mary McGaw Music Building. Two additional parcels of property were acquired on Main Street.

And while buildings were being built, students were being recruited, and the curriculum was being constantly refined to meet the needs of the students, the area, and the changing times.

FOUR-YEAR COLLEGE STATUS RESTORED

Dr. Boswell has said that one of the toughest decisions the College faced during his administration was whether to reinstate a four-year program at Cumberland. He says he "worried that we would not have the money to meet increases in teacher load. It meant an increase in the student body, more buildings." Boswell said he believed, "It was the toughest decision that the trustees have made."[9]

Actually the idea to again seek senior college status was first mentioned at the 24 May 1956 meeting of the Board. The Executive Committee was "directed to investigate the possibilities" and to report at the next full Board meeting.[10]

At the 18 May 1957 Board meeting, the trustees by unanimous action voted "in favor of carrying out at once a publicity campaign and an extensive student solicitation program." Additionally, the Board voted to present a "plan of converting from a junior college to a senior college" to the General Association at their November meeting.[11]

On 8 November 1957, the Executive Committee of the Board met to discuss their upcoming actions at the meetings of the General Association in Harlan. Because Campbellsville College was also going to request approval for conversion to senior college status, it was decided that, if need be, Cumberland's application would be withheld

---

[9] James M. Boswell, Interview, 24 November 1980.

[10] Cumberland College, Board of Trustees, *Minutes,* 24 May 1956.

[11] Cumberland College, Board of Trustees, *Minutes,* 18 May 1957.

until the 1958 meeting. However, it was eventually decided and unanimously approved that if Campbellsville pressed for approval at the 1957 meeting, Cumberland would do likewise.[12]

The General Association's meeting was held in Harlan, Kentucky, on the 12th, 13th, and 14th of November, 1957. During the evening session on the first day, Campbellsville's president addressed the Association and gave his reasons for Campbellsville being changed to a four-year college. It was then moved that Cumberland College also be considered for change to a four-year college and that Boswell be allowed to present reasons for the change. No action was taken on the motion, but the Moderator stated that it would be considered in the afternoon session of the next day.

Before that afternoon session several meetings were held by the executive committee of the Board to discuss what should be done, and it was the consensus that, under the circumstances, the College had no alternative but to present its case. As a result of these meetings the following resolution was presented when the General Association reconvened and called for the issue: "That the General Association give its consent to a resumption by Cumberland College of its status as a four-year college such as it had prior to 1918, if and when its Board of Trustees may elect to resume that status."

POINTS FOR CONSIDERATION

The following points were outlined as worthy of consideration before action on the College's request by the General Association:

It is generally agreed that two basic requirements for the location of a college are financial support and service rendered to the immediate community in which the college is located . . . .

Most of the College's enrollment of 550 [now over 2,000] students come from a section within a radius of eighty miles of the college . . . .

Cumberland's services are needed to provide teachers for the area . . . .

Cumberland was chartered as a senior college in 1888 with the authority to give both the Bachelor's and Master's degrees . . . .

The graduating class now approximates two hundred each year . . . .

As a senior college Cumberland could render much greater service . . . .

Cumberland has had a strong educational program through the years and is regarded as one of the strongest junior colleges in the South. With

[12] Cumberland College, Board of Trustees, *Minutes,* 8 November 1957.

this background on which to build, it is logical to expect that the school could operate as an academically strong senior college . . . .

A motion was made by J. Bill Jones and seconded that the General Association's consent be given for Cumberland to begin a four-year program. It was unanimously passed.[13]

ACCREDITATION

Since 1931 the College has been accredited as a junior college by the Southern Association of Colleges and Schools. It was decided by the Board of Trustees to change to a senior college and to add the junior year in 1959-1960 and the senior year in 1960-1961. It was necessary to graduate three classes before the College could be considered for senior college accreditation. Initial accreditation for the four-year program was granted in December 1964.[14] Reaffirmation was granted in 1974 and in 1985 with no provisions or restrictions whatsoever.

ENROLLMENT INCREASES

With the decision to become a senior college, the junior year was added in 1959-1960, and the enrollment reached 879 students. In 1960-1961, with the addition of the senior year, the enrollment increased to 1,103 students.[15] Cumberland was meeting a real need.

OLD GUARD, YOUNG TURKS

After the transition to senior college status, one of Boswell's greatest tasks was to keep the peace among the "old guard" and the new "young turks" hired to expand the College from junior to senior college status.

Through listening and through communication a state of relative harmony existed more so than otherwise thought possible. Remember this was and is a special purpose College serving primarily, but not exclusively, mountain youth. Remember also that the "old guard" had been here almost from the beginning. Boswell kept things running smoothly, avoiding abrasive and adversarial relationships like the plague.

---

[13] This record of the proceedings at the General Association meeting is filed among the *Minutes,* Board of Trustees, Cumberland College, in order to give a better understanding of the actions taken.

[14] It was during the 1960's that Dr. Boswell served two terms of six years as a member of the Commission on Colleges of the Southern Association of Colleges and Schools.

[15] Cumberland College, *Catalogue,* 1961-1962.

SCHOLASTIC HONOR SOCIETY

In 1961 the Cumberland College Scholastic Honor Society was established to recognize outstanding student achievement. The members of this Society were to be formally recognized at the newly-established Honors Day ceremony. Dr. J. T. Vallandingham served as the first chairman of the Honors Day Committee.

In 1964 the faculty voted to recognize Dr .Vallandingham's personal and professional commitment to the highest academic standard by naming the Scholastic Honor Society for him.[16]

HONORARY DEGREE BESTOWED

Mr. J. B. Gatliff, Sr., of Williamsburg was chosen as the first person to be awarded an honorary degree by Cumberland College after it regained its senior college status. He was awarded the Doctor of Laws degree at Commencement exercises held on 30 May 1966. Mr. Gatliff, who served on the Board of Trustees from November 1918 through November 1964, was chairman of the Board from 30 May 1931 until the expiration of his term in 1964. The awarding of the Doctor of Laws degree was given in recognition of his liberal contribution of time and money to the College, his outstanding contribution in the transition period from junior to senior college status, and his outstanding leadership of the College.[17]

TERRY FORCHT

In the 1930's a good number of acres of land had been given to the College. In 1969 this land was offered by the College on option to the United States Forestry Service for $50.00 an acre. This seemed to be a very reasonable offer at the time, but time changes things.

By 1972 the Forestry Service still had not exercised the option. At this important point in the College's history, Terry Forcht, legal counsel for the College, was able to persuade the Forestry Service to forego its option to purchase the land. Forcht argued that with the passing of time, the property value had appreciated in excess of the value placed upon it some years before by the trustees when granting the option. He brilliantly argued that with the passing of time, in fact an undue amount of time, the land value exceeded what was offered, particularly in light of the Forestry Service taking undue time to survey the land.

---

[16] Membership in the J. T. Vallandingham Scholastic Honor Society continues to be the most prestigious scholastic honor bestowed upon a student at Cumberland College. The requirements for membership are stringent. For a listing of students inducted into the Society since 1961, see Appendix X.

[17] Over the College's one-hundred years of service very few honorary degrees have been awarded, an average of only one degree for every two years of the College's history. For a complete listing of the honorary degree recipients, see Appendix XI.

A PHONE CALL FROM THE WHITE HOUSE

President Boswell wrote a letter to the President of the United States Gerald Ford showing how Cumberland's retention of the land would be of greater value to the people of this mountain region than would the government's possession of the land and asking that the College be allowed to retain the land. Boswell received a call from the White House acknowledging receipt of the letter and stating that the matter would be investigated.

As a result of Forcht's efforts, in particular, and Dr. Boswell's efforts, in general, the option was returned to the College with the agreement that the College would pay the surveying costs incurred by the Forestry Service. The College gladly did so, and as a consequence, Cumberland has enjoyed some income from timber and royalties while maintaining the property which should continue to be of value to the College as it seeks to serve deserving students of limited financial means.[18]

ROTC PROGRAM

Dr. Boswell, in concert with James Crisp (a Cumberland professor and Military Chaplain), announced in 1972 that an ROTC program would begin on the College's campus with the 1973 academic year. This unit would be a branch of the program at Eastern Kentucky University. (Today Cumberland's ROTC program enrolls more students than any other private college's program in the state.)

NURSING PROGRAM

After a thorough study of the need for trained nurses in this area, Cumberland, in 1973, instituted a nurses' training program. The study revealed that nationwide there were 353 registered nurses for every 100,000 people. In our area, however, there were only 128 registered nurses for every 100,000 people. Nationwide there was one medical doctor for every 1,700 people, but in our area there was only one medical doctor for every 3,500 to 4,000 people. There was definitely a scarcity of health professionals in the area.

Two people must be mentioned in particular when speaking about the College's efforts to improve the shortage of health professionals in the Appalachian area: Dr. Jerry C. Davis and Dr. Teresa Sharp, both of whom contributed significantly in their own unique ways.[19]

---

[18] Cumberland College, Board of Trustees, *Minutes,* 14 January 1969; 7 July 1970; 13 July 1972; 26 September 1972; 15 January 1974.

[19] Dr. Jerry Davis earned his Doctor of Philosophy degree from Ohio State University. Dr. Teresa Sharp earned her Doctor of Philosophy degree from the University of Tennessee.

Dr. Jerry C. Davis, now president of Alice Lloyd College, served as professor of biology, as vice-president for development for a time, and would have to be considered the "Father of the Cumberland College Associate Degree in Nursing Program."[20]

Dr. Teresa Sharp assisted Dr. Davis in implementing the nursing program which accomplished much and did tremendous good. With the passing of time, however, and because of changing requirements, the associate degree in nursing was phased out and transformed into a two-plus-two baccalaureate arrangement with Eastern Kentucky University, a program very similar to the three-plus-two engineering program which the College has had with the University of Kentucky. Each year several students take their first two or three years at Cumberland and then complete the appropriate degree at the respective university in engineering or nursing. Large numbers go on to medical, dental, pharmacy, and graduate school after completing their undergraduate study.

HONORED PROFESSOR AWARD AND SERVICE AWARD

In 1976 the Honors Day committee, supported by the faculty of Cumberland College and feeling a need to honor one of their colleagues, approached Dr. Boswell concerning the possibility of establishing an Honored Professor Award. Criteria were established and the award was put into place. In 1983 a Service Award was instituted to recognize an honored member of the staff. Both awards are presented during the annual Honors Day Convocation.[21]

THE OPEN DOOR POLICY

The "open door" policy was a distinctive part of Boswell's administration. Of the policy Boswell said, "Sometimes I feel that establishing the open door policy has been very wise, and other times I feel that it hasn't been so wise." Then he elaborated on the policy:

> I often use time and energy that could be used in promoting the College but as I look back, I wouldn't have it any other way. At times there is business that needs to be attended to, but I see students instead. The good Lord always affords me the time to get my work done. There were times I was

---

[20] Dr. Davis should also be recognized for his fund raising ability which proved beneficial to Cumberland College and now to Alice Lloyd College where he serves as president.

[21] For a complete listing of the recipients of the Honored Professor Award and the Staff Service Award, see Appendix XII.

very tired and busy, but I was always willing to attend to the needs of the people. How can I strive for less?

At times there are students in all sorts of trouble who come to me, and once there was a girl who was so homesick that she sat in my office for almost an hour and cried. We put her on the phone and let her talk to her parents and family. This isn't standard practice but that girl was really in a bad way. She made it through all four years.[22]

Over the years many stories have been told by the students concerning the caring compassion and love shown by Dr. Boswell.

I'LL GO HOME WITH YOU

The College has what is known as a discipline committee composed of various members of the faculty and staff. The purpose of the committee is, as the name implies, to discipline. Discipline might take the form of a fine, probation, or even dismissal. In one case a student had broken a rule severely enough to be sent home. He knew that this would mean facing his parents with an explanation. Following the discipline committee meeting, the student followed Dr. Boswell to his office and told him that he was afraid to go home. Boswell replied, "Son, if you'll wait until morning, I'll go home with you."

POOR DOG

Some years ago President Boswell and one of the College's staff members were on their way to attend an out-of-town meeting. As they went along, the conversation was enlivened by Dr. Boswell relating stories from the College's history, happenings in his own life, or jokes. Boswell, seeing a dead dog lying on the roadside, and hardly without a break in the conversation but with obvious pathos in his voice, said, "Poor dog."

Probably few dead dogs have ever had such a short eulogy delivered over them, revealing such a caring personality in so few words.

DISTINCTIVE TRAITS

Many faculty, staff, students, and others have often commented on the distinctive traits of President Boswell. Once a staff member, in speaking of these traits, noted that he had never seen Dr. Boswell embarrass a student and that he truly lived the Christian ethic and philosophy and instilled such in the faculty as well as the students.

THE ELDER STATESMAN OF RUNNING

Someone has called Dr. Boswell "The Elder Statesman of Running." His life-

---

[22] James M. Boswell, Interview, 24 November 1980.

long interest in athletics has carried over as a large part of his life-style. Up until 1962 Boswell exercised two or three times a week in the gymnasium, but beginning in the fall of 1962, he increased his program of exercise, running at least five miles a day in the gymnasium. Even now he continues to run, but his chief form of exercise is walking three or four miles a day.

Boswell practices the philosophy that ''running may not be for everyone, but if it isn't, walking should be . . . . I do not know if running makes a person live longer, but running will certainly make life more enjoyable.''[23]

HIGH ESTEEM

President Boswell's name has become common-place at Cumberland College and in Williamsburg: the Boswell Art Gallery, the Boswell Tip-off Tournament, the Boswell 10K Run, Boswell Avenue, Boswell Park, and the Boswell Campus Center. Boswell had nothing to do with the naming of these places or events; the names were chosen as a sign of the esteem with which he is held.

CITY SCHOOL PROPERTY OFFERED

The Williamsburg city school system, in the planning process of constructing a new school building, made known its interest in selling to the College its old property and buildings, adjacent to the College's campus. At a special called meeting on 19 March 1980, the Board voted to offer the school system $700,000 for the property and buildings.[24] At a meeting of the Williamsburg School Board on 24 March 1980, the offer was accepted subject to agreement of details by both parties.[25]

---

[23] *Ibid.*

THE STREAKER

The following story appears in the Cumberland College Woman's Club cookbook, *A Taste of Cumberland College.*

''The 1970's were a time of invention and enterprise, and thus the streaker came into being! There had been one incident of streaking on campus already. Henry Morgan, Dean of Men at that time, reported to President Boswell that word was out that another streaking was in the works. At the appointed time, Dr. Boswell, Henry Morgan and several other faculty members were waiting across from Johnson Hall for the 'Grand Appearance.' A car slowed up, and suddenly there were two streakers — dressed casually with merely a grocery sack over their heads. As they raced across the campus, Dean Morgan and President Boswell took off after the culprits. One got away, but Mr. Morgan was able to tackle the other. By the following morning, the story had changed drastically. The tale was that Dr. Boswell himself had tackled the culprit, and after tossing him into a bush, had proclaimed that the indecently clad young man would not move until the authorities had arrived! It does make a better story that way, doesn't it!''

[24] Cumberland College, Board of Trustees, *Minutes,* 19 March 1980.

[25] Actually the author had met with Superintendent J.B. Mountjoy previously. Fortunately the donors to the College's business building project had allowed the College to use their gifts to acquire the city school property in which the business department would be domiciled. This was an answer to prayer for everyone.

TRIBUTES

As Dr. Boswell's presidency was drawing to a close, several occasions were chosen on which to pay tribute to his accomplishments over the period of some thirty-five years.

During the College's Homecoming celebration in November 1979, a "This Is Your Life" program was held for Dr. and Mrs. Boswell.[26]

---

[26] Mr. David Davies, class of 1955, served as Master of Ceremonies. Here are some excerpts from that program.

Arloe W. Mayne, Vice-president of the Ashland Oil Company, member of the class of 1948:
"I think it is fair to say that without his efforts many people, especially those from the Appalachian area, would never have been able to obtain higher education and the opportunities those studies provided. To paraphrase Winston Churchill's famous observation during the dark days of World War II, it is probable that never in the history of Kentucky has one man done so much, so well, for so many, as Dr. Boswell has done for Cumberland and its students during his tenure as president."

Jean Ritchie, folk singer and artist, member of the class of 1944:
"Well, I have just been going through my college souvenirs . . . and came across a snapshot of a young man standing on the gym steps eating an apple, carefree, handsome, smiling, with a little shyness about the eyes. No wonder all we girls had a crush on you and the boys looked on you as their favorite big brother . . . . And I hear that has been going on through all the years since, just as it should have! We all loved you and respected you and went to you for help, for advice, for the joy of your company. That goes for Mrs. Boswell, too."

The Honorable Eugene Siler, United States Congressman, member of the class of 1920, and long-time friend:
"Dr. Boswell, I was present at the Board of Trustees meeting when you were hired to be Cumberland's President. You were a country boy just out of the Navy, so you had a mixture of both hayseed and salt water about your person. I voted for you, we all did in fact, but probably entertained a few lingering doubts about you. You never did thank me for helping you to slide into this job you have held for one-third of a century . . . . Anchors aweigh, Dr. Boswell, you old salt! But don't go too far from us."

David Huff, Trustee of Cumberland College, member of the class of 1953:
"In the 1950's the popular fad at colleges around the country was a small mischievous act called a 'panty raid.' Well, Cumberland students didn't want to feel left out, so they naturally decided to join in the fun . . . . Dr. Boswell got wind of the activity and called a meeting of all men on campus and made it quite plain that there would be no 'panty raid' on Cumberland's campus. The first boy caught in a woman's dormitory would be expelled with not even a trial or disciplinary action to be considered. We had enough respect for this 'mean and hard President' that not one of us took a chance on testing his word."

Bert T. Combs, Governor of Kentucky, member of the class of 1930:
". . . You always make your speeches very personal. You would say that Cumberland was your life and you would be a happy man if someone would like to share in making more of your dream for the school become possible."

William Boswell, brother of Dr. Boswell:
"Much of the early education that prepared him for his position here was gained from sitting around an old-fashioned pot-bellied stove in the country store, listening to the words of wisdom that fell from the lips of the sages of the community who assembled there early every evening to discuss the problems of the world, or at least the ones they knew about. This education was supplemented by attending a one-room school taught by an old-maid school teacher. Growing up in the country was not all together disagreeable. There was always time to play baseball, ride horses, swim in the summer, sleigh ride and ice skate in the winter. We even existed without radio, television, telephones, or electric lights for the early parts of our lives.

. . . Jim and I were almost grown before we realized that the chicken was made up of anything but backs and wings because that was all that was left when we got to the table.

This could go on and on, but it is time to say to my younger brother, congratulations on a job well done and a life well lived.''

Another such occasion was the Cumberland College Commencement in May 1980, when both Dr. and Mrs. Boswell were awarded honorary doctorates in recognition of their years of service and commitment to Cumberland College.[27]

On 27 July 1980, the First Baptist Church of Williamsburg, where the Boswells had held membership for almost fifty years, honored the Boswells by declaring the day, "J. M. and Mary Boswell Day."[28]

And on President Boswell's last official day in office, the faculty, staff, and Board of Trustees of Cumberland College honored Dr. and Mrs. Boswell with a candlelight banquet and "Celebration" program.

That they should ever meet seemed so unlikely. She was a city girl, familiar with the sidewalks and skyscrapers of Chicago; he a country boy, acquainted with the hills and hollows of rural Harrison County, Kentucky.

But Mary Susan Dudley and James Malcolm Boswell did meet at Georgetown College, and the partnership that subsequently developed is what we honor here tonight.

By now the facts of Dr. and Mrs. Boswell's lives are generally well known to us all; we know of their pride in their family, of their love for Cumberland College and the region it serves. We know of the growth and progress of the College under their guidance. Their hard work, dedication and foresight we have all witnessed.

But what we honor most this evening of July 31, 1980, is the humanity of two people whose lives have so naturally coincided with the goals of Christian education, two good people whose many acts of kindness and generosity have endeared them to an entire region.

We are grateful that two people met at a college in Kentucky long ago and that meeting greatly touched our lives.[29]

HE CASTS A SHADOW

Because of James M. Boswell's efforts and those of others, thousands

---

[27] Mrs. Boswell was awarded the Doctor of Modern Languages degree, and Dr. Boswell was awarded the Doctor of Humane Letters degree.

[28] Dr. Boswell had been an active deacon at the First Baptist Church for forty years. He had served in many capacities, including trustee, Sunday School director, Sunday School teacher, stewardship chairman, and pulpit supply. Additionally, he served for eight years, from 1976 to 1984, as a member of the Education Commission of the Southern Baptist Convention.

Mrs. Boswell served her church with loving faithfulness in many ways including: W.M.U. leadership positions, teaching preschoolers in Sunday School, and church hospitality committee.

[29] "A Celebration Honoring Dr. and Mrs. J. M. Boswell," Cumberland College, 31 July 1980, p. 3.

of people are now living constructive and productive lives serving as teachers, medical doctors, dentists, pharmacists, attorneys, scientists, nurses, ministers, missionaries, business men and women, and in an array of other professions.[30]

Ralph Waldo Emerson observed in "Self-Reliance,""An institution is the lengthened shadow of one man . . . ." Of no institution is this observation truer than of Cumberland College under James M. Boswell. Truly James Malcolm Boswell casts a shadow the length and breadth of this beautiful mountain region.

----

[30] At the 1987 meeting of the Education Commission of the Southern Baptist Convention, Dr. James M. Boswell was honored for his very significant contributions to higher educaiton by being chosen to receive the Charles D. Johnson Outstanding Educator Award. Dr. Boswell told this story when receiving the award: "Mr. A.T. Siler always had a cigar in his pocket, wore a rose in his lapel, and carried a cane. One day a gentleman asked Siler why he had a cigar in his pocket since he never smoked, why he had a rose in his lapel since he never smelled it, and why he carried a cane since he never used it for walking? Siler responded that he did these things because they made him feel like somebody." Boswell then remarked that the Education Commission's Outstanding Educator Award made him feel like somebody.

JAMES MALCOLM BOSWELL
Acting President 1946-1947; President 1947-1980

(Photograph from the Cumberland College Collection of a portrait painted by Jack K. Hodgkin)

DR. ANCIL GATLIFF MEMORIAL BUILDING

Before 1950, but specifically in that year, the trustees began to express the feeling of a need for a chapel building. Three sisters, Mrs. N.A. Archer, Mrs. N.B. Perkins, and Mrs. T.E. Mahan, daughters of Dr. and Mrs. Ancil Gatliff, had expressed the wish of giving $50,000 jointly toward the construction of a chapel, classroom, and administration building, provided the building be named the "Dr. Ancil Gatliff Memorial Chapel." The cost of the building, when completed, was around $400,000 and was dedicated on 25 November 1955.

The Trustees in their 15 November 1955 meeting stated in the *Minutes:* "The dedication of this new building will be the final chapter in the story of 'A vision transformed into a reality.' It now stands as a memorial to Dr. Ancil Gatliff, who in 1889 had a vision of the need for a Christian college, where young people in the mountains of Kentucky and neighboring states could be taught 'Vita Abundantior,' more abundant life, and who gave so liberally and sacrificially of his time, talent, and means to make Cumberland College a reality."

The Dr. Ancil Gatliff Memorial Building is a red brick structure with classical columns. Situated on a high hill, it has a tall white tower, which, illuminated at night, is a campus landmark that can be seen for a distance as one approaches the town. In addition to the chapel, the building houses administrative offices and several classrooms.

According to Dr. Boswell, Mr. T.J. Roberts must be given much credit for creating a "nest egg" for this building. Boswell, himself, also solicited gifts to help make the building possible.

(Photograph by Housman Photography)

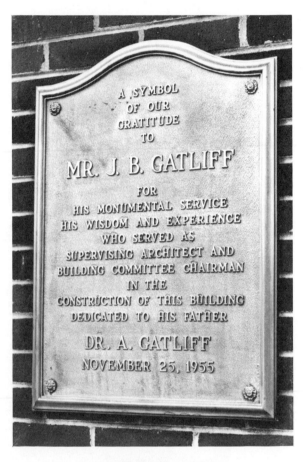

GATLIFF PLAQUE

A plaque at the entrance of the Dr. A. Gatliff Memorial Building pays honor to Mr. J.B. Gatliff, son of Dr. and Mrs. Ancil Gatliff, for his service as supervising architect and building committee chairman in the construction of the building.

(Photograph by Housman Photography)

NORMA JEANNE PERKINS HAGAN

Late in 1957 Mrs. N.B. Perkins indicated her desire to make an initial pledge of $25,000 to the College for the purpose of having a building erected in memory of her daughter Mrs. Norma Jeanne Perkins Hagan, who, with her husband and 46 other passengers, lost their lives in an airplane when it crash landed in the Pacific Ocean en route from San Francisco to Honolulu.

Mrs. Hagan had been a member of the College's Board of Trustees and was the granddaughter of Dr. Ancil Gatliff.

On 20 December 1957, the Executive Committee of the Board voted unanimously to accept the pledge of $25,000 and to erect a library to be known as the Norma Jeanne Perkins Hagan Library as soon as sufficient funds were available to do so.

(Photograph from the Cumberland College Collection)

NORMA JEANNE PERKINS HAGAN MEMORIAL LIBRARY

The Library, located on Walnut Street west of the Gymnasium, is constructed on three levels and houses the College's book collection, offices, receiving and processing areas, the instructional media center, and the computer facilities.

The ground breaking ceremony for the Library was held on 14 October 1959, and the building was first occupied in 1960 and dedicated on 13 May 1961. Thanks to the Steele-Reese Foundation and the Pew Memorial Trusts, the Library has in recent years been modernized and is filled with "state of the art" equipment.

(Photograph by Housman Photography)

THOMAS JEFFERSON ROBERTS
1890-1959

Mr. Thomas Jefferson Roberts, a trustee of Cumberland College from 1936 until his death in 1959, served as treasurer of the College (1942-1959) and as secretary and treasurer of the Board of Trustees (1939-1959). Roberts had served as secretary and treasurer of many coal companies, and since most of the trustees were coal men, they had great confidence in him.

Mr. Roberts was a soft-spoken, tactful man; he did not take credit for the things he did. He was a sound businessman and an advisor to people who had money and authority, yet he was also their friend. His son Gorman Roberts, a Harvard graduate in business, is now a partner at J.J.B. Hilliard and Lyons. Like his father, he is respected by the high and mighty as well as by the common man. A very polite and capable man, Gorman Roberts has also served as a Board member and advisor to the College.

Historically, T.J. Roberts is given the credit by Dr. Boswell as the man who accumulated the "nest egg" for the construction of the Gatliff Building. He held a vision for transferring the College from junior to senior college status. He managed the college's land very well. Respected for his financial genius, his vision still impacts the College today. At the time of his death in 1959, T.J. Roberts was president of the Bank of Williamsburg.

Roberts loved young people, and he felt that Cumberland College was providing a quality Christian education for youngsters who wanted to attend. He was devoted to the College. In May 1960, the trustees decided to name the College's cafeteria as a memorial to Mr. Roberts who had given such faithful and effective service. The building had, in fact, been made possible largely by his efforts and financial genius.

(Photograph from the Cumberland College Collection)

T.J. ROBERTS DINING HALL

The T.J. Roberts Dining Hall is a modern building housing a dining area capable of seating 800, a reception room, and a well-equipped kitchen. With cafeteria style service, around 1,500 people may dine over a two-hour period.

The Roberts Dining Hall, erected in 1958, is named for Mr. T.J. Roberts, who rendered faithful and efficient service to the College. Much thought was given to naming the building for Dr. Creech, the former president, but Mr. Roberts was most deserving, and it was most fitting to have the structure named for him. After all, he had created the "nest egg" for the Gatliff Building and for this building and had successfully guided the College for nearly two decades in its financial affairs.

The Benwood Foundation was also instrumental in assisting with funds for this building.

(Photograph by Housman Photography)

172

E.O. ROBINSON HALL

E.O. Robinson Hall which houses approximately 88 students was completed in 1963. West Hall houses approximately 175 students and was completed in 1965.

These buildings helped to meet the expanding needs of the College. The costs were amortized over time through regular payments.

In 1983 North Hall was given the name E.O. Robinson Hall in honor of Mr. E.O. Robinson and the E.O. Robinson Foundation's past support and continued help for mountain youngsters. Enough good cannot be said about E.O. Robinson, industrial pioneer, philanthropist, and operator of Nowbray Robinson Lumber Company in Eastern Kentucky, 1911-1940, nor of the members of the Foundation's Board including Francis S. Hutchins, former president of Berea College and brother of Robert Maynard Hutchins of the Great Books and the University of Chicago fame, and Lyman V. Ginger, a distinguished educator and statesman.

WEST HALL

(Photographs by Housman Photography)

SCIENCE BUILDING

The biology wing of the Science Building was completed in 1963 and houses eleven classrooms and laboratories, two large storage rooms, and eleven faculty offices. It also contains the Developmental Skills Center.

At the groundbreaking ceremony for the chemistry wing on 8 January 1963, Mr. T.E. Mahan, a trustee and friend of the College, gave a short address telling of the early founders of the College building "on faith." He compared their action with the action of the Board taken for this Building as the trustees had again acted "on faith," not knowing how the money would be raised to pay the construction costs.

The chemistry wing, named in honor of Professor P.R. Jones, was completed in 1968 and houses a total of five lecture rooms, including an amphitheatre which seats 125 people, eight laboratories, eight faculty offices, two storage rooms, three stock rooms, and three utility rooms.

(Photograph by Housman Photography)

RUBY GATLIFF ARCHER HALL

In 1966, a new residence hall was completed to house 172 women students. It was named the Ruby Gatliff Archer Hall as a memorial to Mrs. Archer who had remembered the College through a bequest.

(Photograph by Housman Photography)

RUBY GATLIFF ARCHER
1877-1962

Ruby Gatliff Archer, the wife of Dr. N.A. Archer, was the daughter of Dr. and Mrs. Ancil Gatliff.

Mrs. Archer was the superintendent of the intermediate department of the Sunday School at Williamsburg's First Baptist Church for some twenty-five years. Usually the Young Woman's Auxiliary meetings were held in her beautiful home.

In 1962, Mrs. Archer donated her home, a brick colonial built in 1905 as a replica of the "Kentucky Home" exhibited at the St. Louis, 1904 World's Fair, to the College. Every effort has been made to keep the home as an example of the style, furnishings, and gracious living of the period. The home is the social center of the campus where members of the College's family, town residents, and out-of-town guests are entertained.

(Photograph from *Renfro Revelations,* March 1945)

THE RUBY GATLIFF ARCHER HOME
(Photograph by Housman Photography)

BOSWELL CAMPUS CENTER

The Boswell Campus Center is named in honor of Dr. and Mrs. Boswell "for their dedication and service to the youth of the Mountains."

The Boswell Campus Center opened in February 1972 and was dedicated in November 1972. A challenge grant from the Kresge Foundation provided the leverage to raise the funds for the building.

The Center is located directly across from the Gymnasium. This brick, glass, and cast panel building consists of two full levels and one-half of a third level on the back side. The street level houses a lobby, a complex of offices, a complete kitchen, a large dining area, a conference room, rest rooms, and a space for banquets and private parties. The middle level houses the Post Office, a self-service Book Store, the Student Government offices, rest rooms and a large lounge and recreation area. The third level consists of offices, three all-purpose classrooms and a small chapel.

A plaque on the front of the building bears this inscription, "Plan for the future, persevere through difficulty, be patient and pray."

(Photograph by Housman Photography)

176

THE GEORGE M. ASHER MEMORIAL HALL

The George M. Asher Memorial Hall is a residence hall for women located on Main Street, west of the Ruby Gatliff Archer Memorial Hall. This residence hall housing 156 women was first occupied in the fall of 1976.

Dedication services for the building were held on 12 September 1976. The building was dedicated to the memory of Dr. George M. Asher, a man who was a physician, a surgeon, and a personal friend of the people of southeastern Kentucky for many years. Dr. Asher was vitally concerned with the education of the youth of the mountains and was a benefactor of mankind. Dr. Asher's widow, the wonderful Mrs. Harriet Asher, continues to assist the College even today.

(Photograph by Housman Photography)

DR. GEORGE M. ASHER

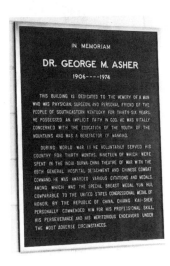

PLAQUE ERECTED IN DORMITORY

(Photograph from the Cumberland College Collection)

THE MARY W. McGAW MUSIC BUILDING

The Mary W. McGaw Music Building was constructed with a gift received from Mr. and Mrs. Foster McGaw, in part. The Booth Ferris Foundation provided the first gift and the incentive to get the campaign underway, and other friends joined in to make this building possible. The building was named in honor of Mrs. McGaw and was first occupied in January 1979.

The 18,000 square-foot facility includes the music office, ten studio offices, two large general music classrooms, a multiple piano-laboratory classroom, an instrumental rehearsal room and opera-musical facility, sixteen practice rooms, a music library, and miscellaneous smaller areas.

(Photograph by Housman Photography)

NICHOLSON-JONES RESIDENCE HALL

This residence hall was acquired by the College in 1959. It has gone by different names since that time, being known as the Sophomore Dormitory or as the Junior-Senior Dormitory.

Since 1982 this building has been known as the Nicholson-Jones Residence Hall. It was dedicated 19 February 1982 in memory of Mrs. Edna Jones Nicholson, Mr. O.T. Nicholson, Miss Lillian Jones, and Mr. and Mrs. George Jones.

(Photograph by Housman Photography)

GRADUATING CLASS, 1961

In May 1961 forty-nine students were graduated. This was Cumberland College's first four-year graduating class since 1918.

(Photograph from the Cumberland College Collection)

ELMER CHARLES MASDEN

Dr. Elmer Charles Masden joined the Cumberland College faculty in 1955 as head of the religion department after serving on the faculty of Carson-Newman College and Bethel College.

Dr. Masden holds the associate degree from Campbellsville College, the bachelor's degree from Georgetown College, and the master's and doctor's degrees from The Southern Baptist Theological Seminary.

When the decision was made to begin the four-year senior college program at Cumberland, Dr. Masden was asked to serve as its coordinator, and in 1961 he was named Academic Dean of the College, a position in which he served well.

On 1 January 1981, Dr. Masden was named Academic Dean Emeritus and senior professor. Since that time he has served as Special Assistant to the President and Director of Special Projects. In this role he conducted a great deal of the research necessary to begin the graduate program as well as the compilation of data for this book.

(Photograph by Housman Photography)

T. ELMER AND UNA GATLIFF MAHAN

T. Elmer Mahan (1891-1976) and Una Gatliff Mahan (1892-1983) were generous benefactors of Cumberland College.

In 1967 Mr. Mahan was awarded the honorary Doctor of Laws degree by the College in recognition of his faithful service as a member of the Board of Trustees (1949-1970), Chairman of the Board of Trustees, and in appreciation of his valuable service as the College's attorney.

A graduate of the Williamsburg Institute and the University of Kentucky Law School, Mahan provided legal counsel for the College without pay for more than thirty years.

Mr. Mahan was very actively involved in Williamsburg's First Baptist Church where he served as chairman of the Trustees, chairman of the Finance and Personnel Committee, and superintendent of the Sunday School. He also served as a charter member of the Southeastern Kentucky Baptist Hospital; director of the Bank of Williamsburg; founder of the Williamsburg Realty Company, vice-president of Gatliff Coal Company, and charter member of the Williamsburg Rotary Club.

Una Gatliff Mahan was the last surviving daughter of Dr. and Mrs. Ancil Gatliff. A graduate of the Williamsburg Institute, Mrs. Mahan was a strong supporter of the College and actively involved in her home, church, and community. Her home and its gardens were a "showplace." She served for many years as president of her Sunday School class which was named for her mother Florida Moss Gatliff. She worked to beautify Williamsburg and even purchased Christmas decorations for the town.

Both Mr. and Mrs. Mahan were generous contributors to the College's building funds and scholarship funds. Following Mr. Mahan's death, Mrs. Mahan established in his memory the T.E. Mahan Endowed Scholarship Fund for pre-law students.

Many of Cumberland's alumni remember Mr. and Mrs. Mahan's concern and generosity toward the Kentucky mountain youth shown time and time again through the years.

(Photograph from the Cumberland College Collection)

ARLOE MAYNE

Arloe Mayne, a native of Whitley County, was graduated from Cumberland College in 1948 and from the University of Kentucky College of Law in 1951, earning the Doctor of Jurisprudence degree. In that same year he was employed as a staff lawyer for Ashland Oil and Refining Company (now Ashland Oil, Inc.) and remained with this company until his retirement in 1981, advancing from staff lawyer to administrative vice president and general counsel with supervisory responsibilities for Ashland's Law, Real Estate, Insurance, Tax, Corporate Secretary, Patent and Trademark Departments. Since retiring Dr. Mayne has been in the general practice of law in Ashland, Kentucky.

(Photograph courtesy of Mr. Mayne)

MYRTLE NICHOLSON

In 1959 following the death of Mr. T.J. Roberts, Mrs. Myrtle Nicholson became the College's Treasurer, a position she held until her retirement. Mrs. Nicholson had served as secretary of the College from 1925 until 1959 and had worked under the guidance of Mr. Roberts.

Myrtle Nicholson was a very capable employee who was extremely dedicated to the College.

(Photograph from the Cumberland College Collection)

MR. TERRY FORCHT

Terry Forcht has his own law office in Corbin, Kentucky, and has provided excellent legal advice and representation for the College on numerous occasions.

(Photograph courtesy of Ted Forcht, Mr. Forcht's son)

RICHARD D. SANBORN
President and Chief Executive Officer
CSX Railway

The College is deeply indebted to Mr. Sanborn and the CSX Railway for their support of the College and its programs.

(Photograph from the Cumberland College Collection)

CHAPTER 6
A MATURING INSTITUTION

OUR TIME IN HISTORY

Cumberland is a maturing institution. Looking back over the College's history, one finds that much credit must be given to the College's faculty, staff, trustees, foundations, corporations, and other friends, not to mention the very significant role the Convention has played in making Cumberland College all it is today. Too much good cannot be said about all the people who have served in leadership positions in the past.

The author followed a man who had served admirably as president for well over a quarter of a century. With the passing of time, however, had come a need to reorganize the College since the institution had grown arithmetically and the budget geometrically over the past quarter of a century. Moreover, with the advent of the microchip, the College had to move from the file cabinet to the cathode ray tube.

On 1 August 1980, the author became president of Cumberland College,[1] standing on the shoulders of all those past presidents, former and current administrators, faculty, staff, students, trustees, and other friends. Today I stand in awe of the presidency. I'm not awed by it, but I stand in awe of it and do all in my power to respect the position and maintain the dignity which is in keeping with the office. I have to chuckle every morning on my way to work to think that someone like me could find himself in such a lofty position. Only in America would this be possible. Only in this great land of the free is it possible for a person to go as high as his or her dreams and abilities and hard work, accompanied by the help of others, will take him. No one does much alone. Needless to say, I'm thankful for all the help I've received and continue to receive along this pilgrimage here below. My goal is to have the College take advantage of its opportunities without becoming opportunistic.

---

[1] The inauguration was held in May 1981 with the following remarks commonly attributed to P.T. Barnum being made:
"Make no little plans. They have no magic to stir men's soul and probably themselves will not be realized. Make big plans: aim high in hope and work, remembering that a noble, logical diagram once recorded will never die, but long after we are gone will be a living thing, asserting itself with ever-growing insistency. Remember that our sons and grandsons are going to do things that would stagger us. Let your watchword be order and your beacon beauty."

Other than being deeply indebted to generous donors, the author shall always be indebted to an array of mentors who've helped along life's way. First, I want to recognize Mr. Richard Fuson, "The Scholar," who was truly a genius, who entered Harvard at the age of fourteen, who spoke several languages, and who took a personal interest in me and encouraged me in both debate and public speaking as well as in the academic disciplines. The second person I should recognize is Dr. Richard Palmer, former

A BURNING DESIRE

As president I have one request and that is to be spared the disappointment of seeing the great opportunities I missed because I lacked the faith to try. "Of all the saddest words from the tongues of men is Oh, what might have been." Today I feel a sense of urgency to promote this wonderful and worthy cause called Cumberland College.

Frankly, the transition in leadership from the previous administration to the present has been smooth and has preserved continuity, interweaving continuity and change. This is in no little way true, thanks to our marvelous administrative staff like Sue Wake, Joe Early, George Ramey, John Duke, Emma McPherson, Topper Criscillis, Jack Stanfill, Doyle Gilbert, Jim Byrge, and Kenneth Shaw, to name a few, who work tirelessly and who are loyal and devoted. There are others too numerous to list here.

As was true in the past, the concern for the curricula, the faculty, and the students is as paramount as it ever has been. Moreover, no one needs to blush when sharing their convictions. We are unapologetic about the One who taught us to love our neighbor as ourselves, even as difficult as that might be, given our human frailties and failures. Today the campus mood is congenial and wholesome if not downright optimistic.

DEDICATED FOLKS

The path to progress has never been easy at Cumberland nor will it ever be. Yet, today as in the past, Cumberland College relies heavily on a dedicated faculty and staff. Tenaciously the College, enduring a lack of facilities and endowment while serving deserving youngsters, has held on to that dream of Christian higher educational opportunities, primarily, but not exclusively for mountain youngsters. Cumberland College runs smoothly with responsibility delegated to responsible people.[2] Our

---

president of Morningside College, Westminster College, and Scarritt College and vice president of Berea College. He taught me the fine craft of institutional development. The third person is Harry Kallas, former president of Lamar University, who taught me worlds of information about development. The fourth group is constituted of trustees who've proven their devotion through thick and thin and who have had confidence in me, especially Mr. David Huff. The fifth and sixth persons are Richard Gaylord Briley and Jerry Huntsinger, both of whom I've admired from afar for years. Dr. J.M. Boswell must be recognized, for it was he who gave me the opportunity to serve this institution known as Cumberland College. Finally, I must mention Mrs. Grover Hermann and Mr. O. Wayne Rollins, both of whom have made a profound impact on Cumberland College. There are others, too numerous to mention.

[2] Talented and capable, our administrative staff aids me immensely. What's more, we seek never to lose our sense of humor. With the coming of the new administration, Mrs. Sue Wake was promoted from secretary for teacher education to administrative assistant to the president and today effectively handles much of the College's development and administrative activities; Dr. Joe Early was promoted from head of the mathematics department to academic dean and has compacted and streamlined the curriculum; Dr. George Ramey was asked to remain as business manager and treasurer and has served as general contractor, planning and drawing specifications for remodeling Mahan Hall, the gymnasium, and the Gray Brick building; Dr. John Duke, chairman of the education department also serves as dean of student services; Miss Emma McPherson was promoted from dean of women

College's Board of Trustees and former trustees[3] are men and women of complete integrity and serve as a bedrock of strength.

This is no thumbs under the suspenders, gather around the cracker barrel, "Ah shucks, boys," operation. No, this is serious business. This College requires more of its faculty than merely being "Good ol' boys," and "Good ol' girls." One person said, "Doggone it, there are right nice folks at the College." Yes, we do work together to achieve our common objective, and we have a clear and crisp vision of what we hope to accomplish in the lives of our youngsters. So, the trustees are just as concerned about academics and the erosion of purchasing power as is anyone else. Today, as in the past, Cumberland's faculty[4] is overworked, carrying exceedingly heavy academic loads while fulfilling heavy committee, counseling, and advising assignments. Additionally, many faculty and staff reach out assisting in the region's high schools and grade schools and assisting in the communities. Cumberland's faculty genuinely cares and gives exceptional time and talent to their chosen profession. The College is bound together by strong threads of commitment. Most faculty and staff wear many hats, giving that extra time and effort which makes all the difference.

A PURPOSE INFINITELY HIGHER THAN SELF-PROMOTION

The faculty are mature scholars, almost half of whom have the earned doctorate from leading universities throughout the nation. They're bright, they're experienced, and most importantly, they're willing to give whatever help is needed. Salaries have never been high, and they probably will never be. But in those qualities that count — in integrity, in academic preparation, in commitment, and in enthusiasm, we'll pit our seasoned faculty and grand student body against the best. You can't have a great college without great teachers, and our professors are exceedingly capable. They live and work for a purpose infinitely higher than self-promotion.

---

to dean of students; Dr. Michael Colegrove was promoted to dean of records and registrar; Mr. Topper Criscillis was promoted to dean of admissions; Mr. Jack Stanfill remains as our director of financial aid; Mr. Kenneth Shaw remains as our director of buildings and grounds; Dr. Robert Schoonover heads our graduate program; Mr. Doyle Gilbert supervises our campus grill and oversees the College's land development; Dr. John Broome works tenaciously as coordinator of advising as well as serving as a faculty member; Mr. Jim Byrge continues as our cafeteria director and chef; Mr. Henry Morgan, formerly dean of men, is now athletic director; Miss Linda Carter was named dean of women; and Mr. Floyd Stroud remains as our dean of men. The list could go on and on. Many deserve recognition; you know who you are.

Others who have worked in administration and/or continue to work are Mr. Richard Brashear, in the area of financial aid; Mr. H. G. Pratt, Mr. Bill Freeman, Mr. Ray Lipps, Mr. Ray Kelly, Mr. Ralph Hopkins, Dr. Oline Carmical, and Dr. Mike Colegrove in the area of student recruitment; Mr. Russell Bridges, Mr. John Heneisen, Mr. John Clinton, Dr. John Lancaster, Mr. Fred Conatser, Mr. Ron Ball, Mr. Maynard Head, Miss Janie Carter, and Mrs. Kay Manning, in the area of development.

[3] For a complete listing of the College's Board of Trustees, see Appendix I.

[4] For a complete listing of the faculty from 1889 to the present and the current support staff, see Appendix IV.

PURITY OF PURPOSE

The administration and the staff, like the faculty, work long hours. The days begin early in the morning and end late at night. But these are exceedingly rewarding days. The College's employees are here in the mountains because of dedication to a cause, and they work together in a friendly, wholesome atmosphere. The College emphasizes individual attention while offering diverse learning experiences. There are no unions, no demonstrations, and little or no self-aggrandizement. The faculty is professional and not amateurish. The academic work will stand up anywhere.

FRIENDS, FUNDS, AND FRESHMEN

Since our College was founded to serve what one man dubbed as "Hillbilly" youth, we've rolled up our sleeves and gone to work. Our College is concerned about the little guy, the underdog, the down-and-outer, as well as the bright and the beautiful, the National Merit Scholars, and the premedical students. We don't make fun of our mountain youngsters' music, dress, or manner of speaking, although we do make every effort to insure that spoken as well as written English is handled correctly.[5]

---

[5] Today Appalachia is commonly popularized by such folklore as "The Beverly Hillbillies," "The Dukes of Hazzard," Daisy Mae and Lil' Abner, Dog Patch, the Hatfields and the McCoys, horse racing, Sergeant York, Loretta Lynn's *Coal Miner's Daughter, The Dollmaker,* Tennessee Ernie Ford's "You load 16 tons and what do you get, another day older and deeper in debt," and of course, Harland Sanders' Kentucky Fried Chicken, which began in nearby Corbin, Kentucky.

In this fairyland of waterfalls, forests, and rivers, folklore images are brought to our minds. Our region gives rise to all the folkways and mores including the spit and whittle clubs, quilt making, bootlegging, dulcimer playing, pottery making, and other forms of crafts. Appalachia is rich in its tapestry with its quilts, dulcimers, and crafts. Yet, we're not all barefoot. The super highways crisscrossing Appalachia like ribbons on a beautifully wrapped package are changing the area. Television and radio make our world smaller.

LOG TRUCKING AND COON HUNTING, NOT SPOT AND JANE

The "hillbilly" has been stereotyped, laughed at, and ridiculed as some have denigrated everyone who hasn't joined the pilgrimage to middle class values. But mountaineers are among those who reject the melting pot theory while turning to their historical roots as a source of pride. Dr. Cratis Williams, a Cumberland alumnus, said, "The older I get the prouder I am that I was born the son of poor mountain people who taught me not to lie, cheat or steal and to give a day's work for a day's pay." Another alumnus, Dr. Tom Cloer, who teaches at Furman University, says that our youngsters should be given books on log trucking and the like when they are first learning to read; they can relate to these topics better than they can to the traditional middle class ideas of Spot and Jane. Log trucking and coon hunting — these are things that have some significance to the Appalachian youngsters.

The story, reportedly true, is told about a youngster in a mountain high school who had trouble staying awake during class. Upon investigation the teacher found he had been out almost every night coon hunting.

The following information is from Robert McCrum, William Cran and Robert McNeil, *The Story of English* (New York: Viking Penguin Inc., 1986), pp. 159-1960. Reprinted by permission of Viking Penguin, Inc.

"Professor Cratis Williams, who has been called 'the father of Appalachian studies' and has devoted years to a study of the speech in that region, considers that the Appalachian people are 'the best storytellers in the world', a tradition he attributes to their Scottish past.

'The Appalachian people love stories. Even when they're in a hurry, they'll stop to hear stories. Children and old people too, when they're relaxed, love to hear long stories . . . . The best stories in the Appalachian tradition are told in the dialect.'

According to Williams, the talk of these hills is now a jumble of Scots-Irish, English and German. But from the

Our teachers don't humiliate youngsters by making disparaging remarks about our mountain culture or our drawl. Here it is all right to be from Appalachia and to be proud of it. What's more, we promote education in a Christian context.[6] While Cumberland can't meet all the needs, it does meet many and seeks to inculcate lasting values. We've never blushed about our faith nor have we trivialized our beliefs by going out of our way to be inoffensive to people of other persuasions. We're courteous but unapologetic about our values though we are trying not to be shallow or simplistic in a world of ambiguity.

THERE ARE NO LITTLE PEOPLE HERE: EVERYONE IS IMPORTANT

Frankly, enough credit cannot be given to those who serve as the backbone of this College, the faculty, staff, and in particular, the hourly employees,[7] and the work-

---

beginning, the Scots-Irish in the Appalachians were especially noted for their speech. In the advertisements of the time, their speech was called 'broad', as distinct from the Irish who spoke with 'the Brogue on his Tongue'. English words borrowed into Pennsylvania German often show archaic forms which could have come from the Scots-Irish; *chaw* for 'chew', *ingine* for 'engine' and *picter* for 'picture'. Writers of the time knew what they were describing. The Reverend Jonathan Boucher, writing in the 1800s, says that it was one of the four distinctive 'dialects' remaining in the States — 'the Scotch-Irish, as it used to be called, in some of the back settlers of the Middle States'.

Many examples of Scots-Irish usage prevail to this day — words like *bonny-clabber* for curdled sour milk (an anglicization of the Irish Gaelic *bainne clabair*) and *flannel-cake* for a thin wheat cake. *Sook, sookie,* or *sook cow* is the local cry farmers use to summon the herd and comes from the Old English *sucan* meaning 'to suck'. The famous Southern *you-all* is a Scots-Irish translation of the plural *yous*. The use of *all* in this context, and in contexts like *who-all was there?* and *tell me, what-all you did?*, is typical both of Ulster and of the (largely southern) states of America.

Most famous of all, perhaps, is the Scots-Irish use of the word *cabin* to refer to the log houses of the frontier. *Log cabin* is first recorded in 1770 referring to the buildings of Virginia, and it is clear that the Scots-Irish, who lived in such buildings (borrowing the design from the German Americans), spread both the name and the building method, until the term entered American folklore.

Cratis Williams says that the distinctive marks of contemporary Appalachian English are clear enough. The word 'there' becomes *tharr*, 'bear' becomes *barr,* and 'hair' is *herr*.

'No one says *hair* the way we do. That's because of the strong influence of the *r* . . . Instead of saying *hair* or *hayre* as other Americans would do, we say *herr* . . . We continue to omit the final *g*. Strictly speaking, we don't really omit it, we never did get around to putting it on. And we continue to use the Middle English *a-* in front of the *ing* words. So we go *a-huntin'* and *a-fishin'* . . . Outsiders are sometimes impressed by hearing us say *Hit* for *it* . . . *Hit* and *it* can both appear in the same sentence. If the word is stressed, its *hit*. If it's not stressed, then it's *it*. One would never say, "I've never heard of *hit*." One would say, "I've never heard of it. *Hit's* something new to me." ' "

SPECIAL PURPOSE COLLEGE

There remains a story to be told about a special purpose college nestled here in the mountains of eastern Kentucky. Today Cumberland College is located in and serving the Fifth Congressional District of eastern Kentucky, one of the lowest per capita income areas of any District in the country. And the College is doing something to try to improve the socio-economic conditions of the area; in the 1985-1986 academic year alone 1,281 students from this area attended Cumberland College, receiving totally more than $3,767,449 in financial aid. Without this assistance, many of these youngsters could not have attended college anywhere and would have lost the opportunity to gain a college education.

[6] The Campus Ministries program sponsors or co-sponsors the following activities: drama and puppet teams, BSU, BSU choir, Love-In-Action, children's ministry, Mountain Outreach, jail ministry, elderly ministry, and mission programs. Additionally, an advisory board composed of ministers and laymen from the surrounding states meets annually on the College's campus to make suggestions and provide guidance for the College. Moreover, one of the highlights of the 1986 year was the publication of Dr. Franklin Owen's book, *The Preacher Remembers: Slightly Soiled Saints.*

[7] Perhaps my proudest moment was when we offered retirement benefits, as precious little as they are, to those who had little

study students, as well as the student spouses, who've worked endlessly and tirelessly at minimum wage doing all of those little jobs which have such a big impact on the College as a whole. Here in the mountains there's no time for an Ivory tower philosophy. In the area of support staff it is largely the minimum wage folks and the workstudy students who prepare and serve the food, maintain the campus, stuff the envelopes, type the letters, and do whatever else is necessary to get the job done. The College is small enough to provide attention but large enough to offer diverse learning experiences.

WE'RE AFTER MORE THAN BUCKS AND BODIES

The College educates the whole person — mind, body, and soul. This liberal arts College offers quality education at affordable prices. Here no professor will snub you, condescend to you, or ridicule you. We do a thorough screening on the faculty we bring to the campus, and this is no inconsequential matter.

GRACE, GRIT, AND GREENBACKS

The College's employees have joined in time and time again to make sacrificial gifts and pledges toward construction projects as well as significant contributions to a quality academic program and a caring atmosphere. It all boils down to grace, grit, and greenbacks.

A JUGGLING ACT

As you can imagine, running a college these days is a real juggling act. Keeping enrollments up, deficits down, admissions standards up, minimum standards down, trying to conserve energy while meeting payroll as well as scholarship and workship needs is no easy task. Somehow one must conserve costs while trying to give the faculty appropriate raises. It's not an easy juggling act, but it's an exceedingly worthwhile enterprise even though most of the higher educational institutions face declining demographics, rising costs, and rising public expectations.

PEOPLE — THAT'S CUMBERLAND'S PURPOSE

Cumberland College has always been concerned first and foremost with people. Our goal is to help each student grow intellectually, physically, and spiritually for the development of the mind, body, and soul. And if students want to see me, all they do is make an appointment, and I see them. It's as simple as that. I've never believed in a high degree of bureaucracy. I believe in keeping things as simple as

---

or none and expanded other benefits to all employees.

It was also a memorable occasion when we distributed to each faculty and staff member an official Policies and Procedures Manual as well as a Benefits Handbook several years ago. These were the first publications of this kind to be distributed to our employees.

possible without a lot of expensive overhead and fancy titles. In fact, I give the students and their parents my home telephone number as the new semester begins each fall, and I want them to call if they need me. You see, this philosophy is important here in the mountains in order to meet needs and to keep things running smoothly. Cumberland is more concerned with people than mere programs or projects. People — that's Cumberland's purpose. We're more concerned about students than cold impersonal statistics. After all, it's the students, staff, faculty, trustees, and other friends, not the buildings, which make this place go. People serving people — that's what's important.

At Cumberland I have noticed little, if any, institutional drift. Faith in God, wholesome values, the sanctity of the family, honesty, the work ethic, neighbor helping neighbor, and a day's work for a day's pay — that's what we're seeking to teach along with our rigorous academic curriculum and its value orientation.

COMMUNITY INVOLVEMENT:
THIS IS NO DOG PATCH, U.S.A.

Cumberland is important to this community[8] and region in other ways besides providing educational opportunities for training its future leaders.

---

[8] Let's say something good about Williamsburg and Cumberland College; there's a lot of good we can say! We appreciate the people of Williamsburg. Williamsburg and Cumberland College are partners in progress. We want to beautify the area. This is not Dog Patch, U.S.A. People want things nice and neat and clean. At Cumberland we're just trying to be good neighbors:

** We are enhancing Main Street and other areas around town by removing old, rickity buildings. This also improves the value of adjacent property. The property on Main Street adjacent to Asher Hall, for instance, will provide more parking space for those who attend Main Street Baptist Church. Reverend Jerry Lowrie has done such a good job there that there isn't enough parking space. And because our lots are fairly empty on weekends, the church's members are welcome to use them. The property across from Lester's Barber Shop on Main Street is a great place for children to play if under supervision. It's crisp and refreshing to see clean, neat, wholesome children running and playing and their parents watching, all on College property. Our College youngsters can also play on this lot.

** We are putting over $40,000 a day into the local community and region.

** Cumberland College's budget is largely spent locally.

** Cumberland College not only buys locally but also hires many of its services locally.

** Cumberland College's faculty members live in and around Williamsburg. They participate in civic organizations and in our churches, and they fulfill other valuable social responsibilities.

** Cumberland College's support staff live in and around Williamsburg. Most of the staff buy locally, and none of these jobs would be available without the College.

** Cumberland College's students each year spend probably $10.00 to $20.00 or so a week in and around Williamburg.

** Cumberland College's faculty, staff, and students rent houses and apartments in and around Williamsburg. Moreover, many of the faculty and staff own or are buying their own homes and cars and are paying taxes on all of these.

** Cumberland College has around 2,000 of its 10,000 alumni living in and around the immediate vicinity of Williamsburg, many of whom are counted among the local doctors, pharmacists, dentists, attorneys, ministers, teachers, and other professionals. Another 8,000 alumni provide needed services throughout

The College assists the community through its Mountain Outreach program.[9] During the summers students involved in this program along with volunteers construct homes for the indigent, the poor, the elderly, the walking wounded. Each home contains approximately 816 square feet and costs around $4,400. A contract agreement for the responsibility of upkeep and payment on the no-interest loan is signed with the loan being based only on the cost of building materials. Schuyler Meyer, Jr., and Martha Innes of the Edwin Gould Foundation must be mentioned for their support of the Mountain Outreach program.

THE HEAD OF A HOLLOW

A College student looking for a particular home to visit traveled far back down a rutted lane to the head of a hollow (where two mountains converge), and he could go no farther. Then he spotted the shack back in the woods at the head of that hollow with a note pinned to the door. The note said: "Gone to the country for the weekend." It's all relative, especially here in the mountains.

Another story is often told of a mountain man who had a "crush" on one of the young ladies who was helping build a new home for him through the College's Mountain Outreach program. The mountaineer told her, "I like you so much I'll brush my 'tooth' if you'll go out with me."

Yet another story is told of a team of sociologists and psychologists who visited in the mountains under one of the "do-gooder" programs. Coming upon a shack

---

Appalachia, the nation, and indeed, the world.
** Cumberland College is always ready to lend a helping hand when it comes to helping the community.
** Cumberland College's property acquisitions have enhanced the community and its property values tremendously.
** Cumberland College offers its facilities (track, gym, campus, fields, tennis courts) and its programs (basketball, non-scholarship football, baseball, and softball games; plays; musicals; lectures; athletic events; religious services) to our friends and neighbors at the appropriate times.

Williamsburg also helps the College:
** Williamsburg provides excellent fire and police protection to the College itself, to our students, and to the faculty and staff living in our community. This is a wholesome community.
** Many Williamsburg merchants and business people are very kind to our students, faculty, and staff, and many of the merchants and business people have special promotions for the College family. These same merchants and business people also help the College financially.
** Williamsburg opens its athletic and sports facilities to our students, faculty, and staff.
** Williamsburg offers a fine city school system in which our young, healthy, curious youngsters receive a good public education.
** The many churches in and around Williamsburg give all of us the opportunity to worship in the church of our choice.
** The quiet, homey way of life in Williamsburg gives our students an excellent place where they can concentrate on their studies and other College-related activities.

[9] The Mountain Outreach program was begun in 1981 by two students Robert Day and Dave Emmert, who saw the need to lend a helping hand to the surrounding communities. From modest beginnings the program has grown into a major summer project with several hundred people giving of their time and talents to assist others less fortunate than they.

back up a hollow they talked with an elderly woman, a matriarch, in a rocking chair on her front porch. They asked her finally, "If you had a lot of money, what would you do with it." She paused, thought, and said: "I reckon I'd give it to the poor."

Another story is told frequently about a team of sociologists and psychologists visiting the mountains. They ran across a barefoot youngster and asked about his family. The youngster quickly pointed out that he had a brother at Harvard University. The sociologist responded by saying, "Your brother must be very smart to be studying at Harvard University." The boy dug his toe into the ground, squinted his eyes, and looked at the man and said, "No, they are a-studying him."

What's more, the story is told of a young man from Hogs Jaw, Kentucky. Asked where his home was located, he replied, "One mile south of 'Resume Speed'."

The story is told of a man named Darrell who worked at a country store and who unfortunately passed away. After some time passed, a traveling salesman came into the store. This traveling salesman had visited the area about once every three months while making his rounds. The salesman asked for Darrell. He was told that Darrell had passed away. The salesman asked who had filled the vacancy created by Darrell's death. The man replied, "Darrell, he didn't leave no vacancy."

Finally, the story is told about a youngster who went to the country school and had quite an odor. The teacher pinned a note to his shirt and sent him home. The note said, "This boy needs scrubbing." The next day the boy appeared at school early in the morning with a fresh note pinned to his shirt. The note said, "This boy doesn't need-a-scrubbing. This boy needs-a-learning."

THE YALE CLUB, THE YACHT CLUB, THE CHEMISTS CLUB, AND THE UNIVERSITY CLUB

Frankly, when traveling I usually stay at a Red Roof Inn or some other reasonably priced or cut-rate motel. However, thanks to people like Schuyler Meyer, Jr., Bill Buice, Senator John Sherman Cooper, and Walter Levering, I've been able to stay in some of the nicest facilities in New York City. The imposing structures with paneled reading rooms, heavy drapes, vaulted ceilings, oil portraits, and leather chairs impressed me when I saw them, and they still do. One of my proudest moments was at a special luncheon hosted at the Yacht Club by Schuyler Meyer, Jr., and Martha Innes during which time our mountain youngsters told their stories to some thirty corporate and foundation executives. As these executives arrived and departed in their limousines I thought surely we are ambassadors for the King of Kings. Later, thanks to the late, great Harold Helm, my wife and I were invited to attend a meeting of the New York Society of Kentuckians at the University Club on 57th Street. This meeting was a particularly proud moment because in the midst of all the "quotable notables" were two Cumberland College alumni who proudly identified themselves as such. My wife Dinah and I beamed with pride as they stood before their colleagues.

After all, the University Club presents quite a contrast to the homes which are built by our youngsters.

OTHER COMMUNITY ACTIVITIES

Each summer the College's students also assist in backyard clubs and recreational programs for the needy youngsters of the community. Other activities open to both the College and the community are various seminars and workshops, a mathematics contest, a science fair, a chemistry symposium, the Madrigal dinner, the Fine Arts series, the Cumberland Regional Theatre, sports activities, career awareness week, cancer awareness week, recitals, and musicals. The College complements the community, and the community complements the College. This has been accomplished through the tireless efforts of many, many people.

A RIGOROUS ACADEMIC PROGRAM

Our academic architect Dr. Joseph Early has brought to the academic program of the College rigorous standards with less fluff. At Cumberland a student finds warmth and friendliness[10] as well as a rigorous academic program with majors in accounting, art, biology, business administration, chemistry, data processing science, education, English, health, history, mathematics, medical technology, music, physical education, political science, psychology, religion, secretarial practice, and sociology. A student may select a minor from the above fields or from the additional fields of biblical languages, drama, earth science, French, geography, geology, military science, philosophy, social work, Spanish, or speech. Degrees offered include Bachelor of Art, Bachelor of Science, Associate in Secretarial Practice, Master of Arts for elementary, secondary, special education, and reading, and Rank I.[11] Pre-professional programs are offered in engineering, military science, mining technology, nursing, dentistry, medicine, law, pharmacy, physical therapy, optometry, and veterinary.

WE'RE NOT LIVING OFF PAST REPUTATION
AND DON'T PLAN TO

Today Cumberland College's program is solid. The College is fully accredited by the Southern Association of Colleges and Schools and offers first-class academic programs. It's an honor to graduate from Cumberland College. Most students who come to Cumberland are serious or they don't stay. Sure, some of our students come to find a life-long companion; some in the hope of obtaining a high paying job; few come just to get away from home; all come to get a first-class education at rates they

---

[10] The Student Government Association plays a major role in student life at Cumberland by offering a medium for enrichment and improvement.

[11] At the 28 January 1981 Board of Trustees meeting, the College's trustees approved the recommendation to begin a master's degree program in teacher education. Courses leading to the Master of Arts in elementary education were begun in 1982, and courses leading to the Master of Arts in secondary education were begun in the summer of 1983.

can afford; few, if any, come just to get their folks off their backs.

Education is serious business at Cumberland. Yet, there is still some time left to enjoy a variety of educational, social, and athletic activities.[12]

WHAT WOULD WE DO WITHOUT OUR FRIENDS?

The support and good will and sacrificial giving of friends scattered from one side of this country to the other is always needed, always appreciated, and never wasted or taken for granted. What would we do without our friends? Every morning and every evening I thank God for our friends who make our work possible. As demographic decline takes place and as tuition increases, we constantly seek outside funds from friends to fill the gap.

ACADEMIC EXCELLENCE

[12] The College is fortunate to have two national honor societies on campus: Phi Alpha Theta and Sigma Tau Delta. Phi Alpha Theta is the national history honor society, and our school's chapter has national acclaim, having won the best chapter award for schools with enrollments of less than 2,500 students eight of the last nine years. The national English honor society Sigma Tau Delta was formed in the 1985-1986 academic year and is already having an impact on our campus.

A wonderful program in developmental skills and writing is maintained. Students are required to write across the curriculum. There are other programs, clubs, and organizations on campus, both educational and social, all of which provide opportunities of involvement and leadership for our students.

ATHLETICS

One of the favorite activities of the student body at Cumberland College is athletics. Whether a student enjoys participating in an activity or just watching from the sideline, there are a variety of opportunities available including basketball, football, (no scholarships here; they pay us to play), softball, baseball, golf, tennis, judo and formerly track, to name a few. For a complete listing of the College's athletic directors, see Appendix IX.

A non-scholarship football program was begun at Cumberland in the 1985-1986 academic year under the coaching supervision of Mr. Tom Dowling, former coach at Liberty College. (Ironically enough, our basketball coach was the former assistant coach at Oral Roberts University.)

During the 1985-1986 basketball season, Cumberland's team was ranked number one for three weeks in the nation's NAIA poll. This was the first Cumberland basketball team ever to be ranked number one in the national poll. The team is coached by Randy Vernon, a very capable man. In fact, during the eight years that Randy Vernon has been head coach of the Indians he has accumulated a record of 218 wins and only 56 losses. His teams have won five Kentucky Intercollegiate Athletic Conference regular season titles, four KIAC tournaments, and five National Association of Intercollegiate Athletics District 32 championships. During the span of 1983-1987, the teams have been ranked between second and thirteenth in the final NAIA ranking.

Since becoming a four-year institution in 1961, the school has a 503-317 record including a sparking 305-85 record in the Gatliff Gymnasium.

Women's basketball coach Henry Morgan, baseball coach Terry Stigall, tennis coach Barbara Doyle, and golf coach Bill Sergeant must be recognized, too, for their contributions to the College's athletic program.

A BRONZE MEDAL AT THE OLYMPICS

Mention should also be made of the national championships won by the College's judo teams over the years. Zafer Roback is considered the father of judo at Cumberland, having begun the program in 1964. Coached by Dr. O. J. Helvey, the College's judo teams have won a host of awards including eight National Judo Championships. Cumberland students have participated in the World University Games in Poland, France, and Finland; in the Pan Am Games; and in other contests in France, Japan, South Africa, Holland, Moscow, and Finland. The College's judo teams hold the distinction of winning the Mid-West Collegiate Championship from 1970 until 1984, when the tournament was discontinued. They also won the Tri-State Judo Championship for three

WE'VE A STORY TO TELL TO THE NATION

We've a story to tell to the nation, and we can't sit back and wring our hands. No, we have to go out and get it to make the place go. When one considers the sacrifice which has gone into making this College possible, it is indeed a story to tell to the nation. We have a "can do" attitude and believe in the free enterprise system as well as helping the down and outer. Here you'll find youngsters from the mountains emerging as leading professionals. This institution is positive.

NATIONAL EXPOSURE IN RECENT YEARS

In telling our story the College is beginning to receive more national exposure. All of this publicity is needed and appreciated and provides good, wholesome exposure.

Time Magazine In 1967 *Time* magazine contributed a full page in its Eastern division entitled, "They Come to Cumberland."

IBM In 1972 IBM selected Cumberland College as one of the colleges for its faculty loan program which has enriched the College through computer training and the establishment of a placement office on campus.

Bing Crosby In 1975 Bing Crosby took a personal interest in Cumberland's program and featured a Cumberland student on the Bing Crosby Pro Am Tournament from Pebble Beach, California.

The Allstate Foundation In 1974 the Allstate Foundation selected Cumberland College's nursing program as one of four programs to support. Now the College cooperates with Eastern Kentucky University in offering the bachelor degree in nursing.

---

straight years and retired that trophy.

Dr. Helvey holds the distinction of being named Judo Coach of the Year three times: 1977, 1980, and 1983. Helvey also served as a member of the U.S. Olympic Committee for eight years.

Three members of Cumberland College's judo team, Eddie Liddie, Leo White, and Doug Nelson, went on from Cumberland to represent the United States in the 1984 Olympics, with Mr. Liddie winning a bronze medal.

CHEERLEADERS

Hardly any athletic event seems complete without a cheering section, and at Cumberland, this is no exception. The College has been fortunate over the years to have many talented youngsters to lead the cheering section, and these cheerleaders have spent many hours in training and practice for the job. Several of the teams have been rewarded for their efforts by being invited to attend both state and national competitions and exhibitions.

194

The Olympics In 1984 three Cumberland College graduates represented the United States as three of six men on the U.S. Judo Team. Eddie Liddie won a bronze medal.

Nationally Ranked Basketball Team The 1985-1986 men's basketball team, under the leadership of Coach Randy Vernon, was ranked as the number one team in the NAIA. In 1986-1987 the men's team was ranked number two in the nation. The women's basketball team also received recognition as winners in Kentucky.

The Teagle Foundation and the Exxon Foundation In 1986-1987 the College was one of four Appalachian institutions selected by the Teagle Foundation and the Exxon Foundation to participate in their alumni development program.

Public Broadcasting System The late, great Cratis Williams, Mr. Appalachia, a Cumberland graduate, was featured on the hour-long program having to do with speech traits and characteristics of the Appalachian people.

Reader's Digest *Reader's Digest* is preparing, we understand, to write an article on the College's outreach programs.

ONE BIG FAMILY

Like a father who must provide for a very large family, my responsibilities as president keep me on the road on the average of about two days or so each week.[13] The remaining four or five days a week are spent at or near the campus. I'm always near the phone. Being president, indeed, is like being the father of a very large family.

———————————————

A WAY OF LIFE

[13] Spending days on the road seeking foundation and corporation support and other types of support has become a way of life, a style of life well worth it because, after all, this College is meeting tremendous human and educational needs. Enough good cannot be said about my wonderful wife Dinah, a home economics graduate from the University of Kentucky, who has been and shall always be my constant source of inspiration and strength. She has labored endlessly and tirelessly and has served as my constant helpmate. Our son Jim, strong in character, has also allowed me to be away from home for sustained periods of time and, like his mother, understands and accepts this as my responsibility.

When I return to campus from a few days on the road, I confront the usual stack of letters. Thank goodness for Mrs. Sue Wake who lightens the load. Incidentally, I tour this campus unannounced frequently. On the other hand, being on campus four to five days a week allows me the opportunity to help mold and shape the direction of the institution. How I wish you could walk with me across this campus and chat with our well-scrubbed, clean-cut youngsters. In the fall of the year I might even be able to help a student overcome homesickness if this is the first time he's been away from home for a sustained period of time.

No matter how hard you try to stretch the budget, there is simply never enough money to meet every need. Turning out the lights a little early won't help a lot. Forming a committee won't help much either. No, there is no substitute for a helping hand!

And I like to think we're concerned about education more than merely providing sports for the alumni, parking for the faculty, and a good time for the students. It's important to show people the overall picture lest we become too preoccupied as a College family with our own little worlds. Balance is important, and I think we have it on the Cumberland campus. As one person said, "Cumberland College is "not an againer," meaning, I suppose, we are not so much against things as for things.

AN AMBASSADOR, NOT A BEGGAR

While I do send out begging letters, I've never felt like a beggar but rather like an ambassador for the King of Kings. We do manage to make ends meet by skimping on some items but never at the expense of the academic program. A gift which would be a mere drop in a bucket to an "Ivy League" university would be a major commitment to Cumberland. At Cumberland we don't distort facts or romanticize or vulgarize to raise funds. We are neither too slick nor too secular. And I've never struggled to develop a stained glass voice. We simply tell our story in the old-fashioned, straightforward way and make no apologies to anyone about it. I normally only rattle the cup once or twice when speaking about the College. I tell myself that heights of fame were not attained by sudden flight but by those who toil upward through the night.

THE DEVELOPMENT PROGRAM

It was in the latter part of 1969 that the development program (constituted largely of minimum wage workers typing letters and stuffing envelopes) began to try to make a dent in the College's need for funds. I can't tell you of the sleepless nights and the never-ending need for money to operate this college. In the decade of the sixties and the seventies, this program was instrumental in raising the funds with which to construct the Campus Center, a women's residence hall, a music building as well as increasing the endowment. Later, in the eighties, it would be responsible for helping in the construction of a classroom building, a business building, and a men's residence hall.

THE MORAL EQUIVALENT OF WAR

While our alumni are good people, wonderful hard-working people, most have entered the service professions and thus have little money to give to Cumberland. Although we appreciate every dime we receive, none of the money comes easily. Quite frankly it's always a battle to make ends meet. For instance, the campaign to construct and pay for the Campus Center was the moral equivalent of war since earlier efforts using professional fund raisers had failed to produce the needed capital. (We sent the professional fund raisers home and have not used them since.) We did the fund raising ourselves, and through faith, hard work, and perseverance in the face of doom and gloom sayers, the Campus Center campaign was on its way with a challenge grant from the Kresge Foundation in 1972, followed by a succession of commitments from other friends.

SUPPORT FROM FRIENDS

The College was beginning to gain some support from its friends, including people like Bing Crosby and Carmel Martin. As is true today, in those early days the College was encouraged on by people like the late Wallace Boyd, Ed Balloff, Bob and Eleanor Behrman, Ralph Denham, Meriel Harris, Bert Combs, Mary Doyle Johnson, Tom Butler, and others far too numerous to list. These folks knew the value of friends, funds, and freshmen. The College had a story to tell; there was and is no need to manufacture a need; we have one.

NO OTHER COLLEGE IS MORE DEPENDENT ON GIFT INCOME

The College had a need for philanthropic support and still does. I know of no other college which is more dependent on gift income for day-to-day operations than is Cumberland College. The College isn't "flush," never has been, and it never will be. But the College is thankful for its friends who make our work possible. Every gift is important, large or small, and every donor is important. We don't turn our nose up at anyone.

A COLLEGE FOR HILLBILLY YOUTH

One person on Wall Street once said to me, "Cumberland College is a great school because of its mission to 'hillbilly' youth, allowing them to earn their own way by doing chores." I said, "Then count me as a 'hillbilly' too, because I've also benefitted from its educational opportunities and also worked my way through."

It was in 1963 that I first read these words about the work program at Cumberland College.

It is the desire of the College that every deserving young person who wants to attend Cumberland shall have the privilege of doing so.

For students who actually need financial assistance to enable them to get through college, Cumberland has a limited number of workships available. For young men the workships involve work in and around the buildings and on the campus. For young women the work afforded is in connection with the culinary department, in various offices, and in the library.

Scholarships and workships are awarded only after the qualified applicant has completed and returned the official application form.

Thus, in order that the College may operate on a balanced budget, extreme caution must be exercised in granting aid to students. Granting aid to a student who does not require assistance may result in the preventing of some deserving student from attending college.

In keeping with the above statements, it has been determined that the total amount of workship aid to be granted is based on the enrollment and is in proportion to the number of students attending.

These factors should be kept in mind when the student requests assistance from the College. Thorough consideration will be given to each request and no decision with respect to aid will be made until full information regarding the student is in the hands of the administrative officials of the College.

In general, the workships pay enough to cover fifty to sixty percent of the cost of tuition.

Either before he leaves home or soon after he arrives here, a student who received a loan from the College Loan Fund will be furnished with a note to be signed by him and his father or some other person acceptable to the College Treasurer, payable to Cumberland College. If, for any reason, the student withdraws with a balance in his favor on his account for board and tuition, such balance is placed as a credit on the note.

It is the purpose of the College to pay students for the work they do through the service scholarships or working positions, such being made possible through special endowment funds for student aid. For these reasons, only students of unusual ability and promise can qualify for a service scholarship or working position.[14]

Little did I know then that I'd work my way through Cumberland College and then become one of its most vigorous exponents.

IN THE RIGHT PLACE AT THE RIGHT TIME OR DIVINE PROVIDENCE?

Shortly before becoming president, the author by pure chance happened upon a man, Mr. Fred Oherlien, a trust officer at the Bank of New York. At the time of

---

[14] Cumberland College, *Catalogue,* 1963-1964, p. 18. This is exactly what I read as an eighteen-year-old when thinking about the work opportunities at Cumberland. After all I'd worked delivering *Pontiac Press* papers at night and *Detroit Free Press* papers in the wee hours of the morning. On Saturday I shined shoes at Pitts Barber Shop or sold Christmas cards or all-occasion cards door to door. At age eighteen I loaded boxcars alongside Teamsters Union men and later worked for the United Auto Workers putting motor mounts on engines going down the assembly line. Earlier in high school I had worked nights at a grocery store. Today I'm not awed by being a college president, yet I stand in awe of the fact that someone like me could attain such a position. I have to chuckle at least once a day.

the first meeting, Mr. Oherlien was in the process of closing out a trust fund which had as its purpose: "service to the disadvantaged." Cumberland College became the beneficiary of that account as well as a subsequent account. These funds helped deserving young people to attend Cumberland College. Mr. Oherlien is gone now, but his influence lives on at Cumberland. Was the meeting pure chance or divine providence? Thank goodness the money came; it's helping to lighten the load.

MEETING CRITICAL NEEDS

Enough good cannot be said for the College's friends. Again and again they have risen to help the College meet its critical needs. The people who've helped us have been men and women of empathy, sympathy, and understanding.

As was true with many, if not most, private colleges, by 1980 Cumberland was facing tremendous deferred maintenance and operational needs. Thanks largely to Jim Rose and his wife Judy, an alumnae of Cumberland and a trustee, the College was able to consummate a transaction which has for a while provided some welcome relief. When I became president I took a long yellow note pad and began to walk around campus filling the pad with notes about shrubs which needed to be planted, construction and renovation projects which were needed, and signs and buildings which had to be painted.[15] Remarkably, the overall result has been well received. Without the help of Jim and Judy Rose at a critical time, we may never have been able to operate on a balanced budget. This is, after all, a cash-thin College.

Also in 1980, the Joyce Foundation provided needed assistance as did the Kettering Family Foundation and the Andrew W. Mellon Foundation, along with sever-

---

RENOVATION, RESTORATION AND REFURBISHMENT

[15] Since 1980 a renovation, restoration, and refurbishment program, both internally and externally, has taken place on the College's campus to keep in tune with the times including acquiring the Williamsburg City School's old properties; improving the athletic field and adding tennis courts; expanding the library; purchasing new boilers; beginning a marching band; renovating Mahan Hall; adding a non-scholarship football program; purchasing the Armory; renovating the Gray Brick Building; air conditioning the College's cafeteria; constructing Boswell Park; installing a central telephone system; restoring the Viaduct; renovating the gymnasium; renovating the Archer home; sandblasting several buildings; installing new windows, guttering, and roofs for several buildings; and erecting a flag pole and marker on Interstate 75. Other property has been purchased, parking areas blacktopped, and the campus grounds beautified. Additionally, a men's residence hall has been constructed, and a new physical education and convocation center is in the construction phase. The College, also, is planning on installing a washer/dryer center for the students.

TODAY THIS PLACE SHINES

Today you won't find paper blowing around on the grounds, and you can almost always see yourself in our shiny floors. Constant management of limited funds is necessary, and every dollar is stretched to the limit to bring about these campus improvements. This College operates on a nub.

tering Family Foundation and the Andrew W. Mellon Foundation, along with several others.[16]

THE ANDREW W. MELLON FOUNDATION

This College was up against what seemed like insurmountable odds when looking for money with which to enhance faculty and curriculum. Fortunately, the Andrew W. Mellon Foundation established at Cumberland College a faculty development program for the liberal arts faculty, thus allowing faculty to complete their graduate degrees and to pursue scholarly and educational research. Without this fund the College could in no way afford to send its faculty for short periods of travel or study or back to school.

Again in 1984, the College was offered an endowment challenge grant from the Andrew W. Mellon Foundation, the income of the fund to be used to assist our exceedingly deserving faculty in a similar manner as the previous grant. A special word of appreciation must be said to Mr. John E. Sawyer and Ms. Claire List of the Mellon Foundation for their work and support of the Appalachian institutions. I don't know what we would have done without this Fund. A great deal of credit must be given to Dr. Oline Carmical for his work on the proposal which resulted in the first grant and to Mrs. Sue Wake for her work on the proposal which resulted in the second grant.

THE PEW CHARITABLE TRUSTS

When I became president I whispered a prayer that we would be able to continue to provide quality academic programs to meet somehow the critical and crying needs in this Fifth Congressional District, the poorest geographical rural district in this nation. Thanks to the Appalachian Colleges Assistance Program of the Pew Charitable Trusts, my prayer has been answered, at least temporarily.

Since 1981 The Pew Charitable Trusts have supported Cumberland College by providing grants to renovate the academic buildings and to enhance the curriculum.

FAITHFUL SUPPORTERS
[16] Mr. Lisle Buckingham has provided needed assistance on numerous occasions. Miss Kate Ireland, a pearl beyond price, is a dear friend and supporter. Mrs. Evelyn Linebery as well as Mr. and Mrs. H. N. Berger have also helped our youngsters interested in the medical professions. Mr. Peter Ryan and Mrs. Alfred Harcourt must be mentioned as well as Mr. Henry See. Mr. and Mrs. George Roughgarden have established a loan fund for our needy students. Mr. Walter Smith provided some welcome funds for maintenance needs as well as an endowed scholarship fund through his bequest. The Bagby Trust must be remembered primarily because of Mr. Joe Leary, a trustee, who helped the College to receive an endowment which helps our youngsters. Mrs. Charlotte Watkins must also be remembered for the funds she has given as a result of the recommendation of another of the College's trustees, Mr. George Griffin. Mrs. T. E. Mahan and her sister Mrs. N. A. Archer remembered the College through their Wills by establishing Trusts, the income of which has helped partially to maintain the cost of operating three buildings as well as providing some loan funds for several students each year. The William Randolph Hearst Foundation has also been a true friend

Words cannot express our gratitude for the assistance which the Trusts have provided to our campus. We are grateful for both the foresight of the Pew family who chose to establish the Trusts and for the sensitivity of the trustees and staff who have responded to the needs of Appalachia's educational institutions.

THE JAMES GRAHAM BROWN FOUNDATION

Many times we have gone, hat in hand, to the James Graham Brown Foundation, and they have provided the needed financial assistance including gifts to support the construction of the Boswell Campus Center and the Mary McGaw Music Building as well as the purchase and renovation of the Williamsburg City School's properties. The following Brown Foundation officers and trustees must be recognized for their support: Mr. Ray E. Loper, Mr. H. Curtis Craig, Mr. Charles F. Wood, Mr. Harold E. Hawkins, Mr. Dan C. Ewing, Mr. Stanley F. Hugenberg, Jr., Dr. Arthur Keeney, Mr. Graham B. Loper, Mr. Joe M. Rodes, and Mr. Robert L. Royer.

THE BOOTH FERRIS FOUNDATION

On several occasions I had visited New York City and rode the subway from Grand Central Station to Wall Street to see Mr. Robert Longley among others. The Booth Ferris Foundation in 1975 provided a challenge grant toward the cost of a new music building. The old building had burned, and we started out with no more than a faith and a promise. Mr. Longley had previously visited the campus, and Mr. Robert Murtagh along with Mr. Longley had been visited in New York by the author. The support of these two men has been most meaningful through the years as they have continued their interest through financial assistance from the Morgan Guaranty Trust's Booth Ferris Foundation and the Charles and Mary Grant Foundation.

HE ALMOST CUT HIMSELF SHAVING

The gift from Mr. and Mrs. Foster McGaw for the Music Building and the endowment came to the College in a peculiar way. For several years in the face of rejection notices, the College's development office continued to write to Mr. McGaw. Finally, we touched a sensitive response cord, and it was like fireworks going off.

---

with special thanks going to Mr. Frehse and Ms. Mack. Mention must also be made of the Eden Hall Foundation for their support over the years. They have been wonderful.

There are others, too numerous to mention them all, who have provided aid at critical times or who have just been faithful supporters of the College.

On the morning of Christmas eve, 1977, Mr. McGaw called Dr. Boswell, then president, at home to tell him that he would give to ensure the construction of the Music Building about which the development officer had written.[17] McGaw also said he would provide an endowment for scholarships. This was an answer to prayer. What excitement and joy! Dr. Boswell was so excited he almost cut himself because he was shaving when the call came.

When the author wrote to Mr. McGaw, he always responded. Here are excerpts from a letter written by Mr. McGaw on 25 January 1983 to the author which gives insight into this great man:

"Dear Dr. Taylor:

". . . I like what I see and hear about your college . . . .

"It is very impressive to learn that some of your graduates in recent years are now qualified medical doctors who have returned to that area to serve their own people. That's a wonderful contribution Cumberland has made to its community. No finer tribute to your college could you find than to know that humanity is the goal of these young doctors rather than money.

"Too many doctors I encounter in the whole Chicago area are out for the bucks, and too many of the young doctors, only a few years in practice, will make a house call only under the greatest duress. I don't like it at all, and that isn't my idea of a real physician.

"I almost envy you living with fine young people with ambitions that they are willing to achieve no matter what it will cost them in time and effort. They will be the real winners and I congratulate you on graduating the kind of people we need for the future leadership of our country. Our Congress is too full of people who vote for their own re-election rather than for the health of our whole society, its morality and its ethics. Keep up the good work and may God bless it richly. I won't forget you.

"Sincerely,
"Foster McGaw"

MEETING HUMAN NEED:
IT'S A CONSTANT STRUGGLE
The numbers, dates, campaign goals, time tables, and construction projects are

---

[17] The person who must be thanked the most for this gift, of course, is the late, great Mr. McGaw. Others, however, should be mentioned including Dr. Dick Palmer and Dr. Harry Kallas, who constantly encouraged me to reach out through development efforts and to broaden our vision. Through extensive consultation and encouragement, these men helped Cumberland College more than words can tell and were partly responsible for this major gift. Another gentleman, the late Mr. Hugh Steely, Sr., also helped through his correspondence with Mr. McGaw.

cold and impersonal and tell little of the constant struggle to meet operational needs and maintenance needs, with perhaps a "tad" left over for the endowment. Furthermore, these objectives say little of the human need seen daily here in the mountains of Eastern Kentucky. There is never enough money to meet all the needs; yes, we operate on a nub. But the College is for Appalachian youth primarily, and we must provide a tremendous amount in scholarship and workship aid to needy but deserving students. This is no small order and could not be accomplished without the generosity of friends. Yet, it's a constant struggle.

FIRST GENERATION COLLEGE STUDENTS

The College is serving first generation college students primarily in an area where the current depression in the coal fields makes it increasingly more difficult for a student to get an education. At Cumberland thousands of deserving youngsters who needed help, received help, and are now helping others.

THE FINAL EXAMINATION CALLED LIFE

Not long ago I had to chuckle when a student told me his finals were over, and he was glad to be getting out from underneath the pressure. Little did he know that soon he will be under the final examination called life, constituted of early mornings, late nights, and an analysis of productivity. College is, indeed, a preparation time in one's life.

WHAT A GROCERY BILL

As you can imagine, it's no easy task to house approximately 1,000 students, to feed them three times a day, and to teach around 2,000 students on almost a five day a week schedule. Just imagine if your grocery bill consisted of hundreds of dozens of eggs, hundreds of loaves of bread, and hundreds of gallons of milk each week!

WHOLESOME KIDS WITHOUT A COCKY SMILE

Today I wish you could walk across the campus, through the buildings, into the library, sit in the chapel and look at the faces of our clean-cut youngsters so you could see for yourself exactly what's happening here at our College, a special purpose college with young people who want an education. Compare our first generation college students with those at an "Ivy League" college. Harvard's president Derek Bok "reports that the stated goals on the applications of incoming freshmen were 'money first, followed by power and then making a reputation.' " L. Fred Jewett, the Dean at Harvard, went on to say, "Once new students are safely aboard, . . . they acquire a certain 'smugness' and 'arrogance'."[18] What a contrast to our first generation College students at Cumberland! Compare our youngsters with those at Harvard. After all, sophistication is a very thin veneer. Yet, our youngsters are more than "country politicians."

THE BEST AND THE BRIGHTEST

Today's students at Cumberland are the best and the brightest students we've ever had, and today our concern is for the individual student as it has been since the beginning. Today, as in the past, Cumberland's mission is to serve Appalachian youth, primarily, but not exclusively, and to do it in a Christian context. We make no apology for the traditional values we seek to inculcate. Historically our young men have volunteered for the military and have served bravely.

IT COULD BRING TEARS TO YOUR EYES

Our average student has an ACT score of 18.6, right up there with other well-known schools. The average student comes from a family of several brothers and sisters, has a family income below $10,000, and is the first in the family ever to attend college. What should I tell these youngsters when they arrive on campus fresh from the mountain communities? I certainly can't say, "Get lost," or "Go home." No, we have no option but to help, and help we do. So I say, "If you're willing to work, come on, and we'll find the money somewhere." And work they do with over 600 students working on campus to help pay their way. And by now each of these youngsters has signed a work contract promising to give a day's work for a day's pay.[19]

HARD WORK UNIVERSITY:
THEY CRACK THE BOOKS

We're old fashioned. In fact, we are a little more than old fashioned. We believe in the work ethic. No one gets credit for work not done. And we don't offer credit for life experiences as a substitute for cracking the books.

Spread across the pages of time one can see the emphasis placed on individual initiative, and even today we have over 600 students who work an average of twelve hours each week. Here they learn attitudes, habits, and ethical behavior along with promptness, dependability, accuracy, thrift, reliance, and integrity. This College avoids

---

[18] Ezra Brown, "Happy Birthday, Fair Harvard!" *Time*, 8 September 1986, p. 57.

[19] Appendix XIII contains a copy of the work contract which is signed by the students who are awarded workships.

the anonymity of massive institutions. At Cumberland work is never demeaned. Over the years a good bit of financial assistance at the College has been given in the form of work, the amount depending upon ability and need.

I COULD TELL YOU A STORY!

Here in the mountains stories abound on every hand about young people and their families who've sacrificed to earn an education. I could tell you about a young lady who put herself through College by using a roadside stand to sell fresh vegetables which she grew in her own garden each summer.

I could tell you about a young man who was put through College by his wife who made and sold handmade dolls and handmade quilts. What a labor of love!

I could tell you about a young man who is now a medical doctor but who was the first in his family ever to attend College.

I could tell you of youngsters who've walked long distances each day to and from home to attend College.

I could tell you about a bright young lady who has seven brothers and sisters. She was going to drop out of College to help her family back home, but because of donors to the College, she is now a successful school teacher.

I could tell you about youngsters who needed eye glasses, shoes, a warm coat for winter, tennis shoes for summer.

I could tell you similar stories about hundreds of doctors, lawyers, pharmacists, and business and professional people, all of whom came from these hills with precious little money, only desire.

WE'RE NOT TOO PROUD TO ACCEPT HELP:
THE COLLEGE OF HARD KNOCKS

Every semester I see even more youngsters who want to join the ranks of others in the work program. And so I write appeal letters to help the down and outer, the underdog, the youngster who wants to go out and make a positive contribution. Sad stories of youngsters, of their neglect and abuse, come across my desk almost daily, and so I make no apology for seeking assistance. I tell the kids that people who know us see us, warts and all. But the sin is not in failing occasionally; the sin is in not trying.

BUTCHER, BAKER, CANDLESTICK MAKER

Students work as janitors, gardeners, cooks, dishwashers, laboratory assistants, clerical assistants, and in numerous other capacities. Can you blame us for being proud? Here at Cumberland there's little time for a serious student to ''goof off'' or to ''loaf.'' Here you won't find a youngster sailing a paper airplane across the classroom or passing notes to his girlfriend. No, this is serious business. Right now Cumberland is sending sixty-five percent of her graduates back into the mountains to serve. Many outstanding alumni[20] have received their education at Cumberland College including two governors of Kentucky, one United States Congressman, doctors, military leaders, teachers, pharmacists, attorneys, business and professional people, missionaries, authors, artists, and the list could go on and on; they are too numerous to mention.

Frankly we could operate more efficiently if we handled students as statistics and if we received funds from anonymous sources, but each student is important and unique in our eyes. These youngsters are the descendents of the proud and heroic pioneers who settled the wilderness. They aren't coming here to protest the American way of life. They have a serious glint in their eyes, and they aren't looking for someone to hand life to them on a silver platter.

One alumnus told me recently, "Many of the most tearful, yet many of the most joyful days of my life were spent on the Cumberland campus." So it was, and so it is.

Since the College didn't assume senior college status until 1961, it isn't flush with wealthy alumni. But if you're an alumnus, think back to when you packed for College. Remember the letters, telephone calls, dirty laundry, your hopes, your dreams. Think about taking the college entrance examination. Remember meeting your new dorm mate or other friends. Remember the nights at the library, the ballgames, the work that went into making your education possible. Cumberland, of course, is where alumni have made lasting friendships, serious career choices, and enduring commitments. Many have selected their life-long mate on this campus. It was here that professors loomed larger than life. To suggest that anything was less than golden to any alumni is heresy, and rightfully so. Cumberland means so much to us all!

ALMA MATER
"Oh Cumberland, My Cumberland"
by Richard E. DuBois

Oh Cumberland, My Cumberland,
A hymn of praise we sing to thee
Our college days will always live
Within our memory.
O Cumberland, My Cumberland,
This be our fervent prayer:
May God from day to endless day
Still have thee in His care.

---

[20] We count as an alumnus any student who has been here a semester or longer.

Oh Cumberland, My Cumberland,
Our days of youth will soon pass by,
But still we know thy fellowship
And faith will never die.
Oh Cumberland, My Cumberland,
Though time will bid us part,
Thy hallowed name will ever claim
Thy love within our hearts. [21]

YOU CAN MAKE A DIFFERENCE

Today the youngsters coming to us fresh from the hills and hollows are descendents of pioneers, of frontiersmen, who settled this great nation. They come as they have been coming since 1889. During this Centennial celebration I want to ask if you will help by sending a gift today to lighten the load? Your gift will be stretched to the limit meeting tremendous educational and human needs. There's a postage paid envelope in the back of the book. Why not sit down right now, take out your pen, write as generous a check as possible, put it in the envelope, and send it today? You'll be glad you did, and you'll like that inner glow that comes from helping others.

---

[21] Richard E. DuBois, "Oh Cumberland, My Cumberland," *Alma Mater.* See Appendix XIV for the words and music.

MOUNTAIN OUTREACH

Here are pictures of a few of the homes as well as some of the children and the student workers.

The family who lives in this home includes three boys, two of whom are twins.

There were two mentally handicapped children living in this home with their parents until Mountain Outreach constructed a new home for them in the summer of 1986.

A disabled veteran lived in the bus shown at the left in this picture. In the summer of 1986, Mountain Outreach volunteers constructed a new home for him, shown at the right in the picture.

Before this home was built by Mountain Outreach volunteers, the family with three children lived in a bus.

(Photographs courtesy of Vicki McEntire, with permission granted by the families)

209

DR. JOSEPH EARLY
Academic Dean

DR. GEORGE RAMEY
Director of Business Affairs
and Treasurer

DR. JOHN DUKE
Dean of Student Services

MRS. SUE WAKE
Administrative Assistant
to the President

(Photographs by Housman Photography)

MISS EMMA McPHERSON
Dean of Students

MRS. EMILY MEADORS
Registrar

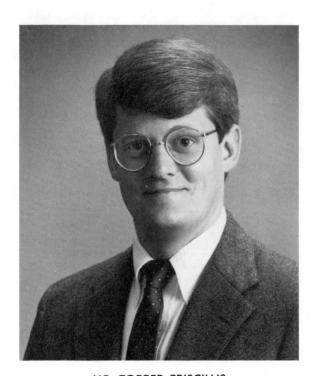

MR. TOPPER CRISCILLIS
Dean of Admissions

MR. JACK STANFILL
Director of Financial Aid

(Photographs by Housman Photography)

MR. HENRY MORGAN
Athletic Director

MR. DOYLE GILBERT
Director of Land Development
Director of Auxiliary Enterprises

MR. JIM BYRGE
Director of Food Services

MR. KENNETH SHAW
Superintendent of Buildings
and Grounds

(Photographs by Housman Photography)

212

MR. JAMES L. ROSE

MRS. JUDY ROSE

James L. Rose is a native of Clay County. He began in the coal business by assisting in a family-owned operation. Later he founded Mountain Clay, Leeco, and Interstate Coal Companies. He currently serves as president of several coal companies in eastern Kentucky. He is also the owner of several banks located throughout the state.

Judy S. Rose is a graduate of Cumberland College. She is also from Clay County. In addition to working alongside her husband in the coal and banking business, Mrs. Rose has owned and operated art galleries in Tennessee and Georgia. Mrs. Rose is also a talented vocalist having performed throughout the United States.

Both Mr. and Mrs. Rose are active in civic organizations and are ardent supporters of Cumberland. Mrs. Rose, in fact, is a member of the College's Board of Trustees.

(Photographs courtesy of Mr. and Mrs. Jim Rose)

MR. AND MRS. O. WAYNE ROLLINS

He's Touched Time

For years I had written to Mr. Rollins and visited his office in Atlanta. However, when Mr. Rollins' jet first touched the air strip in London, Kentucky, I knew for certain he was a warm and caring person, not part of the general public. To be such a powerful man he is a humble man. He is one of the nation's corporate magnets, a man who is a legend in his own time. Mr. O. Wayne Rollins has taken an interest in the College and its Christian work ethic. The College's work manual, in fact, was dedicated to him. Moreover, much credit must be given to Mr. and Mrs. Rollins for their financial support, especially for their gifts toward the construction of what will be the new O. Wayne Rollins Center.

(Photograph courtesy of Mr. and Mrs. Rollins)

MR. GROVER HERMANN   MRS. SARAH T. HERMANN

THE GROVER HERMANN FOUNDATION

In the summer of 1980 the author had the opportunity to visit with Mrs. Grover M. Hermann. She has compassion, as did her late husband, the founder of the American-Marietta Company which subsequently merged with The Martin Company to form the Martin-Marietta Corporation. The construction of the new residence hall for men was made possible in a large part by a generous grant from The Grover Hermann Foundation. Because of Mr. and Mrs. Hermann's caring concern and sharing, young men attending Cumberland have nice, clean, comfortable housing in a beautiful new residence hall.

The Grover Hermann Foundation has also helped with the construction of the new convocation and recreation center, and we are indebted to the Foundation for its generous support.

(Photographs courtesy of Mrs. Hermann)

J. HOWARD PEW

MABEL PEW MYRIN

MARY ETHEL PEW

J.N. PEW, JR.

THE PEW CHARITABLE TRUSTS

The Pew Charitable Trusts are a private philanthropy representing seven charitable trusts created by the sons and daughters of Joseph N. Pew, founder of the Sun Oil Company. Established between 1948 and 1982, the Trusts assist nonprofit organizations dedicated to improving the quality of life for individuals and communities and to encouraging personal growth and self-sufficiency. Support is provided in the areas of conservation, culture, education, health, human services, public policy, and religion.

(Photographs courtesy of The Pew Charitable Trusts)

FOSTER AND MARY McGAW

As mentioned previously Mr. and Mrs. Foster McGaw became generous donors to Cumberland College and helped through their gifts to construct the Mary McGaw Music Building. They also provided financial resources for the establishment of the Foster McGaw Endowed Scholarship Fund, the income from which is annually used to assist many youngsters. While Mr. and Mrs. McGaw have gone on to their reward, their influence lives on.

(Photograph courtesy of Jim Ziv, Northwestern University)

MR. FRED C. ANDERSEN

The Foundation created by the late Mr. Fred C. Andersen has assisted this College unselfishly since 1969, and I can't thank the Andersens enough for their tireless devotion. What would we do without this most meaningful help which has come time and time again to rescue us as we've faced a multitude of needs in providing educational opportunities for our mountain youngsters? Enough good cannot be said of Mr. and Mrs. Andersen, Mr. E.C. Swanson, and this Foundation.

Mr. Fred C. Andersen was director and president of the Andersen Corporation which produces wood window units and vinyl window and door units. Mrs. Katherine B. Andersen, the wife of Mr. Andersen, is currently the Foundation's president and is a caring person.

(Photograph courtesy of the Andersen Foundation)

DeWITT WALLACE   LILA ACHESON WALLACE

Past acquaintances often pay big dividends. The development office had contacted Mr. DeWitt Wallace, founder of *Reader's Digest,* through the mail constantly and to no avail. Through a conversation with Congressman Eugene Siler, it was determined one evening at a Rotary Club meeting in Williamsburg that Mr. Siler was a personal friend of Mr. Melvin Laird who had served as Secretary of Defense for the United States and who was then working as an assistant to Mr. Wallace. Congressman Siler contacted Mr. Laird who in turn spoke with Mr. Wallace about the College's unique mission in Appalachia, and an endowment fund was established which helps needy but deserving youngsters, the DeWitt Wallace Endowed Scholarship Fund.

(Photographs courtesy of *Reader's Digest*)

H.N. AND FRANCES BERGER

H.N. and Frances Berger created and built Oakmont, California, for people over forty-five years of age who wished to live in an active adult community. They are also responsible for the creation of several saving and loan associations in California.

The Bergers have long been interested in young people, especially bright youngsters who, with just a helping hand, can make a significant contribution to society. Mr. and Mrs. Berger have chosen to assist several students to attend Cumberland and then to attend medical school. These students and the College are grateful for the caring concern of these two wonderful people.

(Photograph courtesy of Mr. and Mrs. Berger)

KATE IRELAND

Miss Kate Ireland is a very active lady who always considers others before herself. She is a volunteer for a host of organizations including Frontier Nursing Service where she serves as Chairman of the Board of Governors.

Miss Ireland has received numerous awards for her activities including several honorary doctorates, one of which was awarded by Cumberland College.

(Photograph courtesy of Miss Ireland)

LISLE M. BUCKINGHAM

Mr. Lisle Buckingham was a marvelous person and a compassionate friend of Cumberland College who financially assisted the College whenever possible.

A member of the Ohio Bar Association, Mr. Buckingham served as an attorney for over sixty years. Additionally he assisted his local community through volunteer activities.

(Photograph courtesy of Mr. Buckingham)

BOSWELL PARK

Boswell Park was dedicated on 27 October 1984 during Homecoming activities. The Park is located in front of the new residence hall for men. The focal point of the Park is the bronze bust of Dr. J.M. Boswell sculpted by Barney Bright of Louisville, Kentucky.

(Photograph from the Cumberland College Collection)

WATER FOUNTAIN

Across the street from Boswell Park is a new fountain paid for by gifts from the Student Government Association and other friends.

(Photograph from the Cumberland College Collection)

EUGENE SILER HALL

Cumberland College is most proud of the new residence hall for men. Named for Congressman Eugene Siler, the building was made possible by the contributions of many alumni and other friends and especially a generous donor, The Grover Hermann Foundation. A long-awaited dream came true in 1985 when the new dormitory opened to house over 100 male students.

The building was dedicated on 20 October 1985 and is located on a prominent hill overlooking the College's campus. The building itself, as well as the rolling hills and manicured lawns in front of the building, were made even more attractive after The Hermann Foundation generously contributed additional funds to have the utility lines buried and the poles removed.

(Photograph by Housman Photography)

CLASSROOM BUILDING

Thanks to the Pew Memorial Trusts, the Stranahan Foundation, the James Graham Brown Foundation, and a host of other friends, the College was able to acquire the old City School properties in 1983 for $700,000. It's reasonable to infer that the new City School building would never have been built without the College's purchase. The old City School buildings are now referred to as the Classroom Building and the Business Building.

The two-story classroom building was renovated and occupied in 1984. It houses the departments of art, education, psychology, health, and sociology as well as the College's development offices. In addition, the renovated gymnasium houses the College's intramural offices and several of its programs.

The Business Building was also remodeled and occupied in 1984. The building houses the department of business administration and its faculty's offices.

(Photographs by Housman Photography)

BUSINESS BUILDING

223

PERKINS PLACE

In 1985 the College purchased this property on Main Street for office space. The land surrounding the house was cleared and is now used as an intramural field by the College. Additionally, the local school uses the land for organized activities.

The following information concerning Perkins Place was provided by Olivia Perkins Brisbin in a letter to the author, 13 July 1986.

"Dear Dr. Taylor:

". . . The house was built by my parents, John Wesley and Elizabeth (Kincaid) Perkins, in 1910-1911. The architectural plans were drawn by my mother who said that when she worked on the plans, she envisioned me (then 2 years old) as a bride descending the staircase.

"Construction of the house was somewhat delayed because the brick layers refused to lay the bricks which were of a slightly different size or shape from those they usually worked with. A new contract was negotiated and the house was completed.

"Mother asked the carpenters to install a yard-wide strip of canvas around the walls of the Dining Room and to build the scaffolding on which she stood to paint the mural forestscape. It was in this Dining Room that my husband John Francis Brisbin and I were married on 11 June 1931, 55 years ago.

". . . Following the death of Miss Pauline Kirtley, then resident artist at Cumberland, many students interested in art came to mother's studio for lessons for which they were given college credit . . . ."

(Photograph by Housman Photography)

MAHAN HALL

In 1984 renovation of Mahan Hall was begun, and it is now complete. The building was completely rewired, new stairwells were added, and much repair work was done on the inside. The outside was sandblasted and a new roof added as well as new windows installed.

(Photograph from the Cumberland College Collection)

THE ARMORY BUILDING

The Armory, located on South Second Street, was acquired by the College in 1980 and is used as a maintenance building.

(Photograph by Housman Photography)

THE W.B. WILDER LABORATORY

This laboratory and greenhouse was erected in 1984 with a grant from the Pew Memorial Trusts and was occupied in March 1985.

(Photograph by Housman Photography)

FAULKNER'S MOTEL

The recent acquisition of Faulkner's Motel may just be an answer to prayer. With little expense this Motel can be converted into apartments where our students who are older, married, and have children can live with their families. These are clean, wholesome married couples, but they have little or no money. Our appreciation must be extended to the Faulkners, in particular to Glenn Faulkner and to Howard Faulkner.

(Photograph by Housman Photography)

WOMEN'S BASKETBALL TEAM 1986-1987

MEN'S BASKETBALL TEAM, 1986-1987

(Photographs from the Cumberland College Collection)

228

MEN'S BASKETBALL TEAM, 1985-1986

CHEERLEADERS, 1986-1987

(Photographs from the Cumberland College Collection)

OUR LIBRARY, SECOND TO NONE

Today the College's library is second to none. It is modernized and computerized so much so, in fact, that Cheryl Truman, a reporter for the *Lexington Herald-Leader,* commented on Kentucky Education Television's "Comments on Kentucky," that Darth Vader [for those reading this history 100 years from now, Darth Vader was a fictional outerspace creature who utilized high technology] would feel comfortable in this library. It is incredible."

The library contains more than 40,000 pieces of media material, a book collection of over 170,000 volumes, and a microform collection of over 450,000 pieces. Bibliographic computer data resources, Dialog, Solinet, and many other online networks are available.

Because of the library's advancement, the College's librarians are asked to serve as advisors and consultants to other colleges, universities, and agencies.

(Photographs by Housman Photography)

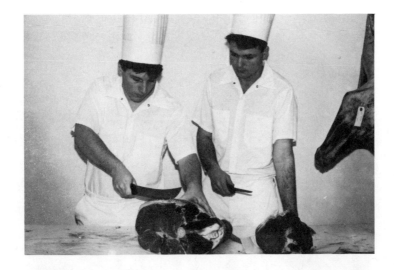

. . . . BUTCHER

. . . . BAKER

. . . . CANDLESTICK MAKER

(Photographs by Ken Prater)

SCIENTIFIC EQUIPMENT

CHEMISTRY

BIOLOGY

PHYSICS

STUDENTS AT WORK

(Photographs by Housman Photography)

CAMPUS SCENES

(Photographs from the Cumberland College Collection)

CHAPTER 7
A PEEK INTO THE FUTURE

NATIONAL AWARENESS

In 1963 President John F. Kennedy invited Kentucky's Governor Bert T. Combs, a Cumberland College alumnus, to the Oval Office for a conference. Kennedy, an avid reader of the *New York Times,* had been reading Pulitzer Prize winner Homer Bigart's articles about the deplorable conditions of life and work in Appalachia, the gasping, dust-choked coal miners, and their children's drawn faces. Bigart, himself, had visited Harry Caudill in Appalachia and was inspired by Caudill's *Night Comes to the Cumberlands* as well as by what he had personally seen during his visit up the hollows. Governor Combs confirmed to President Kennedy the grimmest aspects of the Bigart article. Kennedy pledged support.[1]

Shortly thereafter, CBS television's Charles Kuralt produced a Christmas Eve narrative entitled "Christmas in Appalachia." Caravans of used shoes and clothing were shipped by railway and trucks to the mountains in response to the program.[2] Appalachia was being brought to the nation's attention through well-meaning, but, in some cases, misdirected publicity without regard to mountain pride, our folkways and mores, values, and traditions. Unfortunately, some of the notoriety given to the region exploited the true situation showing "hollow-eyed and hopeless people,"[3] some of whom could just as easily have been found in large metropolitan areas, notwithstanding the real need in many sections of Appalachia. This comes as no real surprise since life is a process of misunderstanding and being misunderstood.

After Kennedy's assassination President Lyndon B. Johnson also pushed for the rehabilitation of Appalachia to conform to Kennedy's pledge. Efforts were made through the "Great Society" and the "War on Poverty."[4] Granted these were well-intentioned programs, but they did not solve the problems. There is no doubt, however, of President Johnson's genuine concern and pure motivation to help the people of this Appalachian area. In fact, Mrs. Johnson still assists the area through donations

---

[1] Harry M. Caudill, *The Watches of the Night,* (Boston: Little, Brown and Company, 1976), pp. 4-6.

[2] *Ibid.,* pp. 7-8.

[3] *Ibid.,* p. 9.

[4] *Ibid.,* pp. 11-16.

to Cumberland College. Here is what she had to say about our work in a letter written to the author on 21 October 1981.

"Dear Mr. Taylor:

"It is always a lift to the spirits to hear about the unfailing good works underway at Cumberland College! I know the fine young people who come to you constantly renew your determination to give them every opportunity to make the most of their journeys through life. Once again, I am delighted to help with one small step.

"With my admiration and *many* good wishes.

"Sincerely,
"Lady Bird Johnson"

SEPARATE FACT FROM FICTION

Appalachia has a wonderful heritage about which we can take justifiable pride. The area is neither drenched in wealth nor constituted of quaint hill folks. The area is populated by people who are trying to make a better life for themselves and their children.

MA AND PA KETTLE ARE NOT CUMBERLAND COLLEGE ALUMNI

While our area has been romanticized and fictionalized by the moonshiner, the child bride, the revenuer, and L'il Abner's Dogpatch,[5] all of this is more fiction than fact. Not much has been written about our mountain patriarchs, many of whom are Cumberland's alumni serving as medical doctors, pharmacists, nurses, ministers, teachers, and other business and professional men and women. These are the people who are making a lasting impact on the region.

WHERE DO WE GO FROM HERE?

The challenge today is no less than it was yesterday, and the answer now is as it always has been. The solution to the problems of Appalachia has to do with educational opportunities and hard work as well as with the capturing and molding of Appalachia's natural resources in water, timber, and energy. Free enterprise zones with special tax incentives for entrepreneurs and industrial development could also help bring jobs to the area.

Granted, the region is rich in arts, crafts, pottery, quilt making, banjo picking, and dulcimer making. Yet, all of these combined won't solve the problem until people take the initiative to lift themselves up high above the mountains, high up over

---

[5] "Poverty, U.S.A.," *Newsweek,* 17 February 1964, 31.

the coal mining camps, and take a look at a brighter tomorrow. Who knows, maybe one day this geographical area can become a vast tourist area along the Interstate 75 corridor; super roadways now provide the access. Television now beams up almost every hollow. Yet, problems persist and the ticket to a brighter tomorrow is educational opportunities today. That's why Cumberland's mission is so very important.

While we cannot be all things to all men, we, nonetheless, are guided by our purpose to provide a high quality, liberal arts education at a minimum cost to students primarily, but not exclusively, from Appalachia. We cherish our traditions.

THE GOALS FOR A MEANINGFUL LIFE

Dr. Arliss Roaden, alumnus of Cumberland College who currently serves as the Director of the Tennessee Higher Education Commission, in an address to our faculty, staff, students, and other friends encapsulated much of the quality and value orientation which Cumberland College seeks to instill into its students.

. . . The great, late Professor Edgar Dale of the Ohio State University stated that for the goals of a decent society there is a hunger for kindness, gentleness, fair play. The men and women whom we admire will put in more than they take out. They are broadly cooperative where others are narrowly competitive. They see life not as a ladder but as a spiraling circle with room enough for everyone to reach a high level. They are 'we' centered, not 'me' centered. They have bifocal vision, can see both the present and the future. They look forward, not backward. They plant trees under whose shade they will never sit. They spend their life working for something that will outlast them. They are mentors for the unloved, the dispossessed, the homeless, the walking wounded. They do not humiliate other people but patiently and wisely help them learn to respect themselves and others. They help people think better of themselves.

. . . Charles Kettering once said, 'No great edifice ever rose to reach the skies unless someone thought it could; someone believed it should; and someone willed it must.[6]

These are the values we seek to instill at Cumberland College. In keeping with these values, one is reminded of the words of Rudyard Kipling in his verse ''If.''

---

[6] Arliss Roaden, Dedication of Eugene Siler Hall, 20 October 1985. Dr. Roaden is the former Vice Provost at Ohio State University and former President of Tennessee Technological University.

If you can keep your head when all about you
    Are losing theirs and blaming it on you,
If you can trust yourself when all men doubt you,
    But make allowance for their doubting too;
If you can wait and not be tired of waiting,
    Or being lied about, don't deal in lies,
Or being hated, don't give way to hating,
    And yet don't look too good, nor talk too wise:

If you can dream — and not make dreams your master;
    If you can think — and not make your thoughts your aim;
If you can meet with Triumph and Disaster
    And treat those two imposters just the same;
If you can bear to hear the truth you've spoken
    Twisted by knaves to make a trap for fools,
Or watch the things you gave your life to, broken,
    And stoop and build 'em up with worn-out tools:

If you can make one heap of all your winnings
    And risk it on one turn of pitch-and-toss,
And lose, and start again at your beginnings
    And never breathe a word about your loss;
If you can force your heart and nerve and sinew
    To serve your turn long after they are gone,
And so hold on when there is nothing in you
    Except the Will which says to them: 'Hold on!'

If you can talk with crowds and keep your virtue,
    Or walk with Kings — nor lose the common touch,
If neither foes nor loving friends can hurt you,
    If all men count with you, but none too much;
If you can fill the unforgiving minute
    With sixty seconds' worth of distance run,
Yours is the Earth and everything that's in it,
    And — which is more — you'll be a Man, my son![7]

---

[7] Rudyard Kipling, "If," in *Rudyard Kipling's Verse, Definitive Edition* (Garden City, New York: Doubleday, Doran and Co., Inc., 1910), p. 578. Quoted by permission of Doubleday.

WE HAVE REVERENCE FOR THE PAST
AND FAITH FOR THE FUTURE

At Cumberland College we have faith for the future and have developed a long-range development plan, *Promises to Keep,* which reflects the past, provides for the present, and prepares for the future.

PROMISES TO KEEP . . .
AND MILES TO GO BEFORE WE SLEEP

Today Cumberland College is unique. Cumberland is different by design. Ours is a special purpose college in the business of salvaging human potential and serving students primarily from the hills and hollows of Appalachia. Cumberland is a college concerned about people. In all of our history we have been concerned with the people of Appalachia; we were concerned long before concern for Appalachia became fashionable.

Here are reasons why Cumberland is different:

1. Cumberland College is one of the precious few colleges left in the nation, and certainly in Kentucky, which neither solicits nor accepts federal aid. We have maintained our integrity as a private college and have used ''shoe leather'' to raise money from the private sector for buildings, equipment, and programs.

2. Cumberland College is located in and serving the Fifth Congressional District, one of the poorest congressional districts in the nation. To use a cliche', the College is genuinely an island of hope in a sea of despair for so many youngsters.

3. Cumberland College provides indigenous leadership for Appalachia. About sixty-five percent of Cumberland's graduates are returning to the Appalachian region to improve the overall socio-economic conditions of the region. And the only way the Appalachian area will ever solve its shortage of professionals is to identify and train the brightest of its native talent. In the past few years six of our graduates, now fully qualified medical doctors, have returned to serve this area. This is remarkable considering the other more glamorous opportunities. Moreover, our College has produced two governors of Kentucky, a host of medical doctors, and other professionals. We feel the success ratio of our graduates reflects the quality of our program.

4. While Cumberland maintains an enrollment of around 2,000 students, size is not what counts. What matters is Cumberland's caring concerns and demanding expectations for the students from the hills and hollows, the mining camps, and isolated mountain areas.

5. Nationwide, we are told, there is a ratio of about one medical doctor for every 1,700 people, and in this area there is a ratio of about one medical doctor for every 5,000 to 7,000 people. Many of the area's medical doctors are Cumberland College alumni. We continue striving to better the health and the health services of Appalachia.

Most of the students coming to Cumberland receive from partial to total aid, and most aren't afraid to get their hands dirty to earn this help. Our kids wash dishes, scrub floors, carry out the garbage, or do whatever else is necessary to earn their own way. And they do this in about the same number of hours most students "goof-off" at the average campus.

Today, even more than before, we believe in the mission of Cumberland College — to provide a quality education at a reasonable cost for the youth of Appalachia.

THE PROMISES OF CUMBERLAND COLLEGE

To offer a first-class educational opportunity within the means of mountain people. Cumberland College's students come primarily from a twenty-county area here in the rugged mountains of Appalachia, an area where modern industry has yet to penetrate, where soil and terrain make farming arduous and unrewarding. These people know what it is to be poor; they've never known anything else. Their children have grown up with hunger; yet, they also hunger for knowledge, for a chance to better themselves and their community. So they come to Cumberland, and they have been coming since 1889.

They come to Cumberland for several reasons: because of the basic soundness of our courses in liberal arts and sciences, because of our nearness to their homes, and because the matter of tuition is never a great problem. Our cost to the student is less than $5,500. This amount covers not only tuition but room, meals, and fees. Yet, even with this low figure, the majority of our students need financial help from us. Soon, however, we may have to begin turning students away, for we are reaching our physical and financial limits.

If you are one of those who can help, you will be heartened to know that you are helping deserving students. Those who receive their degrees from Cumberland are fully equipped for well-paying positions in business and industry. Yet, fully sixty-five percent of our students accept positions within the Appalachian area to do their part in raising the overall educational and community standards of the area they know so well.

Ours is not a big college nor will it ever be. But in those qualities that count: in ambition, in desire, in enthusiasm, in integrity, we'll pit our students against the world.

There is so much need to be answered, so much work yet to be done. We have never failed the youth of Appalachia; we hope we never will. These are the promises of Cumberland College.

To provide an atmosphere which fosters distinctive spiritual growth. National news sources have pointed to a shortage of religious vocation students in our nation's colleges. Most are said to have fewer than one percent of their students preparing for full-time church-related vocations. Cumberland College is a notable exception.

242

A large number of Cumberland's students are preparing for full-time religious service. Cumberland is distinctive in its commitment and has attracted an outstanding community of committed scholars.

Many opportunities for spiritual growth are afforded to the students both on campus and off campus. Every student who graduates from Cumberland must have had six semester hours in Bible courses. Chapel programs are held three days each week. Several Cumberland professors offer non-credit courses in religion and Bible in the surrounding towns and villages. Cumberland supplies many area churches with interim ministers from both its student body and its staff.

For the past several years Cumberland's students have given of their time, even vacation time, to participate in the Mountain Outreach program. This totally volunteer help-your-neighbor activity was designed by students to assist local residents with physical as well as spiritual needs. To date, our students have assisted in winterizing homes, providing electricity and indoor plumbing, and building homes for needy families.

To aid in developing socially responsible citizens. Cumberland College strives to develop within each student a high level of personal citizenship, an appreciation of human values, a sense of deep responsibility to society, and an appreciation of achievements in the development of social graces. While other students from more affluent backgrounds may take for granted an appreciation of the social graces, this is not so for Cumberland College's students. So Cumberland strives to relate to the students through cultural programs an appreciation for the social graces.

In addition to convocation programs which are culturally oriented, the College sponsors a number of musical programs, dramas, films, artists, and lectures by nationally and internationally known individuals. As a contributing member of the Southeastern Fine Arts program, the College provides such cultural activities as recitals, concerts, dramas, and musical programs for the region.

During athletic events and at other appropriate times, the Cumberland College Color Guard reminds us of the debt we owe to this great nation. Cumberland's students have fierce pride and are unusually patriotic. Cumberland's students are also proud of the College. Students are friendly, polite, courteous, and wholesome. The College has not experienced one incident of campus violence. Students know that the administration has full authority to take firm disciplinary action. The use of or possession of alcoholic beverages or narcotics is strictly prohibited.

To urge each student to endeavor to reach full potential. Much effort has been expended in planning academic programs which will meet the special needs of Appalachian students. We have developed educational programs that are tailored to aid in developing persons who have not enjoyed normal advantages. In addition, the College has attracted a faculty and staff who care, who give exceptional time, effort, and imagination to their work with students.

The academic program of the College provides courses of study which will enable students to enter Cumberland at their present academic level and to pursue their area of interest while learning the necessary skills to be successful in their chosen profession. The Learning Skills Center and the Writing Laboratory help students gain better reading abilities, proper grammatical skills, and proper study techniques.

Cumberland's faculty members work closely with each student in order to challenge the average and above-average student and to give remedial work to those less prepared.

Upon the recommendation of the high school instructor or guidance counselor who indicates that certain young people have high motivation and high potential for leadership, some students with latent talent are admitted to Cumberland without records of high academic achievement. The College provides these students with remedial work in reading, writing, spelling, listening, critical thinking, and discussion techniques.

Superior students are challenged by allowing them to do independent work. They also work with weaker students to provide the necessary encouragement for them to succeed in their college work.

Cumberland College has moved into the mainstream of higher education through advanced placement, College Level Examination Programs (CLEP), departmental testing programs, high school junior (rising senior) program, and Appalachian service programs. Additionally, the College offers evening classes for the many students who cannot avail themselves of educational opportunities during the day hours.

To make available opportunities for self-help through workstudy. Since its founding the self-help feature has been an integral part of Cumberland College. We believe that the privilege of a college education should be based upon motivation, ability, character, and purpose rather than upon the amount of money a student or his parents might have. The most wholesome type of financial assistance consists in helping the student to help himself. A student aid program should develop qualities of thrift and self-reliance, as does the workstudy plan at Cumberland.

Much of the financial assistance at Cumberland is given in the form of remunerative employment. The work program is optional and the amount of work depends on ability and need. Continued employment and promotion depend upon the quality of work done. A variety of jobs are available from work in the College's cafeteria or the maintenance department to the positions of faculty assistants, photographers, postal clerks, and secretaries.

Self-help opportunities are afforded to over 600 youngsters who work an average of twelve hours per week under guidance and supervision.

To cultivate an appreciation for physical and mental health. Cumberland seeks to help each student become aware of the importance of physical and mental health and to show how good health may be maintained. Five semester hours of physical education and health are required of all students.

As natives of the area, each summer several Cumberland students work and live in isolated mountain communities. These students provide recreational, health, nutritional, and community development programs for the people of the area. Most importantly, they convey an image of success with which the children of the communities can identify.

Some students complement their classroom learning with meaningful field work experience where they are able to identify problems and suggest solutions, thus developing that sense of community effort necessary to human well-being. In addition, they earn financial help needed to continue their education.

Cumberland's students believe in the lasting values of assistance to the people of the mountain communities. The Appalachian Ministries program, originated by students, seeks to help communities mentally, physically, and spiritually. Appalachian Ministries is a rewarding and meaningful program that has been exceptionally successful since its inception because of its people-to-people concern and its helpfulness to so many less fortunate mountain people.

To help uplift this low income area through Appalachian outreach programs. Recognizing that education affords the only real and permanent solution to the social and economic ills of the area, Cumberland seeks to meet the needs of the area by providing educational programs and by sponsoring specialized community outreach programs. Annually the College sponsors for local high school students, a music festival, a chemistry symposium, a science fair, and a mathematics contest. A regional meeting of guidance counselors in public schools is also held annually. The College considers it an opportunity and obligation to help transform the life of the Appalachian area.

Outreach programs are responsible for creating interest and enrollment in the College, referring of social problems to appropriate agencies, allowing insights into careers by social science and health students, developing indigenous leadership for mountain areas, identifying human needs, and providing people and services to meet these needs, and providing a link between specialized service agencies and isolated mountain communities.

KEEPING OUR PROMISES

Predicting and planning for the future is obviously a task that is filled with many and varied challenges. Those who plan must look with critical judgment upon the past, live creatively in the present, and maintain vision and courage so that significant value may not vanish in the future. Thus, plans for Cumberland's future are made cautiously, with plans and projections based upon the past and present as reflected in the findings of a comprehensive self-study. As the problems and prospects are contemplated, there is a reaffirmation of faith in the purpose and promises of Cumberland College.

As Cumberland looks toward the future, the College is faced with two critical tasks: how to maintain itself as a distinctive, life and work College while at the same time providing needed Appalachian outreach programs; and how to provide urgently needed buildings and facilities without passing the debt retirement and interest payments on to the students to the degree of excluding the very students we are trying to reach.

We firmly believe that the answers to these two concerns are found in our long-range plan. This program will provide the needed funds which will enable Cumberland to continue its historic mission of service to Appalachia. The program was developed from the suggestions, recommendations, and projections made by faculty, staff, trustees, alumni, and students working as members of committees in a self-study of Cumberland College. With your help we will be able to keep our promises.

PROPOSED PROJECTS

The Gatliff Building. The Dr. Ancil Gatliff Memorial Building was built in 1955. Since that time the building which houses the College chapel, major administrative offices, and academic classrooms has served as the primary focus of the campus. There are several renovations needed to keep the Gatliff Building functional: revising electrical services, providing a central air-conditioning system, space realignment, and handicap accessibility.

The Science Building. The Biology Wing, constructed in 1961, houses classrooms, laboratories, and offices for the biology department, the geology department, and the learning skills center. The P. R. Jones Chemistry Wing, built in 1968, houses the offices, classrooms, and laboratories for the chemistry department, the mathematics department, and the physics department. This building presently has many needs for modernization: safety equipment for the laboratories, improved insulation, improved electrical service, improved air conditioning systems, and energy conservation measures.

The Norma Jeanne Perkins Hagan Library. The Hagan Library, constructed in 1959, houses the library, learning materials center, instructional media center, a language laboratory, the department of data processing science, plus conference rooms and offices. The needs are basically energy conservation to make the building more comfortable.

Restoration of Roburn and Johnson Halls. Roburn Hall, Cumberland's first building, and Johnson Hall, the College's second building, have served for almost a century. An ambitious and thorough restoration of these two buildings will enable them to continue to serve Cumberland College's students for another 100 years. These facilities are in need of major repairs: new roofs, new plumbing and bathrooms, new stairways, and structural revisions. In addition, energy conservation measures such as new windows, air conditioning systems, and new heating systems will save utility costs and provide living comfort for each resident.

Hip roofs for Asher, Archer, the McGaw Music Building, and the Campus Center. For functional, architectural, and aesthetic reasons, hip roofs need to be added to these buildings. Hip roofs are very functional and practical, shedding the tremendous weight of rain and snow, and extending the life of the buildings. These roofs will also help beautify the campus and give the campus buildings architectural continuity.

TO PROVIDE BASIC NEEDS

Endowment. Unlike some private colleges, Cumberland College does not have a large endowment to provide much needed income for our students' financial needs. Presently, the College must provide over $2,300,000 in student financial aid. Without this aid many of our students could not attend college. An endowment of $50,000,000 would provide enough income to meet our students' needs and would insure that Cumberland College will continue to serve mountain students for another 100 years. The earnings from an increased endowment will supplement what the students can pay and will help us to keep the educational costs low. It is hoped that much of this goal will be accomplished through wills and bequests and planned gifts.

Scholarships, loan money, and workstudy grants. These funds will be utilized to help meet needs of students, primarily from Appalachia. The loan funds will provide a resource for revolving loans of both short and long duration to be made to students in need of such assistance. The workstudy grants will provide students with the opportunity to work their way through school. The scholarship funds will allow outstanding students to study in the field of their choice.

Gifts for operation, including money for faculty salary increases. Each day it costs in excess of $42,000 to operate Cumberland College. General fund gifts will help the College meet operational costs. The importance of this fund can best be understood when related to an individual's annual budget. The operating expenses of the College are like an individual's expenses for daily necessities. From personal experiences each of us knows how the cost of necessities has dramatically increased in recent years.

Academic chairs. In order to provide true excellence in education, Cumberland College needs to add endowed academic chairs in the areas of free enterprise, music, religion, chemistry, biology, English, history, data processing, and in other appropriate areas. Once established, these endowed funds will provide an annual income that will enable the College to attract the best and the brightest scholars in each discipline. Because the chairs will be endowed, the endowment will provide income for perpetuity.

TO PROVIDE NEW BUILDINGS
AND ADDITIONS TO PRESENT BUILDINGS

Physical Education and Convocation Center. The gymnasium constructed in 1928 contains a basketball arena which also serves as a "make-shift" auditorium. However, since the College has no facility large enough to seat the entire student body, faculty, and staff for special convocation activities and since existing facilities do not adequately provide for the current needs of the physical education department, a new multi-purpose center is needed which can provide for the educational needs as well as for the recreational activities. This center will contain adequate office facilities, concession stand, ticket booth, classrooms, basketball courts, locker rooms, swimming pool, handball courts, and several bowling lanes. This building will also contain an athletic Hall of Fame.

Outdoor track and small football stadium. The current outdoor track needs refurbishing and lighting is needed for night events.

In 1985 the College played its first football game in over sixty years. Football players aren't here for a "free ride." They pay us to play. This non-scholarship football program is no drain on the budget. In fact, these paying students help us assist the students who can't pay. Non-scholarship football increased the male to female ratio, provided a fall activity, and helped recruit paying students. The renewal of this fall sport has brought excitement, entertainment, and revived school spirit to the College as well as increasing student enrollment. Presently our team must play its home games at the Williamsburg City School field. A suitable stadium is needed for the large crowds that attend the games and for the team to have a place to call home.

Mathematics, Physics, Data Processing, Engineering, and Planetary Complex. Cumberland College has in the past and will in the future continue to play a critical role in training and developing indigenous leadership for Appalachia. With the constant forward thrust of technology we are finding it more difficult to furnish the facilities and equipment to prepare our students. For this reason we propose a complex to house and to permit growth in the school's mathematics, physics, data processing, and engineering-oriented areas.

Board Room. Currently we do not have a facility where formal meetings, such as Board of Trustees, the Alumni Board, the Development Board, and others, can take place. Meetings are often held off campus at the College's expense. A designated Board Room would eliminate this costly procedure and make these groups feel more like a part of the College family.

Formal Dining Room. To be located in the T. J. Roberts Dining Hall, a Formal Dining Room will enable the faculty, staff, and special guests of the College to gather for special occasions in the comfort of a family-like atmosphere.

TO PROVIDE APPALACHIAN OUTREACH PROGRAMS

Restaurant, Lodge, and Museum. Because the city of Williamsburg is located on Interstate 75 and is the northbound gateway to Kentucky and the southbound gateway to the South, there is a need for Cumberland, "The College of the Mountains," to open a regional restaurant and to build a Museum of Appalachia where regional arts and crafts such as furniture, quilts, handcrafts, pottery, musical instruments and other items can be displayed and sold. These crafts will be made by our students, and the entire operation will be staffed by our students.

TO PROVIDE EQUIPMENT

Audio-Tutorial Equipment. Audio-tutorial equipment is needed in the Learning Skills Center and the Writing Laboratory, as well as in other areas.

Instructional Media Equipment. Projectors, films, cameras, video recorders/players, and other materials are needed in the Instructional Media Center. These materials can easily be transported to individual classrooms for use to enhance instruction.

Scientific Laboratory Equipment. With almost daily advances in scientific knowledge and procedures, it is of the utmost importance for the College to prepare its science-related majors for successful lives in their chosen professions. In order to do this Cumberland must replace old, outdated equipment with new, up-to-date equipment. To say the least, this is an expensive process.

Computers. In the fall of 1980 the College initiated a data processing science program, and each year the program continues to attract more students. Additional computer hardware and software are needed in order to meet the training needs of the students in this program. This equipment will significantly upgrade our current equipment. Additionally, all personnel, student, and financial records of the College are in the process of being transferred to computer records for more efficient retrieval and processing. This will greatly improve the record keeping of the College.

TO PROVIDE MONEY FOR OTHER PROJECTS

College Master Plans. This fund will provide a means for making plans and designs for College buildings.

Campus Beautification Plan. This fund will provide money for trees, shrubs, flowers, and greenery to help the College maintain aesthetic appeal.

A Grand Entrance. An entrance to the College will provide continuity to the campus and will serve as a directory and information distribution center for new students, parents, and guests to the campus. This entrance will proudly fly the American flag and the flags representing each country or nation from which our international students come. The entrance will serve as "The Gateway to Tomorrow" for all students who enter.

Property Acquisitions. In the past few years the College has been able to acquire some property that is contiguous to the main campus. The result has been a greatly beautified and unified campus. But there is more to be done. Some of the buildings to be acquired could be used for student, staff, and faculty housing or for other needs.

Retirement Village. Many of the College's faculty and staff have served our mountain students long and well. In fact, some have dedicated their lives to the College and to our students. In grateful appreciation and so that we can continue to aid these faculty and staff members, the College needs to build a Retirement Village where these dedicated people may choose to live out their retirement and continue unselfishly to help our students.

WAYS OF HELPING CUMBERLAND COLLEGE KEEP ITS PROMISES

Gifts of Cash. A gift of cash is the most frequently used way through which Cumberland receives financial support. Convenience and simplicity of tax considerations make this manner of giving to Cumberland College a desirable alternative.

Gifts of Securities. A gift of securities is often an attractive way to make a gift to Cumberland. This is particularly true if the securities have appreciated in value over their original cost.

Gifts of Real Estate. You may make a gift of real estate to Cumberland, regardless of its location, and receive a charitable deduction credit. If the real estate is investment property, depreciation may enter into the evaluation of the gift. In such an instance your tax counselor should be consulted.

A Bequest. A gift by Will to Cumberland is a way in which many friends have remembered the College. A testamentary gift to the College qualifies as a deductible contribution for Federal Estate Tax purposes.

Gift Annuity and Life Income Contracts. A gift annuity is an attractive form of gift wherein the donor and/or his beneficiary may receive a life income from the assets given irrevocably to the College. Upon the termination of the life income interest, the remaining assets become the sole property of the College.

Charitable Remainder Trust. A gift may be made to Cumberland College through a living or testamentary charitable remainder trust which may also provide for a non-charitable intermediary beneficiary. Your tax counselor or Cumberland College can provide further information.

Life Insurance. An irrevocable gift of a life insurance policy which has served its original purpose is often a convenient way to support Cumberland College. The tax benefits depend upon the status of the policy at the time of the gift.

Gifts-in-Kind. Contributions of art objects such as jewelry, antiques, paintings, books, and other valuable property may be given to Cumberland College. The fair market value of the property on the date of the transfer is allowed as a charitable deduction if the property is related to the educational functions of the College. The property is efficiently removed from your estate and, therefore, is not subject to the Federal Estate Tax.

Living Memorial. One of the noblest exercises of our freedoms is to make some of our giving immortal by directing it to a special project or objective we cherish. To give a Living Memorial expresses a sense of gratitude for the blessings we enjoy through the goodness of God. A Living Memorial assures everyone that the noble living and the noble dead can forever be bound up in the life, endeavors, and extensions of an institution, such as Cumberland College, which is devoted to the glory of God and to the benefits of mankind.

Cumberland College is, in essence, a living, working memorial. The College honors the foresight, sacrifice, and service of those who have gone before while it serves the living. A Living Memorial contribution will extend its benefits to generations yet unborn.

AN INVESTMENT IN TOMORROW

From the beginning the College has been and continues to be a work of faith. I know of no other College more dependent on gifts for its day-to-day operation than is Cumberland College. Cumberland will continue its quality liberal arts,[8] value-laden mission to students primarily, but not exclusively, from our hills and hollows.

Cumberland is probably the only college in the country which has a fund with which to purchase shoes, clothes, a warm coat for winter, eye glasses, and other needed items for the students. Many of our youngsters could not stay in school were it not for this "extra" assistance. Your help is needed, appreciated, and never wasted or taken for granted. An investment in Cumberland College today is an investment in a brighter tomorrow for our students.[9]

BIGGER — BETTER

The path to greatness in the past as in the future is a commitment to quality, ethics, and values. These commitments have never been confused; nor will they be. As one of the College's early presidents E. E. Wood noted, "But in our efforts to promote its growth let us never separate the word 'bigger' from the word 'better'. . . . An institution grows better by consecration and sacrifice . . . . the aim must always

---

[8] Appendix XV contains a narrative of the College's commitment to the liberal arts as well as the College's purpose and objectives as recorded in the *Catalogue,* 1986-1987, p.5.

[9] The preceding pages were excerpted from the College's long range plan, *Promises to Keep.*

be to make the institution better.''[10]

THE BEST IS YET TO BE

It has been through disappointments and difficulties that this institution has persevered. The College leaders have labored undauntedly through recession and depression, through wars and controversies, and through revenue shortfalls. The history of Cumberland College is one of strength. While future generations will reap where they did not sow, it is equally true that we are beneficiaries today of all of those yesterdays. The past is but a prologue; the best is yet to be. While crisis and conflict are seen on the pages of time, there always have been those few who dreamed the impossible dream and were willing to sacrifice everything to bring it to pass; so shall it continue to be.

In the words of the immortal Daniel Webster:

If we work upon marble, it will perish. If we work upon brass, time will efface it. If we rear temples, they will crumble to dust. But if we work upon men's immortal minds, if we imbue them with high principles, with the just fear of God and love of their fellow men, we engrave on those tablets something which no time can efface, and which will brighten and brighten to all eternity.[11]

REFLECTING ON THE PAST AT ARLINGTON

On 2 February 1986 I stood in front of General Green Clay Smith's tomb at Arlington National Cemetery for the first time, not having known prior to the writing of this book of this man's influence on the creation of Cumberland College. No one could possibly have known the impact this single, solitary life, along with that of R. C. Medaris, would have on this area and, indeed, this nation. In the spontaneity of the moment, and as I made my way to Smith's monument past John F. Kennedy's grave, high and lifted up on a majestic spot at Arlington, I thought of Green Clay Smith's life and of his contribution along with the contributions of R. C. Medaris, E. S. Moss, Ancil Gatliff, and countless others who have passed on the stage of time. Their faith has truly been vindicated. The words commonly attributed to Ralph Waldo Emerson are certainly true, ''What lies behind us and what lies before us are small matters compared to what lies within us.''

---

[10] Wood, ''Dr. Gatliff's Vision,'' in *Doctor Ancil Gatliff*, pp. 15-16.

For a listing of the College's enrollment from the beginning to the present, see Appendix XVI.

[11] Daniel Webster, Speech, Faneuil Hall, 1852, from Burton Stevenson, *The Book of Quotations* (New York: Dodd, Mead and Company, Inc., 1937), p. 1312.

Here's what a few of our alumni and other friends think of Cumberland College, its mission, and *Promises to Keep,* our long-range development plan.

(Photographs from *Promises to Keep*)

FRANCES JONES MILLS
State Treasurer and
Former Secretary of State
Commonwealth of Kentucky

"While a student at Cumberland College, the ideas of truth, loyalty, and progressiveness, and the importance of having Christian principles and concerns for my fellow man were instilled in me. These ideas and principles have helped me to obtain the many worthwhile things I have been able to accomplish."

HOWARD R. BOOZER
Executive Director
South Carolina
Commission on Higher Education

"I attended Cumberland from September 1940 to May 1942 while it was still a junior college. I have attended several colleges and universities since then and have earned four degrees, including the doctorate. In none of my later experiences as a student did I have better teachers than those I studied under at Cumberland College. I became aware later that a large proportion of the students benefited from scholarships that benefactors of the college made available. Such aid made it possible for a number of my friends and fellow students to attend Cumberland College; in most cases no other options were available to them. Cumberland College continues to serve as the path to further educational opportunity, and to training for a number of professions, for large numbers of young people from Kentucky, Tennessee and other states. Many return to their home areas and contribute significantly to the social and economic improvement of those areas. It is most important that Cumberland continue vital and strong."

ARLISS L. ROADEN
Executive Director
Tennessee Higher Education Commission

"Since my graduation from Cumberland in 1949, I have reflected often on the impact of Cumberland on me both while I was a student, and subsequently on the development of my thinking and my career. To be sure, the impact was, is, and will continue to be forceful and positive. What Cumberland was [and I'm sure still is] goes beyond size, affiliation, curriculum, and even the quality of the faculty. Rather, there is an institutional spirit of accepting, caring, and helping. This spirit is contagious and it lives on. In my career I have come in contact with Universities and Colleges throughout this country and abroad. Some institutions emit qualities that inspire students to appreciate themselves, to honor other people, and to sustain a zeal for learning; other institutions don't seem to have those qualities. Cumberland does. As a native of the Appalachian region, I can attest that the institutional spirit which I described is important to a student of the region. Moreover, it is important for all students from all parts of the world."

THE LATE
CRATIS WILLIAMS
Acting Vice Chancellor
for Academic Affairs
Appalachian State University

"It is my understanding that Cumberland has remained steadfast through the generations in its obligation to the promising and deserving but poor young people of the Appalachian region. Had it not been for Cumberland College, I could not have gone to college myself. The oldest of five children in a family trying to survive on a mountain farm far from markets and in a section with inadequate roads, I was fortunate to be able even to attend the county-seat high school where my father paid board and room expenses for me. During the latter part of my senior year in high school my principal told me about Cumberland. I was accepted, awarded a tuition scholarship, given a workship which enabled me to pay for my room and board, and extended a small loan which permitted me to pay incidental expenses. I was not asked to repay the loan until I had completed my undergraduate education later at the University of Kentucky. Officials at Cumberland were not only understanding and helpful, but they were keenly sensitive to the fierce pride of mountain youth. Hundreds of young men and women from the mountains continue to find at Cumberland the same kind of opportunities which I found there. Although I know that the effort of the college must be limited, it nevertheless deserves the fullest measure of support to enable it to extend opportunities to larger and larger numbers of capable, ambitious, and deserving but poor young people from Appalachia."

THE LATE WALLACE BOYD
President, Oakwood Markets, Inc. &
Affiliated Companies

"Cumberland College has many promises to keep. These promises are the same ones the College made to me as a student. The promise of an opportunity to learn, to grow and to excel by developing one's full potential; and the promise of a chance to make a significant contribution to society."

THE LATE MAHAN SILER
Executive Food Broker and Bean Packer

"Cumberland College has contributed greatly to the cultural and economic welfare of the Appalachian region. I know of no school that gets as much per dollar expended as does Cumberland."

BING CROSBY
Loan Fund Established at
Cumberland College

Bing Crosby welcomes Cumberland alumnus Bill Thompson and his wife Susan to the Bing Crosby Open at Pebble Beach, California. Bill was the recipient of the 1976 Bing Crosby Youth Fund Loan which is co-sponsored by the 3M Corporation.

PATRICIA NEAL
Academy Award Winning Actress

"Cumberland College is a shining city set on a hill serving boys and girls coming from the hills and hollows of Appalachia.

While I did not attend Cumberland College myself, I do know of the service the college provides for many Appalachian youngsters who otherwise would not have had an educational opportunity.

If one were to remove all of the medical doctors, attorneys, teachers, and other professional people from Eastern Kentucky who are Cumberland's graduates, there would be a void which could not be filled. That is what Cumberland College is doing, and that is what makes Cumberland College great.

I hope that you will join me and others in your support of this institution."

The great actress Patricia Neal was born at Packard in 1926. Ms. Neal's father, William Burdette Neal, had come from his home in Virginia to visit his sister Maude who had come to Williamsburg to attend college but who stayed here when she married Will Mahan. Patricia's father went to work in the office of the Southern Coal and Coke Company at the mines at Packard. He later married Eura Patricia Petrey. Miss Petrey's father was Dr. Pascal Petrey, the mining camp doctor. In 1929 Ms. Neal and her parents moved to Knoxville.

Ms. Neal's acting has won for her an Academy Award, and her struggle to overcome the effects of a stroke led to her choice as *Good Housekeeping* Woman of the Year.

In referring to her life, Ms. Neal says "My life is only a tiny grain of sand upon this fabulous earth . . . ."

Jones, "Legend and Lore," 8 August 1985; Siler, "Heads or Tales," 8 January 1976 and 10 June 1965.

CAMPUS SCENES

(Photographs from *Promises to Keep*)

APPENDIX I

MEMBERS OF THE BOARD OF TRUSTEES
OF
WILLIAMSBURG INSTITUTE AND CUMBERLAND COLLEGE

The first date following each name indicates the first year of service on the Board while the second date indicates the last year of service. The first members of the Board, appointed at meetings of the Mt. Zion Association in 1887 and 1888, oversaw the founding of the Institute. In 1889 after the school opened its doors, additional members were added. Members of the first Board, then called the Board of Directors, are indicated with an * while current members of the Board of Trustees are indicated with **. In 1960 the College's Charter was changed regarding length of service of Trustees. Since that time Trustees have been elected to serve a four-year term. They are then eligible for reelection for another four-year term. After eight years, however, a Trustee must remain off the Board for a period of one year before being eligible for another four-year, renewable appointment. This process can continue indefinitely. In some of the earlier records the title for the chairman of the Board is listed as president of the Board and the vice-chairman's title is listed as vice-president of the Board.

N.A. Archer, 1911-1946

Robert Asher, 1908-1914

Samuel D. Ballou, 1975-**; Chairman 1981-1982

Charles Barnes, 1970-1986; Chairman 1980

Jesse Bell, 1964-1971

John A. Black, 1889*

Haskell Bolding, 1965-1969; Secretary 1969

William Brown, 1967-1968

Robert Browning, 1986-**

Charles Buhl, Sr., 1966-1986

W.J. Caudill, 1898-1902

Mrs. W.T. Chappell, 1971-1978; Secretary 1973-1978

B.E. Cheely, 1930-1966

W.J. Chestnut, 1961-1968

James Croley, Jr., 1964-1981; Vice Chairman 1969

Arthur Dale, 1969-1978

Robert Daniel, 1957-1974; Chairman 1966-1974

Hywell Davies, 1904-1908

J.H. Davis, 1893-1903; Secretary 1897-1899

E.O. Edwards, 1955; (Elected to serve unexpired term of A.T. Siler)

C.G. Ellison, 1898-1939; Secretary 1900-1939

J.M. Ellison, 1895-1942; Vice Chairman 1906-1907; Vice Chairman and Assistant Treasurer 1907-1910; Vice Chairman and Treasurer 1911-1942

W.A. Ellison, 1940-1942

William Ellison, 1889*

Paul Estes, 1976-**; Vice Chairman 1979-1982; Chairman 1983

J. Donald Faulkner, 1977-1984

W.H. Felix, 1902-1912

Charles E. Freeman, 1969-1980; Vice Chairman 1975; Chairman 1976

H.H. Fuson, 1923-1964

L.S. Gaines, 1927-1928

Gilbert Garrard, 1889*

Charles Garringer, 1964-1965

A. Gatliff, 1888*-1918; Chairman 1888-1918

E.M. Gatliff, 1949

J.B. Gatliff, 1918-1964; Chairman 1931-1964

J.B. Gatliff, Jr., 1946-1965; Vice Chairman 1958-1965

J.G. Gatliff, 1894-1897

George Griffin, 1966-1985; Chairman 1975

H.C. Gentry, 1889*

Bill Hacker, 1982 -**

Mrs. William Hagan, 1957

E.D. Hall, 1949-1953

David Huff, 1969-**; Vice Chairman 1976; Chairman 1977-1980; Secretary 1982-1983, 1987

Billy G. Hurt, 1980-**

J.D. Johnson, 1969-1970

C.H. Keeton, 1893-1899

Ray Kelly, 1987-**

William Lamkin, 1987-**

Raymond Lawrence, 1971

Joseph J. Leary, 1972-1979

Herman E. Leick, 1972-**; Vice Chairman 1977, 1984-1987

J.W. Logsdon, 1900-1902

E.C. Mahan, 1915-1948

J.M. Mahan, 1896-1936

J.P. Mahan, 1888*-1906; Vice Chairman 1888-1906

T.B. Mahan, 1896-1930; Chairman 1918-1930

T.E. Mahan, 1950-1970; Secretary 1960-1961; Chairman 1965-1966

John Meadors, 1889-1896

W.H. Moody, 1916-1918

E.S. Moss, 1888*-1904; Chairman (temporary) 1888; Secretary 1888

George Munro, 1966-**; Vice Chairman 1972

S.W. McComb, 1919-1945

O.G. Nicholson, 1957-1967

James Oaks, 1985-**

Charles Osborne, 1979-1986; Secretary 1984-1986

Robert Palmer, 1961-1968

J.Q. Pearce, 1889*

George Pedigo, 1961-1963

N.B. Perkins, 1917-1955

Mrs. N.B. Perkins, 1957-1964

Calvin Perry, 1987-**

John N. Prestridge, 1893-1896; Secretary 1895-1896

Elmer G. Prewitt, 1968-1975

Floyd Price, 1982-**

William Ramsay, 1961-1969

S.M. Reams, 1946-1948

M.A. Reese, 1972-**; Secretary 1979-1980

A.A. Richardson, 1935-1956

Gorman J. Roberts, 1956-1979

T.J. Roberts, 1936-1959; Secretary and Treasurer 1939-1959

James Roland, 1974-**; Secretary 1981

B.F. Rose, 1911-1921

Judy Rose, 1986-**

J.R. Sampson, 1888*-1915; Secretary 1888

R.D. Sanders, 1960-1978

Carl D. Sears, 1974-1981

N.M. Scales, 1889*

A.T. Siler, 1901-1953; Vice Chairman 1946-1953

E.E. Siler, Sr., 1946-1965

E.E. Siler, Jr., 1966-**; Vice Chairman 1966-1967, 1970-1971, 1983; Chairman 1984-1987

J.W. Siler, 1887*-1912; Treasurer (temporary) 1887; Treasurer 1889-1912

Mahan M. Siler, 1948-1956

M.V. Siler, 1916-1934

C.L. Smith, 1956-1963

Keith P. Smith, 1965-1972

S. Stanfill, 1889-1897

Joe M. Stanford, 1977-1984

E.N. Steely, 1889-1893

Ezra Stephens, 1905-1916

APPENDIX II

PRESIDENTS

William James Johnson, Principal	1889-1890
Edwin Ellsworth Wood, President	1890-1893
John Newton Prestridge, President	1893-1897
Edwin Ellsworth Wood, President	1898-1910
Gorman Jones, Acting President	1910-1912
Edwin Ellsworth Wood, President	1912-1919
Albert Robinson Evans, Acting President	1919-1921
Charles William Elsey, President	1921-1925
James Lloyd Creech, President	1925-1946
James Malcolm Boswell, President	1947-1980
James Harold Taylor, President	1980-

APPENDIX III

ACADEMIC DEANS

Arkley Wright	1920-1926
Parry Raymond Jones	1927-1961
Elmer Charles Masden	1961-1980
Joseph E. Early	1980-

BUSINESS OFFICERS, TREASURERS

John Wesley Siler	1887-1912
James Madison Ellison	1912-1942
Thomas J. Roberts	1942-1959
Myrtle Nicholson	1959-1974
George G. Ramey	1975-

APPENDIX IV

FACULTY AND ADMINISTRATIVE STAFF

The information listed here has been taken from the College's Catalogues (from the first Catalogue in 1889 to the end of the spring semester, 1987). In several of the Catalogues only the department was listed for each individual with no rank being given, so no attempt has been made to list the ranks from those years. If errors of omission have occurred we express our sincere apology. No attempt has been made to locate the names of persons who may have served for interim periods after a Catalogue was published and before a new Catalogue was issued. We recognize this error as well as the error resulting from name changes. No Catalogues were published during the years from 1943 through 1945 because of World War II.

NAME	YEARS	DEGREE	DEPARTMENT
Abbott, Ruth	1978-1979	M.S.N.	Nursing Education
Adair, Paula Jean	1985-Present	B.S.	Senior Accountant
Adams, Constance	1979-1980	B.S.N.	Nursing Education Part Time
Adams, Maude	1907-1908		Teachers Department Third Grade
Adkins, Flora	1914-1915		Piano
Adkins, Leota	1907-1908		Second Grade
Allen, Benjamin Ray	1971-1981	Ph.D.	Assistant Professor of Biology
Allen, Johnnie L.	1979-1981	B.S.	Assistant Professor of Military Science
Allison, William Thomas	1954-1967	M.A.	Part-Time Instructor of Music (Evening Program)
Ambellas, C. Victor	1959-1961	B.A.	Biological Sciences
Ammendolia, Anthony J.	1976-1979	B.S.	Associate Professor of Military Science
Anderson, Agnes	1918		Grade Work
Anderson, Frances Fern	1929		History
Anderson, Nancy Lee Brooks	1976-1986	M.B.A.	Instructor of Business Administration
Angel, Sylvia	1956-1981	B.S.	Librarian, Associate Librarian, Director of Placement, Director of Curriculum Lab, Associate Librarian, Director of Learning Materials Center
Arnett, Mary Ruth	1961-1980	B.A.	Assistant Librarian, Catalog Librarian
Arnold, Mary Alice	1985-1987	B.F.A., M.A., Ed.D.	Assistant Professor of Art
Arp, Florence	1907-1908		Shorthand and Bookkeeping
Austin, Lena B.	1959-1964	M.A.	English
Austin, Willis H.	1959-1962	M.A.	English
Ayers, Erma Loy	1964-1968	M.A.L.S.	Librarian
Ayers, Milas M.	1964-1968	Ed.D.	Director of Orientation, Testing, Associate Professor of Education and Psychology

Bagby, A. Paul	1932-1937	M.A., Th.D.	Literature of the Bible
Bailey, Hazel	1960-1967	M.R.E.	Assistant Dean of Women, Instructor of Religion, Counselor, Part-Time Instructor of Religion
Bailey, Jana	1975-Present	B.S., M.A.	Assistant to Treasurer, Comptroller
Bailey, Kenneth Kyle	1949-1951	A.B., M.A.	History and Social Science
Bailey, Micaiah	1973-Present	B.S., M.B.A., CPA, C.M.A.	Assistant Professor of Business Administration, Associate Professor of Business Administration
Baird, Evelyn	1961-1972	M.A.	Instructor in Physical Education and Health
Baker, E.F.	1896-1897		Tutor in A Grammar
Baker, Franklin D.	1967-1972	M.S.S.W.	Part-Time Instructor of Sociology
Baker, Nannie	1904-1906		Primary
Baker, Pearl	1977-1981		Assistant to Treasurer
Baker, Roger D.	1969-1981	B.S., M.A., Ed.D	Coordinator of Counseling, Instructor in Psychology, Assistant Professor of Psychology, Professor of Education and Registrar
Baldwin, Larry Joe	1985-1987	B.A., M.S., Ph.D.	Assistant Professor of Chemistry
Baldwin, Ray D.	1968-1974	J.D., L.L.M.	Associate Professor of Commerce and Economics, Part-Time Associate Professor of Business Administration
Ball, Ronald	1978-Present	B.S., M.A.	Assistant in Development, Part-Time Instructor in English, Assistant to President for Development
Ball, Ruby Dean	1925	A.A.	Grade Work
Baumgart, John Keppler	1939-1942	B.S., M.A.	Mathematics, German, Dean of Felix Hall
Baumgarten, Michael D.	1985-Present	B.S., M.S.	Instructor of Physical Education and Assistant Men's Basketball Coach
Baxter, Alice	1923-1925		Grade Work, Dean of Johnson Hall
Beams, Rosa Lee	1923-1926		Secretary to Dean, Secretary to President
Beardsley, Thomas B.	1968-1970	M.Ed.	Director of Orientation and Testing, Assistant Professor of Education and Psychology
Bearup, Judith	1982-1983	M.Ed.	Assistant Professor of Nursing Education

Beasley, Modena L.	1974-1976	B.S.	Instructor of Nursing Education
Begley, Joyce	1973-1976	B.S.N., M.A.	Instructor of Nursing Education, Associate Professor of Nursing Education
Best, Billy F.	1973-1976	M.S.	Part-Time Instructor of Sociology (Evening Program)
Bewley, Mable Sadtler	1929	A.B.	Art
Bewley, Ben W.	1929	A.B.	Voice
Beynon, Lisabeth H.	1960-1961	Sc.D.	Head of Department of Chemistry
Bible, Merma	1920-1921		Piano, Harmony
Bingham, W. Edward	1979-Present	B.M., M.M., D.M.A.	Part-Time Instructor of Music, Instructor of Music, Assistant Professor of Music
Bishop, Nancy W.	1948-1950	A.B., B.S.,	Librarian
Blandau, Marcia W.	1972-1973	M.S.	Part-Time Instructor of Education
Blankenbeckler, L.E.	1902-1903	L.I.	Instructor in Algebra and A Grammar
Blasingame, D. Michael	1964-1972	M.A.	Assistant Professor of English and Theatre
Bliss, Alice Caroline	1960-1961		English, Music
Bocock, Gordon	1968-1972	B.S.	Assistant Director of Men's Housing, Assistant to Dean of Men, Instructor of Health and Physical Education, Coach of Track and Cross Country
Bocock, Sue	1971-1972	M.A.	Part-Time Instructor of English
Boppert, M.E.	1910-1911		Piano
Bostic, Paul	1956-1959	B.S., M.S.,	Social Sciences
Boswell, J. Beryl	1977-1978	M.Div.	Missionary in Residence, Instructor in Religion
Boswell, James Malcolm	1931-Present	A.B., M.A., L.L.D., D.Hu.L, L.L.D.	Mathematics, Science, LT. in U.S. Naval Reserve (Active Duty), Acting President, President, President Emeritus
Boswell, Mary Dudley	1945-1984	A.B., M.A., D.M.L.	French, Modern Language, Part-Time Instructor of Modern Language, Senior Professor of Modern Foreign Language
Bowers, Robert Graves	1926	A.B., D.D.	Religious Education
Bowlin, Margaret Meadors	1985-Present	A.A., B.A., M.A.	Instructor in English and Writing Center, Instructor of Learning Skills
Bowman, Robert D.	1948-1951	A.B., B.M., M.A.	Languages
Boyd, Holland L.	1927	M.A.	Education, Dean of Men
Brady, Barbara E.	1979-1980	B.S.N.	Part-time Instructor of Nursing Education

Branson, J.W.	1917-1918		Mathematics
Branson, Mrs. J.W.	1917-1918		Commerce
Brashear, Ginger	1974	M.Ed	Education (Evening Program)
Brashear, Richard	1965-1975		Assistant Dean of Men, Director of Student Aid, Director of Financial Aid
Bridges, Russell	1967-1969		Vice President in Charge of Development
Briley, James E.	1983-Present	B.A., M.B.A.	Assistant Professor of Business Administration
Brock, Bertie	1906-1907		Primary
Brock, Charles R.	1891-1892	B.S.	Instructor in German
Brock, Dan	1976		Director of Student Activities
Brock, Laura E.	1891-1893		B German
Brooks, Anna Beth	1978-Present	B.S., M.R.E., M.A.	Career Planning and Placement
Brooks, Clarence Martin	1978-Present	A.B., M.Div., M.R.E., Ed.D.	Director of Counseling Services Center, Assistant Professor of Religion
Brooks, Oscar Stephenson	1959-1963	Th.D.	Religion
Broome, John David	1966-Present	B.A., M.A., B.D., Th.D.	Assistant Professor of History, Assistant Professor of Religion and History, Associate Professor of Religion and History, Professor of Religion and History
Broome, Mavis	1976-Present	M.A.	Instructor in Special Education (Evening Program)
Brown, Hays	1973-1974		Assistant Treasurer
Brown, Helen P.	1911-1916		Matron of Johnson Hall
Brown, Margaret Ann	1978-1979	M.P.H.	Assistant Professor of Nursing Education
Brown, Peggy Joyce	1971-1972	M.E.	Assistant Professor of Education
Brown, Relis B.	1940-1942	A.B., Ph.D.	Biological Science
Brownlie, M.M.	1906-1911		Instructor in Telegraphy
Bryon, Essie	1924-1925		Dean of Dixie Hall
Bryant, Mary Eliza	1922-1923	A.B.	Mathematics
Bryant, Susan	1984-Present	B.A., M.A.	Head Athletic Trainer, Instructor of Physical Education
Bryant, Thomas Wade	1984-Present	B.S., M.A.	Assistant Football Coach, Instructor of Physical Education
Buchanan, Roxie	1889		Primary Department
Bunch, Lenora Angel	1976-Present	B.S., M.A.	Reading Study Assistant, Learning Skills Assistant, Assistant Professor of Learning Skills
Burgdorf, Charles E.	1979-1981	B.A.	Assistant Professor of Military Science
Byrd, Denny	1974	M.A.	Evening Program
Byrge, James	1971-Present	Master Chef	Cafeteria Manager, Director of Food Services

Caddell, Roxie	1906		D Grammar
Cagle, Julien	1950-1952	B.A., M.S.	Biological Science
Calhoun, Lois	1915-1916		Voice
Camp, Melbaline	1965-1968	M.R.E.	Assistant Dean of Women, Instructor in Religion
Canada, Ray B.	1971-1972	A.B., M.A.	Part-Time Education
Canupp, Billy Jack	1973-Present	B.A., M.Ed.	Director of Publicity, Assistant to President for Promotions
Carlough, Carl D.	1899		Principal and Professor of Mathematics
Carlton, Lessie	1972-1976	Ed.D.	Visiting Professor and Director of Reading Study Center
Carmical, Oline Jr.	1974-Present	B.A., M.A., Ph.D.	Director of Alumni Affairs, Placement and Information, Associate Professor of History and Political Science, Director of Continuing Education, Professor of History and Political Science
Carnes, Barbara Blanton	1957-Present	B.S., M.A.	English, Part-Time Instructor in Education and Psychology, Associate Professor of Education
Carnes, Frank Ferrell	1954-1987	B.A., M.A., B.D., Ph.D.	Instructor of English, Dean of Men, Instructor of English and Philosophy, Professor of English and Philosophy, Head of Department of English and Philosophy and Professor of English and Philosophy, Senior Professor of English and Philosophy
Carnes, Frank Ferrell, Jr.	1978-1979	M.P.H.	Instructor of Health
Carroll, Casey	1980-1981	M.P.H.	Instructor of Health
Carson, Georgia	1977-1979		Assistant Professor of Business Administration
Carter, Janie E.	1982-Present	B.S., M.B.A.	Assistant to President for Development Management, Instructor of Business Administration
Carter, Linda	1977-Present	B.S., M.Ed.	Assistant Dean of Women, Instructor of Health and Education, Dean of Women and Assistant Professor of Education
Caseldine, Mayme	1918		Matron of Johnson Hall
Casey, Jerry	1967-1969	M.C.M.	Instructor of Music
Caskey, Raymond L.	1968-1969		Visiting Professor of Mathematics
Causby, Vickie	1979-1980	M.S.W	Instructor of Sociology

Champion, Michael W.	1974-1980	M.A.	Instructor of Physical Education, Intramurals
Chandler, Marilyn	1975	M.A.	Education (Evening Program)
Churchill, Authur C.	1959-1964	B.S.	History, Economics, Political Science
Clark, Ted B.	1968-1970	M.S.	Instructor of Geography
Clay, Donice	1951-1973	B.S., M.S.	Home Economics, Assistant Professor of Home Economics Teachers Department
Clayton, Mrs. J.M.	1922		
Clayton, Robert David	1964-1970	M.M.	Instructor in Music and Director of Choir, Assistant Professor of Music
Clinton, John	1978-1980	B.S.	Director of Alumni Affairs
Cochran, Mary Elizabeth	1962-1967	Ph.D., L.H.D.	Visiting Professor of History and Political Science
Cochran, Mary B.	1911		Matron of Dixie Hall
Coffman, George L.	1985-1987	B.S., M.S., Ph.D.	Assistant Professor of Biology
Coker, J.D.	1902-1903	B.S.	Instructor in German and Natural Sciences
Colegrove, Donna	1977-Present	B.S., M.M.	Instructor of Music
Colegrove, Michael B.	1973-Present	B.A., M.A., Ph.D.	Assistant Director of Admissions, Part-Time Instructor of Health, Director of Student Enlistment, Coordinator of Student Aid, Director of Admissions, Director of Records and Admissions, Professor of Education and Dean of Educational Services and Registrar
Collett, Ancil	1974-1975	B.S., CPA	Business (Evening Program)
Collett, Dexter	1985-Present	B.A., M.A.	Instructor of English
Colson, Myrtle	1916		Instructor in Teachers Department
Colyer, C.E.	1897-1898	A.B.	Instructor in A & B Grammar
Combes, Linda Jackson	1983	B.A., M.A.	Director of Writing Center Lab
Combs, Ruth Ann	1975-1976	M.S.N.	Associate Professor of Nursing Education
Compton, Esther A	1947-1987	B.A., M.A.T.	Instructor of Mathematics Associate Professor of Mathematics, Part-Time Associate Professor of Mathematics, Senior Professor of Mathematics
Comstock, Marc	1983-1985	M.A.	Instructor of Physical Education, Assistant Basketball Coach
Condray, Charles E., Jr.	1938-1939	B.A., M.A.	French and Dean of Felix Hall
Conley, Larry	1984, 1986	B.A., J.D.	Part-Time Instructor of Business Administration
Cook, Jerry D.	1978-1983	Ph.D.	Assistant Professor of Physics, Associate Professor of Physics

Cook, S.G.	1898-1899	A.B.	Instructor in Mathematics and Astronomy
Cook, Verna Kay	1980-1983	M.S.	Instructor of Learning Skills
Cooper, Ken	1971-1972		Director of Publicity
Corbin, Bertha Benton	1927	M.A.	History and Dean of Women
Cordaro, Richard Brian	1986-1987	Ph.D.	Assistant Professor of Physics
Cordell, James Martin	1974-1975	M.C.M.	Evening Program
Cordell, Jerold	1976	M.A.	Evening Program
Cornwell, Joy J.	1976-1977	M.A.	Assistant Librarian
Cosimini, Hugh	1977-1983	M.A.	Instructor of Physical Education
Cox, Norman J.	1962-Present	B.A., M.S.	Physical Science and Geography, Assistant Professor of Geology and Physical Science, Associate Professor of Geology and Earth Science Teachers Department,
Creech, James Lloyd	1912-1946	A.B., B.S., LL.D.	Instructor in Teachers Department, Dean of Teachers Department, Superintendent of Grades, Dean of Education, President and Teaching Education, President and Psychology, President Emeritus
Criscillis, Arthur Lee	1982-Present	B.A., M.Div.	Assistant Director of Admissions, Director of Admissions, Dean of Admissions
Criscillis, J.H.	1889		Assistant Tutor of English
Crisp, James Allen	1964-Present	B.A., B.D., M.A., Th.M.	Associate Professor of History and Political Science, Acting Head of Department and Associate Professor of History and Political Science, Associate Professor of History, Senior Professor of History
Croft, Ada	1917-1918		Piano, Pipe Organ and Harmony
Croley, Marie Clark	1944-1948	A.B.	Voice, Public School Music, Director of Chorus
Cross, Carlyle	1976-1980	Ph.D.	Librarian and Associate Professor of English, Associate Librarian
Crowe, Richard Godfrey	1975-1977	M.B.E.	Instructor of Business Administration, Assistant Professor of Business Administration and Director of Research Services
Cummings, Lillian A.	1908-1909		Voice Culture and Chorus Work
Curtis, Kate	1892-1893		Instructor in A Grammar

Dale, Gertrude A.	1943-1948	B.S., B.S.L.S.	Librarian
Dale, Gilbert R.	1964-1972	Ed.D.	Visiting Professor of History and Political Science, Education and Psychology
Dalton, H.E.	1917-1918		Instructor in Commercial Department
Darby, Robert W.	1975-1977	Ph.D.	Director of Counseling Services, Assistant Professor of Psychology, Director of Clinical Pastoral Training, Associate Professor of Psychology
Darnaby, E.F.	1898-1899	B. Lit.	Instructor in English Literature and Mathematics
Davidson, Ermal	1947-1970		Dietitian
Davies, W.A.	1901-1902	B.S.	Instructor in German and Natural Sciences
Davis, Alice	1931-1934		Registrar
Davis, Cynthia Alice	1927		Secretary to President
Davis, Cynthia	1897-1898		Librarian
Davis, H.J.	1897-1898	B.S.	Instructor in German and Chemistry
Davis, James L.	1961-1967 1969-Present	B.S., M.A.	Part-Time Instructor in Biology, Director of Secondary Student Teaching and Associate Professor of Education and Psychology, Director of Secondary Student Teaching and Associate Professor of Education
Davis, Jerry Collins	1967-1969, 1972-1976	B.S., M.S., Ph.D.	Instructor of Biology Associate Professor of Biology, Vice-President of Development and Associate Professor of Biology
Davis, Mitzi	1979-1980		Part-Time Associate Professor of Nursing Education
Davis, Nancye C.	1976-1978		Instructor of Nursing Education
Davis, T. Michael	1976-1977	Ph.D.	Assistant Professor of Physics
DeCamp, Wilson H.	1978-1979	M.S., Ph.D.	Associate Professor of Physics
Decker, Mary G.	1918	A.B.	Science
DeGraff, Eleanor C.	1921-1922	B.M.	Piano
Denham, Mary	1917-1918		Grade Work
Denton, Anne	1921-1922		Grade Work
Dillon, Chester C.	1963-1964	M.A.	Health and Physical Education
Diseker, Virginia Marjorie	1929-1936	A.A.	Librarian
Dishman, Myrtle	1924-1925		Piano
Donovan, Mary	1978-1980	B.S.N.	Instructor of Nursing Education
Doane, Nellie M.	1908-1909		Piano
Dorward, M. Dorothy	1926-1927	A.B.	Latin
Dougherty, H.L.	1889-1890		Instructor in Preparatory Department

Dowling, Mary Ann	1984-Present	B.A., M.Ed.	Instructor of Learning Skills Center
Dowling, Tom	1984-Present	B.A., M.A.	Football Coach
Downing, Fred L.	1976-1977	Th.D.	Assistant Professor of Religion
Doyle, Barbara	1983-Present	B.A., M.A., M.S., C.D.P.	Instructor of Data Processing, Assistant Professor of Data Processing, Tennis Coach
Doyle, Donald M.	1947-1952	A.B., M.A.	Education, Director of Athletics
DuBey, Robert E. Lee	1962-1964	Ed.D.	Education
DuBois, Cleo	1949-1951	B.M.	Piano
DuBois, Richard E.	1949-1953	B.M., M.M.	Voice, Choir Director
Duke, Henrietta	1961-1968 1976-Present	B.S., M.A.	Bookstore Manager, Instructor in Special Education (Evening Program)
Duke, John P., Jr.	1959-Present	B.A., M.Ed., Ed.D.	Dean of Men, Physical Education, Health and Physical Education, Dean of Student Affairs, Dean of Men, Associate Professor of Education and Psychology, Dean of College Personnel, Director of Placement, Head of Department and Professor of Education, Dean of Student Services and Director of Graduate Program, Chairman of Department and Professor of Education
Dunlap, William	1982-1984	B.S.	Professor of Military Science
Dunston, Robert C.	1983-Present	B.S., M.Div., Th.M., Ph.D.	Assistant Professor of Religion
Dupier, Charles Mayer, Jr.	1966-Present	B.A., M.A.	Instructor of Geography and Geology, Head of Department and Associate Professor of Geography, Associate Professor of Geography and Director of Continuing Education
Duus, Erling O.	1970-1971	B.A., M.Div.	Instructor in English and History
Dyer, Samuel Coad, Jr.	1986-Present	B.S., B.A., M.A.	Instructor of Speech and Drama Director of Forensics
Early, Joseph E.	1969-Present	B.S., M.M., Ed.D.	Head of Department and Professor of Mathematics and Physics, Academic Dean and Professor of Mathematics
Early, Rubye H.	1960-1970	B.S., M.A.	Education, Director of Placement, Assistant Professor of Education and Psychology, Associate Professor of Education and Psychology

Early, Suanne H.	1981-Present	B.A., M.Ed.	Assistant to Treasurer
Early, W. Blaine, III	1979-Present	B.A.	Chairman of Department and Assistant Professor of Biology
Easterly, Marjorie Donnell	1958-1960	B.A., M.A.	Instructor of English
Edwards, Grace Kleinschmedt	1976-1977	M.A.	Associate Professor of Nursing Education
Edwards, Victor L.	1979-Present	B.S., M.Div., D.Min.	Assistant Professor of Religion, Director of Ministerial Training
Elder, Barbara	1969-1977	M.R.E.	Assistant Dean of Women, Instructor of Religion
Elliott, Elizabeth	1921-1922		Secretary to Dean
Elliott, Henrietta Taylor	1967-1970	M.M.	Instructor of Mathematics
Ellis, M.L.	1908-1909		
Ellison, Josephine	1925-1926	A.B.	Grade Work
Ellison, Lillian	1923-1924	A.B.	Grade Work
Ellison, Lois	1939-1940	B.M.	Piano
Ellison, Marcia	1975-1983		Assistant Comptroller, Supervisor of Personnel Records
Ellison, Maude	1912-1914		Voice
Ellison, Myrtle			Assistant in Piano
Ellison, Ruthella B.	1899-1901		Assistant in B and C Grammar
Elmore, Mary Jo	1967-1971	R.N.	Nurse
Elmore, Roger J.	1966-1973	M.A.	Instructor in Modern Languages, Assistant Professor of Modern Languages
Elsey, Charles William	1921-1925	A.B., D.D.	President of Faculty, President of College
Emert, Reva Joyce	1962-1983	B.A., M.S.	Health and Physical Education, Instructor of Health and Physical Education, Assistant Professor of Health and Physical Education
Engle, F.A.	1918		Teachers Department
Estes, Charles P.	1910-1911	A.M.	English and Botany
Ervin, Robert C., Jr.	1976-1978	M.A.	Instructor of Business Administration
Evans, Albert Robinson	1905-1955	A.B., M.A.	Instructor in Latin and in Teachers Department, Instructor in Latin, Algebra, and Political Economy, Instructor in English and Political Economy, Acting President, Instructor in Latin and Political Economy, English, Latin and Social Sciences, Education
Evans, Wilson A.	1930-1934	B.A.	Physical Education
Falin, Carolyn	1974-1975	M.A., M.S.	Business (Evening Program)
Falin, Paul	1966-1974	M.S.	Instructor in Health and Physical Education, Acting Director of Athletics, Basketball Coach

Farrar, David T.	1984-Present	B.S., Ph.D.	Associate Professor of Chemistry
Faulkner, E.H.	1915-1916	B.S.	Instructor in Agriculture
Faulkner, E.H., Mrs.	1916-1917	A.B.	Mathematics
Faulkner, James Hubert	1947-1969	B.S., B.A.	Bursar, Instructor of Shorthand, Part-Time Instructor of Commerce
Fichter, Thomas A.	1979-1980	M.F.A.	Instructor of Speech
Finley, Harley V.	1985-Present	B.A.	Assistant Professor and Head of Military Science
Fish, Kathryn Griffith	1984-Present	B.S., M.A.	Instructor of English
Fish, Thomas E.	1984-Present	B.A., M.A., M.Phil., Ph.D.	Associate Professor of English
Fitzgerald, J.T.	1906-1907	A.B.	Instructor in Latin and History
Flannery, Clyde	1977-1980		Instructor of Military Science
Fleeman, Gertrude Ollie	1935-1936	B.A., B.S., M.S.	Home Economics (Dietitian)
Fletcher, George Wilfred	1947-1948	Th.B., A.B., M.A.	English and History
Flint, Julia B.	1919-1921	A.B.	Teachers Department
Foley, Louise	1977-Present	A.A.	Assistant to Bursar, Senior Accountant
Foley, Richard W.	1971-Present	B.S., M.A.	Instructor of Geography, Assistant Professor of Geography
Forcht, Terry E.	1964-1966	M.B.A., L.B., J.D.	Acting Head of Department and Associate Professor of Commerce and Economics
	1967-1974		Part-Time Instructor in Economics (Evening Program)
Ford, Sterling, A.	1957-1965	B.S., M.A.	Part-Time Instructor in Education, English, Health and Physical Education (Evening Program)
Foreman, Bessie Orme	1899-1900		Music, Piano, Organ, Mandolin, Guitar
Foster, Kenneth Roger	1966-1975	M.M., Ed.D.	Instructor in Mathematics, Associate Professor of Mathematics
Foster, Wilda	1966-1975		Secretary to Financial Aid
Frazier, Thomas B.	1976-Present	B.A., M.A.	Director of Promotions, Instructor of English, Assistant Professor of English
Freeman, Bill	1960-Present	B.S., M.S.	Director of Public Relations, Director of Student Enlistment, Assistant Director of Admissions, Assistant to President in Community Relations and Associate Director of Admissions, Assistant to President, Associate Professor of Speech

Freeman, Donald	1970-1973	Ph.D.	Assistant Professor of Chemistry, Associate Professor of Chemistry, Acting Head of Department and Associate Professor of Chemistry
Frese, Frank Graham	1961-1964	Ph.D.	Chemistry, Mathematics
Frierson, Rebecca	1981-1982	B.S.	Director of Student Activities and Director of Boswell Campus Center
Fuller, Grady	1957-1960	B.A., M.S., M.A.	History and Sociology
Fuller, Landon Edward	1930	B.A., M.A.	English
Fullerton, Mary	1898-1899		Music
Fuson, Richard E.	1962-1981	B.A., M.A.	English, Associate Professor of English
Gabhart, Herbert C.	1946-1948	B.S., Th.M., Th.D.	Bible
Gaines, L.S.	1927		Religious Education
Gaines, Mary Lewis	1923	A.B.	English and Expression
Gardner, E.E.	1916-1917	A.B.	Instructor in English and German
Garlow, C.D.	1889	A.B., Ph.B.	Professor of Mathematics
Garnett, Jennie Wood	1914-1916		Piano
Gatliff, Nolia	1916-1917		Expression
Gay, Richard L.	1985-Present	B.A.	Instructor of Military Science
Gay, William B.	1984-1985	B.A., M.A., M.F.A.	Assistant Professor of Art
Geiger, Robin	1984-Present	B.S., M.S.	Instructor of Data Processing
George, Doris	1968-1971	B.S.	Part-Time Instructor in Music (Piano)
George, Thomas E.	1968-1975	B.S., B.A., M.A.	Instructor in Music, Assistant Professor of Music
Gilbert, Doyle	1970-Present		Bookstore Manager, Coordinator of Material Purchase, Comptroller, Land Development, Director of Auxiliary Enterprises, Director of Boswell Campus Grill
Gilbert, Kyle	1985-Present	A.A., B.A.	Bookstore Manager
Gillespi, Frances Calvery	1927-1929		Music (Violin)
Gillespie, Richard	1961-1962	M.S.	Physics
Gilliam, Pam	1978-1979	M.S.N.	Part-Time Associate Professor of Nursing Education
Gillis, Elizabeth	1917-1918	A.B.	Grade Work
Girlenghouse, Frank W.	1927-1928	M.A.	Social Science
Glasscock, Annette	1969-1970	M.A.	Instructor of Music
Gleaves, Allie	1907-1908		Music (Violin)
Goebel, Ulrich	1966-1967	M.A.	Instructor and Acting Head of Foreign Language Department
Goforth, David S.	1966-1967	M.A.	Assistant Professor of English

Golden, Connie	1980-1981	M.M.	Instructor of Music
Gooch, Stella	1936-1947	B.S.	Home Economics, Dietitian
Goodman, George Herman	1965-1978	M.A.	Acting Head of Department of Sociology, Associate Professor of Sociology
Gould, Willie	1910-1911		Grade Work
Grandstaff, E.G.	1903-1904	B.S.	Instructor in German and Natural Sciences
Gray, R.D.	1983-1986	B.A., M.A., Ph.D.	Assistant Professor of Physics
Gray, Soporo Faye	1966-1967	B.A.	Instructor in Commerce and Economics
Greene, J.W.	1912-1913		Matron of Dixie Hall
Greeson, Brentley D.	1954-1956	B.M., M.M.	Music (Choir Director, Voice)
Griffin, Ron	1977-1980		Director of Student Activities, Director of Boswell Campus Center
Gross, Rosa Yates	1965-1970	M.A.	Instructor in Mathematics, Instructor in Mathematics and Science, Laboratory Instructor in Chemistry
Gunter, E.I.	1962-1964	M.S.	Instructor in Biology
Hagan, George Dan	1927-1928	M.A.	Social Science, Dean of Men
Hackley, Maggie A.	1889		English and Penmanship
Hague, Grey Lynn	1935-1937	B.M., M.M.	Voice, Public School Music
Hall, Carolyn F.	1902-1903		Music
Hall, Ida Janie	1957-Present	A.A., B.A., B.D., M.A.	History and Religion, Assistant Professor of History, Associate Professor of History
Hall, James Steven	1987-Present	B.M.E., M.M.	Instructor of Music
Hall, Martha	1938-1939		Dean of Johnson Hall
Hamilton, Jewel Boone	1955-1956	B.B.A.	Commerce
Harmon, Judson S.	1969-1971	M.A.	Part-Time Instructor of Psychology
Harp, Debbie	1984-Present	B.S.	Director of Student Activities
Harper, Dee W., Sr.	1957-1960	B.S., M.S., M.Ed.	Biological Sciences
Harris, Eutha	1917-1918		Voice
Harrod, Allen F.	1975-1976	B.D.	Part-Time Instructor of Religion
Harris, W.T.	1917-1918		Matron of Johnson Hall
Hassell, M.D.	1961-1962	M.A.	Biology, Physical Science
Hatcher, Vaughn Hartley	1976-Present	B.A., M.R.E.	Instructor of Physical Education, Assistant Professor of Physical Education
Haviland, Pearl	1903-1904		Music
Hawkins, Mrs.	1910-1911		Matron of Dixie Hall
Hayes, Robert	1978-1979	Ed.D.	Psychology (Evening Program)
Hayner, Jerry	1966-1967		Director of Religious Activities

Haynes, J.J.	1889-1890		Instructor in United States History, Geography, and Physiology
Head, Maynard	1982-Present	B.S., M.A.	Assistant to President for Church Relations and Development
Healey, Doris	1917-1918		Music Vocal
Helvey, Marjorie Wells	1965-Present	B.S., M.A.	Part-Time Instructor in English, Instructor of History, Assistant Professor of History, Associate Professor of History
Helvey, O.J.	1963-Present	B.S., M.S., D.A.S., Ed.D.	Head of Department of Health and Physical Education, Professor of Health and Physical Education, Chairman of Department and Professor of Physical Education
Henderlight, Timothy B.	1973-1977	M.Ed.	Admissions Counselor, Part-Time Instructor of Health
Henderlight, Vivian Siler	1977-1983	B.S.N.	Instructor of Nursing Education
Hendrickson, Eva Allen	1963-1975	B.A., M.S.	Assistant Librarian, Reference Librarian
Heneisen, Jack David	1973-1976	M.S.	Assistant Professor of Physics
Heneisen, John	1966-1969	B.S., M.S.	Assistant to Dean of Men, Director of Men's Housing, Coordinator of Student Activities and Instructor of Education and Psychology
Henry, P.H.	1920-1921		Piano
Herring, Paul E.	1960-1968	Ph.D.	Biology, Assistant Professor of Biology
Herndon, Frances	1927-1929	A.B.	Model School
Hicks, David Bruce	1986-Present	B.A., M.Ed., Ph.D.	Assistant Professor of Political Science
Hicks, Jimmy R.	1970-Present	B.S., M.A.	Chemistry Laboratory Instructor, Instructor of Chemistry, Assistant Professor of Chemistry
Hill, Addie Lawson	1927		Model School
Hill, Alice	1945-1946	A.B.	Dean of Roburn Hall, Assistant Dean of Women
Hill, Benjamin H.	1966-1972	Ph.D.	Associate Professor of Biology
Hill, Clyde	1956-1960	B.S., M.A.	Part-Time Instructor of Nutrition, Social Science, Biology
Hill, Mabel Williams	1966-1971	M.A.	Assistant Professor of English
Hill, Marshall A.	1971-1974	Ph.D.	Assistant Professor of Music
Hill, N.M. Mrs.	1921-1926		Grade Work
Hinant, P. Irvin	1958-1959	A.B., M.A.	Sociology, English

Hinshaw, Bernice	1961-1971	M.S.	Biology, Assistant Professor of Biology
Haben, Frances Bobbitt	1926-1927	M.A.	History, Dean of Women
Hodson, Roger M.	1953-1954	B.M., M.M.	Voice, Choir Director
Hoffelder, Ann McIntosh	1963-present	B.A., M.A.T., Ph.D.	Chemistry, Part-Time Instructor of Chemistry, Assistant Professor of Chemistry, Associate Professor of Chemistry, Head of Department and Professor of Chemistry, Chairman of Department and Professor of Chemistry
Hoffelder, Robert L.	1963-Present	B.S., M.A., Ph.D.	Sociology, Instructor of Sociology, Assistant Professor of Sociology, Head of Department and Professor of Sociology, Chairman of Department and Professor of Sociology
Holbrook, Wyndee	1986-Present	B.S.W., M.Div.	Director of Campus Ministries
Holladay, Alice	1959-1960	M.A.	Assistant Dean of Women, Religion
Holmgren, Byron R.	1982-1983	Ed.D.	Professor of Education
Hood, Mary Nola	1938-1939	B.S., M.A.	Science
Hopkins, Ralph	1973-1974		Director of Student Enlistment, Director of Admissions
Hopper, Edgar	1983-Present	B.A., M.S., Ph.D.	Assistant Professor of Mathematics, Head of Mathematics Department, Acting Chairman of Department of Mathematics
Hosler, Daniel H.	1959-1966	Ph.D.	Chairman Division of Social Studies, Head of Department of History and Political Science, Professor of History and Political Science
Hosler, Russell J., Jr.	1983-Present	B.M., M.M., D.M.A.	Assistant Professor of Music
House, Coleman	1975-1976	M.A.	Special Education - Part-Time
Howard, Connie L.	1976-Present	B.S., M.S.	Part-Time Instructor of Health and Financial Aid Assistant, Instructor of Health, Assistant Professor of Health
Howard, Grace	1914-1915		Domestic Science
Howard, James Merle	1955-1956	A.B., M.A.	Education, Dean of Men

Hubbard, Harold F.	1960-1962 1966-Present	B.S., M.B.A.	Commerce, Acting Head of Department of Commerce and Economics, Assistant Professor of Commerce and Economics, Acting Head of Department and Assistant Professor of Commerce and Economics, Head of Department and Associate Professor of Business Administration, Chairman of Department and Professor of Business Administration
Hudson, W.E.	1910-1911	A.B.	Instructor in Mathematics and German
Hughes, J.W.	1917-1918		Teachers Department
Huston, Fay L.	1918-1919		Voice, Music
Hunt, Lillian	1907-1908		Seventh Grade
Hutchcroft, John C.	1975-1980	M.M.	Assistant Professor of Music
Hyder, Nema K.	1962-1964	M.S.	English
Hyder, Samuel P.	1962-1963	Ed.D.	Education, Director of Evening Program, Education
Inman, James	1924-1925		Grade Work
Inman, L.C.	1906-1907	B.Ph.	Instructor in Mathematics
Jackson, Harry R.	1923-1925		Manual Training, Dean of Men
Jackson, John E.	1959-1963	Ph.D.	Head of Department of Sociology
Jewel, Mark	1979-1983		Instructor of Military Science
Jewell, James W.	1929-1930	M.A.	Education
Johnson, Betty L.	1970-1977	B.M.	Part-Time Instructor of Music
Johnson, Elmore	1905-1909	B.S.	Instructor in German and Natural Sciences
Johnson, Neva Nelson	1950	A.B.	Acting Registrar, Typing
Johnson, Roy	1964-1979	M.M.	Instructor in Music, Associate Professor of Music
Johnson, Sidney P.	1952-1954	B.S., M.A.	Biological Sciences
Johnson, W.J.	1889-1890		Principal
Jones, Clyde	1929-1930		Secretary to President
Jones, Dorothy	1918-1922		Grade Work
Jones, Gorman	1893-1935	A.B., A.M.	Instructor in Greek and History, Dean of Departments of Greek and History, Registrar, Instructor in Greek and History, French and History, Instructor in Greek, History and Political Economy
Jones, Mrs. Gorman	1893-1896		Music
Jones, Grace	1898-1899	B.S.	Assistant in B Grammar
Jones, John	1978-1979	M.D.	Health (Evening Program)

Jones, Lois Sasser	1962-Present	B.A., M.A.	Music and Director of Choir, Part-Time Instructor of Music, Instructor of Music, Assistant Professor of Music, Associate Professor of Music
Jones, Lowell	1923		Piano
Jones, M.B.	1897-1898	A.B.	Instructor in Mathematics and Astronomy
Jones, Mabel	1919-1920		Grade Work
Jones, Parry Raymond	1909-1972	B.S., M.S., L.L.D.	Instructor in Mathematics and Science, Chemistry and Physics, Academic Dean, Acting Head of Chemistry, Associate Professor of Chemistry, Dean Emeritus
Jones, Virginia Ramsey	1922-1942		Piano
Jones, W.D.	1917-1918	B.S.	Principal of Grade Department
Jordan, J.W.	1904-1918		D Grammar and Manager of Boys' Hall, Assistant Teacher and Field Agent, Instructor in Normal Department, Instructor in Manual Training, Assistant in C Grammar and Primary Departments
Juniper, Walter Howard	1938-1939	B.A., B.S., M.A., Ph.D.	French and Latin, Dean of Felix Hall
Karcher, Nancy Susan	1967-1972	B.A.	Instructor in English, Assistant Professor of English
Karr, Mary Alice	1972-1974	M.S.	Instructor of Education and Reading Study
Kazee, Buell H.	1927-1928	A.B.	Voice
Keith, B.F.	1905-1906	Ph.B.	Instructor in Mathematics and Science
Keller, William D.	1953-1955	A.B., M.S.	Commerce
Kelly, Barbara M.	1972-1974	M.A.	Assistant Professor of Modern Foreign Languages
Kelly, Gilbert B.	1962-1966	M.A.	English, Instructor in English
Kelly, Ray	1970-1972	B.S., M.S.	Assistant Director of Public Relations, Assistant Director of Admissions
Key, James B.	1984-Present	B.S., M.S., Ed.D.	Assistant Professor of Physical Education
Kidwell, Jerry G.	1974-1975	NCO	Instructor of Military Science
Kimbrough, James Marion	1961-1964	B.A., M.A.L.S.	Librarian
Kincaid, James Crofford	1963-1964	M.A.	Commerce
Kindoll, William A.	1974-1977		Instructor of Military Science
King, Blanche	1918-1919		Piano, Harmony, Pipe Organ
Kirtley, Georgia	1896-1907	A.B.	B Grammar, Grade Work

Kirtley, Pauline	1905-1918		Teacher of Art and Matron of Girls' Hall, Drawing and Painting
Kleinmann, Richard	1984-Present	B.A., M.A., Ed.D.	Associate Professor of English and Director of Writing Center
Knauper, Beverly Ann	1986-Present	B.S., Ph.D.	Assistant Professor of Biology
Knight, Minta Louise	1941-1942	A.B., M.A., B.S.L.S.	Librarian
Knight, Theresa Marie	1974-1981	M.A.	Associate Professor of Nursing Education
Knowlton, Audrey	1937-1938	B.A., B.S.L.S.	Librarian
Lancaster, John E.	1971-1975	M.A., Ph.D.	Assistant Professor of History, Director of Alumni Affairs and Assistant Professor of History
Lancaster, Keith E.	1947-1948	A.B.	Voice, Choir Director
Lancaster, Sharon B.	1971-1975	A.B., M.A.	Part-Time Instructor of Music
Lane, Michael K.	1973-1976	M.B.A.	Head of Deparment and Associate Professor of Military Science
Lanter, Everett	1923-1924		Assistant in Physics
Lathrop, Robert Morgan	1955-1962	B.S., M.A.	Science, Geography, and Geology
Lawson, Addie	1918-1921		Grade Work
Lawrence, Raymond	1972-1980	B.D.	Assistant to President in Charge of Church Relations and Special Assignments, Assistant to President for Church Relations and Part-Time Instructor of Religion
Lawson, Emma	1967-1968	M.R.E.	Assistant Dean of Women and Instructor of Religion
Lawson, R.E.	1911-1912	A.B.	Instructor in Latin and Teachers Department
Lawson, Reuben Nathan	1927-1929	A.A.	Model School and Dean of Men
Lay, Amon Leon	1977-1978	M.A.	Evening Program
Lee, Ora	1915-1916		Violin and Cornet
Lee, Viola Higgins	1947-1948	A.B., B.S.	Home Economics
Lee, William C.	1972-1975	Ph.D.	Assistant Professor of Political Science
Lefman, Michael D.	1974-1976		Instructor in Military Science
Leger, Glen M.	1967-1976	M.A.	Instructor of Chemistry, Instructor of Chemistry and Physical Science, Assistant Professor of Physical Science
Lewis, Bettie	1889-1900		Music and Elocution
Lewis, Joe O.	1966-1968	Th.D.	Associate Professor of Religion
Lewis, Lavon	1961-1962	M.S.	Physical Science
Lipps, Ray	1970-1971	B.S.	Assistant Director of Public Relations and Assistant Director of Admissions

Litton, Donna C.	1973-1976	B.S.N., M.A.	Instructor of Nursing Education, Associate Professor of Nursing Education
Lockwood, David M.	1959-1987	B.A., M.A., Ed.D.	Art, Associate Professor of Art Head of Department of Art and Associate Professor of Art, Associate Professor of Art, Senior Professor of Art
Lombardo, Jean Madsen	1984-Present	B.M., M.A., D.M.A.	Assistant Professor of Voice
Lombardo, Robert	1977-Present	B.M., M.M.	Instructor of Music, Assistant Professor of Music
Long, Robin	1979-1982	M.S.	Instructor of Physical Education
Long, Virgil E.	1971-1975	Ph.D.	Head of Department and Professor of Sociology
Lopez, Penelope	1978-1979	M.S.	Instructor of Mathematics
Lovett, Virginia Johnson	1955-1984	A.B., M.A.	English, Assistant Professor of English, Part-Time Assistant Professor of English, Senior Professor of English
Lowell, Jennie	1919-1923		Drawing and Painting
Lunsford, Gary	1972-1976	M.A.	Instructor of Health and Physical Education, Assistant Dean of Men
MacFaddon, Channing	1935-1937	B.A., M.A.	French, Latin
Maddox, Elizabeth	1924-1925	A.B.	Home Economics
Maiden, Edgar	1968-1970	M.A.	Part-Time Instructor of English (Evening Program)
Mann, M. Randolph	1974-1976	M.S.S.W.	Sociology
Manning, Claudia Kay	1981-Present	B.S.	Assistant to President for Development Management
Manor, Bertie	1923-1924		Grade Work
Marshman, Judith Kay Manfield	1967-1969	B.A.	Instructor of Sociology
Martin, Mary F.	1893-1901	A.B.	Primary
Martin, Muriel C.	1931-1934	A.B., A.M.	Latin, French
Martin, Vernon	1956-1963	B.A., M.A.	Social Sciences, Head of Department of Political Science
Masden, Elmer Charles	1955-Present	B.A., Th.M., Ph.D.	Bible, Chairman Division of Religion and Philosophy, Head of Department of Religion, Academic Dean, Assistant to the President, Consultant to President, Director of Special Projects, Dean Emeritus, Senior Professor of Religion
Mathes, Walter T.	1961-Present	B.S., M.A.	Physical Education, Health and Physical Education, Assistant Professor of Health and Physical Education, Associate Professor of Health and Physical Education

Matthews, Burrus	1955-1956	A.B., M.A.	Social Science
Mattingly, Dennis W.	1978-1980	M.S.	Instructor of Psychology
Mays, Bill	1981-1982	B.S.	Admissions Counselor
Meadors, A.J.	1895-1896		Instructor in A Grammar
Meadors, Emily	1971-Present	B.S., M.A.	Admissions Supervisor, Assistant Registrar, Registrar
Meadors, Lizzie	1919-1926		Matron of Johnson Hall
Meadors, Millard F.	1904-1906	A.B.	Instructor in Latin, Algebra and A Grammar
Meadows, Roberta	1958-Present		Second Assistant Bursar, Bursar
Mearns, James Thomas	1938-1939	B.S.	Public School Music
Meeks, James L.	1964-1978	M.S., Ph.D.	Instructor in Chemistry and Physical Science, Acting Head of Department of Chemistry, Assistant Professor of Chemistry, Acting Head of Department and Associate Professor of Chemistry, Head of Department and Professor of Chemistry
Meeks, Walter	1951-1956	A.B.	Modern Languages
Meisel, Scott I.	1987-Present	B.S., M.B.A.	Instructor of Business Administration
Mellett, George K.	1963-1964	M.F.A.	Music
Mendell, Edward R.	1968-1976	M.A., Ph.D.	Assistant Professor of Health and Physical Education, Associate Professor of Physical Education and Coordinator of Intramural Activities, Associate Professor of Physical Education
Menges, Paul F.	1985-Present	A.B., M.A., Ph.D.	Visiting Professor of Business Administration
Mickeleboro, Lillian	1899-1901		Art, Drawing, Painting
Miller, Dorothy C.	1938-1939	A.B., M.A.	Science and Physical Education
Miller, Jack	1956-1959	B.S., M.E.	Education
Miller, Linda Rose Cox	1966-Present	B.S., M.A.	Instructor in Commerce, Instructor in Business Administration, Assistant Professor of Business Administration, Associate Professor of Business Administration
Miller, Percy W.	1971-Present	A.B., M.A., Ph.D.	Instructor of English, Associate Professor of English
Miller, Roscoe C.	1961-1979	M.A.	Part-Time Instructor in Education and Psychology, Sociology (Evening Program)
Miller, Wray	1968-1970	Th.D.	Visiting Professor of Sociology
Milton, J.E.	1968-1986	Ph.D.	Associate Professor of Biology
Mitchell, Claudia T.	1983	B.S., M.S.	Assistant Professor of Mathematics

Mitchell, Stephen Harold	1983-1984 1986-Present	B.S., M.S., Ph.D.	Assistant Professor of Education, Associate Professor of Education
Moeller, Warren E.	1950-1951	B.S., M.B.A.	Registrar, Commerce
Monday, Franklin T.	1961-1962	LL.B.	Commerce and Economics
Monroe, Julia Montgomery	1955-1956	B.S.	Commerce
Montgomery, Mary	1947-1948	A.B., A.M.	French, Latin, Spanish
Moore, James E.	1985-Present	B.S., M.S.	Instructor of Data Processing
Moore, John R.	1954-1956	A.B.	Biological Sciences
Moore, Nannie	1905-1907		C Grammar
Moore, O.F.	1901-1902	B.S.	Instructor in Physics and Mathematics
Moore, Nell	1920-1972	B.M., M.M., Ph.D.	Piano, Chairman Division of Fine Arts, Chairman and Head of Department of Music, Head Emeritus and Part-Time Professor of Music
Moore, Susie	1905-1906		Supply in D Grammar
Moore, Wadie M.	1981-Present	B.S., M.Ed., Ed.D.	Associate Professor of Education
Morford, Evelyn	1976-1978	M.S.N.	Associate Professor and Director of Nursing Education
Morgan, Donna C.	1984-Present	B.S., M.A., M.S.	Instructor of Data Processing
Morgan, Elise Fowler	1962-1965	M.A.	Part-Time Instructor in English (Evening Program)
Morgan, Henry	1964-1979 1983-Present	B.S., M.Ed.	Assistant Professor of Physical Education, Assistant Dean of Men, Assistant Director of Men's Housing, Instructor of Health and Physical Education, Dean of Men, Women's Basketball Coach, Athletic Director, Assistant Professor of Physical Education
Morgan, Kenimer H.	1959-1981	A.B., M.Ed., Ph.D.	Chairman of Division and Head of Department of Education, Chairman of Division and Head of Department and Professor of Education and Psychology, Chairman of Division and Head of Department and Professor of Education, Part-time Professor of Education, Senior Professor of Education
Morgan, Marcia Bryant	1955-1960	A.A., B.S.	Music
Morgan, Orena W.	1973-1984	A.B., M.A.	Instructor of Education, Assistant Professor of Education, Senior Professor of Education

Morris, Cecil Arthur	1975-1982	Ph.D.	Associate Professor of Mathematics, Head of Department and Professor of Mathematics
Mosely, A.G.	1919-1923	A.B., Th.M.	Christian Religion
Mosely, A.G. Mrs.	1919-1922		Teachers Department
Mosely, Graham	1923-1924		Assistant in Chemistry
Moser, Shirley O.	1963-1966	B.M.	Part-Time Instructor in Music
Moses, Don R.	1971-1973	J.D.	Instructor in Commerce and Economics
Moses, Ermal Young Davidson	1959-1967		Dietitian
Mosier, Judy	1972-1973	B.S.	Instructor of Health and Physical Education
Moss, Anna Mae	1902-1903		C Grammar
Moss, E.S. Mrs.	1894-1898		Art
Moss, Mattie Bales	1901-1902		C Grammar
Mountjoy, Marcella Faulkner	1946-1949	A.B.	Piano
	1965-1967	B.A.	Part-Time Instructor in Music
Murphy, Joseph H.	1929-1930	B.S.	Science, Director of Athletics
Murphy, Milton	1979-Present	A.B., M.Div., M.A.	Missionary in Residence and Instructor of Religion, Assistant Professor of Religion
McClung, Charles M.,	1978-1982	NCO	Instructor of Military Science
McConachie, Michael	1985-1986	B.A., M.A., Ph.D.	Assistant Professor of Political Science
McConnell, Virginia Eertner	1917-1922		Home Economics, Dean of Women and Home Economics
McCoy, Pamela R.	1978-1980	M.R.E.	Part-Time Instructor of Health
McCracken, Suzannah	1934-1935	B.M., M.S.	Voice, Public School Music
McCreary, Terry W.	1979-1984	M.S.	Instructor of Chemistry
McCullough, Mary	1889-1890 1895-1896	A.B.	B Grammar
McDonald, Harry E.	1952-1954	A.B., M.A.	Education and Director of Athletics
McDowell, Cloyd	1981-1986	B.A.	Consultant to Mining Technology
MacFadon, Channing	1935-1936	B.A., M.A.	French, Latin
McGee, N.W.	1965-1966	Ph.D.	Associate Professor of Sociology
McGuire, Earl Martin	1974-1976	M.B.A.	Instructor of Business Administration
McIlwaine, Eliza R.	1906-1907		Music
McKeehan, Ethel G. Center	1973-1976 1980-1981	M.N., Ph.D.	Associate Professor of Nursing Education, Associate Professor and Director of Associate Degree Nursing Program
McMullan, Cora W.	1917-1918		Matron of Johnson Hall
McNeil, Deborah	1979-1981	M.S.N.	Assistant Professor of Nursing Education
McNeil, W.E.	1914-1916		Instructor in Commercial Department

McNeil, Eliza	1892-1893		Primary
McPherson, Emma	1951-Present	A.A., B.A., M.R.E., M.A.	Dean of Women, Bible, Dean of Women, English, Dean of Women and Part-Time Instructor of English, Dean of Women and Assistant Professor of English, Dean of Women and Associate Professor of English, Dean of Students and Professor of English
Nave, Mary B.	1909-1925		Matron of Girls' Hall, Matron of Boys' Hall, Matron of Felix Hall
Nelson, John Phillip	1974-Present	B.S., M.A., Ed.D.	Co-Director of Reading Study Center, Instructor and Co-Director of Reading Study Center, Instructor and Co-Director of Learning Skills, Assistant Professor and Co-Director of Learning Skills
Nelson, Russell C.	1961-1966	M.A.	Chairman of Division of Fine Arts, Acting Head of Department of Music, Associate Professor of Music, Head of Department of Music, Associate Professor of Music
Nelson, Shirley Louise	1974-Present	B.A., M.A., Ed.D.	Co-Director of Reading Study Center, Instructor and Co-Director of Reading Study Center, Instructor and Co-Director of Learning Skills, Assistant Professor and Co-Director of Learning Skills
Nettleman, A.N.	1904-1905	A.B.	Instructor in Latin and Mathematics
Nelson-Humphries, Tessa	1964-Present	B.A., M.A., Ph.D.	Instructor in English, Assistant Professor of English, Associate Professor of English, Professor of English
Nevels, Chester A.	1964-1984	B.S., M.M.	Instructor in Mathematics, Assistant Professor of Mathematics, Associate Professor of Mathematics
Newell, Edmond Bruce	1946-1950	B.S., M.S.	Biological Science
Nicholson, Myrtle	1925-1974		Secretary to Treasurer, Treasurer
Nickerson, Elathier A.	1950-1956	A.B.L.S.	Librarian
Noe, J.T.C.	1892-1893	A.M.	Instructor in English
Norman, J. Richard	1965-1967	M.A.	Instructor in History

Norton, Cynthia P.	1985-Present	B.S., M.S., Ed.D.	Assistant Professor of Health
Nutter, Laura	1973-1978	M.S.	Associate Professor in Nursing Education
Ogg, C.R.	1900-1901	A.B., B.S.	Instructor in German, Mathematics, and A Grammar
Ogg, Grace Truman	1906-1907	A.B.	Instructor in Science and B Grammar
Olson, Humphrey A.	1968-1975	M.A.L.S.	Librarian
Overton, Shirley	1981-1982	B.S.	Records Supervisor
Owens, Gail	1980-1982	M.A.	Instructor in Psychology
Packard, M. Amelia	1908-1918		Grade Work
Paisley, Lucy	1930-1931		Voice
Palmer, Jeannette M.	1961-Present	B.A., M.A.	Instructor of English, Associate Professor of English
Palmer, Robert Leland	1969-1987	B.A., Ph.D.	Associate Professor of English and Religion, Senior Professor of English and Religion
Parker, Alice	1894-1896		Librarian
Parker, Russell Albert	1961-1984	B.S., M.A.	Assistant Professor of Art, Acting Head and Associate Professor of Art, Head of Department and Professor of Art, Senior Professor of Art
Parr, John D.	1984-Present	B.A., M.S., Ed.Sp., Ed.D.	Professor of Psychology
Partin, Howard	1970-1984	M.A., Ph.D.	Instructor of Biology, Assistant Professor of Biology, Professor of Biology, Chairman of Department and Professor of Biology
Patrick, Norma B.	1985-Present	B.A., M.S.	Supervisor of Student Teachers in Elementary School, Instructor of Education
Payeur, Patricia D.	1985	B.A., M.A.	Instructor of French and English
Payne, Jesse	1905-1906		Instructor in Telegraphy
Payne, Melva Little	1979-1980	M.A.	Instructor in Mathematics
Peace, Irene	1962-Present	B.S., M.S.	Administrative Assistant, Assistant to Academic Dean-Emeritus and Assistant Professor of Health, Assistant to Special Assistant to President
Peace, Lula	1907-1908		Fourth Grade
Pennington, Judith	1986-Present	B.S., M.S.	Instructor of Mathematics
Perkins, Agnes	1959-1969		Assistant Bursar, First Assistant Bursar

Perkins, F.D.	1902-1908	A.B.	Instructor in A Grammar and Preparatory Departments, Instructor in Mathematics and History, Instructor in Logic, Principal of Grade Work, Dean of Teachers Department and Instructor of Mathematics
Perkins, Philip E.	1967-1970	M.A.	Part-Time Instructor of Education and Psychology (Evening Program)
Perkins, Shanda	1980-Present	B.S.	Assistant to Registrar, Postmistress
Perkins, Velma	1939-1942	A.B., M.A.	French and Assistant Dean of Women
Perkins, Wesley	1984-Present	B.S.	Director of Computer Services
Peters, John	1984-1985	B.S., M.S.	Acting Head and Instructor of Data Processing
Petrey, A.S.	1893-1897	A.B.	Instructor in A Grammar
Pickle, Kathleen	1946-1948		Piano
Pope, Anaflora	1923-1924		Secretary to President
Pope, Lela Walker	1966-1970	M.A.	Instructor in English and Speech
Pope, R.L.	1898-1903	A.B.	Instructor in Latin, Algebra and A Grammar
Pope, Steven Douglas	1976-1977	B.S., M.A.	Instructor in Reading Study
Porter, Lyman E.	1965-1970	M.A., Ph.D.	Chemistry, Visiting Professor of Chemistry
Potts, Erwin H.	1927-1928	A.B., Th.M.	Latin
Pratt, H.G.	1958-1960		Director of Public Relations
Prestridge, John N.	1893-1897		President, Instructor in Biblical Introduction
Price, Hattie Mae	1934-1935	B.S.	Dietitian
Price, Alberto	1947-1948	B.S., M.A.	Instructor in Education
Pritchard, Mary Campbell	1958-1959	B.A., M.A.	History
Pulli, Joseph F.	1977-1979	M.S.W.	Instructor of Sociology and Director of ALCOR Program, Instructor of Sociology
Quilling, Emily F.	1936-1937	B.A.	Typewriting and Shorthand, Acting Librarian
Quinn, Jennie	1899-1901		B Grammar, C Grammar
Quinto, Grace Virginia	1963-1984	B.S., B.S., M.S., Ph.D.	Biology, Professor of Biology, Senior Professor of Biology
Ramey, George G.	1968-Present	B.A., B.D., Th.M., Th.D.	Assistant Professor of Religion, Associate Professor of Religion, Assistant to President in Financial Operations, Acting Head and Associate Professor of Religion, Director of Business Affairs and Treasurer and Associate Professor of Religion, Director of Business Affairs and Treasurer and Professor of Religion

Ramsay, Winona	1983-Present	B.A., M.A., M.S.L.S.	Assistant Librarian
Redden, Lolan, Jr.	1981-1986	B.S., M.S.	Instructor of Mathematics
Reed, Walter W.	1930-1932	B.A.	Model School, Dean of Men
Reeves, G. Willard	1963-Present	B.E.E., B.D., Th.M., Ph.D.	B.S.U. Director, Physical Science, Chairman Divison of Religion and Philosophy, Head of Department and Professor of Religion, Chairman of Department and Professor of Religion
Renfro, John E.	1959-1985	B.S., Ed.S., Ed.D	Health and Physical Education, Head of Department of Health and Physical Education, Director of Athletics and Assistant Professor of Health and Physical Education, Director of Athletics and Associate Professor of Health and Physical Education, Senior Professor of Health
Reuter, Vicki	1979-1980	B.S.N.	Instructor of Nursing Education
Rhodes, Charles W.	1952-1953		Public Relations Director, Business Administration
Rice, Alice	1909-1910		Matron of Boys' Hall
Rice, Charles M.	1976-1979	M.R.E.	Part-Time Instructor of Religion and Assistant in Admissions
Richardson, Edwin W.	1977-1980	B.A.	Head of Department of Military Science
Richardson, Margaret	1896-1897		Librarian
Rickman, Kate	1923-1924	A.B.	Home Economics
Riley, Gary F.	1979-1982	Ph.D.	Associate Professor of Chemistry
Riley, Jean	1980-1982		Secretary of Teacher Education and Director of Audio-Visual Center
Riley, Lonnie	1981-1982	B.S.	Assistant to President for Church Relations
Roaden, Ralph	1970-1975	M.S.	Part-Time Instructor of Commerce, Director of Data Processing, Instructor of Library Science
Roberts, Lou Ann	1979-1980	M.S.	Instructor in Health
Roberts, Margaret	1967-1972		Assistant Treasurer
Rodgers, Clyde E.	1959-1969	M.A.	Director of Secondary Student Teaching, Education, Associate Professor of Education and Psychology
Rose, Besse Mahan	1912-1963	A.B., M.A.	English and German, Registrar and English and German, English

Rose, Flora	1974-1980	M.A.	English (Evening Program)
Ross, Bill E.	1954-1961	B.S., M.A.	Education, Director of Athletics
Ross, Helen	1959-1960		Bookstore Manager
Roth, Fred S.	1960-1982	M.R.E., D.R.E., Ed.D.	Sociology and Religion, Coordinator of Counseling and Professor of Religion, Director of Guidance and Professor of Religion, Counselor and Professor of Religion
Rowe, Richard A.	1985-Present	A.B., M.S. Ph.D.	Assistant Professor of Biology
Rowe, Mason Cole, III	1966-1972	M.A.	Assistant Professor of English
Rowlette, Beecher W.	1975-1976		Director of Promotions
Royster, Ralph R.	1961-1962	Ed.D.	Education
Ryan, Ella	1889-1890		Instructor in Normal Department
Leopoldo, T. Ruiz	1966-1967	Ph.D.	Associate Professor of Sociology
Sadler, Frances Elois	1938-1940	A.B.	Librarian
Sampey, Bessie	1894-1895	A.B.	B Grammar
Sanders, Dorothy Barton Booth	1958-1966	M.A., M.R.E.	Psychology and Assistant Dean of Women, Part-Time Instructor in Education and Psychology
Sasser, W.H.	1899-1900	B.S.	Instructor of Mathematics
Scalf, Nora	1947-1951	A.B., M.R.E.	Dean of Women, Bible
Scearce, J.B., Jr.	1946-1948	B.S.	Director of Athletics
Schecter, John C.	1978-Present	B.A., M.M.	Instructor of Music, Assistant Professor of Music
Schoenike, Elmer Louis	1919-1922		Manual Training
Schoonover, Robert	1984-Present	B.S., M.S., Ed.D.	Associate Professor of Education, Director of Graduate Program and Associate Professor of Education
Sego, Lewis P.	1961-1962	M.A.	English, Speech
Senters, P.L.	1919-1921		Grade Work
Sergent, William S., III	1981-Present	B.S.	Director of Sports Information, Instructor of Physical Education and Health, Director of Sports Information, Golf Coach, Assistant Women's Basketball Coach
Sexton, Jennifer Reed	1980-Present	B.S., M.S.	Instructor of Mathematics, Assistant Professor of Mathematics
Shanks, R.H.	1911-1912	A.B.	Instructor in Mathematics and German
Sharp, C.E.	1908-1909		Matron of Boys' Hall

Sharp, Theresa G.	1972-1981	M.S.	Director of Nursing Education, Professor and Director of Nursing Education, Dean and Director of Nursing Affairs, Dean of Nursing Affairs and Professor of Nursing Education
Sharpe, Alvin D.	1971-Present	B.S., M.Ed.	Instructor of Health and Physical Education, Assistant Professor of Health and Physical Education, Associate Professor of Health, Acting Director of Mining Technology
Shaw, Debbie	1967-1968	M.A.	Part-Time Instructor of English and Speech
Shaw, Kenneth	1955-Present		Superintendent of Buildings and Grounds
Shaw, Mary Ruth	1964-1969		Bookstore, Manager of Bookstore
Shaw, Minnie	1916-1917		Domestic Science
Shearer, Gladys	1931-1934	A.B.	Model School
Shearon, Ella Mae	1961-1962	M.A.	Psychology, English
Shearon, Wallace Ethan	1956-1962	B.A., M.M.	Voice, Choir Director
Sheils, Edward Elliott	1944-1976	B.S.	Education, English, Registrar and Director of Admissions, Registrar
Shelley, Ann Renfro	1955-1985	A.B., M.A.	Elementary Education, Director of Elementary Student Teaching, Education, Director of Elementary Student Teaching and Associate Professor of Education and Psychology, Senior Professor of Education
Shelton, Arthur E.	1967-1968	Th.D.	Assistant Professor of Sociology
Shelton, Sarah	1969-1984		Manager of Bookstore
Sherrod, Robert Henry	1937-1938	A.B.	Physical Education
Shields, Rebecca	1984-Present	B.S.	Women's Softball Coach
Shoemaker, Brian	1984-Present	B.S., M.Div.	Director of Alumni Affairs
Sieg, Jerry	1967-1977	M.M.	Instructor of Music, Assistant Professor of Music
Sikes, Mary L.	1917-1918		Teachers Department
Siler, Rhoda	1898-1905		Assistant in Primary Department, C Grammar
Simms, Beatrice	1946-1954	A.B.	Elementary Teacher, Assistant Dean of Women, History, Assistant Dean of Women
Simpson, James Franklin	1977-1980	M.S.	Part-Time Instructor of Health, Instructor of Health, Instructor of Special Education

Simpson, Leon D.	1967-1978	Th.D.	Director In-Service Religious Guidance Program, Assistant Professor of Religion, Director of Ministerial Training Program and Assistant Professor of Religion, Director of Ministerial Training Program and Associate Professor of Religion
Simpson, Marilyn	1969-1978	R.N.	Part-Time Nurse, Nurse
Singleton, James C.	1958-1960	B.A., M.A.	Science and Biology
Singleton, Lynn	1972-1975		Assistant Director of Student Enlistment, Assistant Director of Admissions; Coordinator of Student Affairs, Assistant Director of Admissions, Admissions Counselor and Director of Student Activities
Smedley, M.V.S.	1889-1890		Instructor in the Primary Department
Smith, Charles C.	1960-1978	M.A.	Instructor of Mathematics and Education, Assistant Professor of Mathematics, Part-Time Assistant Professor of Mathematics, Director of Evening Program
Smith, Dorothy B.	1947-1948		Home Economics
Smith, Eloise	1977-Present		Records Co-Ordinator for Department of Military Science
Smith, James Archy	1889-1890	Ph.B.	Assistant Principal
Smith, Wanda Lee	1955-1956	B.S., M.S.	English
Smith, Martha	1907-1908		Third Grade
Smith, Wilma Joyce		B.S.,M.A.	Part-Time Instructor of Education
Snyder, Bertha	1920-1921		Librarian
Spaulding, John A.	1962-1965	Ph.D.	Head of Department and Associate Professor of Modern Languages
Stagner, Elizabeth Plene	1946-1948	A.B., M.A.	Assistant Librarian
Stamm, Opal M.	1927-1931	A.B.	Home Economics
Stancil, Gloria	1979-Present	B.S.	College Nurse
Stancil, John L.	1977-Present	B.S., M.B.A., C.P.A.	Instructor of Business Administration and Track Coach, Assistant Professor of Business Administration
Stanfill, Jack	1976-Present	B.S.	Director of Financial Aid, Associate Director of Financial Aid
Steely, Brance	1981-Present	B.S.	Assistant Director of Financial Aid
Steely, May	1920-1922		Grade Work

Stephens, E.L.	1894-1901	A.B.	Instructor in A Grammar, Instructor of Rhetoric and History, Instructor of Algebra
Stephens, Robert Foster	1950-1951	A.B., M.A.	English
Stephens, Sue Finley	1964-1977	B.M.	Part-Time Instructor in Music
Stephens, Sydney, Jr.	1981-Present	B.S., M.A.	Assistant Professor of Mathematics, Associate Professor of Mathematics
Stephenson, Roy L., Jr.	1959-1961	B.S., M.H.P., E.R.	Instructor of Health and Physical Education
Stewart, Alice C.	1983-1986	B.B.A., M.B.A.	Instructor of Business Administration
Stigall, Laura	1981-1983	B.S.	Admissions Counselor
Stigall, Terry H.	1982-Present	B.S., M.A.	Admissions Counselor, Assistant Director of Admissions, Men's Baseball Coach, Instructor of Health
Stivers, Marie Russell	1923-1927		Librarian
Stokes, Thomas H., Jr.	1986-1987	B.A., M.A.	Modern Foreign Language
Stranathan, Sara E.	1904-1906		Music
Stroud, Floyd	1980-Present	B.S., M.Ed.	Acting Dean of Men, Director of Men's Housing, Dean of Men
Strunk, Dorman E.	1963-1973	M.Ed.	Mathematics and Physics, Assistant Professor of Physics, Associate Professor of Physics
Strunk, Flonnie	1958-1966	B.S., M.S.	Education and Commerce, Associate Professor of Commerce and Economics
Sturgill, Larry Burns	1969-1970	B.A.	Instructor in Physical Education
Sullivan, Hattie M.	1935-1950	A.B.	Acting Registrar, Shorthand, Typewriting, Registrar
Sutton, Linda Clem	1977-Present		Administrative Assistant to Financial Aid Director
Sutton, Raymond Moreland, Jr.	1962-1963		Commerce and Economics
Tankersley, Gayle B.	1973-1980 1982-Present	B.A., M.M.	Assistant Professor of Music
Tarry, Joseph E.	1973-1983 1985-Present	B.M.E., B.C.M., M.M., Ph.D.	Associate Professor of Music, Associate Professor of Music, Head of Department and Associate Professor of Music, Chairman of Department and Professor of Music
Taylor, Carolyn	1954-1956	A.B., M.R.E.	History and Assistant Dean of Women
Taylor, David Dwight	1987-	B.A., M.S.	Instructor of Biology
Taylor, F.F.	1912-1913	A.M.	Instructor in Teachers Department

Taylor, James H.	1968-Present	B.S., M.S., Ed.D., Ed.D.	Director of Development, Director of Alumni Affairs, Assistant to President in charge of Development and Alumni Affairs, Vice-President for Special Financial Projects, Vice-President in charge of Development, President and Professor of Education
Taylor, Joseph, R.	1983-Present	B.S., M.Ed., Ed.D.	Associate Professor of Education
Taylor, L.N.	1909-1910	B.S.	Instructor in Algebra and Teachers Department
Teague, Roy G.	1947-1948	B.S.	Tutor in Mathematics
Thiedeman, Michael H.	1970-1971	M.F.A.	Instructor in Art
Thomas, Hobie Etta	1976-1979	B.S.N.	Instructor in Nursing Education
Thomas, Jerry Douglas	1973-1974	B.S.	Part-Time Instructor in Medical Laboratory Technology
Thomas, Mary	1929-1965	A.B., A.M.	History and Dean of Women, History, Associate Professor of History
Thompson, Carlie	1960-1967	M.A.	Part-Time Instructor in Physical Science (Evening Program)
Thompson, Mildred Ann	1948-1951	B.S.	Home Economics
Thurmond, Charles J.	1959-1964	B.A., M.A.	Director of Guidance and Testing, Director of Orientation and Testing, English and Psychology
Towery, Brooke L.	1963-1964	B.S.	Physical Science, Geography, and Geology
Trivette, Kenneth	1975-1977	M.A.	Basketball Coach and Assistant Professor of Health and Physical Education
Troutman, Charles H.	1974-1975		Instructor in Military Science
Tibb, Hilda	1927-1928	M.A.	Latin and French
Tyner, De Lesline Elberta	1931-1932	B.M., M.A.	Voice, Public School Music
Unthank, Cecil H.	1964-1979	M.A.	Assistant Professor of Biology
Updike, Garland	1971-1974		Director of Food Services and Assistant Dean of Men
Urquhart, Beatrice	1919-1920		Vocal Music
Urquhart, John Richard	1984-Present	B.A., M.A., Ph.D.	Assistant Professor of Speech and Drama

Vallandingham, John Thompson	1913-1975	A.B., L.L.D.	Instructor in Mathematics, First Lieutenant in U.S. Army, Instructor in Mathematics and Dean of Men, Instructor in Mathematics, Captain in U.S. Army, Instructor in Mathematics, Head of Department of Mathematics, Acting Head of Department of Mathematics, Acting Head of Department and Associate Professor of Mathematics, Head Emeritus and Part-Time Associate Professor of Mathematics
Vancil, James E.	1968-1969	M.S.	Instructor in Biology
Van Horn, Clifford	1962-1963	M.S.	Instructor in Physical Science, Geography, and Geology
Varnell, John R.	1962-1963	M.R.E.	Instructor in Sociology
Vaughn, Leslie Jill	1985-1986	B.B.A., M.B.A.	Instructor in Business
Vaught, Roberta	1909-1910		Grade Work
Veach, Charles	1944-1945		Director of Chapel Music, Chorus, and Glee Club
Vernon, Randy	1980-Present		Instructor of Health, Head Basketball Coach, Athletic Director and Men's Basketball Coach, Men's Basketball Coach
Vinson, Fleming G.	1984-Present	A.B., M.A., Ph.D.	Professor of Modern Foreign Language
Waddell, Donna Grice	1972-1973		Part-Time Nurse
Waddell, Jonathan H.	1970-1973	Ed.D.	Director of Vocational Counseling and Assistant Professor of Psychology
Waite, Carelton Frederick	1966-1972	Ph.D.	Associate Professor of History, Professor of History
Wake, Elizabeth Sue	1973-Present	B.S., M.A.	Secretary for Teacher Education, Assistant to President for Administration
Wake, Eric L.	1967-Present	B.A., M.A., Ph.D.	Assistant Professor of History, Associate Professor of History and Chairman of Department, Chairman of Department and Professor of History
Walker, A.J.	1918-1919		Teachers Department
Walker, James Murray	1961-1966	Th.D.	History and Religion, Associate Professor of Religion
Walker, Joan L.	1965-1966		Bookstore Manager
Walker, Leila	1923-1924		Grade Work
Walker, Samuel	1914-1916	A.B.	Instructor in Teachers Department

Wall, Larry Rex	1978-1979	M.A.	Head Basketball Coach, Assistant Professor of Health and Physical Education
Wallace, Carter Harrison	1923-1925	A.B.	History
Walters, Michael Y.	1967-1980	B.S., M.A.	Part-Time Instructor in English and Speech, Instructor in English and Speech, Assistant Professor of English and Speech
Walton, Seth R.	1952-1954	A.B., M.A.	History
Ward, Sallie	1906-1910		Matron of Johnson Hall
Warren, Glenda A.	1984-Present	B.S., M.S., Ed.D.	Professor of Health and Head of Department, Chariman of Department and Professor of Health
Watson, Martha Ellen	1957-1958	B.A., M.R.E.	History and Assistant Dean of Women
Watson, Nellie	1920-1922		Secretary to President
Watson, Walter Elbert	1926-1927	B.S.	Elementary Education, Dean of Men
Watts, Rayford	1968-Present	B.S., M.A.	Instructor in English, Assistant Professor of English, Associate Professor of English, Chairman of Department and Professor of English
Webb, Addie Lee	1921-1923	A.B.	Dramatic Art
Webb, Arnold Henry	1947-1955	A.B., Th.M., M.A.	Education, English
Webb, C. Buford	1928-1929	A.B.	History
Webster, Patricia Chadwell	1986-1987	B.A., M.B.A.	Instructor of Business Administration
Weedman, Kenneth	1968-1971 1972-Present	B.A., M.A.	Instructor in Art, Assistant Professor of Art, Chairman of Department and Professor of Art
Weedman, Sue	1972-Present	B.S., M.A.	Postmistress, Assistant to Academic Dean
Wendt, Robert L.	1950-1952	A.A., B.A., M.A.	Social Sciences
Weninger, John	1978-1979		Purchasing Agent
Wesley, Susan Campbell	1980-Present	B.A., M.S.S.W.	Instructor of Social Work, Assistant Professor of Social Work
West, Merry Jill	1979-1982	B.S.N.	Instructor of Nursing Education
West, Thomas Eugene	1937-1942	B.A., M.A., D.D.	Literature of Bible, Public School Music, Director of Chorus
Whiteside, Mae	1900-1901		Music

White, Meford	1889		Instructor in English, Mathematics and Civil Government
Wiggins, Eugene	1960-1969	Ph.D.	Chariman Division of Languages and Literature, Head of Department and Professor of English
Wilburn, Donald L.	1975-1977	B.S.	Associate Professor of Military Science
Wilburn, William Vaughan	1968-1969	Ph.D.	Assistant Professor of Sociology
Wilder, Hazel Stratton	1962-1984	M.A.	Part-Time Instructor of Art, Instructor of Art, Assistant Professor of Art, Associate Professor of Art, Senior Professor of Art
Wilder, William Baylor	1955-1986	B.S., M.S., Ph.D.	Science, Chairman of Division of Sciences and Mathematics, Head of Department and Professor of Biology, Senior Professor of Biology
Wilkerson, Margaret			Fourth Grade
Wilkinson, Elwyn N., Jr.	1968-1975	B.D.	Director of Religious Activities
Williams, James K.	1963-1967	M.A.	Head of Department and Associate Professor of Sociology
Williams, Lydia	1927-1928	M.A.	History and Science
Williams, Robert Bruce	1980-1986	B.A., M.A.	Head Librarian
Williams, Roy Fowler	1961-1984	A.A., B.A., Th.M., Th.D.	Assistant Professor of Religion, Associate Professor of Religion, Part-Time Associate Professor of Religion, Senior Professor of Religion
Williams, Sandra J. Reeves	1978-Present	B.S., M.S., M.B.A.	Instructor in Business Administration, Chairman of Department and Assistant Professor of Data Processing
Williamson, Jack	1966-Present	B.A., M.Ed., Ph.D.	Assistant Professor of Education and Psychology, Coordinator of Research, Head of Department and Professor of Psychology, Director of Institutional Research, Head of Department and Professor of Psychology, Chairman of Department and Professor of Psychology
Williamson, Lou	1966-Present	B.S., M.A.	Part-Time Instructor in English, Instructor of English and Psychology, Assistant Professor of Education, Associate Professor of Education and Psychology

Wilson, Jane McDonald	1958-1959	B.S.	Commerce
Wilson, Jim	1976-1983	M.Div.	Director of Religious Activities, Director of Campus Ministries
Wilson, John Lloyd	1956-1969 1986-Present	B.S., M.B.A., L.L.B., L.L.M., J.D.	Commerce, Head of Department and Associate Professor of Commerce and Economics, Head of Department and Professor of Commerce and Economics, Professor of Business Administration
Wilson, L. Wingate	1973-1975	Ph.D.	Assistant Professor of Biology
Wong, Hans	1983-1984	B.S., Ph.D.	Assistant Professor of Chemistry
Wood, Burleigh Van Effen	1910-1916		Grade Work
Wood, Edward Ellsworth	1890-1939	A.B., A.M., LL.D.	Vice-President and Instructor in Latin, Methaphysics and English, President, President and Instructor in Latin, English, Intellectual Sciences, Instructor in Latin, English and Philosophy, President Emeritus
Wood, James Wyatt	1931-1942	A.B., A.M.	English, Dean of Men
Wootan, Harry Polk	1921-1922		Voice
Wootan, Harry Polk Mrs.	1922-1923		Librarian
Wortman, Harold	1966-Present	B.A., M.A., Ed.D.	Head of Department and Professor of Music, Professor of Music
Wortman, Lois M.	1980-Present	B.A. M.S.L.S.	Assistant Head Librarian in Charge of Circulation, Reference Librarian, Acting Head Librarian, Head Librarian, Director of Library
Wren, Janice Kay	1984-Present	B.S., M.S.L.S.	Assistant Librarian
Wright, Arkley	1911-1914 1920-1926	A.B.	Instructor in Latin and History, Instructor in Latin and German, Instructor in Latin and Academic Dean, Instructor in History and Academic Dean
Wright, E.F.	1916-1917	D.D.	Bible
Yates, J.A.	1892-1897	B.S.	Instructor in German and Chemistry
Yates, Willard F. Jr.	1960-1963	M.A.	Instructor in Biology
Young, Annie H.	1932-1934		Dietitian
Young, Chester Raymond	1967-1985	B.A., M.Div., M.A., Th.M., Ph.D.	Associate Professor of History, Chairman of Social Sciences, Head of Department and Professor of History, Senior Professor of History

Young, R.P.	1912-1913	B.S.	Instructor in Teachers Department
Young, Virginia Ruth	1986-Present	B.A., Ph.D.	Assistant Professor of Mathematics
Zavecz, Leslie W.	1976-1979	B.S.	Associate Professor of Military Science
Zehr, Earl S.	1983-Present	B.S., M.A., Ed.D.	Associate Professor of Education
Zorn, Ronny Mims	1977-1982	Ph.D.	Assistant Professor of Religion

SUPPORT STAFF

While it was our ardent desire to list all support staff since the College's founding no such list has been kept through the years. Following, however, is a listing of the support staff as of the end of the spring semester, 1987.

	Year of Appointment		Year of Appointment
Adkins, John C.	1975	Freeman, James Edward	1966
Adler, Pamela Fay	1981	Gabbard, Penny	1985
Alder, Richard Dwight	1978	Gay, Patricia Johnson	1986
Allen, Michael R.	1986	Gilbert, Jolene	1972
Asher, Roger Bryan	1986	Goodin, LaTissah A.	1986
Atkinson, Deborah Lynn	1983	Hall, Billy W.	1979
Axten, Lynn L.	1976	Hall, Danny Edward	1986
Barker, George E.	1968	Hall, Melody Lynn	1986
Bennett, Kathy H.	1986	Hall, Tina Marie	1983
Bingham, Ann Marie	1980	Hamblin, Pam S.	1985
Bird, Marcia Gail	1981	Hamblin, Trula Valiere	1984
Bird, Virginia Moore	1982	Hamby, Patricia Ann	1976
Blevens, Melissa Effie	1986	Harris, Annick M.	1986
Boyd, Margie Marie	1980	Harris, Erica A.	1982
Bray, Dallas Elizabeth	1964	Harrison, Doris	1986
Bray, Ruby P.	1980	Hensley, Wanda	1986
Brinks, Michelle	1987	Hill, Isaiah	1986
Brock, Tommy Riley	1981	Huddleston, Ricky	1985
Brown, Deleva	1987	Jackson, Lisa Kay	1983
Bryant, Patsy	1986	Johnson, Patsy	1981
Buhl, Sue	1974	Johnston, Norman E.	1983
Bush, Connie Diane	1981	Jones, Jennifer Gail	1985
Byrge, Billie L.	1976	Jones, Joe Keith	1980
Carpenter, Vickie	1985	Jones, Johnny Lee	1978
Chadwell, Barbara Renee	1986	King, Carolyn Sue	1981
Claxton, Lois	1985	Kinney, William Roy	1985
Conatser, Fred	1986	Lambdin, Jennifer Lynn	1983
Cox, Barbara Jean	1983	Lawson, Kimberly D.	1986
Cox, Lisa Gail	1979	Lawson, Mary Ruth	1982
Creekmore, Doris Emmadean	1978	Logan, Lonnie Joseph	1985
Creekmore, Peggy	1986	Logan, Magdalene Vivian	1975
Croley, William D.	1985	Lovitt, Johnie L.	1972
Douglas, Charles Richard	1977	Lynch, Brenda Diane	1975
Douglas, Sharon Lynne	1985	Lynch, William Harrell	1978
Draper, Heather Lane	1984	Mahan, Opal	1958
Dupier, Georgia Mae	1981	Maiden, John J.	1983
Edwards, Brenda Joyce	1975	Maiden, Violet Irene	1983
Evans, Abigal	1985	Manus, Nerva E.	1974
Evans, Mary E.	1987	Mars, Betty Jean	1984
Franklin, Angel Curry	1985	McEntire, Vicki Joyce	1984

McKiddy, James L.	1986	Rude, Lawrence F.	1984
McKillop, Mable	1982	Rutledge, Rebecca	1987
McKinney, Karen Lynn	1981	Schoonover, Janet Rose	1984
Meadors, Geneva	1964	Shields, Rebecca A.	1981
Meadors, Wesley	1981	Shotwell, Harold Dean	1986
Mehlenbacher, Pauline M.	1982	Shupe, Lois B.	1985
Mehlenbacher, Walter W.	1981	Shupe, Ronald Doyle	1984
Moore, Elizabeth J.	1984	Shupe, Walter Wayne	1985
Moore, Norma Jean	1981	Smith, Melinda Lou	1986
Moses, Louise Rosie	1976	Stanley, Novella Jean	1984
Moses, Shelleigh Lynn	1984	Sutton, A. J.	1975
Mowery, Willie Ulas	1978	Sutton, Linda C.	1974
Opichka, Bess	1987	Swanner, Cassandra Ann	1986
Owen, Hazel T.	1961	Taylor, Harold Lloyd	1986
Owens, Peggie Louise	1978	Taylor, Jeanette	1978
Partin, Avis Fay	1985	Thornhill, Sandra	1984
Partin, Lena I.	1986	Trammell, Francis Marion	1985
Patrick, Tillman	1981	Trammell, Victoria J.	1984
Perkins, Donna Lynn	1977	Underwood, Suzanne	1984
Perkins, Norma Jean	1984	Vinson, Kay Kennon	1984
Petrey, Lula Bell	1973	Wells, Aaron Dewayne	1984
Powers, Caleb, Jr.	1973	Wells, Beverly R.	1984
Powers, Melia Faye	1973	White, Darlene	1986
Powers, Merry Lynn	1985	Whitt, Marc C.	1985
Prewitt, Linda Lucille	1976	Wilkins, Peggy J.	1985
Rains, Tilda Mae	1974	Wilson, Stephanie Jeanne	1986
Rainwater, Irma Vivian	1983	Wilson, Tommy J.	1985
Revlett, Perry Dean	1985	Wingeir, Pearlie	1985
Rhodes, Sandra Bailey	1985	Witt, Ginny L.	1985
Richardson, Wilma J.	1972	Wolfe, Anthony Lee	1985
Rooks, Thomas, Jr.	1981	Wyatt, Bethel	1987
Rose, Denver	1976	York, Charles	1982
Rose, Dorothy	1986	Young, Elmer	1982

APPENDIX V

CONTRIBUTORS TO THE ORIGINAL ENDOWMENT

The following donations totaling $20,058.48 were made to the original endowment of the College in 1891 as a result of the challenge from John D. Rockefeller through the American Baptist Education Society.

Al Mahan	$12.50	H. R. Dillon	$5.00
G. D. Moore	25.00	T. Warren Begle	2.00
William Perkins	12.50	A. Gatliff	10,000.00
J. C. Mahan	25.00	W. J. Johnson, Collections	662.00
J. W. Siler	125.00	B. P. Carpenter	5.00
Joseph Gatliff	125.00	American Baptist Education Society	4,750.00
J. M. Mahan	125.00	Joseph Gatliff	257.50
T. B. Mahan	75.00	E. S. Moss	387.00
C. H. Keeton	25.00	J. W. Siler	387.00
E. S. Moss	125.00	J. H. Davis	154.00
J. P. Mahan	125.00	Joseph Gatliff	129.00
C. W. Alexander	12.50	J. M. Mahan	375.00
Hywell Davis	75.00	G. D. Moore	75.00
J. M. Ellison	100.00	B. P. Carpenter	10.00
H. L. Brummett	25.00	J. T. Slade	10.00
E. N. Steely	25.00	J. W. Waldrop	2.50
E. E. Wood	25.00	R. M. Lowe	2.00
J. D. Adkins	25.00	J. D. Violett	5.00
B. F. Rose	25.00	S. Phillips	1.50
Mike Richardson	25.00	W. R. Thompson	1.00
W. T. Meadors	12.50	Leonard Tingle	5.00
M. L. Davis	12.50	J. C. Wright	10.00
J. H. Davis	50.00	W. D. Bryant	10.00
Milford White	25.00	Sarah B. Cox	2.00
M. E. Mahan	25.00	T. J. Shipman	10.00
A. J. Caddell	25.00	B. Brown	5.00
C. W. Lester	25.00	J. W. Hill	3.00
H. C. King	25.00	W. J. Johnson, Collections	60.00
W. J. Johnson, Collections	150.00	W. H. Fishback	2.00
Sam Freeman	12.50	H. T. Daniel	50.00
J. S. Tye	50.00	W. J. Johnson, Collections	75.00
J. C. Steely	25.00	W. T. Meadors	13.05
W. J. Johnson, Collections	25.00	R. J. Elliott	5.00
S. R. Sutton	12.50	S. C. Jellman	10.00
J. J. Eubanks	12.50	T. J. Slade	5.00
William Baker	12.50	E. C. Kidd	10.00
H. L. Brummett	25.00	T. J. Bigstaff	5.00
I. J. Foley	25.00	B. J. Davis	5.00
William Jameson	25.00	E. N. Steely	77.62
George W. Morgan	25.00	B. Manley	10.00
W. J. Johnson, Collections	22.00	C. H. Keeton	75.00
W. J. Johnson, Collections	280.81	J. C. Mahan	75.00
C. W. Alexander	37.50	Sam Freeman	13.00
J. D. Adkins	25.00	M. White	75.00
William Perkins	37.50	P. Blake	10.00
W. J. Johnson	27.00		
J. R. Sampson	50.00		

CURRENT VALUE OF ENDOWMENT

	Book Value	Market Value
1956-57	805,568	
1957-58	846,767	
1958-59	849,382	
1959-60	851,380	
1960-61	857,357	
1961-62	903,063	
1962-63	1,039,188	
1963-64	1,061,261	
1964-65	1,144,968	
1965-66	1,173,852	
1966-67	1,175,264	
1967-68	1,240,901	
1968-69	1,282,796	
1969-70	1,341,240	
1970-71	1,361,191	
1971-72	1,433,844	
1972-73	1,793,012	
1973-74	1,961,448	
1974-75	2,150,177	4,278,145
1975-76	2,810,380	5,462,090
1976-77	3,676,780	6,426,049
1977-78	3,760,176	6,418,943
1978-79	3,943,106	6,645,729
1979-80	4,217,313	6,775,349
1980-81	5,457,577	7,785,382
1981-82	5,788,343	8,435,846
1982-83	6,177,101	8,920,556
1983-84	7,728,216	9,886,708
1984-85	8,541,435	9,808,914
1985-86	11,211,602	11,867,698
1986-87	11,550,712	11,550,712

APPENDIX VI

LAND AND PROPERTY ACQUISITIONS

GRANTOR	LOCATION	YEAR	USE
John Smith, et al	Main Street	1888	Roburn Hall
J.A. Caddell, et al	Main Street	1892	Johnson Hall
E.S. Moss, et al	Main Street	1892	Johnson Hall
J.L. Bird & T.J. Curd	Sycamore	1893	Mahan, Siler and Robinson Halls
R.D. Hill	Sycamore	1903	Siler and Robinson Halls
Mary Worley	Sycamore	1906	Robinson Hall
American Missionary Association	Maple and Walnut Streets	1907	Mary W. McGaw Music Building, Norma Jeanne Perkins Hagan Library, Gymnasium, Dr. A. Gatliff Memorial, Gray Brick
Theo Terry	Walnut Street	1919	Boswell Campus Center
Nora Hill Gillis	Walnut Street	1919	Boswell Campus Center
Beverly and Florida Gatliff	Main Street	1921	Boswell Park
Beverly and Florida Gatliff	11th Street	1922	Athletic Field
C.G. Ellison	11th Street	1924	Athletic Field
Harvard, Princeton and Massachusetts Institute of Technology	8500 acres Whitley County	1933	Endowment Land
Sam Williams	8th & Elm Streets	1951	Science Building
Whitley County	1 acre - Emlyn, Ky.	1954	Lot
Charlie Buhl, Sr.	8th Street	1959	Nicholson-Jones Hall
Charlie Buhl, Sr.	Main Street	1961	Archer Hall
Hattie Steely	Maple & 8th Streets	1961	Science Building
Rose Lee	Sycamore	1962	Robinson Hall
Ruby G. Archer	Main Street	1962	President's Home
Luke White	11th Street	1964	Athletic Field
E. Thurmond	Walnut Street	1965	Lot
R.L. Brown	Main & 9th	1966	Asher Hall
R.L. Brown	Main Street	1966	Asher Hall & Lot
P.R. Jones	Main Street	1971	Dwelling
L & N Railroad	7th Street	1977	Parking
Ellison Heirs	Main Street	1977	Parking
Bernice Bird Browning	Maple (Three Lots)	1978	Parking
Edna Jones Nicholson, et al	9th & Sycamore	1980	Private Dwelling
State of Kentucky (100-Year Lease)	Ridge and 2nd Streets	1980	Maintenance
E.L. Smith	80 acres - Whitley County	1980	Mineral Land
Joe Patrick	40 acres - Whitley County	1981	Mineral Land
W.R. Rose	2nd Street	1981	Lot-Storage
Heirs of Agnes Perkins	Sycamore	1981	Lot-Boswell Park
Larry Patrick	Main Street	1981	Lot
Retha & Iva Murphy & Jenny Lou West Bixler Heirs	Main Street	1981	Boswell Park

Wade Perkins	7th Street	1982	Lot
Williamsburg City School	Maple and School Streets	1982	Lot
Williamsburg City School	Maple and School Streets	1982	Classroom Building, Business Administration Building
Forestier Nicholson	11th Street	1984	Coach's Office
Link Pennington	11th Street	1984	Athletic Field
Bill and Wanda Freeman	11th Street	1984	Athletic Field
Bill and Wanda Freeman	11th Street	1984	Athletic Field
J.W. Wood	Main Street	1985	Lot
Arthur Dale	Main Street	1985	Office Space
L.B. and Julia Rains	Maple (Two Lots)	1986	Lots
CSX Transportation	Main and Railroad	1986	Old Depot
Barbara Ashby	Main Street	1986	Lot Near Archer Hall
Roger Bruce Stephens	7th and Cumberland	1986	Lot
Louise Howard	7th and Cumberland	1986	Dwelling
D.M. Eddy, Jr.	Corner 7th and Main	1986	Lot
Homer B. Davis	Main Street	1986	Lot
Glenn A. Faulkner	U.S. 25W	1986	Dwelling
Ida C. Campbell	8th and Walnut	1987	House and Lot
Bill Berry	7th Street	1987	Lot
Shirley Lester Harmon	Sycamore	1987	Lot
Barbara Neubert	Sycamore	1987	Lot
Humphrey and Grace Olsen	9th Street	1987	Lot
Bill and Wanda Freeman	9th Street	1987	Lot
James E. Payne	9th Street	1987	Lot

APPENDIX VII

CATALOGUE

OF THE

Officers ✳ and ✳ Students

OF

Williamsburg Institute.

✳FIRST ✦ SESSION ✦ 1889.✳

◄—► INTER-STATE NEWS, JOB PRINT,—◄►
JELLICO, TENN.
1889.

BOARD OF DIRECTORS.

A. Gatliff, President. - - *Williamsburg, Ky.*

J. P. Mahan, Vice-President. " "

E. S. Moss, Secretary, - - " "

J. W. Siler, Treasurer, - - " "

J. R. Sampson, Auditor, - - " "

Wm. Ellison, - - - - - " "

John A. Black, - - - *Barboursville, Ky.*

Gilbert Garrard, - - - *Manchester, Ky.*

J. Q. Pearce, - - - - *Pineville, Ky.*

N. M. Scales, - - - - *London, Ky.*

H. C. Gentry, - - - *Mt. Vernon, Ky.*

FACULTY.

William James Johnson,
(Full Graduate of the South Bap., Seminary, Class '85 and '86.)
PROF. of LATIN and GREEK.

PRINCIPAL.

Carl D. Garlough, A. B., Ph. B.
PROF. of MATHEMATICS.

Miss Maggie A. Hackley,
(Former teacher in Baptist Orphan Home.)
TEACHER of ENGLISH and PENMANSHIP.

Mrs. Roxie Buchanan,
(Teacher of 20 years experience.)
TEACHER of PRIMARY DEPARTMENT.

Miss Bettie Lewis,
TEACHER of MUSIC and ELOCUTION.

J. H. Cricillis,
ASSISTANT TUITOR of ENGLISH.

NAMES ✦ OF ✦ STUDENTS.

COLLEGIATE DEPARTMENT.

Anderson, James Lee., - - - - - - Bush's Store.

Baker, Eli Frank., - - - - - Bryant's Store.

Brummitt, Sarah E., - - - - - Tidal Wave.

Carson, Jennie St. Clai ., - - - - Morristown, Tenn.

Criscillis, J. H., - - - - - Williamsburg, Ky.

Criscillis, Mary., - - - - - - Wild Cat, Ky.

Caddell, A. J., - - - - - Williamsburg, Ky.

Hamilton, E., - - - - - Esco, Tenn.

Jones, J. F., - - - - - - Williamsburg, Ky.

Logan, B. F., - - - - - Bryant's Store.

Meadors, U. H., - - - - - Meadorsville, Ky.

Morgan, W. M., - - - - - Whitesburg, Ky.

Morgan, W. Z., - - - - - - Manchester, Ky.

McGraw, G. W., - - - - - Williamsburg, Ky.

Moyers, W. F., - - - - - - " "

Parker, A. J., - - - - - - " "

Prichard, J. C., - - - - - Bryant's Store.

Sproule, Chas. M., - - - - - Williamsburg, Ky.

Steely, John. S., - - - - - - Meadorsville, Ky.

Stephens, Elisha., - - - - - - Wild Cat, Ky.

White, Nannie., - - - - - " "

NUMBER,....21.

NORMAL ✦ DEPARTMENT.

Adkins, Annie.,	Williamsburg, Ky.
Adkins, Ruthie,	" "
Adkins, Susie.,	" "
Baker, J. M.,	Manchester, Ky.
Bennett, Nellie.,	Williamsburg, Ky.
Bryant, W. H.,	Huddleston, Ky.
Caddell, J. M.,	Williamsburg, Ky.
Caddell, Lulu.,	Holly, Hill, Ky.
Cox, Sabie.,	" "
Davis, J. H.,	Meadorsville, Ky.
Dean, Emily.,	Fiat Lick, Ky.
Dean, Rebecca.,	" "
Fairchild, A.,	Monticello, Ky.
Finley, Anna.,	Williamsburg, Ky.
Freeman, Geo. M.,	" "
Gillman, P. A.,	Jarvis' Store.
Gillman, T G.,	" "
Goans, J. A..	Clinton, Tenn.
Holcomb, J. W.,	Whitesburg, Ky.
Inman, Wm.,	Tidal Wave, Ky.
Jones, L. R.,	Pollyton, Ky.
Kelly, A. Z..	Harlan, C. H., Ky.
Lovett, Melvina.,	Pleasant View, Ky.
Lawson, Charles.,	Williamsburg, Ky.
Meadors, J. F.,	Wild Cat, Ky.
Moore, Mark,	Pleasant View, Ky.
Mahan, Ruthie.,	Wild Cat, Ky.
Mahan, Susie.,	" "
Morgan, Lucinda.,	Williamsburg, Ky.
Martin, J.,	Gregory.....
Martin, E. W..	
Nicholson, G. W.,	Pleasant View, Ky.
Parker, Alice,.	Williamsburg, Ky.
Patrick, Willie.,	Meadorsville, Ky.
Ryan, J. R.	Pine Knot, Ky.
Siler, G. M.,	Lot, Ky.
Steele, M. F.,	Wild Cat, Ky.
Snyder, Julia A.,	Williamsburg, Ky.
Sproule, Ed.,	" "
Trammel Julia.,	Tidal Wave, Ky.
Tye, Katie.,	Pollyton, Ky.
White, Rebecca.,	Wild Cat, Ky.

NUMBER ...42.

PREPARATORY ✦ DEPARTMENT.

Adkins, Nell'e.,	Wms'burg;	Mahan, Eddie.,	Wms'burg'
Adkins, Wm.,	"	McVey, Florence,	
Adkins, Frank.,	"	McCarty, Rosa.,	Kingsville.
Arthur, John.,	"	McCarty, Eddie.,	"
Arthur, Will.,	"	McCarty, Joe L.,	Wms'burg.
Adkins, Walter.,	"	McFarland, Cynthia.,	"
Ballou, Bell.,	"	McCarty, Joe H.,	Jellico, Tenn.
Bruce, Ida.,	"	McCarty, Bertie,	"
Cooley, Frank.,	"	Moore, Markie.,	Pleasant View.
Cox, Annie.,	"	Moody, Clint.,	Wms'burg.
Criscillis, Jerry.,	Wild Cat.	McKee, Sarah J.,	"
Davis, Cynthia.,	Meadorsville.	Patrick, Susie.,	"
Davis, Mary.,	Wms'burg.	Richardson, Ancil.,	"
Davis, Fred.,	"	Richardson, Charles.,	"
Davis, Frank.,	Meadorsville.	Reynolds, John.,	"
Denham, Walter,	Wms'burg.	Reynolds, Josie.,	"
Ellison, George.,	"	Reedy, James.,	"
Foley, John.,	"	Sallee, Alice.,	"
Foley, Lydia,	"	Siler, Cora.,	"
Gatliff, Ruby.,	"	Siler, Joe.,	"
Gatliff, Nannie.,	"	Siler, Virgil.,	"
Gray, Ada,	"	Siler, Tison.,	Lot, Ky.
Hoskins, Monie.,	"	Siler, M. V.,	Pleasant, View.
Hoskins, Lizzie.,	"	Siler, Willis.,	Lot, Ky.
Hamlin, Judith.,	Wms'burg.	Sisk, Floyd,.	Wms'burg.
Hogan, John.,	"	Smith, Dempsey,.	Meadorsville.
Hogan, David.,	"	Snyder, Ben,.	Wms'burg.
Hampton, Ca,.,	"	Sproule, Ermine,.	"
Jones, S. L.,	"	Sproule, Evert	"
Jones, Ellen,	"	Stee'e, Siler,.	"
Jones, Susie.,	"	Sutton, Flora,.	"
Jones, Mollie.,	"	Tinsley, Willie,.	"
Jones, Andrew.,	"	Tinsely, Carrie,.	"
Jones, Oen.,	"	Walters, Annie,.	"
Kinner, Lillie.,	"	Walters, Jennie,.	"
Kinner, Katie,	"	Walters, Maggie"	"
Lawson, Nann'e.,	"	Webb, Bertie,.	"
McCleod, Cora,.	"	Webb, James.,	"
McCloed, Jennings.,	"	Weesner, Biddie.,	"
Moore, Mattie.,	"	Weesner, Newel.,	"
Myers, Carrie,	"	Weesner, Fronia,.	"

NUMBER .... 82.

PRIMARY ✦ DEPARTMENT.

Adkins, Elbert.,	Williamsburg, Ky.
Adkins, Flora.,	" "
Arthur, Eddie.,	" "
Arthur, Emma.,	" "
Ballou, Halleck.,	" "
Ballou, Mollie.,	" "
Barnes, Bertie.,	" "
Barnes, Nellie.,	" "
Cooley, Alma.,	" "
Cooley, Emmett.,	" "
Croley, Berry.,	" "
Croley, Nannie.,	" "
Croley, John.,	" "
Croley, Wm.,	" "
Criscillis, George.,	" "
Crouch, Cora.,	" "
Davis, Ancil.,	" "
Davis, Robert.,	" "
Davis, Sam.,	" "
Denham, Bessie.,	" "
Denham, Sam.,	" "
Foley. James.,	" "
Gatliff, James.,	" "
Gray, Flora.,	" "
Hoskins, Eva.,	" "
Jones, George.,	" "

PRIMARY DEPARTMENT.-Continued.

Jones, Tavie.,   -   -   -   Williamsburg, Ky.

Jones, Arnetta.,   -   -   -   -   "   "

Jones, Frank.,   -   -   -   -   "   "

Jones, James.,   -   -   -   -   "   "

Jones, LaFayett.,   -   -   -   -   "   "

Jones, Lawrence.,   -   -   -   -   "   "

Jones, John.,   -   -   -   -   "   "

Jones, Mollie.,   -   -   -   -   "   "

Jones, Sarah.,   -   -   -   -   "   "

Mahan, Carrie.,   -   -   -   -   "   "

Meadors, Eliza.,   -   -   -   -   "   "

Medaris, Lizzie.,   -   -   -   -   "   "

Medaris, Wayland.,   -   -   -   -   "   "

Moody, Willie.,   -   -   -   -   "   "

McCleod, Whitley.,   -   -   -   -   "   "

Owens, Albert.,   -   -   -   -   "   "

Richardson, Eddie.,   -   -   -   -   "   "

Sampson, Willie.,   -   -   -   -   "   "

Small, Linsey.,   -   -   -   -   "   "

Sowders, Frank.,   -   -   -   -   "   "

Sutton, Fannie.,   -   -   -   -   "   "

Sutton, Joe.,   -   -   -   -   "   "

Sutton, Nellie.,   -   -   -   -   "   "

Tydings, Talbert.,   -   -   -   -   "   "

Tydings, Alma.,   -   -   -   -   "   "

Webb, Louis.,   -   -   -   -   "   "

Webb, Forest.,   -   -   -   -   "   "

NUMBER ...54.

SPECIAL NOTICE.

Students arriving in town should call AT ONCE upon J. P. Mahan, who will give all desired information.

BUILDING.

Williamsburg Institute is a Three Story Brick Building, 90 x 55 ft; Modern style, well ventilated and comfortable; will accommodate about 300 pupils. It is located on a beautiful and healthy plateau above the town, convenient and easily accessable.

LOCATION.

The Institute is located in Williamsburg, a thriving town, of more than 2,000 inhabitants, situated on the Cumberland River and L. & N. R R., and is accessable from all points. Being a mountain town, and surrounded by the everlasting mountains, as Jerusalem of old, it is a great health resort both summer and winter. The pure water and fresh air make it a very healthy place, especially for those who suffer from weak lungs and bronchital diseases. That the morals of the town are good, no one will question, when it is known we have four prospering churches, and that Prohibition prevails in both town and county and is put into force by the good people. Parents, in thinking about sending their children off to school, should remember that Williamsburg is free from whiskey and many other temptations which lead young men astray. Children coming to this school are surrounded by a moral and religious atmosphere.

MATRICULATION.

To be admitted into the Institute, the applicant must furnish satistactory.evidence of good moral character. The school is open to both sexes and all ages. While it is HIGHLY DESIRABLE that students enter at the opening of the session, yet one may enter at any time and take up such studies as will be most advantageous. Students are allowed to select their own studies with the advice and consent of the faculty.

EXAMINATIONS.

Examinations are of two kinds, viz:

1st. Daily Examinations in class, which are searching and thorough, and the success of the student is noted according to a certain numerical rule, and this report will be preserved in the Archieves of the Institute.

2nd. WRITTEN EXAMINATIONS near close of each half session.

Much stress is laid upon these written examinations as they will be thorough tests of the students' knowledge in the respective studies.   No one is allowed to absent himself or herself from these examinations without consent of teacher.   The papers of each will be carefully graded according to a certain numerical rule, and result preserved.   The standing of every pupil will be read out at end of each half session, and parents furnished with report of same.

Two kinds of honors are used to stimulate students; one ascertained at the end of each MONTH, called the "ROLL OF MERIT"; the other known at the close of the session, known as the Roll of Honor.

The following are the conditions for place on the ROLL OF MERIT:

1. Average class standing must be .85 per cent. or more.   2. It must not fall below .75 in any single study.   3. Deportment must not be below .90 per cent.   5. Punctuality must not be less than .90 per cent.

For ROLL OF HONOR, the same must be true of his session standing and written examination must not fall below .85 per cent.   All on Roll of Honor will receive nice PRESENTS

SESSION ✦ AND ✦ EXPENSES

There is one session of about forty weeks, begining the first Tuesday in September and closing the second Friday in June. One week's vacation during Christmas Holidays.

Tuition in College Course, $30.00, per session; one half IN ADVANCF, the remainder the second Monday in January—that is $3.00, per month.

Tuition in Normal Course, $20.00, per session or $2.00, per month, one half in advance, the remainder second Monday in January,

Tuition in Preparatory Department $1.50, per month payable monthly IN ADVANCE.

Tuition in Primary Department $1.00, per month payable monthly in advance.

The expenses are much cheaper than most Colleges, but we have done so that no one may be deprived of the advantages of a first-class education.

No money refunded except in case of protracted sickness. No incidental fees

Books can be procured through Prof. Johnson at less than wholesale prices, thus students are enabled to get their books at greatly reduced prices, which is no small item in going to school.

Board can be had at from $2.00, to $2.50, per week in private families, including lights and fuel.

A number of students can rent rooms together and board themselves for less than $1.00, per week,

Every effort will be put forward to have a boarding hall ready by September, where students can board very cheap.

Parents, who have children to educate, are urged to move their families here, buy property and send them to school. Several are doing that this year and they say it pays them. LOTS AND HOUSES FOR SALE CHEAP.

So great is the need of education in this country that parents should be willing to make any sacrifice to have their children educated. The age has passed away when ignorant men and women can rise to eminence. 'WE MUST EDUCATE OR WE MUST PERISH."

DISCIPLINE.

The purpose of this institution is to train boys and girls, young men and young ladies in knowledge, morality, and religion. The students are graded in deportment just the same as they are in their studies. Manners and politeness are taught. Some of the rules of the Institute are as follows:

1. Every student is required to attend chapel exercises in the morning; also public worship at some church on Sunday.

2. Every student shall regularly and punctually all his recitations.

3. No student will be permitted to leave the town on any pretext whatever, during term time, without previous permission from the Principal.

4. Damage done to any part of the Institute property must be repaired by the offender.

5. No student is allowed to molest the property of others, or associate with idle or vicious company, or to engage in any disorderly conduct.

LITERARY ✦ SOCIETY.

The Smithsonian Literary Society meets every Friday night for debate. Much importance is attached to this Society by the Faculty, as a means of improvement in oratory declamation and general literary culture, as well as imparting a knowledge of parliamentary law. All the young men are expected to belong to this Society until another is formed.

A Library will soon be attached to the Society and Institute. Any book given will be gratefully received. Persons having cheap second hand books for sale are requested to write to Prof. W. J. Johnson, who is getting up the Library.

PROSPECT OF AN ENDOWMENT.

The trustees have applied to the Baptist Educational Society for an endowment of $20,000, which they are confident will be secured through the Society and personal contributions.

Any amount given, however small, will be THANKFULLY received.

COLLEGIATE ✦ DEPARTMENT.

SCHOOL OF ENGLISH LANGUAGE AND LITERATURE.

JUNIOR.—English Grammar, Composition Rhetoric. Each member of this class is required to write at least one original composition a week, which is criticized privately and before the class so that each pupil is made to see his own faults and the remedy.

INTER.—This class studies Composition and Rhetoric-- the art of thinking and expression- -Anglo Saxon, Early English, Chancer, History of the English Language. Words are analyzed and traced back to their original source.

SENIOR.---A. S. Hill's Rhetoric, Jevon's Logic, and Welsh English Literature. This class reads largely from the best English authors both of Prose and Poetry. Much time is given to Shakepere, Bunyan and Milton.

The styles of the se different authors are studied and criticized. Weekly compositions are written by members of the class. No one is allowed to graduate in the Institute unless he speaks nd writes accurately and can write a good composition.

As English is our own language, the one with which we have to do all our lives, and the one about which most people are shamefully ignorant, this school is one of great importance.

SCHOOL ✦ OF ✦ LATIN.

Three years are required to complete this school. It is divided into three courses.

JUNIOR.---This class studies Latin Grammar, roots and forms of words; weekly exercises of English into Latin; reads Ceasar, Cicero's Orations and Virgil.

INTER.---Latin Prose Composition, History of Ancient Rome, with Lectures and reference to the best histories. The books read in this class are: Horace, Ovid, Terence, Cicero de Offices an Sallust.

SENIOR.---This year is given largely to reading Latin Author's; De Amicitia, Senica, Juvinal, Livy, Tacitus, Pliny, and reading the Latin Bible (Vulgate) at sight. Weekly Original exercises of English into Latin.

SCHOOL ✦ OF ✦ GREEK.

JUNIOR.—Harkness First Book of Greek, Xenophons Anabasis and Memoribilia of Socrates. Much attention is paid to the roots and forms of words. Hadley & Allen's Greek Grammar is used.

INTER.--Greek Prose Composition. Grammar especially Syntax. This class reads Lysias, Homer, Heroditus and Theocritus, Grecian History and Antiquities are studied and Lectures by the Professor.

SENIOR.—This class reads largely from the best Grecian writers, studies History, Literature, and Philosophy of the Greeks. Original exercises from English into Greek. Much attention is given the Greek New Testament.

Books read are: Demosthenes, Plato, Thucydides, Sophocles, Euripedes and Greek Testament.

The study of Greek is highly important in three respects: 1st. As a mental training. 2nd. Because it is the language in which is locked the profoundest philosophy of the ages. 3rd. It is impossible to understand much of the New Testament without a knowledge of the Greek.

SCHOOL OF POLITICAL SCIENCE.

This school embraces Political Economy, Constitutional Government, Political History.

1. Chapin's Wayland's Political History.

2. Civil Government.

3. Political History, Swinton's History. Lectures on Ancient Medieval and Modern History. Church History and Old Testament History are studied.

☞Book-keeping is taught, but outside of course and $2.00 per month extra.

SCHOOL OF MORAL and MENTAL PHILOSOPHY.

This school embraces Psychology, Ethics, Mental Philosophy and Evidences of Christianity.

Text books not yet selected.

The aim of this school is to teach the pupils the great doctrines of Morality and Christianity with reference to the life that now is and that which is to come.

SCHOOL OF MODERN LANGUAGES.

This course is made to occupy two years. The object is to learn to read and speak these Languages.

GERMAN.

JUNIOR.—Campbell's Complete German course is thoroughly studied until student can speak, read and write German fairly well. Frequent conversations in German are held in the class-room and students are recommended to speak to each other as often as possible in this language. Besides Schiller's "William Tell" a private course of reading is pursued.

SENIOR.—This class studies Whitney's Grammar, reads largely in the German language. Goethe's Antobiography of Faust and Schiller's Works are read. Exercise into German. A private course of reading is given.

FRENCH.

JUNIOR.--Paule Girrade's Complete Course is so thoroughly studied that the pupil can speak, read and write French fairly well. A private course of reading is recommended.

SENIOR.--This class reads Moriere, Racine, Voltaire, Tainis Angeleterre, with an additional course of private reading. Weekly exercises of English into French.

SCHOOL OF MATHEMATICS AND PHYSICS.

The study of Mathematics excels all other departments of study in its power to develop the reasoning and thinking faculty of the mind. An able thinker says;" Mathematics include a perfect system of reasoning whose premises are self-evident and whose conclusion are irresistible. While it is before all as a useful attainment it especially adapts itself to the cultivation and improvement of the thinking faculty, and is alike necessary to all who would be governed by reason or live for usefulness."

This school consists of four classes and includes the study of Algebra, Plane and Solid Geometry, Plane and Spherical Trigonometry, Surveying, Analytical Geometry, Calculus, Mechanics, Astronomy, and Physics.

The Freshman Class completes the study of Algebra and Plane Geometry. This class gives special attention to the subjects, Logarithms and Theory of Equations in Higher Algebra, and to original work in the Geometry.

The Sophomore Class studies Solid Geometry, Plane and Spherical Trigonometry, and Surveying. Special attention is given to the study of surveying. The class is required to solve a a number of problems taken from other sources than the text book and involving the principles most frequently met with in practical surveying.

Junior Class; Analytical Geometry Differential and Integral Calculus.

Senior Class; Mechanics, Physics, and Astronomy.

SCHOOL OF NATURAL SCIENCES.

The work of this school embraces two years of careful and diligent study. The course arranged with the special object of leading the student to independent thinking. No department of study is better adapted to teaching the real object and end of life.

The work of the first year is begun with the study of Inorganic followed by Organic Chemistry. Numerous experiments are performed before the class and frequent lectures given by the professor. The study of Chemistry is followed by twelve weeks in Botany, in which each student is required to devote sometime to the analysis of the various species of plants found in this locality. The many rare and beautiful flowers in the mountains afford a special advantage for profitable and pleasant work in this department of Biology.

The second year opens with the study of Zoology. Sixteen weeks are then devoted to Human Anatomy, Physiology and Hygiene. This branch of study receives special attention. Many experiments are given and dissections made to enable the student to form a clear conception of the principles of the science. Lectures are frequently given before the class upon special subjects of Physiology and Hygiene. This coarse is closed with the study of Geology. This locality is rich in specimens which afford excellent opportunities for practical work in Geology.

NORMAL ✦ DEPARTMENT.

FIRST YEAR.—Arithmetic reviewed, Elementary Algebra to Quadratic Equations, Physiology, History of United States, Civil Government, English Grammar, Geography, Theory and Practice of Teaching. Reading, Spelling and Penmanship.

SECOND YEAR.—Higher Arithmetic, Complete Algebra, Plane Geometry, Rhetoric and Composition, Physical Geography, Natural Philosophy, Geology, Shorter Course in Astronomy, Outlines of History, Shorter Course in Moral and Mental Philosophy.

The object of this department is to prepare men and women thoroughly for teaching in common or graded schools. Those completing this course will be entitled to a Teacher's Diploma.

DEGREES AND DIPLOMAS.

1. A TEACHER'S DIPLOMA will be granted to each one who shall complete the Normal Course.

2. The Degree of Bachelor of Science (B. S.) is conferred upon those who shall complete the School of English, Mental and Moral Philosophy, Natural Sciences, Political Science and History, Mathematics, through Solid Geometry, Plane Trigonometry and Surveying, and one year of Latin.

3. The Degree of Bachelor of Arts (A. B.) conferred upon those who shall complete all the schools of the Institute except Modern Languages.

4. The Degree of Master of Arts (A. M.) conferred upon such as shall have pursued with marked success the full course prescribed for A. B., with French and German.

MUSIC AND ELOCUTION.

(MISS BETTIE LEWIS.)

MUSIC —Piano and Organ.

TERMS.—($4.00). Four Dollars per Month. Voice-

CULTURE—($4.00). Four Dollars per Month.

☞Lablache Italian method used for Vocal, or Voice Culture.

ELOCUTION.—Dramatic and Oratory. Terms $2.00 per Month. Monroe's Physical Vocal Training used for instruction.

The services of MISS LEWIS have been secured by the Faculty in Training the Students for entertainments and public occasions. Thus a great deal of Elocutionary training is given to all the pupils FREE GRATIS.

PREPARATORY DEPARTMENT.
◄FOURTH GRADE.►

READING.—Fourth Reader or some supplementary reading suitable for this grade. Position, articulation, pronunciation and punctuation receive attention.

Spelling and Defining. Written work including the use of capitals and formation of sentences.

ARITHMETIC.—Mental and Written Arithmetic complete to Percentage.

GRAMMAR --Elementary Grammar and Composition.

GEOGRAPHY. --Primary Geography finished and Advanced commenced.

HISTORY.---Parley's Universal History finished.

Child's Book of Nature.

FIFTH GRADE.

READING.--Fifth Reader or supplementary reading of same grade. Drills on inflections, pitch and force of voice.

Grammar.---English Grammar. Parsing and Analysis. Original composition and Letter-writing.

ARITHMETIC.---Mental and Written complete.

GEOGRAPHY.---Complete Geography by out-lines.

HISTORY.---History of United States.

Familiar Science or Science of Common Things.

Writing and Spelling.

PRIMARY ✦ DEPARTMENT.

✦FIRST GRADE.✦

READING.—Chart and First Reader. Attention given to combined methods, Alphabetic Words and Phonetic.

SPELLING.—Words in reading lessons.

ARITHMETIC.—Oral Arithmetic, adding and substracting small numbers with and without objects.

Slate work in different studies.

SECOND GRADE.

READING.—Second Reader, Capitals and marks of Punctuation taught.

SPELLING.—Spelling by sound and written work.

ARITHMETIC.—Primary Arithmetic, Writing and Reading numbers.

Oral Geography, taught, cardinal points, form and motions of the earth, location of places near the child's home.

THIRD GRADE.

READING.—Third Reader. Special attention to teach the pupil to grasp thought.

SPELLING.—Spelling and Defining. The pupil taught to look in the dictionary for meaning of words.

LANGUAGE.—Lessons with much written work.

ARITHMETIC.—Primary Arithmetic finished and Elementary Arithmetic through the four fundamental rules.

GEOGRAPHY.—Primary Geography with map drawing.
Parley's Universal History commenced.

Primary teaching should be thorough. The foundation should be laid well, broad and deep. Then if followed up by good building how strong and valuable the structure when reared.

CHARTER.

(An Act to incorporate the Williamsburg Institute.)

Be it enacted by the General Assembly of the Commonwealth of Kentucky:

1. That, J. W. Siler; J. P. Mahan; E. S. Moss; A. Gatliff; Wm. Ellison; S. Stanfill; H. C. Harman; G. C. Brassfield, and J. R. Sampson, of Williamsburg, Ky; John A. Black, of Barboursville, Ky; J. Q. Pearce, of Pineville, Ky; Gilbert Garard, of Manchester, Ky; N. M. Scales of London, Ky; and H. C. Gentry, of Mt. Vernon, Ky; and their successors, be, and they are hereby, created a body-politic and corporate, to be known as the Williamsburg Institute, with its place of business at Williamsburg, Ky.

2. The business of said Institute shall be the establishment and maintenance of an Institute of learning at Williamsburg, Ky., in which is to be taught the English literary and scientific branches, the same to be under the control of Mount Zion Association of Baptists, as herein provided.

3. The capital stock of said Institute shall consist of such funds or property as may be given it, or be purchased by such funds, and the income and increase thereof, which shall be used for the exclusive benefit of said Institute.

4. Said Institute shall have power to make contracts, sue and be sued, take and hold property of any sort by purchase, gift, bequest or devise; may sell any property, real or personal, it may own for benefit of said institute; may make any investment of its funds from time to time which is authorized by law, or lend the same at interest; it may purchase all necessary grounds and erect all buildings to carry out the purpose of its incorporation; it may establish such school as it may see proper, and provide terms of admission and of pupils and course of study therein; and shall have power to do any and all acts necessary for the management of its school and property: Provided, That, it shall at no time owe an indebtedness greater than one third the value of its assets, and to that extent may, if necessary, mortgage any part of its real estate.

Said institute may graduate students and confer upon them the several degrees of "Master of Arts." "Bachelor of Arts," and "Bachelor of Science." It may adopt a seal and change it at pleasure.

5. The officers of said institute shall be a board of trustees, not exceeding fifteen in number, a President, Vice President, Secretary and Treasurer, and such other officers as may be provided for in the by-law.

6. The incorporators herein named shall constitute the first board of trustees, and may meet at any time they may agree upon, and organize hereunder by the election of officers herein named. The said board of trustees and officers elected by them shall serve until their successors are appointed and enter upon the duties of the office. The board shall, by its by-laws, fix some day in the month of October of each year upon which all officers other than trustees shall be elected, who shall hold for the term of one year. A bond may, by the by-law, be required of the treasurer, upon which said institute may sue for any breach thereof. The Mount Zion Association may, at its next annual meeting, and at each annual meeting thereafter, elect a new board of trustees or change the same as it may see fit, and those so elected may immediately enter upon the duties as such.

7. Said board of trustees shall have full control and management of all the affairs and property of said institute, and as such board, is invested with all the powers herein granted. All the property of said institute shall rest in said board of trustees in trust for the uses herein named, and all conveyances, gifts or devise to said institute shall so rest in said board. No conveyance of any real estate of said institute shall pass title unless first directed to be made by

an order on the record of said institute, and unless conveyance be acknowledged by the President of said institute. Said board of trustees shall, at each meeting of the said Mount Zion Association, make full and complete report to the same, showing fully the condition of said institute, financially and otherwise, and showing account of all money received and expended. Said board of trustees may make all necessary by-laws, and thereby provide for all officers and agents necessary to carry on the institute; Provided, Said by-laws are not in conflict with the laws of Kentucky or of the United States. It may fill vacancies occuring in the board until the next meeting of said association thereafter. A majority of said board as constituted at the time, shall constitute a quorum for the transaction of any of its business.

8. Should the Mount Zion Association at any time be disorganized or cease to exist, then the powers herein conferred upon said association shall vest in any association of Baptists which is agreed on by a vote of two thirds of the members of the board of trustees as then constituted.

9. The private property of the incorporators herein named, and that of all officers and others in any way connected with the management of the affairs of said institute, shall not be liable at any time for the payment of corporate debts against said institute.

10. That this act shall take effect from and after its passage.

(Approved April 6th, 1888.)

APPENDIX VIII
ENDOWED FUNDS AVAILABLE FOR SCHOLARSHIPS AND LOANS

The George I. Alden Endowed Scholarship Fund

The Alexander's Incorporated Endowed Scholarship Fund

The Mrs. Virginia Hill Allen Endowed Memorial Scholarship Fund

The Sylvia Angel Memorial Endowed Scholarship Fund

The Dr. N. A. Archer Memorial Endowed Scholarship Fund

The Ruby Gatliff Archer Endowed Scholarship Fund

The Jacob and Gertrude Arronson Memorial Nursing Endowed Scholarship Fund

The George Bagby Endowed Scholarship Loan Fund

The Mr. and Mrs. R. M. Barry Endowed Scholarship Fund

The Clyde Bennett Endowed Scholarship Fund

The H. N. and Frances C. Berger Foundation Endowed Scholarship Fund

The Stuart Blazer Endowed Student Loan Fund

The J. M. Boswell Presidential Scholarship Fund

The Wallace Boyd Endowed Memorial Scholarship Fund

The Attorney R. L. Brown Endowed Scholarship Fund

The William Jennings Bryan Endowed Scholarship Fund

The John T. Burgess Endowed Fund

The Abner L. Bushnell Memorial Endowed Scholarship Fund

The B. E. Cheely Memorial Endowed Scholarship Fund

The O. L. Clark Endowed Loan Fund

The Donice Clay Memorial Endowed Scholarship Fund

Gwynn Cornell Helping Hand Endowed Scholarship Fund

The Clyde and Cora Ellison Creech Endowed Scholarship Fund

The Jasper C. Creekmore Endowed Scholarship Fund

The Mr. and Mrs. J. A. Dickinson Endowed Scholarship Fund

The Charles M. Dupier, Sr. Endowed Scholarship Fund

The Mr. and Mrs. Walter B. Early Biology Endowed Scholarship Fund

The Reva Joyce Emert Memorial Endowed Scholarship Fund

The Grace L. Eyrick Endowed Emergency Loan Fund

The Hubert Faulkner Memorial Endowed Scholarship Fund

The J. W. Faulkner Family Endowed Scholarship Fund

The John Wesley Faulkner Memorial Endowed Scholarship Fund

The Mrs. Dorothy McComb Finley Memorial Endowed Scholarship Fund

The Desiree L. Franklin Endowed Scholarship Fund

The Ben D. Gatliff Endowed Scholarship Fund

The J. B. Gatliff, Jr. Endowed Scholarship Fund

The Edwin Gould Foundation for Children Endowed Scholarship Fund

The Catherine C. Graves Memorial Endowed Scholarship Fund

The Harry Lee Green Memorial Endowed Scholarship Fund

The Mary Kent Griffin Endowed Scholarship Fund

The Mrs. Jake Hacker Memorial Foundation Endowed Scholarship Fund

The Ethel Harmon Endowed Scholarship Fund

The Paul H. Harp Endowed Scholarship Fund

The Meriel D. Harris Endowed Scholarship Fund

The Ralph Hickey Memorial Endowed Scholarship Fund

The Millard H. and Mary E. Highland Memorial Endowed Scholarship Fund

The T. Russ Hill Endowed Scholarship Fund

The Anna M. Hoffeld Endowed Scholarship Fund
The Billy G. Hurt Endowed Scholarship Fund
The J. B. Johnson, Sr. Endowed Scholarship Fund
The Charles W. Jones Memorial Endowed Scholarship Fund
The Gorman Jones Memorial Endowed Scholarship Fund
The P. R. Jones Endowed Scholarship and Loan Fund
The Beulah Marsh Kennedy Endowed Scholarship Fund
The Kentucky River Coal Corporation Endowed Scholarship Fund
The Vera Hogg Lentz Endowed Scholarship Fund
The Virginia Lovett Endowed Scholarship Fund for Superior English Students
The Colonel E. T. Mackey Endowed Scholarship Fund
The Mahan-Ellison Coal Company Endowed Scholarship Fund
The Florence Mahan Endowed Student Fund
The T. E. Mahan Memorial Pre-Law Scholarship Fund
The Una Mahan Memorial Endowed Scholarship Fund
The Maude and Fred Mason Endowed Scholarship Fund
The R. C. Medaris Memorial Endowed Scholarship Fund
The Dr. R. C. Miller Loan Fund for Outstanding Students from Eastern Kentucky
The R. C. Miller Endowed Scholarship Fund
The Raymond Miller and Mary Lou Miller Gray Endowed Scholarship Fund
The Lewis Mitchell Endowed Scholarship Fund
The Ermal Davidson Moses Endowed Scholarship Fund
The Eva Murphy Endowed Scholarship Fund
The William A. McCall Memorial Endowed Scholarship Fund
The S. Jameson McComb Endowed Fund
The Mary W. McGaw Endowed Scholarship Fund
The Frank McKeehan Endowed Fund
The Chester Nevels Endowed Memorial Mathematics Scholarship Fund
The Edna J. Nicholson Endowed Scholarship Fund
The Mr. and Mrs. O. G. Nicholson Endowed Scholarship Fund
The Franklin Owen Endowed Scholarship Fund
The Lee B. Parker Endowed Scholarship Fund
The Carl D. Perkins Endowed Memorial Scholarship Fund
The Jerome A. and Agnes P. Perkins Memorial Endowed Scholarship Fund
The Pearl Gatliff Perkins Endowed Scholarship Fund
The Ruth Ramey Endowed Scholarship Fund
The Milton M. Ratner Endowed Scholarship Fund
The Charles Reed Athletic Endowed Scholarship Fund
The Dr. A. A. Richardson Endowed Scholarship Fund
The B. P. Roach Endowed Student Loan Fund
The Dr. Mack Roberts Endowed Loan Fund
The Dr. Fred Roth Memorial Endowed Scholarship Fund
The George C. and Nita Roughgarden Endowed Student Loan Fund
The Kara Wiman Scarborough Endowed Scholarship Fund for Nursing
The Auldean Moses-Seibert Memorial Endowed Scholarship Fund
The Ann R. Shelley Endowed Scholarship Fund
The Mr. and Mrs. A. T. Siler Endowed Scholarship Fund
The John Skeen Memorial Endowed Scholarship Fund
The W. I. Smallwood Endowed Scholarship Fund
The James Archie Smith Memorial Endowed Scholarship Fund

The Paul Gentry Smith Endowed Scholarship Fund
The Walter A. Smith Memorial Endowed Scholarship Fund
The Walton Smith Endowed Scholarship Fund
The Lena Snyder Nursing Endowed Scholarship Fund
The Southern Harlan Coal Company Endowed Student Fund
The Mindia Steely Endowed Scholarship Fund
The Mrs. Effie Jimmerson Story Endowed Scholarship Fund
The Steely Terrell Memorial Endowed Scholarship Fund
The J. L. Tigue Endowed Scholarship Fund
The Harold Trowbridge Endowed Scholarship Fund
The Casandra Tuggle Memorial Endowed Music Scholarship Fund
The Lillian South Tye Endowed Loan Fund
The Cecil Unthank Endowed Scholarship Fund
The J. T. Vallandingham Endowed Scholarship Fund for Mathematics Students
The Dr. L. F. Waggoner Endowed Loan Fund
The Dewitt Wallace Reader's Digest Endowed Scholarship Fund
The Mary Clynch Hunnicutt West Endowed Memorial Scholarship Fund
The Phyllis Wood Memorial Endowed Scholarship Fund for Music
The Don Worley Memorial Endowed Scholarship Fund

APPENDIX IX

ATHLETIC DIRECTORS

J. W. Jewell	1929-1930
Joseph Murphy	1929-1930
Wilson Evans	1930-1931
James M. Boswell	1932-1942
J. B. Scearce, Jr.	1946-1948
Donald M. Doyle	1948-1952
Harry E. McDonald	1952-1954
Bill E. Ross	1954-1961
John E. Renfro	1961-1985
Randy Vernon	1985-1986
Henry Morgan	1986-

APPENDIX X

J. T. VALLANDINGHAM SCHOLASTIC HONOR SOCIETY

To be eligible for membership in the J. T. Vallandingham Scholastic Honor Society, a student must have completed at least 94 semester hours of credit as a full-time student and have a standing of 3.50 or better for each semester since entering college. The date given is the year of induction.

1961
Jeanne Blevins
Patricia Jones
Shelby Pennington
Brenda Rains
Georgia Robinson
Edsel West
Hazel Wilder

1962
Lois Duncan
Patricia Hopkins
Jeanne Jackson
Anna Laura Johnson
Ruth Sharpe
Christine Stephens

1963
LeOra Childers
Russell Franklin
Thomas Hays
Orvetta Hines
Carol Teague

1964
Phyllis Estridge
Jana Sue Hill
Patsy Smith

1965
Sandra Johnson

1966
Delora Frazier
Judith Mayfield
Gary Warrix

1967
Jesse Kidd
Bobbie Littrell
Bobby Ross

1968
Geraldine Locke
Sherry Meadors

1969
Bonnie Bryant
William Edwards
Angelo Kidd

1970
Phillip Armstrong
Sue Bocock
Nancy Kelley

1971
Kathy Carson
Gayle Clifton
Ancil Collet
George Cox
Michael Perkins
Gaila Ann Stephens

1972
Annie Saylor
Ronald Steward

1973
Janet Adams
Cynthia Angier
Barbara Carnes
Julie Scheick

1974
Derma Berg
Ramona Faulkner
Linda McDonald
John Moore
Richard Ross
Jolly Sharp
Richard Stephens
Edwina Walker

1975
Henrriann Allen
Betty Collett
Linda Ford
Vickie Gilbert
Andrew Helvey
Gayle Hicks
Rosemary Hicks
Ada Phillips
Clara Reed
Rita Smith
Doris Taylor
Larry Taylor
Teresa Thomas

1976
Corrine Burns
Catherine Carnes
Arthur Criscillis
Thomas Croxton
Kenneth Dryden
James Ehrhard
Lana Frye
Belinda Hall
Debra Hanson
Jacqueline Harris
David Haun
Geraldine Phillips
Belinda Randolph
Thelma Sasser
Ricky Shoemaker
Douglas Williamson

1977
Sandra Adams
Edward Begley
Regina Bowling
Nancy Brooks
Alice Darnell
Danny Egner
Karen Gordon
James Lowe
Sheila Siler
Patricia Williams

1978
Richard Adams
Karen Arnett
Leigh Brooks

Kathryn Carson
Kevin Castleberry
Gail Childers
Debra Croley
Jane Faulkner
Debra Froendhoff
Betty Hensley
Brenda Kegley
Wanda Keith
Billie O'Neal
Charlene Powers
Kathy Simpson
Rhonda Stephens
Lee Tate
Leila Thomas

1979
Sharon Arnett
Laura Baker
Mary Bowman
Catherine Branham
Harry Brittian
Helen Cornett
Tammy Deaton
Lou Ann Hairston
Karin Hitch
Darrell Halcomb
Richard Mays
Timothy Osborne
Della Schafer
Deborah Scharber
Dennis Sherziner
Jeffrey Siler
Russell Steele
Sheila Underwood

1980
Stephen Ball
Donald Ballou
Kathleen Batson
Nathan Bryson
Kimberly Cornelius
Don Derose
Rebekah Earls
Janet Hicks
Nina Hicks
Randall Milwood
Jeanne Schaar
Marianne Williams
Virginia Young

1981
Latin Beets
Sherry Couch
Linda Dees
Rebecca Frierson
Carol Harris
Margaret Hopkins
Donna Jones
James Manning
Anthony Melton
Jana Swanner

1982
Tony Adams
Joye Barnes
Tommie Blankenship
Kevin Collins
David Combs
Paula Estes
Debbie Hopkins
Brenda Ledbetter
Jane Keating
Janice Manning
Debra Sexton
William Shepherd
Kathy Spears
Debbie Tharpe
Shirley Wilder

1983
Robert Carnes
Andrea Couch
Lois Davis
Jerry Denney
Tammy Foley
Sandra Harper
Joyce Helton
David Hubbard
Linda Hubbard
Eugenia Jones
Michelle Kellogg
Gary Kirby
Claire Knight
Marta Long
Karen Maggard
Carolyn Mills
Michael Mills
Colleen McMahan
John Taylor

1984
Penelope Abraham
Lori Albro
Deborah Atkinson
Lisa Gilreath
Karen Goss
Steven Hoblit
Catherine Nichols
Bonnie Partin
Judith Pennington
Basil Shorrosh
Lynnelle Spear
Chooi Khim Tan
Johnny Thomas
Benita Trapp
Kimberly Trivette
Thomas Wicker
Jeffrey Wilder
Vickie Winchester
David Witt
Wendall Worley
Cheryl Yandell

1985
Steven Canada
Michael Clark
Martina Cromer
Paula Emmert
Jacqueline Fowler
Georgetta Gannon
Kimberly Garrison
Patricia Jackson
Charlotte Keith
Arlene Leach
Donna Matney
Jackie Maxey
Melissa Mullins
David Popham
Donna Rutherford
Steve Scudder
Bishara Shorrosh
Donna Thornton
Paul Walker
Robin Williams
Sandra Wilson

1986
Essam Ackleh
William Byers
Dawna Grimes
Karen Helton
John Mobley
Ruth Morgan
Kenneth Sims
Sheila Terrell
Robin Thompson
Lisa Westerfield
Lori Whitlock

1987
Shannon Adams
J. Douglas Adkins
Janet Bentley
Linda Cowherd
Sherry Cox
Stuart Lockhart
Pamela Mahan
James McDowell
Jonathan Ramey
Raed Shorrosh
Cynthia Skaggs
Joni Skiles
Gina Smith
Charlene Wells
Marlene Wells

APPENDIX XI

HONORARY DEGREE RECIPIENTS

NAME	DATE OF AWARD	DOCTOR OF
Aldridge, D. M.	May 1981	Divinity
Balloff, Edward	May 1984	Humane Letters
Bays, Karl	May 1981	Humane Letters
Berger, Frances C.	April 1987	Humane Letters
Berger, H. Norwood	April 1987	Laws
Bolding, Haskell	August 1969	Divinity
Boswell, James M.	May 1980	Humane Letters
Boswell, Mary D.	May 1980	Modern Languages
Boyd, Wallace	August 1973	Laws
Buckingham, Lisle	August 1985	Laws
Combs, Bert T.	August 1983	Laws
Cooper, John Sherman	May 1985	Laws
Crawford, John L.	May 1984	Letters
Denham, Ralph M.	August 1986	Humane Letters
Denney, Edwin	August 1984	Humane Letters
Dunaway, John	April 1980	Divinity
Early, Jack	May 1981	Administration
Finch, Edward	August 1985	Science
Freed, Clyde	February 1960	Divinity
Gatliff, J. B., Sr.	May 1966	Laws
Griffin, Orville	August 1982	Divinity
Harbert, John III	May 1987	Laws
Harmon, Ethel	August 1970	Humane Letters
Hermann, Sarah T.	May 1982	Humane Letters

Ireland, Kate	May 1986	Humanitarian Pursuits
Jones, Charles	August 1981	Divinity
Jones, P. R.	August 1967	Laws
Kincaid, Garvice D.	August 1970	Laws
Mahan, T. E.	May 1967	Laws
Marshall, William	May 1986	Humane Letters
Martin, J. E.	May 1914	Divinity
McGaw, Mary	May 1981	Fine Arts
Miller, R. C.	April 1980	Laws
Mitchell	May 1913	Divinity
Moore, Barkley	August 1981	Laws
Moore, Nell	August 1973	Humane Letters
Roaden, Arliss	May 1986	Pedagogy
Rollins, O. Wayne	May 1985	Laws
Rose, James	August 1983	Administration
Rose, Judy	August 1985	Humane Letters
Sanborn, Richard Dyer	August 1986	Laws
Siegel, Betty	May 1985	Letters
Slusher, William M.	May 1971	Laws
Siler, Eugene E., Sr.	May 1973	Laws
Stacy, Charles B.	May 1982	Science
Stivers, Randolph	August 1984	Laws
Stone, W. Clement	August 1985	Laws
Swanson, Donald	May 1985	Science
Terrell, Robert S.	April 1980	Laws
Todd, Russell	May 1982	Laws
Vallandingham, J. T.	May 1969	Laws

Whitaker, Elmer	May 1987	Laws
Williams, Cratis	August 1984	Pedagogy
Winchester, M. A.	August 1986	Humane Letters
Wilson, Mary Asher	May 1983	Humane Letters
Wright, E. J.	May 1913	Divinity

APPENDIX XII

Honored Professor Award

1976	Mrs. Mary Boswell, Assistant Professor of Modern Languages
1977	Mr. Rayford Watts, Associate Professor of English
1978	Mrs. Jeannette Palmer, Assistant Professor of English; Miss Emma McPherson, Associate Professor of English
1979	Dr. Ann Hoffelder, Professor of Chemistry
1980	Dr. Eric Wake, Associate Professor of History
1981	Dr. Ron Zorn, Assistant Professor of Religion
1982	Mrs. Barbara Carnes, Associate Professor of Education
1983	Dr. Fred Roth, Professor of Religion and Counselor
1984	Mr. Walter Blaine Early, III, Associate Professor of Biology and Acting Head of the Biology Department
1985	Dr. Chester Young, Professor of History and Head of the History Department
1986	Mr. James Davis, Associate Professor of Education
1987	Mr. Tom Frazier, Assistant Professor of English

Special thanks should be given to Robert Michael Duncan, an alumnus and President of the Inez Bank, for his generosity in providing financial support for the Honored Professor Award.

Service Award

1983	Mrs. June Creekmore, Assistant Manager of the T.J. Roberts Cafeteria
1984	Mr. Jim Byrge, Director of Food Services and Manager of the T.J. Roberts Cafeteria
1985	Mr. Kenneth Shaw, Superintendent of Buildings and Grounds
1986	Mrs. Jana Bailey, Comptroller
1987	Mrs. Opal Mahan, Assistant Manager of the T.J. Roberts Cafeteria

APPENDIX XIII

CUMBERLAND COLLEGE WORKSTUDY PROGRAM
WORK CONTRACT

The work contract agreement records the basic commitments of the student and the College to the College's Workstudy Program and should be read carefully. To understand this contract, students should also read the policies and procedures of the Workstudy Program recorded in the Workstudy Manual and other College documents. The Workstudy Program is an important part of the total educational program of the College and knowing its conditions and requirements can contribute to a happier and more productive stay at Cumberland College.

THE STUDENT, IN ACCEPTING A WORK ASSIGNMENT, AGREES TO:

A. abide by the policies and procedures as provided in the Workstudy Manual and other documents containing related policy statements.

B. make a long-term commitment to the job and the assigned duties.

C. work the hours awarded and adhere to the work schedule as required by the position and arranged with the supervisor.

D. recognize that the assignment is a job and that in order to receive an hour's pay, there must be an hour's work performed.

E. secure approval for absences from work and arrange to make up hours with the job supervisor in advance of the absence if possible and to notify the supervisor of an unexpected absence.

F. strive to meet duties, responsibilities, and standards required by the job and defined by the supervisor.

AND THE COLLEGE AGREES TO STRIVE TO:

A. provide each workstudy student with opportunities for meaningful work experiences.

B. review, and, whenever possible, match student skills with the requirements of the available jobs.

C. provide financial assistance to the qualified students approved for workstudy.

D. conduct individual work evaluations.

E. promote equal opportunity and comply with related laws.

F. provide a grievance procedure whereby complaints about the Workstudy Program can be resolved.

STUDENT STATEMENT.

In signing this contract, I agree to carry out my job assignment to the best of my ability. I understand and agree to the conditions set forth in this contract. In addition, I am aware that failure to meet the requirements and conditions of this contract can result in disciplinary action as stipulated in the Cumberland College Workstudy Manual. I also understand that this contract is effective for the period that I am participating in the Workstudy Program and that I will receive a copy for my records.

COLLEGE STATEMENT

Cumberland College agrees to the conditions and requirements set forth in this contract and will make every attempt to insure the fair and equitable administration of the Workstudy Program. The College reserves the right to revise procedures and/or forms for the implementation of the above agreement.

_____   _____
Student's Printed Name   Signature for Cumberland College

_____   _____
Student's Signature   Date

APPENDIX XIV

Cumberland College Alma Mater

Words and Music by Richard E. Dubois

APPENDIX XV

CUMBERLAND COLLEGE
Commitment to Liberal Arts

In the belief that freedom is the result of respect for truth and concern for humanity, Cumberland College, through a traditional liberal arts program, attempts to foster in its students a heightened awareness and sensitivity to the search for truth and a deepened responsibility toward mankind.

The college seeks to graduate men and women with Christian values derived from spiritual and intellectual experience within the college community as well as from the traditional academic disciplines.

PURPOSES AND OBJECTIVES

Cumberland, "the College of the Kentucky Mountains," was founded in 1889 to provide indigenous leadership for the southern Appalachian region, based upon a quality educational program sustained by Christian values. To accomplish this purpose the College has the following specific objectives:

1. Cumberland seeks to perpetuate, by word and deed, those values which are derived from the Christian faith and thereby encourage students to develop a sense of self-worth and to establish patterns of personal integrity, self-discipline and social responsibility.

2. Cumberland seeks to equip each student with a liberal education which will encourage the student to think critically, appreciate broadly, and act intelligently and unselfishly.

3. Cumberland seeks to assist each student in understanding the cultural traditions of which each is a part.

4. Cumberland seeks to teach each student the importance of physical and mental well-being and how each may be maintained.

5. Cumberland seeks to provide academic specialization, insofar as it is possible within the broad framework of a liberal arts education, in order to develop each individual for effective leadership in his chosen profession, in the church of his choice, and in the geographical area where he will serve.

With respect to the members of the faculty and administrative staff, our purpose is:
to maintain a sense of community which maximizes acceptance, mutual respect and individual worth;
to serve as models of ideal persons and professions;
and to pursue the most effective means of teaching and learning for the benefit of the entire academic community.

With respect to the larger community, our purpose is:
to offer educational opportunities to students, regardless of race, religion, age, or financial status.

APPENDIX XVI

ENROLLMENT

The following enrollment figures were taken from the Catalogues of the Williamsburg Institute and Cumberland College as well as from the Registrar's Office. The first enrollment listed for 1889 is for the session beginning January 7, 1889; the second listing for 1889 is the headcount enrollment for the school year. Enrollments for the year 1890 through the year 1951 are headcount enrollments for the school year. Beginning with the listing for 1952, the enrollments are given for the headcount of the fall semester.

One should remember that from the fall of 1918 to the fall of 1961 the College was of junior college status. The grade department was discontinued in 1934 and the high school department discontinued in 1941.

ACADEMIC YEAR	STUDENT ENROLLMENT	ACADEMIC YEAR	STUDENT ENROLLMENT
1889	199	1925	340
1889	373	1926	382
1890	333	1927	405
1891	377	1928	395
1892	422	1929	376
1893	408	1930	372
1894	349	1931	278
1895	411	1932	293
1896	357	1933	Unknown
1897	386	1934	245
1898	404	1935	236
1899	426	1936	240
1900	510	1937	234
1901	459	1938	185
1902	396	1939	268
1903	523	1940	152
1904	494	1941	208
1905	581	1942	197
1906	752	1943	143
1907	1023	1944	146
1908	372	1945	151
1909	425	1946	324
1910	428	1947	432
1911	431	1948	402
1912	419	1949	474
1913	395	1950	215
1914	419	1951	327
1915	393	1952	274
1916	426	1953	305
1917	395	1954	351
1918	420	1955	454
1919	439	1956	521
1920	486	1957	533
1921	518	1958	731
1922	532	1959	881
1923	523	1960	1103
1924	444	1961	1268

1962	1226
1963	1117
1964	1225
1965	1250
1966	1536
1967	1621
1968	1771
1969	1873
1970	1858
1971	1807
1972	1751
1973	1716
1974	1777
1975	1751
1976	1856
1977	1907
1978	1979
1979	2073
1980	2162
1981	2033
1982	1747
1983	1950
1984	2106
1985	2094
1986	1927